A NEW ENGAGEMENT

A NEW ENGAGEMENT

Evangelical Political Thought,
1966 — 1976

by
ROBERT BOOTH FOWLER

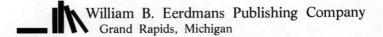William B. Eerdmans Publishing Company
Grand Rapids, Michigan

To Gama

Copyright © 1982 by William B. Eerdmans Publishing Co.
255 Jefferson Ave. SE, Grand Rapids, Mich. 49503
Printed in the United States of America

Library of Congress Cataloging in Publication Data

Fowler, Robert Booth, 1940-
  A New Engagement.

  Bibliography: p. 289
  1. Christianity and politics—History of doctrines—
20th century. 2. Evangelicalism—United States—
History—20th century. 3. Sociology, Christian.
I. Title
BR115.P7F68 1982   261.7'0973   82-11389
ISBN 0-8028-1929-X

CONTENTS

PREFACE

THE IDEA OF PURSUING the recent political and social thought of evangelical thinkers in the 1960s and early 1970s grew out of two related experiences. The first was my interest in the Carter phenomenon and related events, which alerted me like many others to the existence of the world of evangelicalism. The second was my own personal quickening of interest in religion. Both came at a time when my commitment to study post–World War II intellectuals in America continued as strong as it had been in the years when I researched and wrote *Believing Skeptics: American Political Intellectuals 1945–1964* (1978). But now I wanted to listen to some American voices that were not the voices heard in the dominant intellectual forums in the United States. None seemed of more potential significance than those of expanding evangelicalism.

I discovered that the political and social ideas of evangelical writers in the 1960s and early 1970s were far more complex and challenging than I had dreamed. The sheer volume of evangelical writing on public issues was as extensive as scholarly analysis and interpretation on it is scanty. Moreover, the evolution of evangelical perspectives toward increasing diversity, a result I had not predicted, made the task more demanding than I once had imagined—but also a far more intriguing one than I had anticipated.

After introducing the evangelicals my study proceeds in two parts. The first is a discussion of different clusters of evangelicals, whom I have, with some diffidence, divided according to their general social and political thought. This is a strategy which many thoughtful evangelicals find distasteful. Donald Dayton in *The Other Side* objects that such an approach can be simplistic.[1] There is, however, no escape from it if one seeks to begin to perceive the patterns of arguments within the multisided world of evangelical political argument today. The second part tries to comprehend evangelical political thinking by quite another approach. It looks at selected issues in the evangelical debates in the late 1960s and early 1970s to uncover the diversity and resonance of the discussion. Taken together these two approaches expose the richness, the diversity, and the complexity of evangelical political and social thought in the age from the New Left to the election of Jimmy Carter.

I wish to thank the Graduate School of the University of Wisconsin-Madison, which on several occasions generously supported my research. I wish to thank the American Philosophical Society, which kindly supported my efforts to supplement my research with essential interviews. Some particular evangelicals I want to mention, with thanks, are the following: David O. Moberg, who aided me enormously with his wisdom early in my work; Richard Martin, Tom Schussler, and David Cook, who represented the local evangelical community and gave me support as well as insight; the people of Wheaton College, who were of special help, from Hudson T. Armerding to the generous Robert Webber and the colleagues he assembled for my benefit; Harold Lindsell, whose remarkable and pointed conversation with me was a delightful and enlightening experience; Robert Culver, whose thoughtful reflections with me at his Minnesota farmhouse on a lovely summer afternoon were much appreciated; Lucille Sider Dayton and Donald Dayton, who talked long with me in the midst of their preparations to move; Paul Henry, Nicholas Wolterstorff, Stephen Monsma, and Richard Mouw, who made my visit to Grand Rapids and Calvin College such a stimulating intellectual experience; Wes Michaelson, who kindly spoke with me of his vision in the midst of a hot and busy Washington afternoon; Carl F. H. Henry, who did not give up on me; and Paul King Jewett, who flexibly made time for a visitor uneasy about California's freeways. I am grateful to them all.

I also wish to thank the following for reading parts of my work and providing me the criticism I much needed: Charles Anderson, Bonnie Cook-Freeman, Emily Albrink Fowler, John Harman, Mark Kann, Michael Kirn, Sandy Levinson, David McConnell, and Gregory Schneider. Finally, much appreciation goes to Paul Feldman and Andy Aoki, who helped in the final stages. Of course, they and the rest are completely free of any share of my full responsibility for errors of fact and interpretation.

Chapter One

INTRODUCTION

IT WAS IN THE YEAR 1976 that America discovered the evangelicals. National news magazines began reporting the explosive growth of the evangelical movement. Charles Colson, a leading culprit of the Watergate affair, became an evangelical and published his best-selling story *Born Again*. Eldridge Cleaver was home from Algeria and home from black revolution; his conversion to evangelical Christianity received widespread attention. Yet it was the political campaign of 1976 which more than anything else put evangelicals before the average American's consciousness. The leading contenders for the Republican nomination for president vied with each other to establish their evangelical credentials, but of course it was the meteoric rise of Jimmy Carter, a small-town Southern Baptist, that was most responsible. Carter's race for the nomination and his election to the presidency established for many the arrival of a new force on the American scene: the Protestant evangelical. It was ironic that though the majority of evangelicals who cast ballots in the 1976 election did not vote for Carter, his election ensured that they would at last be counted by the larger society.[1]

The events of 1976 which were so important to the emergence of modern evangelicalism in the American mind were actually the culmination of a process of almost two decades of remarkable evangelical growth. By 1960 signs of rapid evangelical growth were evident to informed observers of American religion, and both the signs and the numbers continued to multiply over the next fifteen years.[2] Yet the dominant American culture was slow to become aware of this increasingly substantial element in American life. Partly it was the fault of a media and intellectual culture which chose to ignore evangelicals. Partly it was the evangelicals' own fault, since, as one evangelical spokesman put it, "evangelicals have failed to exert a telling influence on modern culture."[3] Those days are, for better or worse, part of the past.

Though evangelicals are more and more important in American life,

1

most educated Americans know surprisingly little about them—including
the intellectual perspectives which provide the form, substance, and history
of evangelical political beliefs and aspirations. This book fills that gap by
exploring the political and social ideas of leading evangelical thinkers during the decisive years of rapid evangelical expansion, from the middle 1960s
to 1976. My argument is that evangelicalism underwent a historic inner
change at exactly the time that it stepped into the larger American culture.
As evangelicalism grew during the stormy years from the New Left to Carter
and came more and more often into contact with the broader culture, the
political and social reflections of many thoughtful evangelicals increasingly
changed. The old evangelical consensus on conservative values in all aspects
of life gave way to a spreading social and political diversity in a process of
fascinating change. Growth eliminated isolation; more and more, intellectual evangelical debates resembled those in the nation as a whole. As a
group evangelical spokesmen are often conservative, but the age of monolithic unity (perhaps always exaggerated) is now as dead as the idea that
evangelicals are an obscure group of religious fanatics to whom no serious
observer of American life need pay any attention.

WHO IS AN EVANGELICAL?

The first task facing any explorer of modern evangelicalism is to define an
evangelical. As many observers have noted, this act of definition is not easy.
There is no formula which somehow arranges firm and unquestioned
boundary lines. Evangelicalism is too dynamic for that, though there are
those in the movement who have insisted that one or another test is the
proper one. We can usefully pursue three approaches to definition. One is
to look closely at doctrinal lines. Another is to see evangelicalism as its
universe of dominant people, churches, places, publications, preachers, and
intellectuals. A third is to look at the numbers of evangelicals themselves
and the streams of faith which feed them.

Evangelicals in the 1960s and early 1970s usually shared several convictions. They affirmed that all people were born sinners. Their ultimate
fate was likely to be grim unless they responded to God's offer through
Christ to make a "decision for Christ." That decision might date from a
conscious conversion experience, or it might mean continually affirming a
lifelong religious conviction. Such a faith commitment necessarily involved
the most profound examination of one's beliefs, attitudes, and behaviors.
The act of choosing Christ and the transformations that were to follow
were described by some evangelicals as the famous process of being "born
again."[4]

Second, evangelicals affirmed the truth of the scriptures. While there
were disagreements over exactly what that meant, the disagreements took

place in a shared context which took for granted that all evangelicals were biblically oriented, all acknowledged the Bible's divine authority, and all claimed to be determined to worship and live by its commands. Many, probably most, evangelical spokesmen insisted that the Bible was "inerrant." They meant that the scriptures were both absolutely true and completely authored by God. Some supporters of the dominant inerrant position felt their strength within the movement weakening in the early 1970s and struggled to uphold it. Such figures as Harold Lindsell, editor of *Christianity Today* in the late 1960s and early 1970s, or Francis Schaeffer, popular evangelical intellectual, waged an untiring battle for the inerrant view. They had the support of a good many others, some of whom carefully stressed that they did not favor it "in a petulant or antagonistic spirit."[5] Still others, increasingly, favored "limited inerrancy." This view held that biblical inerrancy always applied on matters of religious faith and ethics, while it did not always do so on matters of historical and scientific fact. The respected intellectual evangelical publication *The Reformed Journal* was in the forefront of those who "expressed much disdain for the total inerrancy position."[6] Another perspective, enunciated by those clustered around the radical publication *Sojourners*, insisted that Christians must be biblical, but not inerrant. Their readers certainly received the impression that writers in *Sojourners* believed themselves to be at least as biblical as those in *Christianity Today*. Always the focus was on the authority of the Bible.

Third, evangelicals insisted that they were intensely dedicated to spreading the word. Evangelism was at the center of evangelicalism. They felt this was Christ's command to his disciples and they were determined to carry out his injunction. The evangelical sense of mission and its frequent lack of inhibition in proselytizing is as famous as it is a distinguishing mark separating evangelicalism from "mainstream" Protestantism or Catholicism.[7]

Fourth, intellectual evangelicals in particular had a commitment to reason and the intellectual process. They looked at Christianity as a whole as something more than experience, to which charismatic Christians seemed to reduce it. They respected the role of love and faith, but suggested that rational knowledge mattered also. They applauded Christian action, but remarked that scholarship had its role to play, too.[8] Christianity had to take the Bible seriously on intellectual terms. It had to take theology seriously. It had to take critical perspectives seriously. This concern explains why the student of evangelical thought discovers how pervasive intellectual interest and controversy is in this world, whether the subject is theology or the political and social implications of the Bible. This was (and is) not a group composed simply of naive believers.[9]

It was true enough, however, that there had long been a streak of anti-intellectualism within evangelicalism, and no one doubted the "angularity of trying to be an evangelical and an intellectual."[10] But by the 1960s there

was a concerted drive, which was one salient feature of the new evangelicalism, to eradicate such an attitude. Francis Schaeffer, *Christianity Today*,
reform-oriented evangelicals, and radicals agreed that evangelicalism had
to recognize the significant place of thought and of reason within this faith.
Their combined efforts increased the respectability of intellectuals in evangelical life. One result was that their systematic reflections on politics and
society flourished without any necessary sacrifice of orthodoxy, denigration
of the centrality of faith, or repudiation of the Bible. What it meant was
that the old tension within evangelicals between faith and the snares of
reason softened. The suspicions remain, especially as reason edges toward
matters of faith. But there is little doubt that the campaign for the intellectual side to evangelicalism lowered those suspicions in the 1960s and early
1970s, except among determinedly anti-intellectual fundamentalists.

Somewhat less widely shared, and not even a subject of concern for
many, was the question of pre- and postmillenialism. The majority of evangelicals were premillenialists, a position which had some import for political
and social thought. The premillenialist view held that the Book of Revelation established that Christ would return to earth and rule for a thousand
years before the final judgment. Its proponents looked for his return to be
signaled by decline and collapse in all aspects of human affairs. The post-
millenialists, on the other hand, interpreted the thousand-year period described in Revelation as the era since the Incarnation, a period of the spread
of God's Kingdom on earth, which will culminate in Jesus' second coming
and his final judgment. A third view, the amillenialist, also did not believe
in a literal thousand-year reign but interpreted the current age as the mil-
lenium. Like the premillenialists, however, they expected a period of trial
and tribulation before Christ's second coming. Many premillenialists suggested that we are able to look forward to little that is good prior to Christ's
return and that we can hardly expect to accomplish good while awaiting
him. To them the point as well as the prospect for significant political or
social reform before Christ's return was slight. Others saw it differently.
Premillenialism, they claimed, suggests that sin will be hard to fight, but it
did not negate the duty to fight anyway.[11]

Finally, one other doctrine must be considered. It is of central importance to this study. This was the evangelical position toward social change
and social action. One leading interpreter of Protestant American religion
speaks of two parties in our religious history: one party stressing individual
change both in terms of religious conversion and ethical life; the other
stressing a more social gospel, a religion oriented more toward social groups
than individuals and one that relies on social activism to meet their needs.
Using the terms of this two-party model, evangelicalism entered our period
firmly committed to the first party.[12] The evangelical mood was not congenial to social change or social activism. Its emphasis was on individual

conversion and individual action and witness in daily life. Traditionally many factors worked toward this result. Its stress on individual faith, its premillenialism, its concentration on the next world, its belief that finding Christ was so much more important than any other charge, its devotion to separation of church and state, its tradition of hostility to social action all had the same consequence. The result was, as we know, that evangelicals were leery of major social and political changes. The common sentiment was conservative.

We can gain perspective on the traditional conservative attitude by examining another model proposed for the history of Protestant religion in America. H. Richard Niebuhr suggested that there were really three varieties of Protestants in our history.[13] One, exemplified in the Pilgrims, Puritans, and early Quakers, focused primarily on the absolute rule of God, the sovereignty and wisdom of God, and our necessary dependence on him. It also stressed that human beings were sinners and thus quite unable to achieve a dramatically renewed human life or utopia. Such a perspective was and is very much alive in evangelical circles today. At the same time, though, Niebuhr's second current also described American evangelicals. It described a tradition which focused on the achievement of a new person through Christ, or being "born again." This type of religion was more immediate, more individually oriented, and was dominant among the classic nineteenth- and twentieth-century revivalists. In the nineteenth century this form of Protestantism was often radically hopeful, but it was not so by the mid-twentieth century. Sin loomed larger. Overall, the stress on sin matched with a hope of being born again represented an uneasy dialectic suggesting a cautious message about the importance and the possibility of social and political change.

Niebuhr's third variety of Christianity was the Social Gospel. This did not attract evangelicals. Even in the late 1960s the most radical evangelicals were at pains to demonstrate that they did not proceed in the manner they felt plagued the Social Gospel in the late nineteenth and early twentieth centuries. In evangelical opinion the followers of the Social Gospel often naively ignored the reality of sin and placed the cause of human problems entirely in the social environment. They also seemed to ignore Jesus as God and to replace him with a gentle yet somehow revolutionary example of how to live earthly life. This was not being born again in the divine Jesus Christ.

Thus modern evangelicals came into the 1960s opposed to the Social Gospel, stressing the sovereignty of God and the reality of individual sin, the impossibility of earthly utopia, the importance of individual change and individual salvation, and the illusions of the Social Gospel. They were often allied with a politics which was as conservative about the means of change as it was about making substantive social alterations. As late as the middle

1960s evangelical clergy were four times as likely to be Republicans as Democrats, and even more likely to be Independents than Democrats (R, 62%; D, 15%; I, 22%). Lay evangelicals had similar loyalties, except for Southern Baptists. Though Southern Baptists were often Democrats, they were among the most conservative evangelicals in their political and social attitudes.[14] These attitudes were shared, as we will see, by many of the leading evangelical thinkers and writers who espoused political conservatism.

The second approach to defining evangelicalism is also important in understanding the modern-day movement. We might call it a focus on the culture of evangelicalism. The center of that culture, for better or for worse, lies now, as it did in the 1960s, in the organization, voice, and evangelism of Billy Graham. While Graham is not an intellectual, and has never claimed to be, in the 1960s and early 1970s thoughtful evangelicals often closely followed and sometimes eagerly courted his stance on the issues of the day. His influence was enormous. No wonder, since Graham, born in Charlotte, North Carolina, in 1918, has been an active evangelist for over thirty years and has preached to perhaps eighty million in person and countless millions more on television and radio.[15]

While Graham is the most important evangelical today, Wheaton, Illinois, may be the physical center of evangelicalism. It is the location of Wheaton College, alma mater of many thoughtful evangelicals, and also the location of Billy Graham's religious center. Wheaton College no longer states in its catalogs that it is "conservative in its religious, political, and economic views," but it continues to be a crucial base for mainstream intellectual evangelicalism. It is in Wheaton as well that *Christianity Today*, the dominant periodical of interdenominational evangelicalism, is published. Wheaton now is an actual as well as a symbolic link of many branches of evangelicalism, a little hub of a large wheel.

The two editors of *Christianity Today* during the 1960s and the earlier 1970s were (and are) both central figures in the world of informed evangelicalism. Carl F. H. Henry, the subject of Chapter Five, was significant as a pioneering voice for more devotion to social action. Harold Lindsell, whose thought Chapter Two considers, was the editor of *Christianity Today* during most of the time from the emergence of the New Left to the election of Carter. His major preoccupations for our purposes were (1) battling elements within evangelicalism who did not affirm absolute inerrancy of the Bible, and (2) defending traditionally conservative evangelical ideas in political and social life. Both men were often involved in controversy and both had a deserved wide respect.

Francis and Edith Schaeffer were also extremely important in the universe of popular evangelicalism in the 1960s and thereafter. No voice within evangelicalism had more admirers among reflective young people than did Francis Schaeffer. His wife, who served as a weekly columnist for *Chris-*

tianity Today during part of the 1970s, had many admirers also. Though American, the Schaeffers guided a Christian center in Switzerland called L'Abri Fellowship. It was the source of a stream of books, articles, films, and students who spread its teachings with remarkable impact.

Another source of much of the intellectual direction and excitement within evangelicalism during this period of intellectual and religious growth was Calvin College, the Christian Reformed college in Michigan. This college had associated with it at various points such important evangelical thinkers and activists as Paul Henry, Stephen Monsma, and Richard Mouw. A third institution of considerable importance was Fuller Theological Seminary in Pasadena, California. Founded in 1947 as a traditional evangelical institution, it rapidly rose to importance. It became a locus of considerable controversy as some of its teachers and students identified with reform-oriented evangelicalism in the late 1960s and early 1970s; some of its founders, such as Harold Lindsell, consequently became critical of the institution.[16]

While there were many periodicals and individuals who acted as advocates of a new social concern, producing such journals as *The Other Side*, the most discussed and the most radical of the evangelical (they preferred to say biblical) publications was *The Post-American*, later *Sojourners*, which became an established publication in the early 1970s. Its editor, Jim Wallis, and those associated with him attained a controversial reputation as radical representatives within evangelicalism. Their ideas were well known and widely argued.

These base points within intellectual evangelicalism are only a beginning, necessarily limited and subjective. There was a far richer world which this book will discuss. But even this introduction should give some sense of the range which composed the evangelical world. Taken together its diverse parts are a brief definitional map: the people, the centers of learning, and the publications of thoughtful evangelicals which were the flesh of the intellectual church.

A third way to get a sense of evangelicalism is to understand what groups of religious Americans are evangelicals—and what their total number of members are. Robert Webber suggests in his book *Common Roots* that there are at least fourteen different bodies of evangelicals.[17] His categories are inclusive but not implausible, and they recognize the fact that today vast numbers of Americans consider themselves evangelicals, remarkable in an era in which church affiliation in America has declined to less than two-thirds of the population.[18] At the present time one in three adults claims that he or she is "born again" in Jesus Christ.[19]

Of course, evangelicals have grown in number enormously in the last few years, but they had been "very numerous previously, as can be seen by tracing statistics of evangelical denominations, associations, missions, and other groups back over half a century."[20] Then or now, however, it has never been easy to state with confidence exactly how many people in the United States are evangelicals. Informed analysts agree that perhaps forty million Americans are evangelicals. Some suggest the correct figure is higher, nearer fifty million. The search for more precision confronts several problems.

There is no single evangelical church, though there are clearly evangelical denominations. The Southern Baptist Convention is by far the largest with more than twelve million members. Many other of the thirty or so Baptist groups are also clearly evangelical. The total number of Baptists in the United States today approaches thirty million, including both black and white Baptists. Also important are the some thirty thousand Lutheran churches of the Missouri Synod, whose members number three and a half million. The Missouri Synod Lutherans have been in the news in recent years because of their intrasynodical struggle over the inerrancy of the Bible, a contest traditional evangelicals won completely.[21] While there are several varieties of Presbyterianism, and it continues to suffer division and dissension, some branches of this diverse church are firmly evangelical, and many of the most prominent leaders in the evangelical world are Presbyterians. It has influence beyond its numbers. This is even more pointedly true of the Christian Reformed denomination, which numbers no more than a few hundred thousand communicants. Their Michigan—still largely Dutch—base has been particularly important in the evangelical world.

In addition to these evangelical denominations and their members, there are also a good many evangelicals among Episcopalians, Methodists, and (non—Missouri Synod) Lutherans, some of whom are well organized, as in The Fellowship of Witness within the Episcopal Church. Many observers would add the pentecostal churches, holiness churches, and Protestant charismatics. Their respective numbers are not entirely clear. The number of members of pentecostal churches is not known, since so many are independent, small, and widely scattered. But the largest body of pentecostals, The Assemblies of God, has over a million adherents. Nazarenes, whose origins lie in Methodism, are by far the biggest single group among the holiness churches, with perhaps upwards of 500,000 members. The number of Protestant charismatics is a matter of pure guesswork but probably runs into the millions, though many are already affiliated with evangelical churches. There are also an unknown number of evangelicals in the more separatist fundamentalist churches.[22]

Many evangelical churches belong to the National Association of Evangelicals, the counterpart of the well-known National Council of Churches, and there is a recurrent tone of hostility among evangelical writers toward the National Council. There is also a National Negro Evangelical Association. It is important to keep in mind that blacks represent a substantial proportion of evangelicals, a fifth or more, and most black Christians are evangelicals. Certainly one of the most significant and fascinating aspects of evangelical history in the 1960s and early 1970s was the discovery by white evangelicals of the millions of black evangelicals.[23] The interest in blacks was obviously at its high point in the late 1960s, but it did not end there. Blacks became a significant, no longer unheard, element in evangelicalism. Moreover, as we shall see, intellectual blacks became agents of the new black consciousness, which entered into black evangelicalism as it entered the black experience generally.

SPECIAL CONSIDERATIONS

A sense of who is an evangelical (and who was in the 1960s) and an exploration of their numbers hardly resolves all the problems associated with comprehending the contours of the complex world of evangelicalism in even outline form. Several problems deserve more consideration for the reader to have a sense of the terrain ahead. The first and surely the most urgent is the necessity of discussing the relationship between evangelicals and the "fundamentalists." Informed evangelicals know that most people in the larger world are not familiar with "evangelicals"; they routinely describe all Christians who take the Bible inerrantly (literally, they say) as "fundamentalists." Many evangelicals are comfortable with this assumption. As one put it, "a fundamentalist is marked by adherence to . . . the inerrancy of the Bible. To me, this is also the mark of a self-professed evangelical. Evangelical is merely a nice way of saying fundamentalist."[24] In recent years, however, some evangelicals and some fundamentalists have tried to distinguish the two groups. They may not have succeeded fully, but it should be noted that there are sometimes points of tension between those who identify with evangelicalism and those who call themselves fundamentalists. Evangelicalism and fundamentalism are not always two names for one body of believers.[25]

The term "fundamentalist" was first coined in the independent Baptist weekly, the *Watchman – Examiner*, in 1920. Yet fundamentalists existed in all but name long before. They began to appear as far back as the late nineteenth century, fueled by the belief of some clergy and lay people within the main Protestant denominations that their churches were slowly but surely forsaking orthodox Christianity. From then to now fundamentalists insist that the crucial issue is the same: will Christians succumb to the assault on the guiding rule of the Bible? "Historic Fundamentalism is the literal exposition of all the affirmations and attitudes of the Bible and the militant exposure of all non-Biblical affirmations and attitudes."[26] One early attempt to stem the tide was the publication of twelve volumes of orthodox interpretations, called *Fundamentals*, in the years just before World War I.[27] It was during the 1920s that fundamentalism emerged as a publicly distinct movement. While sometimes it is said that theologically liberal Baptist Harry Emerson Fosdick's "Shall the Fundamentalists Win?", a call for an inclusive and doctrinally relaxed Christianity in 1922, marked the moment when skirmishes metamorphosed into open warfare, there was no such single moment. Yet a serious and intense battle did take place in the 1920s between biblical literalists and more "modern" Protestants. Despite the celebrated 1920s image of Darwin's defeat in Dayton, Tennessee, most centrist denominations repulsed the fundamentalist efforts.[28]

In these conflicts it is, of course, never self-evident who was being faithful to the old truth and who was not. The fundamentalists were not, for example, especially "fundamental" from a Roman Catholic perspective based on the historic church of Christianity. They were modernists in their accent on biblical supremacy, in their downgrading of the traditional sacraments, and in their belief in premillenialism. From within the Reformation tradition of Protestantism, however, fundamentalists were traditionalists, and from the 1920s on they did face in American Protestantism a gradual weakening of a firm commitment to the Bible as read by many old guard Protestants who saw themselves in the Reformation tradition.[29] By the 1930s and 1940s, Protestantism in the United States was clearly divided between the "fundamentalists," often but not always outside the central denominations, and the conventional Protestants, such as the Methodists, Episcopalians, Congregationalists, and many Lutherans.

Evangelicalism as a term for many self-consciously conservative Protestant Christians rapidly replaced the term "fundamentalist" in the 1940s and 1950s. The founding of the National Association of Evangelicals in 1941 was a significant step in this process. The remarkable growth of evangelical Christianity after World War II brought in more and more people who called themselves evangelicals and who took it for granted that their fold's common name was evangelicalism. Yet they did not necessarily place themselves in opposition to the dwindling numbers who still preferred to call themselves "fundamentalists."[30]

However, there were (and are) tensions between evangelicalism and some forms of fundamentalism which it is important to understand. Despite these tensions, both groups assumed agreement on what was most vital: commitment to orthodox Christianity and an intense biblical focus. The tensions, then, should not be exaggerated—nor ignored.

1. Many evangelicals were suspicious of leading figures in some branches of fundamentalism. Often this was a clash over style more than doctrine. A clear example was Carl McIntire, the most aggressive representative of fundamentalism in the 1960s and early 1970s. *Christianity Today* specifically singled him out for censure because to them he advocated extreme

political and social positions, because he inveterately and eagerly participated in disputations, because he chose more often than not to be a politician rather than a religious leader, and because he took himself and his
dicta so seriously, acting as if he were a "pope."[31]

Many evangelicals also began to shun the Bob Joneses (father and son),
who obtained an unsavory reputation as racists for their very reluctant
relaxing of the color bar at Bob Jones University. The Joneses were part of
the significant proportion of Baptists who identified with fundamentalism.
They were proud of their outlook and sure that the "real danger is not
strong Fundamentalism but a soft and effeminate Christianity."[32]

More important was Billy James Hargis. His flamboyant career and his
spectacular fall were covered — with some disdain — by *Christianity Today*.
Hargis felt his anticommunist crusade ought to inspire every true Christian.
He realized that he was not an easy man to get along with and that his
personal independence and resistance to all dictatorships, including religious ones, made him seem schismatic and troublesome to those who wanted
to rule or be ruled. But Hargis knew he had talents too. He could recount
a charming story, such as his tale of growing up as a hard-working, God-
fearing boy who followed his parents and aspired to do God's work, and
did so without appearing to be a complete prig. He always advanced his
personal belief that God did not call him to replace God as supreme judge.
Hargis's humility before judgment explained, he observed, why he married
people who were divorced: let God assess their sin. This tolerant mood,
however, was never evident whenever a communist, socialist, or liberal
appeared.[33]

Yet it was Carl McIntire who more than anyone else symbolized fundamentalism and explained why so much of evangelicalism stood apart
from its origins. McIntire's fanaticism was a cause of alienation, whether
he showed it in his obsession with communism in his *The Christian Beacon*
or in such incidents as his harassment of Queen Elizabeth upon her visit
to the United States in 1976. So were his questionable intellectual com-
mitments and the shoddy standards of the educational institutions he headed.
Christianity Today, for instance, carefully but critically reported the fact
that New Jersey had removed the accreditation of McIntire's college.[34]

The major issue was McIntire's — and other fundamentalist leaders' —
religious separatism. McIntire contended that the evangelical world had
become willing to compromise with sin, even on occasion to cooperate
openly with it. The irony was that McIntire thought that some evangelicals
were silly in their verbal insistence on literalism. They had a bad case of
"Bibliolatry." They were like the Old Testament scribes Jesus had denounced. They often did not have enough sense to see and understand a
biblical metaphor. Meanwhile, in practice evangelicals had a horrifying tendency to walk with the forces of evil. It was only one more sign of a modern

age in which McIntire believed the "saints" were filled with "a general drowsiness."[35] How could it be otherwise when such great figures as Billy Graham engaged in disgraceful "unscriptural fellowship and cooperation with liberal leaders and their groups."[36]

McIntire charged that Graham was busy promoting a single Christian church united by a watered down Christianity despite God's specific admonition in Revelations 17 and 18 that such a church would meet God's doom. It was tragic, he thought, that the ambitious Graham would not listen, but it was not surprising. It was an old story: "few heed prophecies when they interfere with their programs."[37] While McIntire respected Graham's powers as an eloquent and effective evangelist, Graham's error remained. So did McIntire's harsh and sustained campaign against Graham and his tie with the "killing force" in modern evangelism, the "spirit of inclusiveness as most notably practiced by Billy Graham."[38]

Modern evangelism's false path was not, of course, solely the fault of Billy Graham in McIntire's view. It was a pervasive, movement-wide problem. Carl Henry and Francis Schaeffer, other significant voices, were also guilty along with Graham. Francis Schaeffer drew McIntire's fire because he supposedly lusted for ecumenism even though he said he did not. Carl Henry, founding editor of *Christianity Today*, received criticism on this score also, though the situation with Henry went beyond that. It involved a tangled web of bad relations which led McIntire to accuse Henry of showing him no Christian love. Their conflict was deep.[39]

McIntire's commitment to separatism has involved him in a stormy career, one that is almost legendary, and one that has included many a schism. He has lived out his philosophy just as he has urged others to do. As a young Presbyterian clergyman in the 1930s, McIntire began to build his record of opposition to what he took to be the pervasive corruption and sin among Christians. The Presbyterian Church eventually expelled him; he went on to form his own denomination, which much later was in turn to push him out. In 1941 he founded the American Council of Christian Churches as an alternative to the World Council of Churches and the National Association of Evangelicals, and in 1948 he created the organization he called the International Council of Christian Churches. These were always small bodies, loyal to his version of Christian purism, fighting the scientific doctrine of evolution, defending the war in Vietnam, and the like. In 1970 McIntire was ousted from the leadership of the ACCC in yet another schismatic struggle.[40] So it has gone, with McIntire convinced his conflicts are for the glory of God and his choices for separatism fully justified: "As in the first century, so in the twentieth century—we must go outside the camp and do all for the glory of God."[41]

2. Evangelicals sometimes also criticized fundamentalists, apart from the actions of one leader or another, for their militant separatism from the

society around them. The fundamentalists often found little that was acceptable in the world, preached rigid separation from contact with it, and yearned for the end of time. Evangelicals in general were uncomfortable with such a radical alienation. They were hardly in sympathy with all features of the American order, but they did not usually understand the Bible, their situation, or sheer practicality to teach the wisdom of the fundamentalist view.[42]

The most obvious point at which this separatism offended evangelicals was the fundamentalist treatment of other Christian groups. Evangelicals were hardly ecumenists. They were often critical of Roman Catholicism and liberal Christianity, and many evangelicals welcomed conflicts such as the bitter controversy within the Lutheran Missouri Synod in the 1970s. They respected a Bible-believing Christianity too, after all, and endorsed efforts to preserve it. Yet they usually refused to be as contentious, as open to schism, and as devoted to complete religious purism as they judged fundamentalists to be. Nor were they inclined to express their religious disagreements in the scarring language fundamentalists occasionally employed. One fundamentalist characterization of evangelicals as a "party to compromise, evasion, and capitulation to Satanic forces" was a good example of the rhetoric that separated the two groups.[43]

3. Some evangelicals spurned what they saw as fundamentalist anti-intellectualism. It was one thing to support the Bible. It was quite another to promote an attitude of disrespect for thinking, research, and exploration in religious subjects — or any others. Evangelical thinkers frequently insisted that their own commitment to intellectual pursuits formed a major boundary line in the 1960s and 1970s (as it had in the 1940s) between them and the fundamentalists.[44]

4. Finally, evangelical spokesmen often suggested that fundamentalists confused Christianity with far right-wing politics. It was by no means rare for even politically conservative evangelicals to express this uneasiness. *Christianity Today* objected to Bob Jones University, a center of fundamentalism, because of its racism and unvarnished devotion to right-wing causes. They had less use for Billy James Hargis's Christian Anti-Communist Crusade, because the crusade could not discover any difference between the United States and Christianity. Mark Hatfield shared this view and attacked Hargis, among others, for addiction to fulltime anticommunism, conspiracy theories, and a virulent American nationalism which equated America with the cause of Christianity.[45]

If there were undoubted tensions between mainstream evangelicals and what might be termed fundamentalist evangelicals, the fact remained that many key opinion leaders frankly admitted that they did not mind the term "fundamentalist" for themselves as long as it did not carry the connotations they disliked. They *were* fundamentalists and they were allies of the fundamentalist movement in what really mattered: their support of biblical orthodoxy.

Since there was a historic link between fundamentalism and evangelicalism, there was at least a common background to share. This basis for mutuality was not as clear in regard to a second and far more recent phenomenon which we need to understand in its relationship to evangelicalism. This is the rapid rise of the charismatic movement in the 1960s and especially the 1970s. It is not unusual to class the charismatics as belonging under the general rubric of evangelicalism, but it should be understood that even today, and unquestionably in the early 1970s and before, there is considerable uneasiness between the "new charismatics" and the evangelical center. The charismatics believe one discovers God by experience, usually by an intense "baptism in the Holy Spirit." They express their faith by the assorted "gifts" of God, including speaking in tongues. They contend that the results of their experiences are a tremendous renewal of Christian faith and commitment, including a heightened involvement in worship and service to God. Among the most well-known evangelical charismatics are Pat Boone and Ruth Carter Stapleton.[46]

While the number of charismatics has grown rapidly in recent years, this is only the culmination of a steady process which accelerated in the 1960s. Until then relatively few mainstream evangelicals were charismatics. Charismatics and evangelicals both shared a profound allegiance to the classic doctrines of Christianity, but many evangelicals disapproved of the irregular, sometimes spontaneous nature of charismatic worship and the use of the "gift" of glossalalia, or speaking in tongues. The experiential side of the charismatic approach came into conflict with the evangelical adherence to reason, to the "rational evangelical god of the intellect—the great giver of propositional truth."[47]

Moreover, some more reform-minded evangelicals expressed skepticism in the 1970s about the depth of the charismatics' interest in the social teachings of Jesus. *The Post-American*, the organ of radical evangelicalism, carried several articles suggesting that charismatics tended to be too cut off from the struggle to realize God's will in a pain-filled world. Some evidence of change appeared in the 1970s. For example, Larry Christenson's *Social Action: Jesus Style* (1976) represented an attempt to relate charismatics to social change. Christenson urged change, even drastic change, for every Christian as well as the larger institutional environment. But he was careful to indicate that evangelism itself, the calling of souls to Christ, was by far the best method of social amelioration and the least likely to trap Christians into the snare of this world. This perspective was not exactly what reform-oriented evangelicals had in mind, and even it was far more oriented to social action than most writings by charismatics.[48]

On the other hand, much of the teaching in charismatic circles attempts to help people learn how to live lives of wholeness. While this focus does not commonly appear to proceed out of a "sophisticated" sociological analysis, it constitutes a tacit recognition that life in our modern society tears people to pieces. It also expresses a commitment to alleviate that problem. While it does so through the characteristic approach of individual change, modern charismatics in many cases are intensely involved in the goal—and sometimes the reality—of community. Charismatic groups aspire to be loving, Christian communities, an endeavor which should, perhaps, appeal to the most radical evangelicals.[49]

It is not so clear, however, that either the charismatic focus on community or their serious concentration on healing is entirely consonant with the evangelical mainstream. Yet by the middle 1970s charismatics were more acceptable to the evangelical world than ever before. Not all the tensions had disappeared, but charismatics were too numerous and too familiar now for quick evangelical rejection. A serious question remained as to whether charismatics outside traditional evangelical domains, especially Roman Catholic charismatics, were somehow evangelicals. There were those who said they were, but evangelical opinion has long leaned against this view. The ancient belief that Roman Catholicism is not evangelicalism, and cannot be, has remained strong.[50]

THE MISSING EVANGELICALS

No matter how one defines evangelicalism, its rise is the most important event in the history of religion in the United States in the past twenty years. Yet what is astounding is how little systematic attention observers have accorded the evangelical phenomenon. Virtually no one has written, for example, on their political and social thought. There are serious studies of evangelicalism from within the camp, which are sensitive to their new prominence, of course, and which are alert to the divisions and controversies within the movement. I draw on these works. But the larger point is that until very recently there was little interest in the evangelical story among most other writers on religion in American life; especially neglected were its ideas about politics and social action.

The reasons for this are numerous, and we will look at five. First, the sociology of religion did not focus on this phenomenon in the 1960s or 1970s. A fair illustration may be found in the impressive and thoughtful works of the distinguished sociologist of religion J. Milton Yinger. There is much to be said for his reflections on religion in America and elsewhere, though his sociological perspective which interprets religion in terms of need rather than truth poses obvious problems for evangelicals. Yet Yinger, unlike many sociologists, recognized that there are genuine problems with any simplistic analysis which links religion to functionalism. This was an approach worlds away from the crude work of Marxian sociologists on religion, for example. This is true not least because Yinger assumed "that religion is a natural expression of man as an individual and as a member of society."[51]

Yinger, as we might expect, was alert to many aspects of American religion. For instance, he considered black religion thoroughly, even if at times he reduced it to four-cell boxes and the questionable enlightenment they provide. Yinger also carefully avoided falling into the comfortable cliches of many secular intellectuals. For example, he well realized that religious fundamentalism and the political right wing could not be too quickly or snugly linked. He sensed what this study will demonstrate, that such an assertion is too sweeping and ignores a host of conceivable intervening factors. Above all, Yinger represented sociology at its best when he frankly acknowledged that his discipline can only approach religion from one side and thus can only provide one of several pictures of religion. Such modesty is rare in sociologists and therefore all the more welcome.[52]

Yinger is a good illustration, then, for us to explore. His prominence in our period and his own relatively open and judicious orientation to the study of religion are evident. Yet Yinger just did not catch the evangelical revival. Certainly he knew that the evangelical world existed, though he was clearly out of touch with its theology. He did refer to evangelicals and fundamentalists in several places, however, unlike some sociologists who ignored them altogether except to denounce them as the worst remnants of a receding past. But Yinger's treatment was one which was increasingly misleading as a description of reality. He tended to consider them as "sects"—there are too many evangelicals to label them sects any more—and he was inclined to classify them into different types. He found three types in one version: "acceptance," "progressive," and "avoidance" sects. It was not a helpful or aware analysis.[53]

Why Yinger, who represented in some ways the best among sociological discussions of religion, did not grasp the evangelical story or devote much attention to it is an important question. It is one that in one form or another evangelicals continued to ask in this period, long before *Time* and *Newsweek* and even the broader intellectual world were to discover them in 1976. They found few satisfying answers, but Yinger himself provided insight into this problem. He suggested that evangelicals and the more secular intellectuals often had strikingly different class and—we may add—educational backgrounds. While it is clear that evangelicals have broken out of class barriers that once seemed to divide them neatly from their Episcopalian or Unitarian fellows, the class difference Yinger recognized still remains.

Even more relevant was the lack of interest in religion among most intellectuals in America in the 1960s and early 1970s. Moreover, what interest there was often felt sympathy for a kind of religion very different from that which the evangelicals offered. Yinger was frank on this score. He was not, unlike many other sociological writers on religion, hostile to religion, but he did not like orthodox religions and he frankly declared that he wanted a new reformation which would demythologize traditional religion and develop new ideas leading toward "a world ecumenicalism." This was not exactly what the evangelicals had in mind![54]

A second factor which worked against scholars seriously investigating the growth of evangelicalism was the fashion of studying civil religion. The energy for this activity undoubtedly derived from the intellectual mood of the late 1960s in the United States, a mood disillusioned with belief in nation. There was a search for why the United States had so long been so self-confident — some said imperialistic — in world affairs. Blame fell on many causes, including our "civil religion," our national faith.

The leader of the professional study of civil religion was (and is) Robert N. Bellah, who became the leading sociologist of American religion in the era of the New Left. He continues to be so in the present time. His publications were numerous, from his landmark article, "Civil Religion in America," in a 1967 issue of *Daedalus*, to such books as *Beyond Belief* (1970) and *The Broken Covenant: American Civil Religion in Time of Trial* (1975).

The enterprise which intrigued Bellah, what he called "civil religion," was, he argued, the means by which *every* people and *every* nation described and explained their historical life in connection with the transcendent. Bellah emphasized American civil religion in particular. He noted the power and the persistence of the idea that we were a specially chosen people; he pointed out how many of our major public documents and great events were wrapped in our sense of the interconnection between America and divine purpose. The Second Inaugural of Lincoln, the Inaugural of John Kennedy, and so many other great speeches in America, reflected a sense of God's will and the belief that God's support was with America. Bellah was also fascinated by what he considered to be the tension within our civil religion, a dialectic between our several visions, our several aspirations, between the individual and community, liberation and freedom, conversion and covenant. His analysis was intriguing and its illumination expanded over time. Certainly it was far more complex and multidimensional than any short introduction can adequately represent.[55]

Bellah's discussion stimulated a number of other observers to consider the role of civil religion in the United States and led to a revival of earlier ideas which were along somewhat the same lines. A large academic debate, not entirely pointless, broke out concerning the nature of civil religion in America. Will Herberg drew a picture of it as a kind of folk religion celebrating the American way of life. Sidney Mead saw our civil religion in-

volving a critical God who selected America as his ark in history and
therefore expected much of us. Leo Marx saw it in terms of a pervasive
democratic faith. And there were many more versions.[56]

From an evangelical perspective, Bellah and the new focus on the wider
social roles of religion left something to be desired. It did not take Christianity seriously as a system of truth, as evangelicals naturally wanted everyone to do. Bellah did appreciate that civil religion would continue to be a
force in American public and political life even after the turbulent 1960s,
during which public piety fell from favor. Its role was too important to slip
away silently. But he did not direct his investigation to the evangelical
renaissance in the 1960s or after. Moreover, what religious life and "renewal" Bellah could find "has come outside the Protestant tradition."[57]
Evangelicals knew that judgment to be wrong, but there seemed no way to
deflect Bellah and others away from their interest in civil religion.

Yet, compared to many sociologists, Bellah was sympathetic to religion
defined as "that symbolic form through which man comes to terms with
the antimonies of his being." It "has not declined, indeed, cannot decline."[58]
We needed it even more as we struggled in a context which starved our
religious-ethical side, a context of science, technology, capitalist organization, and utilitarianism. In this general sense he appreciated religion and
unquestionably he did provide genuine illumination about a role religion
played in America.[59]

Third, those caught up in the New Left mood and its aftereffects who
turned to think about religion showed no more interest in evangelicalism.
Ironically, it was during this very period that so much of the evangelical
renaissance took place. The New Left in religion as elsewhere dominated
the scene to the extent that it obscured developments taking place outside
its confines. This was especially true perhaps in university communities,
where the controversies generated over Vietnam and the New Left were so
real and evangelicalism seemed so far away.

It is unfair to pick a single author or book to use as an example,
especially when there are so many. One might have profitably looked at
Harvey Cox, the most celebrated popular religious thinker in America in
the last fifteen years. His works have been a part of intellectual fashion
from his abandonment of traditional religion in the *Secular City* (1965) to
his recent flirtation with Eastern religions in *Turning East* (1977). But Cox
does not purport to be a descriptive student of American religion.

He is typical to the extent that he crystallized and celebrated each
manifestation of what evangelicals might consider faddism in American
religion as it happened, while he ignored the serious and lasting change in
religion in America in the last twenty years, the growth of the evangelicals.
In the 1960s Cox acknowledged there was a "New Breed" in the church in
America. It was the social activist whom he saw, but it was not the rise of

social activism within evangelicalism that caught his notice. He saw nothing of the growth of social activism in that world, but then he saw little of that world in any way.[60]

Cox's opinion, expressed by his neglect of the rapidly growing evangelical movement, was routinely shared by many other observers of religion in the United States who operated in the shadow of the New Left era. It was not uncommon to read articles which routinely stated what they considered obvious, that the "irrelevance of traditional Christian teachings has been acknowledged" among religious Americans, though "practice probably outlasts faith." These judgments were no doubt true of many within liberal Protestantism in the 1960s, but they hardly characterized the ignored evangelicals, who already were more numerous than their "mainstream" fellows.[61]

William G. McLoughlin was one respected historian of American religion who could hardly be accused of neglecting evangelicals. But he concluded in a famous article, "Is There a Third Force in Christendom?", that evangelicals and fundamentalists had reached their peak and were no longer going anywhere. He dated their apogee at 1964 and doubted if they would ever see such a heyday again.[62]

A classic dismissal of evangelicals in the aftermood of the New Left was Sontag and Roth's *The American Religious Experience* (1972). They represented an effort to report on religious thinking in America, yet they had not a word to say about either fundamentalism or evangelicalism. Those Christians were not worth these authors' time, one gathers, since they were hardly likely to take part in the religious mood of the age: "America has started off on a new trip. Fasten your seat belts. The journey will be rough."[63] Nor were they candidates for a view which hopes for something Sontag and Roth termed "free theology" and a "democratic God."[64]

Fourth, interest in assorted unconventional religious expressions in America continues to be one popular pastime for students of religion in America. For example, Sontag and Roth took up every "religion" which was intellectually respectable to them (as evangelicalism apparently was not), including John Dewey's "religion," Alfred North Whitehead's process theology, the Death of God theology, and, of course, black theology. Each received substantial discussion and each was accorded respect. They showered the highest praise on black religion in America, since it might have the answer. What the authors had in mind, of course, was not the actual religion of most black Americans (usually one version or another of fundamentalism or evangelicalism), but "a theology of revolution" which they hoped blacks would produce.[65]

More recently, of course, the study of cults continues to fascinate, as Jonestown in our own time reminds us. In the earlier 1970s other cults were thought as worthy of exploration as evangelicalism was not. For ex-

ample, Robert Bellah coedited a work which, like many others, claimed to
be about "the new religious consciousness" and gave considerably more
attention to Hare Krishna, the Guru Maharaj Ji, among others, than it did
to such campus Christian groups as Inter-Varsity. This study concentrated
on the Berkeley area, but one doubts if that mattered much. The fact is that
many studies of current religious developments focus on what are religious
expressions of only a tiny element of the population, while largely or entirely
ignoring the explosion of evangelical strength.[66]

It is not self-evident why Meher Baba, Zen, Tibetan Buddhism, or the
religion of Alpha Waves should appear to be so fascinating. They have a
kind of esoteric interest, but their attraction goes beyond that. They appear
to many professional students of religion to be more legitimate than Christian evangelicalism. In some American universities today it is easier to find
people prepared to take Sufi, Zen, or American Indian religions more seriously than evangelicalism.

Fifth, some work has, in fact, been done on evangelicalism, but it is
not always good. Often, the focus is on the fundamentalist stream of the
movement and it is rarely even understanding. For instance, one important
collection stressed a good deal how alienated and confused fundamentalists
were.[67] It also attacked them because they choose private approaches to
problems and thereby (dare to) "support the existing social structure." This
simplification shows little actual knowledge of developments in the last
decade and a half within evangelicalism. It does indicate, however, the
biases which some observers bring to the study of contemporary religion.[68]

Other students of contemporary evangelicalism and/or fundamentalism appear to consider their main task the creation of distinct categories
by which the assorted denominations may be classified. This search for a
discrete set of categories provides endless possibilities. Indeed, the various
essays in classification are of limited use because they are so numerous and
so often in disagreement with each other. But it is evident that the attempt
is popular, though *usually* singularly devoid of enlightenment.[69]

Occasionally, other modern analyses are sadly implausible. One article's explanation as to why people participate in faith healing or speaking
in tongues suggests that it aids those who are out of touch with their normal
middle-class habitat and who need such extreme religious practices as com-
pensation and support. These people teem with "covert hostility," "pervasive masochism," "frequent use of paranoid mechanisms," and the like.
Such an argument appears very weak in the light of millions of all classes
who have now taken an interest in faith healing and/or speaking in tongues.[70]

Exceptions which look at the evangelicals and do so with at least an
evenhandedness are few—and they rarely examine the political and social
themes which this book considers. The exceptions tend to be church historians much more often than they are sociologists, pursuers of civil reli-

gion, or New Left faddists. Martin Marty's work definitely takes account of the evangelical phenomenon. Marty has written a number of books which show his awareness and his lively, informal publication *Context* repeatedly reports on evangelical activities. So did Sydney Ahlstrom's magisterial *A Religious History of the American People* (1972). Recent work by historian Paul Carter also deserves mention. Carter recognizes that evangelicalism has been and is extremely important in American culture. He notes wryly that because most intellectuals have dismissed this movement does not mean for a moment that it has gone away. He is amused by the fact that liberal thought in the 1920s (as today) has had fundamentalist-evangelicals both "dying in ill repute and at the same time dangerously threatening."[71] He also contends that time has made clear that the fundamentalist predecessors of modern evangelists were right when they contended in the great Fundamentalist-Modernist controversy of the 1920s that the defenders of orthodoxy and liberal Protestantism would grow less and less committed to traditional doctrines. Carter has much more to say; significantly, his stance is always that of a frank revisionist challenging the conventional wisdom.[72]

That is the point. Carter is one more acknowledgment that outside their precincts, evangelicals simply have not been taken seriously. They deserve to be—and so does their political and social thought. They are now an important part of American religious and political life.

Chapter Two

CHRISTIANITY TODAY AND THE EVANGELICAL MAINSTREAM

T HE MAJOR VOICE of traditional, conservative evangelicalism in the late 1960s and 1970s was the influential *Christianity Today*. Read by many clergy, professors, and other evangelical opinion leaders, this twice-monthly publication first appeared in 1956. It was published first in Washington, D.C., and later in Wheaton, Illinois (it is now in Carol Stream, just outside Wheaton). The magazine was in part the brainchild of Billy Graham and his father-in-law, L. Nelson Bell, long-time columnist of *Christianity Today*. During the 1960s and 1970s the magazine had two editors-in-chief. The first editor-in-chief, Carl F. H. Henry, still served at the beginning of the New Left era, but Harold Lindsell formally succeeded him on September 27, 1968.

Lindsell was the controversial voice of *Christianity Today* and an important spokesman of mainstream evangelicalism through 1976. He was a logical successor to Henry, having long been an associate of Henry's. He and Henry had been classmates at Wheaton College and colleagues at Northern Baptist Seminary, Fuller Theological Seminary, and *Christianity Today*, where Lindsell was associate editor from 1964 to 1967. Earlier Lindsell had served as best man in Carl Henry's wedding.[1]

Lindsell was the major force directing *Christianity Today* in the years from the New Left to Jimmy Carter. He was both a religious and a political conservative, and *Christianity Today* during the 1960s and earlier 1970s became a pole around which conservatives in the fold rallied as political consensus broke apart after the mid-1960s. *Christianity Today* followed, to be sure, no simple pattern—it was a more interesting and more sophisticated publication than that—but it is fair to describe it as the most important center for the old values resisting the new tide of ideas, intellectuals, and activists.

It is well to understand, though, that the path *Christianity Today* followed was not one constantly directed toward the ethical, political, and social controversies of the age. It was, above all, a religious publication, more devoted to reporting news about the world of faith and to discussing questions of faith than anything else. It was conservative most of all in religious terms, though it contended that conservatism on religious issues led to conservatism on a broad range of social and economic questions. For example, Harold Lindsell argued that his conservatism was less a matter of politics or economics than it was a question of fighting for what he held to be the proper evangelical position on the Bible. Lindsell was committed to *The Battle for the Bible*, the title of his controversial book written during his editorship of *Christianity Today*. All social and political questions were secondary. The Bible was first, and its defense was, Lindsell said, "perhaps the most crucial issue in Christianity now."[2]

Lindsell praised those who, like Billy Graham or Carl Henry, remained true to biblical inerrancy, but he spent more of his intellectual effort on identifying and criticizing those who strayed from the fold. Lindsell was always on guard against those who tried to weaken the dogma of absolute biblical infallibility: "In recent years evangelical Christianity has been infiltrated by people who do not believe in inerrancy. This penetration into the evangelical spectrum is my deep concern."[3] Lindsell's use of the word "infiltrated" was no accident. He meant just that. The danger as he saw it lay in the growth of theological liberalism, which gradually slipped into the precincts of evangelicalism, corrupting honest believers. He recognized that arguments such as the frequent suggestion that modern science contradicted biblical religion fueled its power. Yet why should we take such assertions seriously, Lindsell asked? After all, science had changed its mind with an astonishing frequency in the course of human history. *It* was hardly infallible.[4]

In Lindsell's opinion, evidence of backsliding was widespread. The Southern Baptists had admitted ideas which were not faithful to the Bible. So had Fuller Theological Seminary. So had other groups and schools. But there was also hopeful evidence of a backlash on behalf of an inerrant Bible. The best illustration was the revolt in the Lutheran Church, Missouri Synod, a movement which drove out those trying to undermine an inerrant Bible.[5] Less hopeful, he thought, was the emergence of the reform-oriented evangelicals in the 1960s. Lindsell disagreed with them often enough politically, but his chief concern as always was theological. He worried whether or not as they rushed to advance social action they were faithful to the Bible and whether they humbly acknowledged its importance and its inerrancy. He claimed to see indications that some preferred Marxism to Christianity. Others had a utilitarian affinity for denying the Bible when they found it inconvenient.[6] This bothered him particularly in the 1970s when the writings of St. Paul on women came under fire from many feminist evangelicals. They began dismissing Paul's teachings on the subject, a flagrant example of a rejection of the inerrancy of part of the Bible when it conflicted with fashion.[7]

Lindsell understood that his overwhelming concern with the authority of the Bible was controversial even among the faithful. His insistence that it was the matter of first importance in an age in which many intellectuals thought differently and his insistence on absolute inerrancy were far from universally popular. He was, to this extent, right that there was a "battle for the Bible." He tried at times to be moderate and granted that those who did not support complete inerrancy "are still relatively evangelical. [But] I do not for one moment concede, however, in a technical sense anyone can claim the evangelical badge once he has abandoned inerrancy."[8] When critics said his crusade was divisive, Lindsell accepted that fact. He declared that faithful Christians must always elect to answer the call to truth over the call to unity.[9]

Lindsell and *Christianity Today* operated on the belief that "once inerrancy goes, it leads, however slowly, to a further denial of other biblical truths."[10] It was no surprise to Lindsell that disloyalty to the Bible was matched by moral and political decay, which also bothered him greatly. Lindsell was extremely upset about moral permissiveness in the age, especially regarding sexual practices. He felt there was little realization that life is a struggle to the death between God and the devil. One had to choose. There was little chance to defeat the devil if we did not adhere to God's commands regarding sexual life. Nor, he warned, could one comfortably leave these matters up to the schools. They could not be—and should not be—trusted to know and follow God's teachings.[11] As Lindsell told the "new evangelicals," every Christian had a solemn responsibility to avoid being "soft on premarital sex, homosexuality, pornography, and foul language."[12]

The teaching of the Bible, as Lindsell read it, regarding politics was conservative. This meant not only that Lindsell fully supported such standard American conservative ideas as a balanced budget and the prevention of any more erosion of America's traditional freedoms. It also meant a determination to see the good sides of the United States in an era in which many thoughtful people saw nothing good.[13] It included as well Lindsell's reluctance to press for much change. To be sure, he believed that as a Christian he had a responsibility to urge all the faithful to move themselves and their society closer to God's ideal: "Every believer . . . ought to be involved in seeking the improvement of society."[14] Irresponsible smugness was not Christian: "I hope you will always be critical of the status quo."[15]

Yet, like his *Christianity Today*, Lindsell frequently admonished his readers that there was no utopia in this world of sin, and there was going to be none.[16] He thought that at best we would arrive at a place far short of utopia. Moreover, he contended that we were really here not to reform the world but "to endure tribulation in the world,"[17] a fate that ensured the wisdom of "the truism that the world is filled with evils about which we can do nothing."[18]

It followed that Lindsell, like his *Christianity Today*, was ambivalent about the rise in evangelical enthusiasm for social action. Social action was not the central mission of Christians, nor was it very realistic in many cases. The answer for most social problems was devotion to Christ and individual actions by transformed, "born again" Christians. The only exception which Lindsell made was on the racial question. Individual Christians were to act, but he agreed with other writers of almost all persuasions who asserted that laws, and a good many of them, were also required to confront directly the ungodly reality of racism in America.[19]

Lindsell and many other conservative evangelicals were not necessarily unconcerned with society. It is important to understand that they believed that the discovery of Christ by individuals would have a beneficial and needed transforming effect on the social order through transformed Christian men and women. Excessive focus on social action diverted people from the meaningful social change that ultimately proceeded from finding Christ to the involvement with social structures and their age-old record of limited success at best.[20] Moreover, Lindsell and other conservatives contended that Christian individuals who were trained to fulfill useful roles in society were in their way demonstrating social concern and having social impact by doing a good job in their respective callings. Service in one's occupational calling was often the very best thing one could do both to serve God and to aid mankind.[21]

CAPITALISM, FREEDOM, AND ORDER

At the heart of the conservatism of the evangelical mainstream was its devotion to "free enterprise" and its sense that capitalism faced dangerous enemies under the banners of the Left, enemies who preached freedom, promoted anarchy, and would eventually impose a chilling form of order. Harold Lindsell and *Christianity Today* were deeply involved in this struggle. From one perspective, they saw it as a crusade to defend and celebrate the glory of human freedom. Writers from *Christianity Today* consistently enunciated a conservative position on freedom and order. On the one hand, they often defended the reality and value of human freedom, or choice, against determinists from Skinner to hard-line Marxists.[22] Usually they had in mind a definition of freedom in the classic negative liberty framework.

Freedom was the absence of restraint, and *Christianity Today* interpreted restraint to mean government and other forms of collective action. Why negative freedom was good was rarely explicitly explained, but it was assumed that only a free person in this sense could choose Christianity and otherwise lead a moral, responsible life. This kind of freedom was an assumption behind Lindsell's attacks on socialism in the World Council of Churches or elsewhere. It was also the basis for predictably glowing reviews of striking, libertarian work, such as Robert Nozick's *Anarchism, the State, and Utopia.*[23]

Above all, *Christianity Today*'s devotion to negative freedom led to sharp attacks in the magazine on the trend toward growing government, whether that growth came under President Johnson or President Nixon. Jesus, one writer declared, cared only for the individual. He never cared for the state nor approved of its relentless imperialism, which restricted economic liberty by imposing an ever-growing welfare state—and its inflationary costs. At one point in 1972 *Christianity Today* went so far as to attack the social security system, edging close to the position that it be abolished. The result was a storm of letters and complaints to the magazine, which reacted with surprise. Why did its criticism provoke such anger, it asked? In an editorial, it solemnly warned that social security had grown too important to too many people and that "the attempt to create an infallible security on earth easily slips over into a kind of idolatry."[24]

For *Christianity Today,* to defend freedom very much included supporting capitalism. *Christianity Today* could be counted on in strike situations to support business and to criticize strikers. It even suggested that labor unions were not compatible with a free country, since labor unions, like many forms of government, impeded the liberty of business. The idea that modern American capitalism was hardly an unambiguous source of increased individual choice received no consideration. *Christianity Today*'s model of economic life in America often seemed to be unaware of modern corporate economic life and its forces.[25] Yet there can be no appreciation of the view of Harold Lindsell, *Christianity Today*, and the evangelical mainstream in these years which does not *accent* their sense that capitalism and with it freedom and order needed defense. Over and over they returned to this theme, determined to save "free enterprise" from the sometimes naive and sometimes malicious forces on the Left which would destroy it.

It was in this context that *Christianity Today* crusaded against domestic lawbreakers. Its favorite target was the New Left, but it criticized many others. The magazine's tone was shrill in its judgment of radicals who had no respect for law or anything else: "We *are* sick! For one thing, we are sick of unasked, unruly potheads who shoot from the lip at our generation."[26] The sad thing about the lawless New Left, hippies and the like, L. Nelson Bell argued, was that these young people were missing the op-

portunity to know Jesus. That was the real loss, though Bell was philosophical about this (he hoped temporary) situation. No matter how many
youths rushed about after one fad or another, truth endured: "God's moral
truths are changeless."[27] Bell and *Christianity Today* were not inclined to
be philosophical, however, about "mobbism" and anarchy: they were in-
tolerable. Drastic action had to be taken to alter the spirit of disorder which
the New Left and ghetto riots manifested. Moreover, 1984 lay on the horizon and we had to decide to live in orderly freedom now.[28]

Christianity Today's excitement had more calming alloy than it sometimes seemed. Some writers in the magazine tried to offer a moderating
perspective, especially in the highly charged New Left years. One author
urged readers to relax about what he called the "new propriety" among
youths, including evangelicals, such as the new fashions of long hair for
young men and the like. Such fashion did not necessarily signify a new
morality. Another tried to explain to readers that campus tensions in the
new age would require flexible responses, which at least in Christian colleges should endeavor to reinforce basic Christian values, but by modern
means. On the one hand, "business as usual" just would not work; the
pressures for change in the New Left era required response. On the other
hand, the favorite technique of too many evangelicals—"vigorous repression"—hardly was the answer either.[29]

Against such views, however, was quite another. *Christianity Today*
quite comfortably quoted former Attorney General John Mitchell in support
of the most strident attacks on student riots and other forms of lawlessness
in the 1960s. While in retrospect he was an embarrassing authority, *Christianity Today* found his hard-line sentiments when he was attorney general
to be very appropriate. His opinion was welcome in *Christianity Today*,
and J. Edgar Hoover's was even more so. He "wrote" several articles for
the periodical during his last years, bewailing the disorder of the times. We
were now reaping the whirlwind of our permissiveness in life, which had
yielded violence, lawlessness, and widespread "civil" disobedience.[30]

J. Edgar Hoover's access to *Christianity Today* is significant. The magazine spoke for the many evangelicals who did not believe God's message
condoned disorder or force if it were directed against established institutions. There was a kind of uncomplicated faith in *Christianity Today*'s
pages. No matter how much was wrong in America—and it saw much
trouble—traditional liberty and order deserved our support as Christians
cognizant of Paul's admonition in Romans 13 that God ordained government and as Americans cognizant of our treasured past. With such a view—
in that age—J. Edgar Hoover seemed a natural ally. He was one of the
verities who still endured.

In the fight for order, to preserve free enterprise in particular, *Christianity Today* was hardly alone in its struggles. Many evangelicals joined

them. One well-known, militant illustration, present in all the religious bookstores, was Russ Walton's *One Nation Under God* (1975). The only real difference between his view and *Christianity Today*'s was a stridency not favored by the conservative journal. Walton, like so many others, contended that the United States was on the way to "A New Slavery," for which he blamed Franklin D. Roosevelt and the New Deal and the administrations which had succeeded his in Washington. Government appeared to be ruthlessly forcing its will on all kinds of Americans. Less and less often did it serve the people; more and more often people served government. The new world was one of "Controlled People and Uncontrolled Government." An example which Walton particularly bemoaned was the huge bite of taxation which government exacted from its citizens. Walton proposed abolishing high "progressive" taxes, fixing a low and flat rate of taxation, limiting government spending, forbidding budget deficits, and even returning to the gold standard.[31]

Walton declared that further steps toward statism were merely additional moves toward the "junking of the American idea."[32] They were also sacrilegious. They created a despotic power; they established and celebrated "Big Brother" and "Caesar" over God. Idolatry lurked in the background, and no true Christian could accept that. Finally, the expansion of the state unmistakably threatened private property. To do so was to deny God's will in the most direct manner possible. Walton here as elsewhere cited scripture to illuminate the tie he saw between Christianity and his political-economic values. In this case, Acts 5:4, which clearly does assume a concept of private property, and Luke 12:13–14, which does the same by a discussion of inheritance, confirmed for him that Jesus supported private ownership. For the state to undermine free enterprise and maximum individual freedom was to challenge Christianity itself.[33]

Walton and other conservatives' idea that God endorsed their economic libertarianism should not lead anyone to conclude they approved of the "greed, ruthlessness, monopoly, and coercion" critics often associated with capitalism.[34] Far from it. Walton said such practices were manifestations of self-centered sinfulness. Similarly, Walton took it for granted that all property belonged ultimately to God. It was God's universe. But this fact, he remarked, was no argument for casually limiting private property. On the contrary, it was a potent argument against such a practice, one more reminder that the state's growth ensured the parallel growth of idolatry.[35]

It was also a firm belief of conservatives like Walton that a free economic life was not to be confused with general permissiveness. Economic freedom was not the same thing as individual liberty to do whatever one willed. Economic freedom was right because it was God's law. Nowhere, even in economic life, did Christianity legitimate irresponsible freedom.

Freedom when and where God's laws provided for it was one thing, anarchy another. God's freedom certainly did not include abusing employees, or supporting abortions, or encouraging homosexuality. This was freedom gone mad.[36]

Occasionally *Christianity Today* observed that capitalism should not matter to a Christian ultimately. No economic system should. The Christian's primary job was not to rally to the aid of any single economic order; it was to gather souls for Christ. This emphasis was less obvious in books like *One Nation Under God*. *Christianity Today* also occasionally remarked that there was another form of freedom than the conservatives' notion of earthly liberty. In the last analysis *Christianity Today* held that Christians were to opt for "positive liberty," the idea that true freedom lay in the possession of absolute truth: "you will know the truth and the truth will make you free." Genuine freedom was knowledge of God and faith in him.[37]

Yet to understand *Christianity Today*'s outlook, one must appreciate that it saw no conflict between seeking souls for Christ and serving ultimate truth on the one hand and a generous amount of ordinary freedom and strong support for capitalism on the other.

AMERICA: PATRIOTISM AND CONSERVATIVE POLITICS

The sad fact, *Christianity Today* believed, was that the United States was not the country it had once been. It was not as welcome an environment for those who sought freedom, for those who supported capitalism, or for those seeking to live a Christian life. As a result, *Christianity Today* articulated an ambivalence about the United States that was characteristic of conservatives in the 1960s and 1970s. Their love for the American nation and its past was deep, but at times it seemed best to them to describe their love as an unrequited love for a no longer beautiful lover.

In the era from the New Left to Carter, *Christianity Today* denounced developments in the United States in unqualified terms. Its writers often agreed that "perhaps never before has sin been so flagrant and so bold."[38] By far the fiercest denunciations were directed at America's materialism. Their indignation over the inexhaustible covetousness in American society knew few limits. Everywhere *Christianity Today* looked the signs abounded. Materialism corrupted pervasively. It was inextricably imbedded in the culture. So were other forms of egoism, all of them eating away at the United States. We were increasingly "hedonistic, materialistic, . . . hungry for profits, pleasure, and affluence."[39] The editors of *Christianity Today* got so upset at the mess of modern America that they openly posed the question of whether or not America was through as a moral, or even a viable, nation. It asked, was "America on its knees?," was "America over the hill?" There were few reassurances vouchsafed on the editorial pages. The writers never gave a final no, but *Christianity Today* typically analyzed the situation as dire. Not hopeless, but dire. We had the choice: did we want God or decadence and destruction? The years rolled by, but the magazine did not see the answers it sought.[40]

The other side of this anxiety about America was the commitment of *Christianity Today* to the nation. The magazine consistently thought in a nation-state framework. Patriotism was a value it respected very much, and *Christianity Today* urged its readers to fly the flag on national holidays. Americans, especially in tough times, had a special responsibility to "rally behind our flag" and to defend "responsible protest and high-principled patriotism."[41] High-principled was an important adjective in that *Christianity Today* did not—indeed could not—indulge in patriotism of the fanatic kind which blindly defended every national want, or shouted support for "my country right or wrong." But it did insist that patriotism and Christianity were perfectly compatible. Moreover, *Christianity Today* argued that America, despite all, had much to be patriotic about. The depth of this belief was clear in the spirited arguments against communism that the periodical mounted. It was even more obvious when evangelicals like Mark Hatfield bore in on America's weaknesses. Then *Christianity Today* turned to the defense of the United States. All was not well in America, *nor elsewhere*. Yet our society, including our capitalist economic system, remained the best.[42]

This ambivalence may be compared profitably with the judgment of fundamentalist evangelicals. There has long been much disapproval of the "chauvinistic religious nationalism" supposedly prevalent among fundamentalists, of the idolatry it implied and the conflation of church and state it suggested. Observers note, for instance, that Billy James Hargis declared that Christianity and America were—and ought to be—intimately intertwined. His image of the United States held that it was a uniquely Christian nation.[43]

Yet, while Hargis claimed that "America is still God's greatest nation under the Living Son," he felt ambivalence in the midst of his praise. There were, he said, "problems, and there are many."[44] He and others in the late 1960s and well into the 1970s were highly upset about America. They were not admirers of what they saw. They were, indeed, harsh critics. Hargis was angry at what he saw as the frightening progress of communists and their liberal allies in all aspects of American life. They were destroying the American dream and American Christianity. Our government was already in the hands of enemies of a Christian America. There was an urgent need "to purge the church of an apostate leadership and to eliminate the subverters and destroyers who undermine our American way."[45]

Another spokesman for religious fundamentalism also attested that all was far from well in the United States. It was distressing to him how much America was in love with money and how little with God. It was disgusting how many Americans had a taste for decadence. We chased after "self-indulgence through amusement, . . . drinking, and drugs" and whatever else we could find.[46] We were far away from Jesus.

He was clearly sympathetic to Christians committed to what he termed "patriotic movements." They undertook the essential mission of rekindling the bond between the United States and Christianity. They stood for American rediscovery and regeneration. More were needed, however, a point on which Hargis agreed, since he contended that there was a desperate need for Christians to mobilize to bring back a Christian America. Hargis believed he had been annointed by God to launch a crusade among the American people to struggle against our fallen politicians, our polluted Christianity, and our drift toward communism. This, of course, Hargis expressed in his Christian Anti-Communist Crusade. Hargis also felt prayer was another important weapon. So was voting—correctly. So was running for office, whether it was the local school board or higher positions. So was tackling broader public opinion by television and radio programming. All of these instruments together might stem, or even reverse, the tide.[47]

In short, as Hargis's thought suggests, the fundamentalist perspective was not only conservative but also radical. It not only loved a certain Christian America, but also recognized that there was a long road to travel before that vision was vigorous and healthy again in an America gone wrong.[48]

The more fundamentalist wing of conservative evangelicalism was more shrill than their mainstream brethren. They saw more dangers, greater corruption, and more communism. But their analysis was the same: a damaged America was no longer as great as it had once been. Yet it must still be loved, cared for, and ultimately—like the fallen sinner it was—reborn.

This conviction underlay *Christianity Today*'s explicit attitudes toward the political choices that faced America in the age of the New Left, Watergate, and Carter. *Christianity Today* did not openly endorse candidates. Its interest in electoral politics was keen, however, a fact which reflected continued conservative belief in the flawed American System. The 1968 presidential campaign coverage in *Christianity Today* was fairly typical. The journal viewed the election partly in the frame of obvious contemporary events such as the riots at the Democratic National Convention in Chicago in 1968. It reported whom various "star" clergy supported, that leading evangelicals such as Billy Graham and L. Nelson Bell were for Nixon, while more socially active clerics often endorsed Humphrey. The magazine avoided overt criticism of any candidate, even George Wallace, though it remarked that for Christians Wallace's stand on race constituted a roadblock, and it did not support any candidate. Editor Harold Lindsell made it clear that he would not endorse anyone. Indeed, he could not even vote because he had moved recently.[49]

The 1972 election received more attention. The magazine was unusually partisan, though once again it did not officially support either aspirant. Harold Lindsell did note that his personal choice was Nixon, but he did so in an easygoing fashion. A number of news reports slanted toward Nixon, including one that painted Nixon as a safe centrist and suggested that McGovern was an extremist and another which ridiculed McGovern's pretensions to honesty in the light of his behavior in the Senator Thomas Eagleton affair. A third dismissed Democratic Party claims that their convention represented a new politics as an old story which merited much skepticism. A fourth article announced the existence of "Evangelicals for McGovern," including such figures as Tom Skinner, David Moberg, and Stephen Monsma, but also indicated that Billy Graham favored Nixon and predicted that most evangelicals would follow his example in the voting booth.[50]

Christianity Today, in its coverage of the 1968 and 1972 elections, showed general support for the political process and bias against candidates who appeared radical in ways it did not like (McGovern). The periodical did not see either 1968 or 1972 as a contest between the forces of change and the forces of the status quo. In both elections they appeared to view Nixon as a force for order, which they anxiously sought, *and* a force for change. Nixon, in their mind, was trying to bring America back to its classic values of individualism, capitalism, patriotism, and Christian fellowship. These changes would produce a better society, the magazine suggested, and a more orderly one.

The magazine displayed no trace of alienation in its reflections on the 1976 presidential election either, not least because both presidential candidates openly courted evangelicals. *Christianity Today* was more sympathetic to Ford than to Carter, but there was no concerted animus against Carter in its articles. There was no suggestion that he was another McGovern. He was hardly the enemy of evangelical America, and *Christianity Today* never pretended otherwise.[51]

Watergate did not crack *Christianity Today*'s relatively sanguine evaluation of the American political order, especially since 1976 produced candidates Ford and Carter, who breathed a different and better spirit. Watergate was a warning about the corruption of flexible morality and situation ethics which currently infected America. It could—and had—corrupted the top. But it had not soiled the whole. It was a basis for ambivalence about America, but not yet for a retreat from loyalty to an imperfect nation and society.[52]

Here and there, though, *Christianity Today* showed signs of being more in sympathy with critical conservatism than their reputation for the politics of the bland middle might have suggested. For example, *Christianity Today* praised J. Howard Pew on his death in 1971, lauding him extravagantly as a man and as a benefactor of *Christianity Today*. It did not mention that he was also a zealot of extreme right-wing causes nor that he financed the early deficits of *Christianity Today*. The magazine also closely followed Campus Crusade's Bill Bright and his involvement in Christian conservative politics. It sympathetically described his intervention in 1976 Republican politics in Arizona. It also reported, however, that Billy Graham did not especially welcome Bright's mixing in politics.[53]

The book reviews in *Christianity Today* usually had nothing to do with politics, but occasionally they did. One could encounter such surprises as Russell Kirk, the active conservative, reviewing a book—or having a book of his favorably reviewed. Ronald Nash's *The Conservative Intellectual Movement in America Since 1945*, the most able work by a conservative on the postwar era in conservative thought, received a warm review in *Christianity Today*, though its reviewer complained that the book neglected the realm of religious conservatism (which *Christianity Today* often exemplified). Finally, on the occasion of the tenth anniversary of *The National Review*, *Christianity Today* carried a laudatory article celebrating the controversial organ of intellectual conservatism in America.[54]

These examples hardly add up to a relentless campaign by *Christianity Today* to expose its readers to the names, books, and magazines of organized conservatism. Yet the bias was definitely there. The magazine showed no favorable interest in liberal or radical movements. There were no links with important liberals nor did works by liberals receive generous praise in the book review pages; such attention was invariably reserved for conservatives.[55]

SOCIAL ACTION

Christianity Today in the later 1960s reflected the traditional conservative suspicion of Christian social action. It respected fundamentalist denunciations of the heretical idea that "sin is essentially social and should be saved socially" and their belief that what mattered was "the ministry of the local church . . . souls saved, converts baptized, spiritual growth."[56] Of course, it also approved of fundamentalist objections to the "social gospel, human betterment" movements and "the graveyard of social salvation and do-goodism of all kinds."[57]

More than anyone else in *Christianity Today*, L. Nelson Bell, former China missionary and father-in-law of Billy Graham, developed the conservative case in his regular and effective column in *Christianity Today*. He resisted the rising voices within evangelicalism calling for increased social concern, suspecting that the cost of this new emphasis would be surrendering the duty to win souls to Christ. Bell suspected that many in the 1960s were no longer interested in saving souls and did not realize that "it is impossible to reform the social order apart from personal redemption of individuals."[58] While they should aid the needy, true Christians were never to forget that their main responsibility was to offer all "the Bread of Life."[59] Bell and others were confident that when people discovered the truth of Christianity, they would grow so much spiritually that they would necessarily affect and improve their immediate environment. They would be healed personally, and society would gain from that process.

By the 1970s Bell had passed from the scene, but his point of view still obtained a hearing. Editorials in *Christianity Today* reflected it when they complained that many social reformers lacked a realistic understanding of the world. The reformers, said the editorials, often were downright silly in their utopianism. But they were not alone. It was a lamentably pervasive disease: "Contemporary Americans seem obsessed by a passion for social utopia and look to politico-economic forces to provide it."[60] The facts were that the complexity of modern society and the inexorable power of sin ruled out utopias and allowed for only gradual change.

Christianity Today worried about the enthusiasm for social action particularly when it swept up clergy and churches as it sometimes did in the 1960s. The periodical invariably castigated clergy who plunged into politics, and it had little sympathy for any efforts to urge denominations to take political stands. The church, it argued, should not usurp a role that was proper, if not central, for the individual Christian. God's call to the church was a call to save souls. Moreover, the social teachings of scripture were hardly so self-evident that the church could stride confidently forward.[61]

Yet these anxieties, doubts, and worries about social action were not the entire story, especially in the 1970s. The traditional stance remained important, but *Christianity Today* showed a growing inclination to suggest to its readers that as individual Christians they had social responsibilities. They were to be healers. As *Christianity Today* reminded its readers in 1976, the bicentennial was a good time for Christians to ask themselves the hard question of whether they were matching "doctrine with deed."[62] The magazine warmly endorsed the Lausanne Covenant of world evangelicals in 1974, including its proclamation: "Evangelism and socio-political involvement are both part of our Christian duty. . . . Both are necessary expressions of . . . our love for our neighbor and our obedience to Jesus Christ."[63] A number of book reviews in the 1970s were surprisingly supportive of the work of such reform-oriented figures as David O. Moberg and often suggested that evangelicals might do more in the social side of life. This was, as an article published in 1972 observed, what the early church had left as a legacy, and no one should ignore it.[64]

Though the magazine sometimes urged individual Christians to serve social needs, its appeals were often vague and general and offered largely in passing. Two exceptions were the areas of race relations and environmental concerns. We discuss the role the race issue played in the entire movement in Chapter Nine, but it is worth noting here that *Christianity Today* often discussed racial problems and repeatedly declared that racial prejudice was wrong. Much less clear was its commitment to suggesting specific actions or to accepting active state intervention or to welcoming the tactics of blacks and whites who did demonstrate a determined, concrete witness to work for racial change. As always, the failure of *Christianity Today* to follow up its general affirmations in the area of social action suggested that its conservative impulses remained strong.

While *Christianity Today* continued discussing the race problem through 1976, it also looked to other social issues in the 1970s. Environmentalism in particular came into its own, a shift which closely paralleled developments in the larger culture. Many articles and editorials appeared in the periodical urging that sensitive Christians learn God's teachings about the environment—and then change their own attitudes. According to writers in *Christianity Today*, God taught that we must love and respect his creation, not plunder and pollute it. Human history told a tale of such desecrations. We now had to alter our attitudes and behavior to follow God's different norm. The real problem was the sin of selfishness. People *used* nature to get what they wanted at a terrible cost to God's earth. Stewardship had to replace selfishness, not least because we now had to face the practical consequences of our rapaciousness.[65]

This analysis was characteristic of *Christianity Today*. It placed the blame on individuals and their sinful actions—and thus on all of us. The editors of *Christianity Today* were little inclined to the view that capitalism, or government, or one or another nation was at fault. We were at fault. They dismissed such "social" explanations as superficial just as they rejected "solutions" which proposed dependence on government control. The editorials did not deny the advantage of selected steps of government intervention, but they warned of the insatiable thirst of the state for human liberty. Moreover, *Christianity Today* doubted that government could alter individual attitudes, which were often greedy and careless. Nor did it believe the state could lead individuals to a simpler life, which *Christianity Today* often urged on readers. Americans ate too much. They used too much gasoline. They wasted too much. They needed to learn that less *was* more. Government could not teach that lesson.[66]

What were the implications of the periodical's enthusiasm for environmental sensitivity in the 1970s? It did involve considerable social awareness, though its insistence that coping with environmental issues should best come through individual actions suggested its limitations in social analysis. To its critics such a proposal was one more reminder that *Christianity Today* routinely tamed every potentially disturbing issue in this fashion. Each became a subject for individual action and an occasion for the castigation of the state. Whether it was intentional or not, the result was a fundamentally conservative response that might have some beneficial consequences for a problem such as pollution, but not consequences that were likely to transform the complex economic and social practices and institutions which ultimately encouraged pollution. Other critics noted that *Christianity Today* usually directed its exploration of the environmental crisis away from the problem of famine and world hunger, or poverty; its environmentalism seemed to have little connection with these evils. To critics, environmentalism in the hands of *Christianity Today* became no more than a vague cause with few significant implications, one which mainstream conservative evangelicals could safely — and meaninglessly — support. Finally, some skeptics went so far as to ask if the magazine had any authentic commitment to the simple life it often lauded. This was a good test, they suggested, of its willingness to witness. By this test, they said, *Christianity Today* obviously failed. They claimed to see no sign in the lives of the staffers that demonstrated a radical reformation toward a simple life.[67]

COMPANIONS

Christianity Today was hardly alone in the evangelical mainstream. Even in the diversity which the times spawned in the 1960s and 1970s, it had many allies. Some of those who shared its conservative political perspective were not particularly sophisticated, or at least their works did not aim at an especially sophisticated audience. While writers in *Christianity Today* took seriously the task of reaching an educated and intellectually demanding audience, other authors reached out to different publics. The result was often writing which those associated with *Christianity Today* would not have produced for their publication, yet which was in one accord with its conservative political message.

One of the most breathless examples was Richard M. DeVos, author of *Believe* (1975). The founder and president of Amway Corporation, DeVos did not pretend to be an intellectual. His emphasis on the value of positive thinking, the importance of practical action, the need for bold entrepreneurs, and the necessity of persistent workers identified him as an aggressive businessman. DeVos mixed his belief in free enterprise, Jesus, and American patriotism in a fashion in which enthusiasm substituted for disciplined thought. There did not seem to be much difference in his enthusiasm for America or Jesus, both of which were central to his notion of truth. To him belief in Jesus and in an "old-fashioned, hand-over-heart, emotional brand of patriotism" could not, in fact, possibly conflict.[68]

Writers such as DeVos liked their arguments uncomplicated. This was clear when DeVos discussed his theory of human beings and human freedom. DeVos had absolutely no doubt that the human person was fully accountable for his actions in life. He did not take into account background factors even to the modest extent that *Christianity Today* did. Thus DeVos insisted that justice must be founded on merit. We should get in life based on what we achieve as human beings. This doctrine soon emerged as a defense of "free enterprise," which he considered "a gift of God to us."[69] The connections were rarely clear, but the affirmations were always intense.

DeVos was hardly the likeliest candidate from the world of conservatism for an intellectual award, but he was a fair enough example of a sincere and earnest popular perspective which shared many ideas with *Christianity Today*. At quite another level, one compatible with the thoughtful approach of *Christianity Today*, were other writers such as Robert Culver of Trinity Evangelical Divinity School, Deerfield, Illinois, and Harold O. J. Brown, one-time associate editor of *Christianity Today*. *Christianity Today* strongly recommended both men's writings to its readers as examples of the best thinking being done on political and social questions in their age. Both men ably argued for a conservative, Christian politics. Harold O. J. Brown, a conservative Christian published by the conservative firm Arlington House, followed one approach in his defense of conservative evangelicalism. Robert Culver, the best single conservative Christian political theorist of the era, followed another.

Brown spoke in terms of the issues of the day, always informed, of course, by what he deeply believed to be the teaching of scripture. His topical conservatism expressed itself, for example, in strong support of the Vietnam War and deep anger with protesters who took part in "the domestic agitation for peace in Vietnam at any price." He was convinced that they had "played into the hands of our external enemies."[70] He was bitter when it became clear that, as he put it, the "so-called doves now appear to have won their battle to force the United States to yield to the Hanoi government and the N.L.F."[71] Doves were only one aspect of an American civilization which was increasingly secular and soft, overwhelmed by growing materialism and the love of a "dreadful thing," secular equality.[72]

Much of this sort of thing was absent in Robert Culver's impressive *Toward a Biblical View of Civil Government* (1974). Culver was far more scholarly than Brown. Culver also stayed closer to biblical texts, the teachings of the Old Testament, the Pauline epistles, and the ideas of Jesus. Culver, like Brown, forcefully argued his point of view, but he was better able to put what he had to say into what he took to be biblical language and biblical truth.

Culver and Brown explored two issues of particular interest for our study of the conservative evangelical outlook: the proper relationship between the Christian, the state, and authority, raising fundamental questions about the tensions between freedom and authority; and the appropriate evangelical attitude toward social reform in an age which experienced the New Left and the opening in evangelicalism toward more social commitment.

The issue of the state and authority was not necessarily an easy matter for many conservative evangelicals. One popular view that the evangelicals were libertarians was completely off the mark. They were authoritarians, devoted believers in following God and his will. Moreover, they denied that God taught that we could do without authority in any aspect of life. God's plan for us hardly included anarchism. Certainly God taught reverence for his authority, which was not to be confused with secular notions of freedom. True freedom, Brown suggested, was adherence to God and had nothing to do with secular images of liberty. The "flight from authority," which perceptive conservative evangelicals recognized in our period, bothered Brown.[73] He placed most of the blame not on right-wing libertarians and celebrators of the free enterprise system, but rather on the American left. Its older members praised freedom in academic studies to naive students while writing sociology and psychology textbooks that enunciated environmental or psychological determinism. Its younger members in the New Left era, on the other hand, set about smashing every existent authority in the name of a vague but intense commitment to human liberty.[74]

Conservative evangelicals like Brown carefully tried to delineate where God's authority required state action. There was no biblical mandate for state interference with ordinary social and economic activities. God did not propose that laws control the economic life of people, but he did require state action in certain areas of personal moral life. Brown had no enthusiasm for bluenoses, but when wild, undisciplined self-indulgence began to run unchecked in the late 1960s and early 1970s, he believed that the state had to step in. We faced a situation of "unbridled license." Moreover, we should not let our efforts to enforce God's laws be derailed by the notion that "freedom-of-choice" was a sacred value. It was not, Brown argued, as he attacked those opposed to state regulation and those in favor of abortions. This was a secular ideal, not basic to Christian purposes.[75]

In this attitude, Culver suggested, he was in accord with the teaching of the Bible. It did not teach anarchism or libertarianism. Nor did it teach disrespect for rulers or hate toward governmental authority. This was not the model Jesus' behavior demonstrated.[76]

Culver thought it was manifest that no one could summon Paul either to support disrespect for the state. Culver had in mind not only the injunctions of Romans 13, to accept and obey the divine institution of government, but also Paul's behavior as a Roman citizen. Paul, Culver pointed out, always honored the Rome which eventually executed him. He clung to his Roman citizenship and its privileges. He knew that government, established in God's will, was far more useful to every individual than the anarchy which was its practical alternative.[77]

Brown and Culver and other more thoughtful evangelical conservatives were far more in an Augustinian/Calvinist tradition than they were in a Millian liberal tradition. The state was something of worth and not lightly scorned. To be sure, the state would not be necessary if we were not sinners; given our sinful condition, however, it was needed. But their defense of the Christian use of the state in moral matters (as opposed to social policies) did not mean they approved of state programs to make people Christians. Such a policy was never supported by conservative evangelicals. To do so would conflict with Jesus' instruction that one must choose Christianity freely. Nor did respect for governmental authority lead them to deny the prophets' warnings about the dangers of unchecked power. All people were sinners, government rulers and bureaucrats no less than New Leftists and libertarians.[78]

One of the most interesting marks of conservatism among such evangelicals as Culver and Brown, and one of the signs of their attachment to the broader conservative world, was their explicit sympathy for tradition. They did not claim tradition was right in all areas of life or at all times, but they had deep affection for conventional ways of doing things. They claimed biblical support for such an attitude: "The general focus of biblical wisdom in the social sphere is conservative. . . . The best things are to be preserved. . . . Stable institutions, stable social relationships, strengthening of civil order and authority are supported. Disruptive agitation, revolution, and active civil disobedience all are condemned."[79]

Perhaps it was equally significant that these evangelical conservatives did not make more of traditionalism. It was an aspect of their thought, but not the bedrock. The explanation lay in their Protestant evangelical background. In politics and religion tradition was a guide, but in importance it hardly replaced the Word of God found in the Bible.

Brown and Culver discussed the relationship between Christianity and social action in sharper outline than *Christianity Today* did. But they shared the same general evangelical orthodoxy. Salvation and redemption could only be individual acts guided by God's beneficent grace. The only way there could be any genuine improvement in society was through a Christ-centered change in individuals; only "changed men can change society."[80] Mass political movements accomplished little that was good and did not speak to human hearts.

Predictably, they concluded government was not the best agency for godly change, however much he instituted it. The most that conservative evangelicals would grant government, and some were not enthusiastic about granting even this much, was that it should provide a basic minimum of safety and liberty for every citizen. Beyond that, government should not step into what should be the individual's realm, under God's wisdom. To be sure, Brown and Culver were hardly unaware of original sin, and they often cited the dangers of "excessive individualism"—individualism undirected by God's laws. But there were also other dangers, dangers that could come from government interference. They were "the dangers of collectivism," which included the substitution of a secular governmental decision for God's judgment and the collapse of individual choice and responsibility before the whims of state bureaucrats who claimed to act for the larger community.[81]

Conservatives such as Culver also faulted the tone of many social reform enthusiasts. They brimmed over with too much hatred of the rich, which was not a biblical emotion. Did the reformers of the Old Testament teach such animosity? Moreover, as Culver said, the prophets did not want "to despoil the rich. The prophets were not advocates of social and economic leveling."[82] Was Jesus a teacher of such heresy? No, Jesus "had no poor man's prejudices against the well-to-do and the privileges accompanying wealth and property ownership." Brown and Culver agreed that the New Testament clearly provided for the existence and legitimacy of private property. No wonder "there is small comfort for economic equality or socialism in Jesus."[83] This biblical message was far indeed from the position of political liberals or leftists, who seemed bent on destroying both gospel truth and the upper economic classes.

The nature of proper social concern was readily apparent. On a one-to-one basis, insofar as possible, we were to aid widows, orphans, and others who were suffering in life and to act through the state to block serious immorality like abortion. All social concern had to proceed with two caveats. First, Christians had to remember that the first function of the Christian was to spread the good news of Jesus Christ and prepare for the next world. Second, Christians had to remember that Jesus' view was that his kingdom was ultimately not of this world. The danger of a social gospel was the substitution of secular social action for Christ's word. Never, warned conservative evangelicals, must we lose Christ as we concern ourselves with social betterment. Never must we fall under the illusion that in social action will we really know and live like Christ. Such a belief led away from Christ and his sacred call to evangelize.

Chapter Three

THE PERSPECTIVE OF BILLY GRAHAM

WHAT *Christianity Today* represents for conservative, mainstream evangelical opinion leaders, Billy Graham represents for the wider evangelical fellowship. Both stood together for a more open but fundamentally conservative Christianity as it translated into political and social action in the 1960s and 1970s. Graham has long been *Christianity Today*'s favorite evangelical and his political conservatism has often paralleled the line taken by *Christianity Today*.

Billy Graham was born in 1918 in Charlotte, North Carolina. Unlike the others we will discuss in this book, his status as a religious celebrity and his role as a widely popular leader have ensured him numerous biographers and students of his activities. His career has received microscopic examination, as have his utterances over the years. Graham came from a comparatively well-off, but hardly rich, farm family. He became a minister only after struggling through several crises and several colleges, finally being graduated from Wheaton College, where he met his wife Ruth. His service as a minister took several forms, including work in the major Youth for Christ movement from 1946 to 1949. It was in 1949 in a Los Angeles crusade that he caught on with the national media and his emergence as a famous evangelist began. Today he (unlike his Presbyterian wife) is a Baptist and significantly a member of the largest Southern Baptist church, First Baptist of Dallas, whose pastor, W. A. Criswell, is also a well-known evangelical and a vigorous proponent of political conservatism.[1]

Graham's ministry has not been a particularly intellectual one. He insists he speaks to the heart, not to the mind, and he believes this is as it should be. But Graham is not hostile to religion which can also speak to the mind. His substantial role in the founding of *Christianity Today* in the 1950s was testimony to his interest in this objective, though Graham is no intellectual and does not claim to be.[2]

But Graham's undeniable popularity with the bulk of ordinary evan-

gelicals and his close contacts with many leaders—and intellectuals—within
his religious universe establish the reality of his enormous influence. He is
a key figure in exploring the traditional forces in evangelicalism because of
this influence. One can hardly ignore so central a figure. In the 1960s and
early 1970s he joined with those associated with *Christianity Today* to
defend a conservative perspective, albeit with a certain modern admixture.

His enormous influence, even among many evangelical thinkers, is hard
for many nonevangelical intellectuals to believe. Some ridicule him as one
whose "intellectual grasp of the complexities of modern life remained child-
ishly simple and superstitious."[3] Others dismiss him as a performer of
questionable quality and dubious honesty. And political critics link him
with "ultra-conservative politics and economics," perfectionist individualism, rabid patriotism, and fanatic anti-Communism.[4] More recently, his
intimate connections with the Nixon White House cast another shadow
over him: involvement with the darker side of the American power
establishment.[5]

One unmistakable measure of Graham's importance was *Christianity
Today*'s very warm treatment of Graham throughout the 1960s and middle
1970s. While *Christianity Today* and Graham benefited from their alliance
with each other, the endless stream of laudatory articles on Graham in
Christianity Today reflected as well as encouraged his standing among all
evangelicals. In fairness, *Christianity Today* was merely accurately reporting
the reality of Graham's prominence by covering him far more than any
other evangelical. It demonstrated its own judgment on this fact, however,
through its consistently flattering coverage of Graham. Whether Graham
went to Seattle, Berkeley, Northern Ireland, New York City, Korea, or Raleigh, North Carolina, *Christianity Today* reported his trip with every bit
as much enthusiasm as local audiences displayed.[6] For the editors of *Christianity Today* as for the mainstream of the evangelical movement, Graham
was a great man and his work God's work. He and Harold Lindsell were
personal friends, and Lindsell frankly admired Graham and assessed his
contribution to evangelicalism in glowing terms even as Graham acknowledged the assistance he received from Lindsell.[7] The celebration of Graham
reached its height during the twenty-fifth anniversary year of his ministry
in 1974. Laudatory stories on him appeared in several issues of *Christianity
Today*, and almost all of one issue was devoted to *Christianity Today*'s
"long-time friend." That issue included a glossy full-page picture of Graham, a warm biography which spared few adjectives of praise for Graham
as a man of "winsome personality and patient sincerity." The magazine also
put on an anniversary party for Graham—in the Hollywood Bowl.[8]

To some observers even within the evangelical movement all this was
excessive. The left-wing *Sojourners* chose to attack Graham in the late
1970s in a way that was unthinkable before then. It reported that the Billy

Graham organization had given *Christianity Today* $240,000 in the period
1971 to 1975, the very years when *Christianity Today* was most enthusiastic
about Graham.[9] The implication was obvious, though a reading of *Christianity Today* and a knowledge of Graham's importance in the evangelical
movement does not confirm the sinister suspicions. After all, Graham and
Christianity Today were allies on a broad range of questions from inerrancy
of the Bible to the race issue. They engaged in no conspiracy, but rather
shared a meeting of minds and hearts. This is why Graham gives us a good
sense of the mainstream's political and social inclinations on one level in
the age of the New Left, Vietnam, and Watergate, just as *Christianity Today*
reveals those inclinations at another, somewhat more complex and developed level.

Graham's ministry was an obviously popular one—his implicit and
sometimes explicit religious and political conservatism reached many ears
and eyes. Graham was partly his organization, its elaborately disciplined
rallies around the world, its network of over 900 radio stations which
broadcast his weekly Hour of Decision program, and his incredible personal
ministry with his listeners in person or on radio and TV. Graham's organization was the result of many hands, obviously, but it has long been a
superbly efficient organization for which Graham deserves a hefty share of
the credit. Graham, a former Fuller Brush salesman who says he would
have gone into politics had the Lord not called him to religion, may lay
claim to be the founder of an organization which any Fuller Brush executive
might well wish to equal.[10]

To understand Billy Graham in the 1960s and early 1970s, it is important to realize that Graham gave no indication that he saw himself as
a political figure. His approach and his mission had political implications,
but he saw himself primarily as an evangelist for Christ. His task was not
political reform or social action so much as it was delivering what he and
others called "the Good News." He proclaimed that faith was what mattered if one sought the ultimate goal of salvation, and he was as rigorous
as Harold Lindsell or any theological conservative could wish when he
defended the inerrant scripture or insisted on the necessity for a person to
be born again through faith.[11]

Graham's presuppositions had inevitably conservative results. His emphasis on evangelism led him to accept the status quo in practice even as
he undertook to lead souls to be born again in Christ. Graham knew we
would have a transformed world if our globe fell under the sway of Christians, although his premillenialism expected no such achievement prior to
Christ's return. For now Graham thought we should concentrate on individual salvation and evangelism and largely avoid politics. His message was
unmistakable, and we should recognize the powerful legitimacy Graham's
ministry gave to this conviction of conservative evangelicalism.

But personal salvation was not all. Graham's crusades, his sermons, and his popular writings should demonstrate to any skeptic that Graham cared a good deal about living an ethical life as well as achieving personal salvation. The discovery and propagation of the good news was first in importance, but Graham always declared that the Christian had a solemn and urgent duty to live rightly in witness to God's word. He always demanded that his listeners and readers do so. However, throughout his ministry Graham's interpretation of this responsibility followed standard evangelical views. Graham's ideal concentrated on personal morality reached by individual action; only infrequently did he evidence a broader social or political sensitivity. Graham talked about individuals living a Christian life by adhering to a disciplined, self-denying personal road where sin had little sway. To do this Christians had to avoid confusing "liberty with license" and "freedom for the bondage of self-indulgence."[12] The major trap designed to snare people into a life of sin was sexual lust and the immorality which often accompanied it. Graham's favorite theme was his lamentation of the growing national scandal of sexual "impurity," the spread of extramarital sex, and the consequent tragedy of divorce. Sometimes Graham's intense concern with these problems excluded other issues and lent strength to the suggestion that personal sin and individual change was the sum and substance of his social vision.[13]

Early in his career and continuing into the 1970s, Graham demonstrated commitment to *one* question which leading mainstream evangelicals saw as a social issue of importance: the problem of race relations. Graham consistently articulated his conviction that every person deserved equal dignity as a child of God and he insisted that society as well as individuals must change to realize this goal. Graham was in fact a pioneer. His focus on the race question and his effort on behalf of equal treatment of the races began before the civil rights revolution started. He was far ahead of his time and of his (at first) largely southern constituency. Beginning with his first purposely integrated crusade, in Chattanooga, Tennessee, in 1953, he talked only to desegregated audiences; he later gave complete support to the Civil Rights Acts of the Johnson years. He developed and maintained an integrated staff. He even made TV spots urging people to obey the law regarding school integration.[14] He insisted that his rallies in South Africa be open to all races and he condemned the South African system in unequivocable language: "I don't think anyone anywhere in the world could possibly excuse apartheid."[15]

Graham told his fellow Christians that they had to deal with the race relations. But he reacted in perfect step with the mainstream of evangelicalism in his caution over many of the specific moves made in the name of the civil rights revolution for blacks in the late 1960s. Graham did not always support all civil rights activists any more than *Christianity Today* did. In fact, as the pace of racial turmoil stepped up in the middle 1960s, events bypassed Graham and his sympathies for a time; he began proposing, for example, that King "put the brakes on." Graham even made the mistake of speculating that the bulk of the black community in Birmingham did not support King's efforts to break segregation there. Whenever racial rioting broke out Graham expressed great unhappiness, and he always took a strong law and order position.[16] After King's death, however, Graham began quoting Martin Luther King, and he gradually grew more in touch with black aspirations — though in no way altering his opposition to rioting — through his expanded contacts with black evangelical thinkers and activists.[17]

Graham's forthright stand on race was an early testimony to at least some openness on his part to social action. In the late 1960s and the 1970s Graham went further and endorsed the necessity of broader social responsibility: "The new man should have a new social concern."[18] He began to devote time and space to this theme. There were so many arenas in which the believing Christian could work. The sick, the prisoners, the discriminated against, and above all the poor cried out for a demonstration of the Christian witness. Graham had rarely discussed the poor before — at least with any understanding. That he did so now was the mark of his modestly expanding social awareness and suggested that he too caught something of the spirit of the age. The plight of the poor, he declared, "causes an ache in my heart constantly," and he proposed that Christians follow scripture (e.g., Proverbs 21:13 and Psalms 41:1) and exercise "a responsibility to the poor."[19] Although Graham particularly had in mind the poor who were eager to find work but could not do so, he still preached that all the poor merited concern, as did the hungry. Every Christian had to move actively to demonstrate love for people struggling to survive in the sometimes cruel and painful world. It was a tragedy that the relative wealth of the rich and poor should count for so much in life, since in Christ it did not matter who was rich or poor.[20]

Exactly what did Graham propose Christians do about the impoverished? Graham did endorse Lyndon Johnson's war on poverty, but generally he shied away from making specific policy recommendations. His critics suggested that this was a typically conservative response. All he offered was generalized sympathy for the disadvantaged in society, but that concern did not really mean anything concrete. Without both specific plans to help the poor and a strong social analysis which explained why they were poor in the first place, his words meant little. Some even suggested that Graham had no choice: he was so unhelpful because he was in bondage to the rich in order to support his ministry, or even his personal lifestyle. This was too cynical, though there was hardly any doubt that Graham was a conservative. His relative lack of interest in government solutions to such social problems as poverty had more to do with conservative views about the means

of change than it did with obvious callousness. The fact was that Graham
expected individual Christians to take the lead toward solutions. Government could not replace, or even begin to equal, the effective role of the
individual. There was an unmistakably spiritual dimension to every problem, including poverty, and knee jerk advocates of government solution of
every social ailment were all too slow to learn such a basic truth about life.
The state had its role, to be sure, but only spiritually based social action,
no matter how much the state helped, could conquer perplexing and serious
social problems.[21]

This point obviously applied to those who thought the solution to
poverty and materialism was the abolition of private property. Graham
judged this approach to be a mechanical solution foreign to Jesus and
doomed to end unsuccessfully. What was needed was something else: people had to fight their own selfishness and replace it with Jesus' spirit. Selfishness was the principal cause of evil; one economic order or another was
not. The spirit of Jesus in an individual, in reformers, in a society could
indeed work miracles. This spirit was, above all, one of love. Love was the
greatest of all the agents of change. It was essential. Without love a Christian died. Without love Christian social concern was empty.[22]

This warning was characteristic of Graham's entire approach to Christian social action. Every mention of social action was circumscribed with
a number of similar warnings to show caution. He emphasized the caution
far more than he did his occasional urgings for social concern or his infre-
quent specific suggestions as to how to serve. Those ubiquitous warnings
give us a good sense of his essential political conservatism and of his participation in the evangelical mainstream.

Five points, common to traditional evangelical thought, illustrated the
caution which permeated Graham's views. First, Graham frequently remarked that all social action, however pressing its need and however consuming its purpose, must be kept in perspective. Of course, as we know,
Graham never budged for a moment from the orthodox position that the
first mission of every evangelist was the spreading of the good news. Everything else was secondary for Graham, even in those early years of the late
1950s and early 1960s when he stood for racial equality or later when he
discovered the poor: "Let us rejoice in social action, and yet insist that it
alone is not evangelism, and cannot be substituted for evangelism."[23]

He repeated this belief at the Lausanne Conference on World Evangelism in 1974. But he appreciated that there was a proper role for social
action also. His best-selling book Angels (1975) once again indicated his
overwhelming commitment to evangelism and his remarkable, continuing
lack of interest in Christian problems in this world. It suggested that Graham's modest interest in social reform in the late 1960s and his endorsement of social concern after that date had waned. This is not really the

whole story, though. True to his commitment to individual social action, the Graham organization in the 1980s is active in several social ministries, and Graham himself has spoken out about the arms race and nuclear destruction.[24]

Second, people had to remember that now, as it always had been and always would be, the great problem remained sin. The root cause of evil was not poverty, not race, and not war. Therefore, any means of change that did not modify the sinful proclivities of our vulnerable human hearts was unlikely to succeed.[25]

Third, while Graham knew that Christianity decreed that we make revolutionary changes in life, he insisted that they be made recognizing that "Christ is the only answer." Many of the revolutionary dreams that misled so many people were remote from Christ, bubbles bound to burst, allowing their naive advocates no satisfaction. Graham admonished all visionaries, for example those who dreamed of ultimate world peace, to recognize that their goals were impossible short of God's direct intervention. Those who dreamed of an economic utopia were particularly confused. They did not comprehend that such a utopia was quite impossible by human efforts alone, and their confidence that such a world could fulfill the human being's basic needs betrayed a lamentably materialist misunderstanding of man.[26]

Fourth, it followed that Graham felt that politics must be used gingerly, just as he believed government should be. Both the 1960 and 1964 elections embarrassed him, because they were instances in which large numbers of religious people hurled themselves into politics with an energy, indeed fervor, that belied a Christian awareness of the restricted value and significance of politics. He made the same observation about the New Left era. Politics was a most limited means to accomplish social change. It was more than unfortunate that "people have become addicted to sitting, squatting, demonstrating, and striking for what they want."[27]

Fifth, Graham castigated churches which did not understand that the church must be careful as it operated in the realm of social action and proposed to take public stands on social issues of the day. Only where the scripture was unequivocally clear was there a mandate for the Christian church to act. There was no room for the Vietnam era social activists, who had lost all perspective, had become "angry with the world and are determined to use violence to change social structures of society."[28] They did not know prudence and they did not follow Christ's injunction that we are, in the end, to accept life, however painful its dimensions.[29]

GRAHAM, AMERICANS, AND THE AMERICAN STATE

In the 1960s and early 1970s, Graham was active in his praise of American patriotism and attained a wide reputation as a consort of powerful Amer-

ican political figures. This was the Billy Graham who was himself a part of
the established order, who participated with Bob Hope and *Readers Digest*
in an elaborate 1970 Honor America Day or who was Grand Marshall of
the Tournament of Roses Parade in 1971.[30] Above all, this was the Billy
Graham who became the friend of presidents, their ally, and, his critics
said, their tool. He appeared to be the very symbol in practice of evangelicalism's reputation as the defender of the American status quo.

Graham was eager to speak on behalf of patriotism and "honoring
America." He insisted that Americans had a need to be positive about their
country, especially amidst all the cynicism and criticism that washed over
the nation in the late 1960s. Here was a nation generous beyond human
experience, deservedly famous for its open doors, and much more. And it
was, in any case, our nation led by our government which 1 Peter 2:17
instructed us to honor.[31]

But Graham's enthusiasm for America had its limits. Graham had a
deep love for America but he also had fear. It was not just that we had
problems such as pollution, poverty, and moral permissiveness; we were
making efforts to deal with them and these efforts were much to our credit.
It was rather that the situation *at times* appeared too grim for any patching
efforts. He sometimes wondered whether America was a dying culture.[32]

The crucial element in this fear was his anxiety and anger over what
we know he considered to be spreading immorality. The late 1960s and
1970s were to Graham unmistakable years of moral disintegration in a
"democracy gone wild. Freedom has become license."[33] Permissiveness,
after God, became Graham's most invoked word, and much of his argument
consisted of the contention that the two were in irreconcilable conflict. The
permissiveness in America that most concerned him, of course, was sexual—adultery, sex before marriage, pornography, homosexuality. There were
other signs of moral degeneration as well. Honesty was in decline. Materialism was on the rise. Slavery to mass fashion was characteristic of the
age. Everywhere one looked in America one found nothing like perfection.
Even as Graham did "honor" America, he cried out against the sinful
Americans.[34]

However, Graham did not single out the structure and the major policies of the American system as the culprit. On the contrary, the system
and its policies (usually) were good—and he supported them. In the 1960s
this was most obvious (and most controversial) in the support he gave the
Vietnam War. In fact, Graham had less to say regarding the United States
government's entanglement in Vietnam than some of his critics thought.
What he did say made him a target for those who claimed that he could
not separate his affection for America and for his powerful friends, Johnson
and Nixon, from the Vietnam situation. He emerged as a supporter of war
and a man who lacked perspective.

Graham in the late 1960s at times did give the impression that he wished that the United States would go in and win the Vietnam War. Such opinions from Graham, however, were rare. More often Graham's analysis had little to do with what strategies to follow. His concern over the spread of communism motivated him far more. He insisted that communism represented the most serious threat to the Christian world in two millennia, and it could not be taken lightly wherever it appeared to be on the march. It was in this context that Graham long supported the Vietnam War. He was a firm anticommunist, and to him Vietnam was part of the ongoing struggle against communism. Graham disagreed with those who suggested his support was not in accord with Christian teachings. The truth was that Christ was a determined and vigorous fighter, one who would not give up and one who did not. Graham's Christ was not at all "weak," much less a pacifist.[35]

Nonetheless, for Graham as for others the time came when Vietnam no longer was worth the cost. No doubt this time came later for him than for some other evangelicals because of Graham's conviction that his friend Richard Nixon was "motivated by a desire for peace," and therefore had to be pursuing policies in Vietnam that would lead to a peace even as they halted communism. But by the early 1970s Graham's enthusiasm for Vietnam, though not for Nixon, was gone. By early 1973 he explained that he had long been praying for peace in Vietnam and now believed that the war had gone on too long at too great a cost to the United States. There was never any more evidence in Graham than in other conservative evangelicals (see Chapter Eleven) that they regretted Vietnam, except insofar as it proved to be a war that could not be won. Graham gave no evidence that the war was morally wrong; he did not believe it was.[36]

Graham's close link with the American political establishment derived from his association with important political leaders. He had never seen Washington as an enemy and never felt apologetic about the American political system. Ours was an order of government which "has come close" to perfection. He had always believed that Christians must pray for all rulers, since God established them for our benefit. Given this Christian duty and the excellent political system we had, Graham deplored those who were apathetic or disrespectful to our political order and its rulers. He reminded them that Jesus had no grudge against Rome and "never said a word against Rome."[37]

Graham's association with the politically powerful had its beginning during the 1950s and the Eisenhower presidency. Graham had much contact with Eisenhower and often was at the White House in those years. He had little contact with Kennedy, but when his long-time acquaintance, Lyndon Johnson, succeeded Kennedy, Graham's White House contacts resumed, though relations between Graham and Johnson were never intimate nor trouble free. Of course, it was with Richard Nixon that Graham achieved what he thought was a close friendship. Graham and Nixon had much contact with each other over the years before Nixon attained the presidency in the 1968 election. They were friends, had gone golfing together, and knew each other's families. In 1960, when Nixon made his first race for the presidency, Graham composed an article for Henry Luce's *Life* magazine that sang Nixon's praises. It was, of course, a thinly disguised effort to assist Nixon's election, though it carried no formal endorsement by Graham. At the last minute, however, Luce killed the article—a great relief to Graham, who was uneasy about his projected step into party politics. Yet Graham could not quite resist, since he chose to appear at a campaign rally for Nixon in Columbia, South Carolina, five days before the general election. Not surprisingly, many observers saw this act as a Graham endorsement, even though he insisted it was not.[38]

In 1968 Nixon claimed that Graham was a factor in his decision to run for the presidency again, and five days before the election Graham announced he had voted for Nixon by absentee ballot. Graham was present during some of the deliberations in the Nixon camp at the 1968 Republican convention over who should be Nixon's vice-presidential nominee. His choice was Mark Hatfield, the Republican senator from Oregon and a widely respected evangelical politician. Nixon of course picked Spiro Agnew, a person Graham defended as a man who was "making a great Vice President" until it became clear he was just another boodler. But Graham was not a close friend of Agnew and really did not know Agnew well. His favorable treatment of him undoubtedly had to do with his support of Nixon and his respect for those in power.[39]

After Nixon's 1968 victory Graham was often in Washington. Graham gave the inaugural prayer in 1969 and he urged God to give Nixon "an uncompromising courage to do what is morally right. Give him a cool head and a warm heart. Give him compassion. . . ."[40] He actively associated with Nixon in the first term, preaching at the White House on several occasions.

Graham was basically silent on Watergate until after Nixon's reelection in 1972. Then he assured Americans that Nixon had told him personally that he would be "putting a lot more emphasis on moral and spiritual affairs" in his second term of office because "the greatest problem we're facing is moral permissiveness and decadence.[41] There was no hint that Graham suspected or even dreamed that "permissiveness and decadence" had occurred in the Oval Office. When the forces seeking to investigate and clean up the mess began mounting an increasingly powerful campaign, Graham insisted that Nixon had done nothing evil. Only a few months before the president's fall Graham was at the White House preaching for Nixon.[42]

But the clouds around Nixon grew. Graham realized this fact. The

January 4, 1974, issue of *Christianity Today* carried a long discussion by Graham on Watergate. He understood that people faulted him for preaching at a White House now shrouded in suspicion, but he insisted that he had a mission to preach anywhere he could, including the White House—where, he continued to believe, he was heard by a group who still deserved to be termed a "distinguished audience." Graham did make it clear he was disgusted by Watergate. It was illegal. It was unethical. It "has hurt America."[43] But he did not see what it had to do with him or the evangelical movement in any way. The major culprits as he knew of them in early 1974 were, with the "possible exception of one," not evangelicals, nor was it true or fair to suggest that he agreed "with everything the Nixon administration does" and was therefore somehow responsible for it.[44] For that matter Graham did not see how the affair tarnished the reputation of his friend Richard Nixon in any major way. He pointed out that Nixon had not been found guilty of any crime; the most that could be said was that he had made judgment errors which should not reflect on any man's integrity and were "not wrong, or not sin."[45]

He reminded his readers that Nixon was only human and thus fallible just as other persons were. And he contended that he, and by implication the rest of us, knew too little of the full story of Watergate to be suspicious of Richard Nixon, or to rebuke him. While he said that anything he might say to Nixon would be in private, there was no indication Graham felt called upon to speak to Nixon in that context because he did not feel it was appropriate for him to second guess the president of the United States. To the end, the position and power of Nixon obviously impressed Graham.[46]

Graham also felt it was inappropriate to accuse or even to suspect Nixon in part because he thought Nixon was his friend. He felt much sorrow for Nixon, no doubt of that, for Graham sincerely believed that Nixon was a decent, nonmanipulative man. Graham had even thought Lyndon B. Johnson would not try to use Graham's prestige for his purposes, and he certainly believed that Nixon would not. He knew that people thought both had done so, but he still could not accept the truth that they had used him.[47]

Yet Graham was more than merely an apologist for Nixon over the Watergate scandals. He was appalled by the sordid mess, and he declared, as so many other evangelicals did, that we must learn a lesson about the reality of permissiveness in our time and its ability to creep anywhere. We had to learn that there would never be any substitute for the verities of God's absolute commands. Those who thought they could dispense with them were doomed to begin the downward slide. Watergate was also a lesson for Graham on the abiding insight of eternal truths such as honor, honesty, and fair dealing.

After the fall of Nixon in 1974, Graham's association with the government and leading figures there underwent an obvious change. He no longer continued to be seen frequently in the precincts of Washington or with the politically powerful wherever they were. He turned away from this arena back to his continuing love, evangelism for Jesus Christ, before mass rallies around the world as opposed to "distinguished guests" in the East Room.

There was no doubt that Graham had paid a price by close contact with Nixon, and he had taken with him a lesson he well knew reemphasized that sin was everywhere. His disposition to support American political institutions did not decrease, but clearly his perspective on those who ran them was changed. Moreover, Graham could not ignore the criticism he received for his extended defense of his associate Richard Nixon. Yet he did not apologize for his relationships with the powerful and never apologized for his devoted service to Nixon in particular. This was not his way. The period after Watergate was not the first time that Graham came under heavy fire for his affiliation with the mighty. Many of his southern backers had not received well his earlier association with Lyndon Johnson. They had been eager to have Graham endorse Barry Goldwater in the 1964 presidential election, but Graham did not do so, continuing instead his contacts with Johnson.[48]

The Nixon association, however, was something else and, beginning with the presidency of Gerald Ford, Graham ceased to travel so often and so quickly to Washington. Moreover after the election of Jimmy Carter, Graham's contacts with key people in the national administration declined. He was perceived in official, Democratic Washington as something of a Republican evangelist — which was not quite fair, although he did keep in touch with some of the exiles from Carter's Washington, most notably Henry Kissinger.[49]

GRAHAM AND SOCIAL ACTION IN THE 1970s

The early 1970s were not Graham's best years for forays into the public realm. Nor were they years in which Graham pushed on to new frontiers of social commitment. He once again focused less on controversial statements and more on his obvious evangelistic gift for seeking souls for Christ. While he seemed to forswear politics and politicians to a large extent after Watergate, he did not sidestep all the social issues of the 1970s. For example, he took a clear position on the role of women. His stance closely paralleled that of others in the conservative mainstream such as Francis Schaeffer and the editors of *Christianity Today*. It was reasonably predictable given his own past. During their courtship he and his future wife had both wanted to minister for Christ, and their individual plans did not mesh. Graham, for his part, just did not feel he received a calling to follow his wife, but she eventually did respond when he told her, citing scripture, that

"The Lord leads me and you follow." She gave up her plans to be a religious missionary and became a housewife and mother.[50]

Graham did endorse equal pay for equal work and he praised Jesus as the world's greatest liberator of women. But he vigorously opposed what he saw as the dangers of women's "liberation." He was afraid it would damage the family because it denied God's teachings about the proper role of husband and wife in the family. "God has appointed you husbands to be the head of the home. . . . When a woman opposes that order, she rebels against the will of God."[51] There could be no other conclusion, Graham repeatedly declared: "The husband is the head of the home!"[52] Other views were just new outcroppings of the old problem of permissiveness, which women's liberation reflected and encouraged. Despite its moral advocates, it was, at least in its more militant forms, a gospel of selfishness. It would meet no deep need nor address any basic problem, and only feed the American taste for moral license at the expense of our already shockingly weakened national moral fiber. For Graham, women's liberation was, in short, just the latest example of moral corruption in America.[53]

LEIGHTON FORD

It was fitting that at the end of our period, as at the beginning, Graham saw as his principal social function the struggle against moral corruption and license. The texture of a society was always for Graham a matter of individual and family loyalty and decency under God, and the great social struggle was to preserve this objective against the powerful tides of sin. Broader social issues occasionally caught his eye, but his evangelism as it reached beyond saving souls stayed firmly within traditional boundaries.

Despite his great influence, his cautious, conservative approach, as well as his strong urge to consort with the politically elite, eventually attracted critics within evangelicalism. They were usually careful, balanced, and, before the late 1970s, reluctant to mount an all-out attack on Graham and his ministry. Usually Graham's skeptics pointed to examples of what they took to be his most serious shortcoming—his relative unconcern about Christian-sponsored social change. This in fact remains a sticking point between him and some radical evangelicals today. In the 1960s and 1970s his critics also unfavorably reviewed Graham's tendency to hobnob with the powers that be; faulted his practical activities which encouraged civil religion instead of a prophetic faith; charged that he stressed individual change too much; suggested he was inconsistent in objecting to using the state to deal with many social problems while welcoming it as an ally to deal with pornography; and complained that his use of star athletes and beauty queens in his rallies gave the impression that competition and Christianity were perfectly compatible. All of these objections illustrated the suspicions among the "new" evangelicals of recent years that Graham was deeply conservative. All reflected his allegiance to the leaders and institutions of the status quo, his nonsocial means of change, and ultimately, his distance from concerted Christian reform. Yet the critics' remarks were usually muted, and even among them the context usually was—and is—one that refused to give up on Graham. The hope remained that he might come around, another powerful measure of his hold and influence on the evangelical movement in the 1960s, the early 1970s, and thereafter.

Those who were most eager to have Graham involved in social action admitted Graham's theology of change and his modest record of involvement disappointed them, but they invariably felt they had a solid ally within Graham's world in Leighton Ford. Ford was Graham's Canadian-born brother-in-law, actively involved as an evangelist in the Graham organization. He was significantly more receptive to change than Graham while recognizably within Graham's fold.[54]

Some observers viewed Ford as a man who suddenly introduced a whole new ethos into the Graham organization in the late 1960s. This opinion was wrong on several counts. It was wrong because it overlooked Graham's long-time interest in selected social questions and Graham's own growing interest during the 1960s in moral reformation, social and personal. It was correct in that Ford found that many people who welcomed Graham resisted some of Ford's teaching, a message which some felt was sometimes too strident, too prophetic, too radical, or too political. Yet Ford pushed on, both in his programs, such as his prison work, and in his preaching under the Graham umbrella. And he saw evidence that Graham responded, perhaps most famously in the joint endorsement by Graham and Ford of the poverty program of the Johnson administration.[55]

Ford's position was that Christianity could not ignore the times. The times called for change, especially in the late 1960s and early 1970s. No serious Christianity could avoid this situation. Such blissful ignorance would be folly—and immoral. There could be no excuse for those who "strain at gnats while the camels of revolution are marching."[56] Ford determined that Christianity could do better than Rip Van Winkle, and he set out to make his belief come true.[57]

He did not see that anyone could deny how much people and the world as a whole needed change and cried out for change. He believed Christianity could meet this contemporary need. He was annoyed that evangelicals had "soft-pedaled" the "revolutionary implication of Christian faith for too long."[58] It was time to turn the situation around and proclaim the truth that Christianity was something very different from an insular and blind devotion to the status quo. It was relevant to times of crisis. It was also time to discover that evangelism and social action must go together in the life of a complete Christian just as they did in the life of Jesus.[59]

While Ford declared he wanted to be understood as a devotee of revolution, one of the militants for change, it should be equally clear that he wanted a Christian revolution, and no other. "Christians agree with Karl Marx! The world does need to be changed. But to what end, and how? That is the point."[60] The only purpose could be to serve Jesus, as far as Ford was concerned; that would be a "constructive rebellion," for it was "Christ who is the true revolutionary."[61]

Christ was a revolutionary, make no mistake about it, but he was not just another revolutionary. His was the only way. This meant, for example, that Christians were not uncritically to join in all aspects of the New Left, especially the aimless and immoral wallowing in drugs and sexual abuse. Such practices were only "substitute saviors" that would not succeed. Nor could there be unity with Marxists and communists. While one had to recognize that communism had its origins in real social injustices and communists deserved love like anyone else, their cause was not the true revolution. It was just the opposite, though this fact should not allow us to become "a crude, sword-rattling anti-Communist."[62] It was just the opposite because a communist revolution involved demonic forces, not God.[63]

Ford knew that an authentic Christian revolution in any person and in any society was a hard road to travel: "The cause of Christ is far more . . . demanding than any other revolutionary movement."[64] One reason this was true was the kind of spirit in which change must occur. A decision had to be made about "which revolution: the revolution of hate and violence or Christ's revolution of love and spiritual power."[65] Violence was hardly necessary in the United States, Ford maintained, since change was possible here by far less drastic means. But even if it had not been, violence was a forbidden option. It clashed with the living spirit of Christ and was hardly the means of improving people's lives or speaking the word. The Bible taught clearly, in any case, that the "last resort is not violence, but martyrdom."[66]

Ford also assessed the general, anarchical ambience of his age. It offered no path to an effective realization of Christ's word. The Bible, not one's personal conscience or whim, was one's guide. It taught respect for one's rulers. One had to repudiate anarchy as a statement that one did not recognize and accept God's complete sovereignty.[67]

Ford devoted considerable energy to the issue of how to bring about this revolution for Christ. Opposing violence and anarchy and endorsing love was certainly a start, but he knew that this was not enough. Like traditional evangelicals, Ford thought any revolution in Christ had to start with the individual and with every individual. He meant it when he wrote: "LORD, START A REVOLUTION AND START IT IN ME!"[68] He took it for granted that without a genuine conversion to Christ there was little hope for any broader social changes, because of "the heart of the problem, which is the problem of the human heart."[69] There could be no escape from sin, to be sure, but Ford believed that much could be accomplished by sincere repentance. Such an attitude was, indeed, essential: "Before there can be real revolution there must be genuine repentance."[70] Only such an act would open the eternal road back toward individual and social change: "the human heart."[71]

Where Ford differed from many traditionalists was not in his starting point, but in his determination to go further. This objective was built on his conviction that personal conversions alone could not and would not resolve many social ills, and only the most naive conservative could believe they would. Conversion and repentance were vital, but they were not enough for a Christian: "Conversion is a beginning, not an end."[72] Two other things were needed. First, the devoted Christian had to demonstrate Christ in his or her own life, be a "kind of preview" of the loving and just society that Christ would eventually bring to earth. Such individual witness was essential. Second, the Christian must attack social evils. Too few Christians did this. Ford urged them on: "Speak. Tell it like it is. Plead. Provoke. Make us mad if you have to. Do it with love and humility. But do it!"[73] This had been the practice of the early Christians. They were driven with their message and their determination to live it and build communities which demonstrated it. They showed what passion for human change in the service of God could do.[74]

Ford's extensive analysis of the *methods* of change did not lead him to neglect formulating goals for his Christian revolution. What social changes did he seek? Racial equality was vital. Like Graham, Ford believed this was a benchmark for those who purported to speak for change in Jesus' name. There was little chance that churches which did not welcome blacks could be taken seriously as Christian, no matter how orthodox the sermons or how ancient the hymns. Welcoming blacks to church was not enough, however, for Ford, who contended that racial growth must speak to social conditions. Ford suggested that the heart of the problem lay in housing patterns. Housing was the painful area in which those really committed to alleviating the racial tension and hate that was so contrary to God's will should address their attention.[75]

Ford went beyond Graham and toward reform-oriented evangelicals in emphasizing the importance of a new order in a second area: property relations. Ford said he could not get excited either about the hammer and sickle OR the dollar sign of American capitalism. Neither should be the symbol of a faithful Christian. While he knew that modern evangelicals rejected the fallacies of communism, he was not convinced that they had the same attitude toward the dollar sign. The fact was, Ford declared, everything anyone owned was theirs only as a trust from God. It was hardly something they had any right to. That was why a Christian revolution was needed "in our thinking about money and possessions." Another reason was the enormous gap between the rich and the poor in America and the rich and poor nations of the world. There was too much evidence that famine stalked the world. And there was too much evidence that the rich were indifferent.[76]

Ford rarely moved beyond these general criticisms to suggest specific remedies for society or particular actions for Christians who acknowledged the problems he saw. Where his critics saw the characteristic caution and vagueness of those in the orbit of Graham, Ford's admirers had another explanation. He was an evangelist for Christ who as part of his broad mission had the responsibility to aid people's consciousness and to activate their consciences, not serve as their policy maker. In his years of closest contact with the Graham organization, there is considerable agreement that he fulfilled this definition of his vocation.

CONCLUSION

It would be a mistake to place Ford against Graham or either of them against the mainstream of their faith. At times, Ford was on the edge of the Graham organization's political attitudes, but he shared its fundamental concerns and purposes. No more than Graham did Ford challenge the basic value structure they shared. He developed no alternative theoretical frameworks. He clearly was less conservative than Graham politically and more socially aware. He represented the forces of moderate change within the fold but he did not reject the old ways. He stressed evangelism far more than all else, and he did not depart far from the usually cautious conservatism of the Graham world when specific political and social issues arose.

Chapter Four

THE SCHAEFFERS OF L'ABRI

IN THE LATE 1960s through the middle 1970s Francis Schaeffer was to many literate younger evangelicals what Billy Graham was to the larger fellowship, an inspiration and a leader. Schaeffer's books sold over two million copies, and his talks, movies, and records spread his influence far enough that he began to attract critics.[1] Compared to Graham, Schaeffer was far more intellectual and cultural, but he aggressively proclaimed the same message: the importance of absolute faith and an inerrant Bible; he too decried those Christians who retreated before skeptics into "defensiveness."[2] Schaeffer was also like Graham in responding to the social issues of the 1960s and early 1970s in a form which, although something more than a routine recapitulation of traditional conservative platforms, was still basically a modernized defense of mainstream values. He struck the old chords, but in a new key.

In the years from the New Left to Carter, *Christianity Today* often praised Schaeffer's works and his articles found a ready outlet there. Moreover, his wife, Edith Schaeffer, had a regular column in *Christianity Today* in the last years of Harold Lindsell's editorship, during the middle 1970s. The contacts between the Schaeffers and the people at *Christianity Today* were close, though the Schaeffers were independent people, zealous in resisting efforts to edit their work and not at all social intimates of the magazine's staff.[3]

The Schaeffers' outreach went well beyond the pages of *Christianity Today*. Francis Schaeffer and his wife operated L'Abri Fellowship in Switzerland, an institution where they welcomed fellow Americans and believers from other countries to participate in their ministry and their training. From L'Abri, which they founded in the late 1940s after Schaeffer left previous pastorate work in the United States, this "evangelist to students and intellectuals" exercised ever increasing influence.[4] Especially in the 1970s, Schaeffer gained respect among Christians of his persuasion for his ministry to the mind — but also the heart — of his fellow Christians.

In considering Schaeffer's essential conservatism, we should begin by remembering that Schaeffer, like *Christianity Today*, was not basically political in focus. It followed that the most powerful cement between Schaeffer and *Christianity Today* was their agreement on crucial theological points. We should not overlook the significance of this fact. *Christianity Today* during our period always used as the ultimate test of evangelical orthodoxy a nonpolitical standard: its conviction that the Bible was the inerrant word of God. This was a test which Schaeffer met nicely. It is true, of course, that such a standard is hardly innocent of political implications in that it ranks politics and social action as decidedly secondary for Christianity, itself a very political conclusion. This conclusion led some to say that *Christianity Today* and Francis Schaeffer necessarily became subtle apologists for the established order. This view argues that those who did not think it important to attack the established order therefore bolstered it, a view that at the least misunderstands how the Schaeffers and *Christianity Today* saw themselves.

Over and over again Schaeffer campaigned for a Christianity distinguished not by its commitment to social action or political commitment or anything else except its trust in the full truth of scripture. This was what truly mattered, a theme he enunciated in his books and such major addresses as his keynote speech to the National Association of Evangelicals in convention in 1976.[5] This was the basis for all else. There was, he contended, no substitute for true Christian doctrine rooted in the certain word of the Bible. It was quite impossible to "compromise our view of Scripture."[6] Like Harold Lindsell, he believed that the great battle ahead for the Christian church was the fight over scripture and whether Christians were prepared to confess its infallible truth. Against this issue other, outer matters, Schaeffer declared, paled into insignificance. Thus Schaeffer was convinced that "the real battle for men is in the world of ideas, rather than in that which is outward."[7]

Schaeffer was explicit in rejecting anything which could possibly be construed as even the least bit theologically liberal. Liberal and existential theologies were inadequate because they left human beings lost and on their own. Such theologies tried to destroy God and his Bible in smooth and sophistical words. But the alternative was right at hand. All people had the soaring truth of the Bible available to them if only they would affirm it. Schaeffer felt he also had to spurn all efforts toward ecumenism. Support for ecumenism meant asking evangelicals to accept those who blatantly tolerated or promoted error. This was exactly what a Christian must not do, exactly what he must avoid at all costs.[8]

Schaeffer also stressed the reality of sin and the reality of human choice in creating sin: "The problem of man is moral, for by choice he stands in rebellion against God."[9] He adamantly opposed social and psychological explanations of sin. He was equally opposed to those who denied human choice and responsibility for whatever reason and was therefore naturally critical of B. F. Skinner. Skinner's conclusions, derived from his behaviorist psychology, rendered human choice meaningless, a doctrine which denied Christianity and its faith in a responsible being. Schaeffer admitted that everyone was conditioned to some extent, but he insisted that each also had a mind of his own through which he could influence things in the larger world. We had an autonomous realm as well as a determined one.[10]

Schaeffer's rebuttal to Skinner demonstrated his contemporary awareness. More than *Christianity Today* and more than many compatriots, Schaeffer was in touch with the modern intellectual world. His understanding was not necessarily deep, but it was wide. It was characteristic of Schaeffer to applaud a Christianity where the mind played a major role, where intellectuals were welcome, and where there was "no final conflict" between the rational science of the modern world and the Bible. He always maintained that Christianity as he understood it should not be based in "experience or emotion" but rational truth. He was critical of those in the Christian community who he held too involved in "superspirituality." This was common, he felt, in the American church. Its practitioners invariably downplayed the vital scriptural substance of Christianity and often showed little interest in the human mind.[11]

Schaeffer's sympathy for an intellectual Christianity and his insistence that "Biblical Christianity rest upon content, factual content"—"It does not cause people to react merely emotionally"—appeared also in his open attitude toward many cultural and other intellectual pursuits.[12] Schaeffer was obviously enthusiastic about culture. He was unusual in his keen interest in art, architecture, and music as well as history. He did not consider such interests snares of the devil, but rather signs of life. Schaeffer acted on his conviction that history or art could provide great enlightenment. For example, both history and art helped us understand that the Renaissance was a crucial era of human declension. It was the age in which the attention of men and women dangerously shifted from God and toward the human person. Glorious as the Reformation was, it could not and did not overcome this movement. We could observe the contemporary results all around us in economic life, in politics, and in the arts. License and moral drift lay over us. We had few values that were strong, when we had any at all, and we demonstrated this truth in the anarchic and "impoverished" culture we displayed.[13]

Schaeffer's confident and energetic defense of the human mind (so long as it was faithful to divine truths) was significant not only in explaining his appeal to many reflective, young evangelicals in our period but also in symbolizing the emergence of a robust side of evangelicalism which was not reducible to emotion or pietism. Schaeffer's acclaim marked the rise of an approach, even if he sometimes was merely its popularizer, which helped give legitimacy within evangelicalism to intellectual argument about political and social ideas, human culture, and the nature of the faith of a Christian.

For Schaeffer, respect for the power and importance of the human mind was no new ideal in Christian history. He recognized many greater predecessors in his effort and seemed to have a special regard for Paul. Indeed, Schaeffer cited Paul, who engaged more in theological and metaphysical subtlety than Jesus did, far more often than Jesus.[14]

But Schaeffer was far from being a cold intellectual. Quite the contrary. Schaeffer often sounded like the Jeremiah—or Paul, for that matter—he so obviously admired. He was not always "reasonable" in the world's terms—unlike *Christianity Today*. Schaeffer could be angry, aggressive, enthusiastic, but he was rarely dull. Moreover, Schaeffer was also like Jeremiah and Paul in that, for all his defense of the mind, he stood ultimately for faith. Reason was important, but it was no substitute for faith in Jesus Christ.

Reason and faith, Schaeffer contended, led him to orthodox Christianity. Perhaps it was his intellectual side which, despite his insistence on inerrancy and orthodoxy, made his faith less rigid and divisive in its consequences than it might have been. Certainly Schaeffer rejected a mood of unending religious factionalism, which sometimes gripped the fundamentalists. He refused to indulge in expressions of personal hostility toward those with whom he disagreed. He said he would not take the road of hate, because he did not believe that his efforts for what he judged to be Christian orthodoxy were consistent with a contemptuous treatment of opponents that necessarily denied Christian principles. Moreover, he was temperamentally unsuited for controversy. Disagreements over doctrine were sometimes necessary, but they were never to be welcomed. They were always painful and sad and should never occur "without regret and without tears."[15]

What bothered Schaeffer was that too few evangelicals displayed this respectful attitude toward others. The unpleasant truth was that too often "we rush in, being very, very pleased, it would seem at times, to find other men's mistakes."[16] We needed to be reminded that God created all of us and that he cared for all of us, and we should not lightly undo his work by dividing into "ugly parties."[17] We also needed to be more forgiving—as Christians should be. We too often showed that we had "lost compassion. We are hard. Hard!"[18]

SCHAEFFER'S POLITICAL IDEAS

Schaeffer displayed this perspective on Christian doctrinal disputes when he approached the political and social realms. His ultimate position was that every Christian had to have two things: a "clear doctrinal stand and an exhibition of real, *observational* love."[19] These two goals were not in conflict. The question relevant to politics and society was what doctrine and love meant in political and social terms.

Schaeffer was insistent on one matter above all in his search for a living Christianity which manifested the word of God: a faithful Christianity could not be at peace with the world. The Christian must inevitably be in conflict with his environment, since that environment obviously did not take Jesus or his scripture seriously as its guide. "We are all too easily infiltrated with relativism and synthesis in our own day. We lack antithesis."[20] The resulting mood was bound to be negative, but that was the kind of message we needed in our age as we recognized the failure around us and accepted the awesome fact that we were under God's exacting judgment. Schaeffer was explicit on the absolute necessity of opposition to the ways—and wiles—of the world. Though many of his followers did not appear to comprehend his message, he declared that the teachings of God and the standard middle class life were hardly the same. He protested, on the other hand, that no one should delude himself and believe that drugs or similar escapes from the world were a solution. Nor was radical political action, following the social gospel, the proper route. All of these were the pathways of the world in the end, and Schaeffer condemned them all.

The trouble with people was that even when they saw the fallacies of one worldly trap, they escaped only to erect another earthly god in its place. We should remember, Schaeffer argued, that we dwelt in what God had proclaimed as a "lost world." We were to have compassion for our common human plight and not yield to the temptation to hate our earthly existence. We were also to understand that our world was doomed. We were not to celebrate it or conform to it.[21]

Schaeffer declared that the way many ordinary Christians lived their lives convinced him that the average Christian often did not understand these truths. Too rarely did Christians avoid the evil of the world. He noted two particular pieces of evidence. First, there was the matter of race relations—especially *Christians'* treatment of other races. In a remarkable article in *Christianity Today* in 1974 Schaeffer reported that he had erred in his earlier writings in not sufficiently underlining the importance of racial problems. They were very serious. His conviction was that racism was an evil which Christians could not tolerate. They were actively to oppose it as a concrete demonstration of their devotion to the love of Christ and of their neighbor as their self. Schaeffer often proclaimed that he counted himself among those "opposed to any form of racism."[22]

Schaeffer lamented what he considered the appalling past record of Christians in the area of race relations. Individual Christians as well as the Christian church had failed regarding slavery and had subsequently neglected to fight racial prejudice. A start toward remedying this record was to acknowledge it frankly. Schaeffer tried to make the point in his article on the subject in *Christianity Today* by asserting that the past record was "non-Christian, repeat non-Christian," but the periodical refused to allow such a claim to appear in its pages. It was too blunt, too controversial. Schaeffer had a number of opportunities to make the same observation in other forums and he took them, but he knew the significance of the "editing" at *Christianity Today*. Evangelicals often did not want to look too closely at the past. It was, after all, their past.

In racial matters Schaeffer appeared to be much in tune with the forces of change. Of course, almost all leading evangelicals spoke for racial equality in the late 1960s; *Christianity Today* did so and felt it was an exemplar in this regard. But Schaeffer pursued the issue more vigorously than *Christianity Today*, with fewer qualifications and hesitations. His conflict with the magazine over the editing of his article on racial justice was no accident.[23]

Schaeffer favored complete integration. He opposed any attitude of "toleration" among races because he wanted race not to count at all. Moreover, just as he objected to white supremacists, so he had no patience for the prophets of black power or for those who suggested there was or should be a black Bible, a black Christianity, or a black God. It was only natural that everyone would perceive a somewhat different scripture, but that fact should not allow anyone to get off the track about scriptural truth. There was only one truth; there could never be one truth for blacks and another for whites. Similarly, there could be only one Christian attitude toward the new, often racially influenced theologies of the 1960s. Schaeffer proposed to assess all of them in the light of the single truth of Jesus. No perspective could receive immunity from a thorough scrutiny of its theological claims just because blacks — or whites — authored it. Members of any or all races could and should probe and criticize any so-called Christian theology. Race was, and had to be, utterly irrelevant to truth.[24]

Second, Schaeffer attacked the widespread materialism of the modern age. Everywhere he turned he noticed people who worshipped money and the things it bought. Even those who pretended to be Christians were swept up in this tragic corruption. "The danger of materialism in a Christian's life" was too often a reality. Few understood how important it was to employ their "money wisely before the face of God."[25]

Yet Schaeffer's concentration on the evil of materialism did not suggest he was somehow a covert socialist or even the advocate of government programs beyond those reluctantly accepted by typical evangelical conservatives. He proposed no repudiation, for example, of capitalism, as long as it resembled the capitalism he saw in the Bible, one "that cares for people," and as long as its leaders followed Jesus Christ. In fact, Schaeffer had no patience with those who endlessly carped at the existence of private property. There was, he contended, a sharp distinction between the question of the appropriate use of wealth and the question of ownership. What mattered was the use of property. Schaeffer's standard always was the "compassionate" employment of wealth. Exactly what "compassionate Christianity" meant never was entirely clear, but he gave some hints. He indicted the Industrial Revolution as the worst example of the "lack of compassion" which often continued to characterize our approach to wealth. It involved rapacious accumulation by a few at the expense of the many and, even more, the failure of the rich to utilize their resources to aid the less fortunate, the failure to act as Christian stewards.[26]

Schaeffer called on every individual to reach out to the needy. People should open their homes to help others, when necessary. Clergy had a special obligation to assist the less fortunate, Schaeffer contended, though he acknowledged this task would not be easy to fulfill. He knew that clergy who acted in this way could face hostile comment from church members, but he had little patience with clergy who professed to be upset at that prospect. Serving God hardly meant avoiding sacrifice. The church, Schaeffer declared, had been timid too often. A clear witness to the needs of the less fortunate was a Christian duty. Yet the church had been "very, very weak in the matter of compassionate use of accumulated wealth."[27] It had not stood for a more caring, Christian ideal either in its clergy or in its laity.

This failure was a tragic denial of Jesus and his word in the scripture. It was also fraught with explosive, practical consequences. The costs were already evident within the evangelical fold; the church's lack of witness had "opened the door to the rather left-wing swing among some of the younger evangelicals, some of whom are beginning to equate the Kingdom of God with an almost socialistic program."[28] Schaeffer could already see in many reform-oriented and radical evangelicals the hope that the state would promote radical economic and social change.

Statists who thought in socialist or welfare state terms obviously were not Schaeffer's alternative to the church's failure to grapple with materialism. They were not even close to what Schaeffer took to be Christ's message. They were themselves materialists, followers of a philosophy which "gives no basis for the dignity or rights of man."[29] They also promoted a confusion which Schaeffer always resisted. The state was no solution to ultimate problems and could not be. Political institutions and ideas, like all other dimensions of the external world, had to take a clear second place to our inner world of thought and allegiance to Jesus. The ultimate answer to our problems lay only in that inner world. Schaeffer had as little use for radical political activists in the church. Their priorities were wrong; they thought externals counted. Authentic Christianity was about the truth of Christ, not "external signs."[30]

Yet Schaeffer's quite conventionally conservative view did not ignore the outer world. He wanted priorities kept straight, but he granted that Christians had a divine mission to "bring" a society toward the truth by "applying the law of God" as much as possible.[31] The most important sign of a Christian, surely, must be "love." Every Christian was to acknowledge that each person is a creature of God, that we were all brothers and sisters under God, and that we must love one another. To love God and our fellows did not mean a mere abstract faithfulness; it had to involve a genuine, concrete love of God and his creatures as individuals.[32] Schaeffer predictably criticized those who based their notion of love on an idealized, humanist love of mankind. Christians must do better, he asserted. They must love particular men and women and treat their neighbors as themselves, as God expected. This conviction explains why all the works of this deeply biblical Christian project a strong plea for "warm-heartedness" as well as adherence to formal doctrine. As he put it, the Christian had to undertake the challenging task to "show forth the love of God and the holiness of God *simultaneously.*"[33]

In his mind, Schaeffer's opposition to materialism and racism were expressions of his loyalty to God's requirement that Christians concretely love men and women and oppose those things which led to their destruction. Yet his views were not especially unique among thoughtful, conservative evangelicals. *Christianity Today* and Harold Lindsell routinely denounced racism and materialism. Schaeffer's belief that sin was the principal cause of such follies and his notion that individual action to defeat them was the most appropriate response were hardly unusual in orthodox circles either.[34]

Yet Schaeffer was more congenial to the reform elements within evangelicalism in the 1960s and early 1970s in several ways. His convictions about racism and materialism were far more explicit than those usually expressed in more restrained terms in *Christianity Today*. His convictions here had a ring of authenticity, of depth of conviction, not always obvious in other orthodox voices. Moreover, Schaeffer aligned himself with the fashionable calls for a revolution popular among many evangelical intellectuals in the late 1960s. To be sure, he never tried to suggest that the revolution he had in mind was anything other than "a Christian revolution," one that was strictly "biblical."[35] Behind these affirmations lay Schaeffer's conviction that a true revolution must fashion two achievements, neither of which could be reached by violence. Revolution must guarantee (1) "a restoration to pure doctrine," *and* (2) "a restoration in the Christian's life."[36] He often described this twofold commitment to the Bible and to a clear witness to it in the world as a *reformation*. This term was far more congenial to him than *revolution* and was perhaps far more accurate as well. By using the word "reformation" Schaeffer obviously meant to evoke the Protestant Reformation of the sixteenth century. To Schaeffer, that Reformation had achieved the rekindling of a Christian religion pure in faith and intense in witness. So must any twentieth-century reformation. It had to involve "pockets of individuals turning back to the Bible, looking at the world through its eyes, and basing their whole lives on the Bible."[37] Such a reformation was impossible without God's grace, of course, "though hope in God was no excuse for quietism."[38]

The phrase "pockets of individuals" is important, for Schaeffer felt that biblical Christianity required living life in community, a condition that too rarely existed. Like the New Left, Schaeffer decried this absence of community in modern life, including the Christian order and its many churches. Schaeffer declared: "I don't think a church is a real church unless it is a practicing community."[39] Not surprisingly, his aspirations for L'Abri reflected this faith. Schaeffer wanted it to be a special place expressing the Christian ideal, a witness to both Christians and non-Christians of what Christianity should be when actually *lived*. It would be a community united in the Spirit, forsaking materialism, scorning racism, and practicing love of God and its neighbors.[40]

Schaeffer's sense that a Christian existence must be different from ordinary life in the West, his call for "revolution" (reformation), his condemnation of racism, and his sympathy toward community, among other attitudes, provided him with a basis of empathy with the student turmoils of the late 1960s and a feeling of disappointment with the peaceful 1970s. The truth was, he said, that the "young people had been right in their analysis, though wrong in their solutions."[41] The young rebels of the 1960s saw many of the faults of modern society, though they hardly proposed Schaeffer's Christian reformation as the way out. Schaeffer sometimes was more sympathetic toward them and sometimes less so. When he felt more critical he noted that they had not learned the lesson of the French and Russian revolutions, that human-centered revolutions were terrible and bloody failures. Even more, they had not discovered that every revolution retaught the reality of the intransigence of sin and the inadequacy of a belief in environmental and state manipulation. Every true revolutionary, Schaeffer warned, must know that the "problem is not outward things. The problem is having, and then acting upon, the right world view" — the right world view of evangelical Christianity.[42] Ideas made moral and lasting revolutions.

Examining Schaeffer's approach to one issue, pollution, may provide a better sense of his overall analysis of faith and life in the late twentieth century. Schaeffer gave detailed attention to pollution because it was a

problem he clearly cared a good deal about. Schaeffer said he identified
with all those citizens the world over who were enraged about the environmental abuse so frequent in their nations. He even went so far as to
praise the hippie movement on this matter, some of the few words in the
evangelical literature of that age ever spoken favorably about the hippies.
Schaeffer judged they had no idea what to do about the situation, but they
did have a precious "sensitivity to nature," and they understood how little
in the "plastic culture" around us conformed to nature or respected it.[43]

The hippies and so many other nature lovers, though, were confused,
Schaeffer maintained, in that the modern, polluting culture they condemned
trapped them too. They lacked secure alternative values. Schaeffer, as we
know, took it for granted that "one can never have real morals without
absolutes."[44] In this way, the hippies were no different from pragmatic men
who destroyed the environment for their immediate needs or pleasures. On
the other hand, insofar as hippies and others who were concerned about
the environmental crisis were pantheists, they made other errors. They
made nature an absolute. They had only a partial view of nature, one that
falsely eliminated the dark in nature and wrapped nature in a soft glow of
romantic illusion. Moreover, the value of nature did not lie in its being
somehow the substance of God, but in the fact that all of it, good and bad,
had its origins in God's plan. Nature had no worth in itself. It had value as
part of a whole which had worth because God proclaimed that it did. Thus
"we really *are* one with the tree!", not for ill-founded sentimental reasons
but because God put us together on this earth.[45]

Since nature had no independent value, and certainly was not valuable
because we decided it was, the Christian's attitude toward nature had to be
guided by the fact that it was of God. In the light of this truth, Schaeffer
asserted that Christians must be environmentalists. How could Christians
be desecrators of God's magnificent bounty of nature? How dared they?
To do so, Schaeffer eloquently argued, was to attack God and his works.
We "should treat nature with an overwhelming respect" due all of God's
creation.[46]

Schaeffer thought that the church should demonstrate this by acting,
so to speak, as a "pilot plant" in the fashion in which it treated nature.
Ordinary Christians should do the same. What this meant was not entirely
clear. It did not imply any assault on capitalism or on the gospel of economic development. There was no point, Schaeffer claimed, in suggesting
that people should discard a profit motive. Schaeffer did think there was
a point in teaching Christians that how they acted toward the environment
was essential. People must be taught to love and protect God's bounty.
More importantly, his program urged Christians to be active in healing
divisions in all of life, divisions between individual people, divisions between man and nature. The alienations of the world loomed large. So did

the responsibility, for Schaeffer, to act to meet them, including reducing pollution and other abuses of nature.[47] Predictably, Schaeffer did not have in mind a vast net of government programs to end pollution or to combat broader alienations. Here as elsewhere Schaeffer did not think they were useless, just that they were very far from the main answer.

Significantly, Schaeffer believed that Christians had an especially weighty responsibility regarding pollution and other human problems when they dealt with other Christians. He was very concerned that the individual Christian and the Christian church both live up to their ideals on this as on other issues. He did not scorn Christian sensitivity for the larger human community, but in combating pollution or any other evil the first task was to root it out among Christians and then turn to others. The "Christian is called to understand that there are two humanities, and to love his brothers in Christ especially, and yet Christ also lays upon us the love of all men, as our neighbors, because we *are* one."[48]

Thus Schaeffer's inclinations about social action were not simple. Certainly he shared the apparent unease over the paucity of evangelical witness evident among his fellows in the late 1960s and after. He was not warm to those who were instinctively conservative. He recommended teaching children the wisdom of listening for the possibilities of change and being open to the future. They should not be taught to be conservative about change. Schaeffer never appeared frightened at the prospects of change even as he was no uncritical reform-minded evangelical.

Yet Schaeffer's mood was actually much closer to mainstream evangelical conservatism than his emphasis on "revolution" or openness to change suggested. His reactions were always intensely conservative whenever other voices recommended going outside conventional evangelical strategies of individual transformation. Schaeffer was as critical of the state as the most enthusiastic capitalist evangelical. He feared political liberalism and the welfare state, not to mention his strong antipathy to any hint of state socialism. Moreover, the genuinely utopian mind was clearly abhorrent to Schaeffer. There was no possibility of achieving Christ-like perfection on this earth for any of us. He spurned the New Left not least because it was a utopian movement that sunk fo "totalitarianism" as it tried to overcome the facts of human sin and went its literally hell-bent road to utopia. Utopianism, he suspected, was really a form of "cruelty." Its costs to a society were cruel when totalitarian molders came to power and sought to remake people and social systems. Manipulators were everywhere cruel, though the manipulation unleashed by the lust for utopia was the worst. All utopian impulses were both dangerous and ungodly.[49]

Schaeffer warned that the craving for utopia in any society would ultimately involve its citizenry in a world of power and its fearsome attributes. God has told us to do otherwise, "not to seek power." Humility, not pride, the low place and not the high one, was for the Christian. This truth applied to all of those interested in any form of social action as well. Christians were to be active, but always on guard to preserve their Christianity. Action which was humble and which avoided the corruptions of pride and power was the only way.[50] We were not at the heart of the universe. We could not be what God was. It was presumptuous, and also tragic, to attempt it.[51]

That power would not go away even if Christians ignored it was a fact Schaeffer fully realized. But he did not see it as his primary function to argue the consequences of his admonitions to Christians. They had their duties to follow, and they were not to let the powers (or would-be powers) of the world be their guide — or scare them. That the practical consequence of such an attitude might be less a flirtation with utopianism than an acceptance of the powers currently dominating societies did not occur to Schaeffer, though even that realization would not have moved him. In truth, Schaeffer had as little enthusiasm for politics as he had for the state.

Always Francis Schaeffer sought to direct Christians back to Christ. God was central, not us, not our material possessions, not the earth, and not our personal or social plans for utopia — or reform. The hour was late. We were now under "the wrath of God" and we were living "in a post-Christian world" about which we have to be "realistic."[52] There was "*death in the city!*"[53] And few, as the Bible had warned, were likely to be moved "by a church and by a culture in revolt."[54] We needed to pray not for justice for ourselves, but for mercy. We were badly in need of repentance. Our minds were weak, our wallets full, and our gospel was man-centered. Yet there was still a chance for the revolution, the reformation. God's grace was, as always, mankind's only hope.[55]

Within evangelicalism this essentially conservative position assumed by Schaeffer began to attract critics by the 1970s. In a more diverse universe it was bound to do so. Clark Pinnock, a former associate at L'Abri, faulted Schaeffer for presenting the same old conservative political ideas. Schaeffer had scant interest in serious social change, Pinnock charged, and any concrete demonstration of his concern for the poor, the Third World, or any environment outside his comfortable Nordic world of the North Atlantic community did not exist. Such a critique in an antiestablishment journal like *Sojourners* surprised no one. Criticism of Schaeffer in *The Reformed Journal* was something else. While political labeling was not the style of that sensitive and intellectual publication, it did criticize Schaeffer on other grounds. One article suggested that, despite his reputation, he substituted "personal conviction" and "great rhetorical power" for scholarly and intellectual arguments, an argument which Pinnock also made in *Sojourners*. The conclusion in *The Reformed Journal* that Schaeffer should be honored not so much as an intellectual but more as an evangelist was ironic given Schaeffer's intellectual commitment and influence; it was, however, not necessarily an insult to Schaeffer, whose goal, after all, was to evangelize the world for Jesus Christ.[56]

It did suggest that from the Reformed tradition, a tradition which Schaeffer himself reflected, the standards of *intellectual* and *cultural* sophistication were likely to be far higher than in many branches of evangelicalism, including the world of Billy Graham and many famous exponents of the faith. The uneasiness that Schaeffer generated among some intellectuals, quite apart from political disagreements, was predictable in the increasingly and openly pluralistic evangelical world of the 1970s.[57]

By now even *Christianity Today* spliced a few objections into its praise for Francis Schaeffer. Critics there never felt he was remarkably profound.[58] One article, for example, lauded him, but did remark that his logic was often weak, his arguments hardly invulnerable, and many of his claims too grandiose. Overall, the periodical's appreciation for Schaeffer remained strong, however, in a largely apolitical context. He was an admired soldier for Christ at *Christianity Today* as he had long been.[59]

Schaeffer believed he made an impact. He believed that he brought the message of Christ and reformation to people both in small groups and, as he grew more famous, to much larger groups—and he contended he did so effectively. He insisted that no one could deny his influence.[60]

EDITH SCHAEFFER

The criticism of Schaeffer's intellectual credentials demonstrated how important serious claims to intellectual sophistication were among some evangelicals in the 1970s. It also suggested that even the most respected evangelicals could expect less than fully reverent treatment in the new, more pluralistic era.

Francis Schaeffer's work was, of course, the core of the L'Abri influence on evangelical thinking in the 1960s and 1970s. But L'Abri was more than one person. Schaeffer's wife, Edith, was an active participant in several ways, including Christian writing. In the middle 1970s she was a regular columnist for *Christianity Today*, contributing primarily devotional pieces. They were rarely even remotely connected with political or social topics, though it was clear that she was hardly in sympathy with reform-oriented evangelicals. *Christianity Today* and her husband had far more to say on these subjects than did she.

Most of her columns were pious in a clever fashion, building from an incident or a Bible verse to a modest teaching of one sort or another. A steel building in Pittsburgh was an analogy for God, the cornerstone for Jesus, and the columns for the martyrs. Harvests led her to discuss the question of what the individual has sown and not sown before God. There were some hints of other interests, including the proper role for women, but generally Schaeffer confined herself to warnings such as the danger of careless conversation in one's life or the sinfulness of the snob.[61]

She was the author of several books, as well, books which should be read on more than one level. On the one hand, they were genial, folksy discussions of the history of L'Abri or the way to mold a successful family. At a more penetrating level they were essays on the nature of community, what it was like, how one might achieve it, and what its pitfalls were. Like her husband, Edith Schaeffer was profoundly concerned with the goal of Christian community, especially in the family, the form of community which more evangelicals wrote about than any other. Her lively description of the founding and nurturing of L'Abri, however, also operated as a tale about community. Her story of L'Abri was very much a report on a larger family, and both books made much the same argument.

When a family achieved its potential life, Schaeffer believed, something truly remarkable took place. The resulting community was worth all the hard, devoted work which, of course, was necessary for success. Then the family was near its ideal form: "Families are meant to be a . . . beautiful art from which will in some tiny way picture the beauty of the gigantic art form of the complete 'Family' of those who have come to God."[62]

Such a family was, above all, a relationship of sharing: the joys, the burdens, the work. This was its essence as a community. Merely living in the same house did not guarantee sharing. Talking with each other, making things together, and building mutually was the goal. This meant, and Schaeffer was very emphatic about this point, that the philosophy and the life of those involved in a family had to have a commitment to giving; it could *not* consist of the continual demanding of rights. She believed that the rights approach to life might yield "justice" or strengthen individuals, but it could create no communities and never had. It followed that Schaeffer felt a genuine family community had to be bound together by loyalties that transcended everything but loyalty to God. Obligation to family was a sacred and central value. It was also a practical one for her, since she thought that commitment by family members to each other and to the "oneness" of the family was desperately needed if the family was to endure. Moreover, she judged that only if the family was a community of commitment could it be a shelter from the storms and stresses of outer life. Then it would be the place where the pleasant words were heard — quoting Proverbs 16:23 – 24 — "like a honeycomb, sweetness to the soul and health to the body."

All this might sound a bit too secure and comfortable, a bit too insulated, but Schaeffer's sense of family was not at all rigid, stuffy, or closed. The good family was a place for creativity, not an environment where life was discouraged. It was a place where laughter and joy often resounded. It was also a place which reached out and welcomed others, a community which cheerfully acted on the Christian duty of aid to the needy.[63]

Edith Schaeffer was perhaps even more effective than her husband was in concretely illustrating their common goal of community. She had an almost inexhaustible number of stories and incidents to provide flesh to her vision. Much of what she said could hardly be controversial in or out of evangelical circles—but there were limits to her noncontroversial image. On one topic she was unmistakably controversial: the role appropriate for women.

Edith Schaeffer was an unabashed opponent of women's liberation, as her articles in *Christianity Today* occasionally hinted and other writing made very clear. She was critical of those who made an "exaggerated emphasis on equality of men and women," and she felt the entire controversy led away from more important questions. She preferred to discuss the urgency of sustaining the doctrine of the virgin birth rather than the issue of the ordination of women.[64] But her main thrust was that women's liberation was *wrong*. It was a moral doctrine which, according to Schaeffer, confused women. It undermined their true vocation, which was family life, because it led too many women to the outrageous conclusion that family life was not a vital and sacred calling without equal. Schaeffer protested that she too believed that husbands as well as wives had to put their families before all else.[65] Yet, Schaeffer asked, who "can make the family a career? The natural person provided with the attributes for that is the woman."[66] The woman with children who tried to work was bound to hurt her family badly. She would produce a pattern of life just not likely to foster genuine community. "Two people with two separate careers and living in one house, but infrequently together—with children who are more frequently cared for by other people than by their parents—have not really formed a family."[67]

Schaeffer was reluctant to consider role reversals. She had definite—and conventional—images of what men and women ought to be like and to be doing. Her critics noted that she herself had hardly had a life which came close to her traditional model for a woman. She was no conventional homemaker. Moreover, the many trips which she and her husband took in pursuit of their mission, leaving their children in the care of others, did not appear to do anyone great harm. Yet such observations missed her point. She had built a family and she insisted that God called women to this vocation in building community. This was their great task. They were to follow him just as they were to follow their husbands, devotedly and loyally, as they undertook to craft a community out of a family.[68]

CONCLUSION

The Schaeffers saw themselves as proponents of genuine change in the world around them. Francis Schaeffer was proud of his stands against racism, against the abuse of wealth, and for community; and Edith Schaeffer waged a campaign for community that was even more active than her husband's. Both not only talked on behalf of community but participated in constructing several. They had a record of action that matched their words.[69]

But they did not emerge as the heroes of the new, reform-oriented evangelicals of the late 1960s; social action was not important enough for them, and their critiques did not run deep enough. The Schaeffers fit comfortably in no camp, but in the end they emerged as religious conservatives who were, somewhat unwillingly, part of the mainstream conservative political coalition involving *Christianity Today*, Harold Lindsell, the Billy Graham organization, and others in sympathy with traditional evangelical politics.

They were, however, uneasy members, somewhat detached at L'Abri and somewhat less happy with traditional evangelical stands than many of their compatriots. Yet the gap between them and those for whom social action and commitment was vital and essential and at the core of Christianity was great. To this world of "new evangelicalism" we turn now.

Chapter Five

CARL HENRY: PIONEERING MODERATE

FRANCIS AND EDITH SCHAEFFER were effective spokesmen of the conservative world of traditional evangelicalism. They reflected the greater openness regarding social commitment characteristic of recent years among some traditionalists just as they demonstrated its limits. Their emergence in the 1960s was a reminder of the continued vitality of Christian intellectuals whose themes and tones *Christianity Today* could welcome. At the same time, the story of evangelical thought in the 1960s and into the 1970s must include the remarkable surge to prominence of a wide variety of opinions about social action which were until then muted. These voices never constituted the majority in the years of Vietnam, Watergate, and Carter. But they undoubtedly transformed the map of evangelicalism as its more intellectual spokesmen saw its political and social implications shift from a monolithic conservatism into a new pattern. Agreement disappeared. What some saw as healthy diversity and others regarded as disastrous fragmentation took its place.

THE PIONEER

The pioneer of the movement within evangelicalism for a new gospel of social concern was Carl F. H. Henry. Many reform-minded brethren and even radicals acknowledged Henry as their trailblazer, but in an oft-told tale, many also became sons who rebelled against their father who they saw as a latter-day "conservative." The essence of Henry's once rather lonely teaching was that the "social implications of the Gospel are integrated to evangelistic fulfillment, and social concern is an indispensable ingredient of the evangelistic message."[1] Upon such a belief, reform and radical evangelical intellectuals of the 1960s and early 1970s could and did unite, creating a demand for confronting social questions which Henry could hardly have anticipated.

While Henry's views on social activism were hardly popular, perhaps hardly taken seriously, in informed evangelical circles before the late 1960s, Henry was in other ways a significant thinker and leader in the movement long before then. After all, Henry, born in 1913 and a minister of the American Baptist Church, was the editor of *Christianity Today* in the 1950s and 1960s. Moreover, he continued to be widely active in religious circles after Harold Lindsell succeeded him at *Christianity Today* in 1968. He wrote frequently in *Christianity Today* after he relinquished his editorship, though on several issues he was not fully in agreement with the drift of the magazine he once headed. At the same time he wrote numerous books and was busy at national and international evangelical meetings. He was undoubtedly one of the leaders of his movement in the 1960s and 1970s, though he was always more a thinker than an activist.

Social activism in Henry's vision was an urgent responsibility for every Christian. The responsibilities of a Christian had to go beyond encouraging the spread of the "Good News" of Jesus Christ. Evangelism was not enough to demonstrate Christ's injunction to love one's neighbors; evangelism alone was not what he meant when he said that such as one did to the least of them one did also to Christ. Christians had to help others and reject the social "passivity" which was "no strategy at all," except insofar as it structured a dangerous "setting where left-wing strategists can more easily gain their political objectives."[2] It was necessary for evangelicals to get out and fight for a decent social life for all people. They would have to lay aside the mean-spirited and selfish "restrictive social vision" which was too prevalent in the world, including the evangelical world.[3] This endeavor was not hopeless, he argued, and the emergence of the new evangelicalism in the late 1960s reaffirmed his optimism. He saw evidence that his own efforts, among others, to some extent had succeeded, and "the dichotomy between evangelism and social concern has broken down."[4]

It was not a matter of left or right ideologies. What should motivate Christians was not ideology, but God and God's scriptural word. Henry was convinced that the Bible overflowed with injunctions to social action to make human lives closer to God's ideal: "We must stand courageously . . . in championing the Gospel's irreducible relevance to oppressed multitudes, and actively identify evangelical Christianity with the justice God demands in all areas of human exploitation and oppression."[5]

The crucial agent of social change had to be the individual Christian or ad hoc groups of Christians. Individuals were to act in their own life and in groups in the broader social milieu. Without these efforts all other strategies would fail. From first to last, Henry did not place his hopes in the state as the best means of change. The state could not be what an individual Christian could be: an agent of love. Only through love could long-lasting change be effected. Henry felt that the state could play a role, but it would be of necessity a circumscribed one. It was not the role of the state, for instance, to attempt to force Christian views on everyone else; neither state nor society should be active in "forcing the fruits of regeneration upon unregenerate men."[6] One had to appreciate the ugly fact that the state could do great evil as it sought to do good. The Amish had learned that. And the average American citizen learned that as he saw the results of federal welfare programs that failed at their intended purpose while putting the government into the business of trying to make human beings love each other. It was sheer folly to rely on "compulsive techniques" to transform human beings and their society.[7]

Nevertheless, Henry wanted nothing to do with those who saw no function for the state. God established the state, and Christians needed "a positive spirit toward the state."[8] Henry wanted Christians to be active in politics and government. Government service was a legitimate career choice for young people. He looked to the state for what he called justice. His justice included the maintenance of the God-given rights of every individual citizen in America and, more broadly, the preservation and advancement of order and peace at home and abroad. But he always returned to his master distinction between justice and love. The state had its role, and Henry respected it. But it should not be expected to be the agent of transforming love. That goal lay beyond its ken. God had commissioned each citizen of the Christian community to demonstrate witnessing love. Laws were often needed and could aid love, but alone they were and could be nothing.[9]

Henry was not particularly convinced that the answer lay in the organized church either. To be sure, he was sharply critical of those churches whose "sole preoccupation is private saintliness, preaching 'Christ crucified' in absolute isolation from socio-political affairs, and promoting the piety of the local church in total unconcern over social disorders and evils."[10] He knew that this attitude put him in opposition to many conservative church figures who had been "wrong in minimizing the importance of the church's witness to the social order."[11] But the church had the awesome and demanding mission to "proclaim" the "abiding truths and ultimate loyalties" which God expected from it.[12] It had to speak to the state and assess the state's "divinely intended role" to "maintain order and justice."[13] It also had to "address rulers and the populace on the theme of proper social principles" as long as they were truly "enunciated in the Scriptures," as he sincerely believed racial equality was.[14] Moreover, Henry thought each church ought to be actively involved in helping people. It had to have a vigorous program of Christ-like concern for people both within and without its group as a living witness to its religious faith.

Yet as he formulated the role he wanted the church to play in social and political affairs, Henry was always careful to state that the Christian

church was "not revolutionary" and could "not initiate movements for political independence."[15] Henry was always anxious to make sure there was
no conflating his position with those who sought a "political" church. He
was not really in favor of appeals from the pulpit on particular issues of
public policy or concern except when great, biblical principles of Christianity were at stake. Even then the church should be careful not to descend
to offering detailed advice concerning a given policy. It was best for it to
stick to principle, to urge discussion and prayer, and to encourage its members to enter the political process to resolve issues.[16]

From some angles Henry's stance seemed cautious. His enthusiasm for
social commitment always turned out to be sharply tempered, as his advice
to Christian churches clearly demonstrated. Yet in the context of the 1950s
and 1960s when Henry first advanced his ideas about the church and social
involvement, his cautions received less attention than some reform-oriented
evangelicals gave them later. It was his overall goal which attracted controversy, since it clashed with the evangelical mainstream which was intensely suspicious of the church having any role in the larger political,
social, and sometimes moral controversies of the age. Back then Henry
seemed radical, though time relieved him of a hardly accurate label that
surely made him most uncomfortable.

There were several reasons for Henry's cautiousness. Henry inclined
to the view that even the most socially involved Christians must keep priorities in mind. They had to "give no quarter to the illusion that Christianity
is primarily an ethical idealism engaged in denouncing political and social
injustice."[17] Their first goal was evangelizing souls for God. The other side
of this point was the danger of a fall to secularism, to the world, to the
devil. Were the church to take itself seriously as "the conscience of the
State, or the pulsebeat of the body politic," it would err fatally in "thus
directly merging its interests with those of the world."[18] Moreover, Henry
suspected that there was a line between political and social policies and
personal moral rules. God's will was that the church be more active when
it came to moral rules, which often appeared in detail in scripture, and less
so on social or economic policies upon which he had much less to say
except in broad terms.[19]

The question always came back to individual Christians for Henry.
They were the primary spearhead for progress and for the alleviation of
human suffering. At times the church or the state could complement them;
never could they replace them. This conclusion remained firm even as
Henry's sense of urgency grew as he looked at his world around him and
he pressed more and more vigorously for social action by Christians.

Henry was deeply disturbed at the world around him in the late 1960s
and the early 1970s. He had some interest in prophecy, and the dark signs
he saw convinced him that the end was near. *"The last days are here* —let

us make no mistake about it."[20] Ours, he thought, was "a carnal age" in which few could not see that the "savages are stirring again; you can hear them rumbling and rustling in the tempo of our times."[21] There seemed to him to be no way around the fact that "we live in the twilight of a great civilization, amid the deepening decline of modern culture."[22] The evidence of sin, selfishness, violence, greed, sexual immorality, and political corruption were everywhere at hand.

Henry's conclusion was not to wait passively for the end. As we know, he wanted Christians to become active to fight sin in all its guises, including social problems. His enthusiasm for struggling naturally made him delighted by one aspect of modernity: the rapid expansion of evangelical interest in social action in the late 1960s and early 1970s. He welcomed the declaration by many evangelical intellectuals in Chicago in 1973 that their faith required them to attack social evils from a Christian perspective. Henry was also pleased with the Lausanne Declaration of World Evangelism's 1974 statement on social action, though it fell short by leaving unclear how important social concern had to be to a full Christian life. Yet Henry by no means saw only good signs. The in-fighting at Lausanne, for example, was fierce when it came to taking a general stand for social action, and this both disappointed and disturbed Henry.[23]

Henry's own affection for social concern, expressed as it usually was in general terms rather than in specific goals, produced criticism. But a good part of Henry's impact on the "new evangelicalism" of recent decades derived from Henry's support for social action as an activity rather than particular goals or specific means. His contribution might well have been less decisive had he pushed principally to advocate a program, a particular content to social action. Yet his contribution was widely agreed to be very significant in laying the groundwork within evangelicalism for the legitimacy of social action.

It would be misleading to imply, however, that Henry never left the high road of philosophical principles. He did have programs he favored and he did take positions. He knew criticism was not enough and he was hardly afraid of taking a stand. Even so, his positions tended to be general ones: racial equality, decent health care, and sufficient economic sustenance for all. While he was not given to issuing lengthy position papers in support of these general goals, his commitment was there. They were objectives endorsed, he believed, by Christ in the Gospels.[24]

Henry took other stands which exposed the tensions between him and his reform-oriented offspring of the 1960s and 1970s which lay just beneath the surface of their praise for his pioneering support for social action.

First, Henry's consistent sympathy for old-fashioned patriotism, reaffirmed on numerous occasions well into the 1970s, often attracted dissent from other social action evangelicals. Henry carefully distinguished his patriotism from blind and fanatical nationalism, and then argued strenuously that his modest patriotism was something no one should apologize for. In his view genuine love of country did not require him to be a defender of every aspect of the United States. It did not prevent him from being critical of materialism, hypocrisy, and degenerating moral standards in the United States. Nor, in his view, was there any conflict between loyalty toward his country and his obligation to God. No Christian could deny that the obligation to God was higher than his obligation to his nation. But Henry accepted a world of multiple obligations, and he rejected the notion that one obligation cancelled all others. God ranked far ahead of nation, but he did not eliminate obligation to one's country.[25]

In the bicentennial year of 1976 Henry understood more than many evangelicals how much damage Agnew and Nixon had done to the cause of patriotism. They had used patriotism, as they had used so many things, for their own purposes, and their dirt had stained patriotism as an ideal. But Henry continued to believe that it was too early for patriotism to die. He continued to suggest that his critics among radicals within the evangelical movement open their Bibles. Scripture did not prohibit patriotism; indeed, in the Old Testament it was a central ideal.[26]

Second, the gap between Henry and some of those who admired his ethic of social concern was more pronounced on women's liberation — by the middle 1970s a controversial question within evangelical circles as elsewhere. No one singled out Henry for attack, but his ideas were hardly congenial with the direction many "advanced" evangelicals wanted to take.

It was typical of Henry that he did not duck the issue when it began to receive considerable attention. He frankly stated his conviction and he did so with a gentleness that was, unfortunately, unusual in the arguments that swirled around the issue in evangelical circles. Henry did try to reach out to feminism. He declared that evangelicals needed to rethink their patriarchal ideas of marriage. He supported the idea that when women wanted to contribute their talents in more public roles, they should have the chance. They had much talent which society could use, and he maintained that there must be new and creative attempts to serve the needs of working mothers. He undertook to defend Christianity to the women's movement. After all, he asserted, if it had not been for Christianity, women's condition would have been much worse. All we had to do, he remarked, was compare the condition of women in simpler and more primitive societies. Christianity was all about respect for persons, and it had fought a war of two millennia for the sacred principle that we were all equal in Christ.[27]

Yet Henry argued we must be honest and admit that the Bible teaches that men are to lead in marriage and women to follow. Moreover, men are to make the living while women are to take charge of the home. There would be exceptions and these were fine, but God's basic plan for us was in the Bible for all to see. These were also permanent patterns, established for all time. Henry did not see how he or anyone could pretend that some of Paul's pronouncements in the Bible about the role of men and women were simply cultural artifacts of Paul's time. To suggest this was to deny the Bible's inerrancy. Henry was adamant that the standard for conduct must be the Bible, not the latest fad in social issues.[28]

Third, Henry did not appreciate the potential uses of the state as a means to achieve Christian social action. As many reform-minded evangelicals saw it, this was a lingering attitude of past evangelicalism which needed to be revised in the face of modern social problems. Henry just did not agree, and he was quite prepared to carry his message into the inner sanctum of reform-minded evangelicals. Consider Henry's review of a book by Mark Hatfield, who was widely admired among those evangelicals committed to social reform. Henry complained that Hatfield did not know the difference between the maintenance of basic order and liberty, the proper function of the state, and an endless array of social programs designed somehow to make human beings loving and decent to each other. Moreover, Henry suspected that Hatfield also wanted the state to make people economically equal. This was not only unrealistic, Henry declared, it also bordered on materialism. The Christian ought not to glory in material goods, nor lust after them. Ideally, the Christian should not be concerned about them at all. It was, therefore, inappropriate for a Christian to struggle to gain for himself or others an equal share of wealth. Hatfield did not quite understand that only Christ would bring the millennium: "Political salvation is not the answer."[29]

Despite his criticism of Hatfield, Henry respected Hatfield as a responsible Christian looking for meaningful change. Henry obviously admired Hatfield, but he did not want to see their common cause, the recovery of social concern in the evangelical world, degenerate into statism rather than Christianity. He constantly repeated his conviction that much of the new evangelicalism had his hearty support. It had to speak out against the tendency of establishment leaders to ignore social needs and social criticism. It had to have a perspective which "demands a radical commitment to social justice."[30]

Yet no matter how urgent social concerns were, Henry always returned to his doctrine of limits, which he felt too many of his newfound allies ignored. They did not seem to know that Jesus was not primarily a radical killed for his social activity. They did not know that he "founded neither a party of revolutionaries, nor a movement of reformers."[31] They did not seem to know that one could get too involved in politics just as easily as one could become too withdrawn from it. They did not seem to know that many conservative evangelicals were trying to help others and were hardly simple hypocrites deserving of dismissal. They did not seem to realize that government was not to be more than "a means of preserving justice in a fallen and sinful order."[32] They did not seem to recognize the ignorance in the view which "confuses capitalism with the devil."[33] Finally, they did not always seem to know that one should approach change with a healthy sense of sin and seek a realistic hope, "a hope unblemished by hallucination."[34]

It is not surprising in light of such criticism by Henry that in the 1970s negative judgments about Henry's ideas began to appear in other quarters than the usual mainstream conservative ones. Self-styled radicals turned on Henry and charged that his social and political ideas had lagged behind the times. He was now too conservative. Controversy boiled over in 1974 when Jim Wallis, editor of the radical journal *Sojourners*, openly objected to Henry's political and social stance. Wallis held that Henry's position was basically a defense of the status quo. Henry was not prepared for radical change, he was not eager for it, and in fact he was afraid of it. To Henry, this was nonsense after all his years of urging social action to aid the poor, the racial minorities, and other oppressed groups.

But Henry never denied that he was unhappy with those like Jim Wallis and *Sojourners* (earlier *The Post-American*). He refused to have anything to do with the haters of the United States — just as he did not like the superpatriots. If the new test for reform-oriented evangelicals was to be loyalty to "post-Americanism," Henry did not intend to participate. He sought change, yes, but to a better world, not a new world.[35]

On the other hand, we must remember that Henry shared reform-minded evangelicals' unease with mainstream conservative thinking. He too was impatient with its temporizing on the question of social action. He too thought many evangelicals overemphasized personal Christianity and personal piety. He too lamented what he called the "restricted social vision" which encased many evangelicals. They were just too conservative both in their conception of religion and of politics.[36] He was also dissatisfied more and more in the 1970s with the leadership of *Christianity Today* as editor Harold Lindsell tried to make biblical inerrancy the central issue among Christians. Henry thought this emphasis came at the tragic cost of downplaying the social and political side of Christianity. He complained that the "battle over the Bible has become more central than the effective statement of the Bible's claims upon man and society."[37] And he returned again and again to this theme especially in *Christianity Today*.[38]

Henry did not know how to work out of the box in the 1970s which had trapped many thoughtful evangelicals. To the outer world evangelicalism was growing rapidly and enjoying great success. But at the same time, as Henry said, there was a struggle within evangelicalism between those who thought all efforts must go to evangelism and defending biblical inerrancy and those who wanted a more open evangelicalism, including one open to social and political involvement. This conflict bothered Henry, but though he was not always a supporter of all the passions of the "new" evangelicals who often praised him, he did not blame them. He tended to blame Harold Lindsell and those who cared so much about inerrancy. We needed, he thought, an evangelicalism which had room for many views, all biblical, but not all tied to some rigid, separatist definition of inerrancy. Surely there were other objectives biblical Christians should be busy with, including helping people, rather than testing everyone else who was an evangelical to make sure that they fit Harold Lindsell's test for orthodoxy.[39]

In Henry's mind evangelicals had to decide whether they wanted to exert a powerful Christian influence on modern culture or whether they wanted to remain a separatist and divided cult. Their numbers had grown, but he did not see any comparable growth in their influence in the citadels of modern culture. Evangelicals were still not heard there. They tended to stay away from such places, secure in their separatism, when not actually "defensive and reactionary." Were evangelicals prepared to "resign ourselves to a subculture" or were they going to enter the broader world?[40] Henry yearned for a greater influence on the broader culture, but he knew it was possible only if evangelicals showed more love toward each other, found again "the larger sense of evangelical family," and determined to resist the mood "that aligns believers against believers." This could hardly be done when "some key evangelicals are not even on speaking terms, let alone learning terms with each other."[41]

It was the potentially broad influence of evangelicalism which Henry sought, including a wider impact on social ills. Despite his cautious attitude toward change and his complicated relations with the "new" evangelical thinkers of the 1960s, Henry's substantial significance in the intellectual history of evangelicalism in his age derived from his efforts toward that objective. Henry was the careful moderate whose devotion to a socially alive evangelical Christianity promoted a political and social diversity which altered the once monolithic political message of evangelicalism in the 1960s and early 1970s. He was the pioneer.

CONGENIAL SPIRITS

One of the most obvious truths about the influence of Carl Henry is that he spoke to people across party and factional lines. His voice reached out across many barriers and into many places where it might not be expected to gain a hearing. One consequence of this was the wide respect and the generous hearing he often obtained. Another, perhaps, was that there was no movement which Henry led in any direct sense. Though he inspired many and he enlightened more, few were his direct followers. Henry seemed to welcome this state of affairs, since he was determined to preach to the world, not to build a faction of his own.

Henry was not alone in the general stance which he took toward the world—a socially concerned Christian, critical of the slim evangelical record of social action, and yet resistant to the movement of the "new evangelicals." There were numerous other writers in the 1960s and earlier 1970s who were of very nearly the same mind. Each was independent and not in full agreement with any other. But they had a real if often unintentional similarity, captured in their description of themselves as moderates.

They shared Henry's mood: openness to change, convinced that evangelicals must play a role in the social and political world around them, but unready to throw themselves into fashionable crusades without hesitation. There were many examples. John Warwick Montgomery, a Missouri Lutheran, was certainly the most prolific, and he was clearly quite impressive. Congressman John Anderson of Illinois spoke from this perspective, as did Elton Trueblood, the prominent Quaker, and many more. None formed a school or became well known outside of their evangelical circle. But collectively they developed a balanced point of view which was one of the characteristic modes of thought of evangelicalism in our period.

In another age they would have been on the cutting edge of evangelicalism on political and social action. As it happened, others had gone further than they had gone in the 1960s and early 1970s. Yet these thinkers and writers were part of the story of developing evangelicalism in that era. They were rather like Henry, a quiet part, but quite possibly influential beyond their apparent reservation. Closer to the average evangelical, perhaps, their gentle push toward social commitment came in appealing accents and dressed with characteristic doubts that made it a more authentic, if less flashy, expression of the opening toward social concern within evangelicalism in the years from the New Left to Carter.

Many of these figures openly acknowledged Carl Henry as the prophet of the path they wanted to follow, but they were often as likely to praise Billy Graham and other evangelical leaders. The respect for Graham was a sign that many of these observers were at pains to establish the closeness of their own perspectives with the mainstream while making the declaration that devoted Christians had to play a much expanded social role and join the fight against social evils and political injustice.[42] Their message was that evangelicals could no longer "concentrate exclusively on personal conversions and personal morality." Such narrow concentration led to a "blind spot" which, as Montgomery put it, built on "confusing the *Zeitgeist* with the Word of God." Christians had to break from their parochialism if they were to help. They had to pull back "the cultural web in which we Caucasians are caught."[43] The result, said Congressman John Anderson, could be "a new and vital evangelical social ethic." It would be based on a mature appreciation that "we cannot escape the fact that we are our own brother's keeper," and it would recognize that "sin and righteousness are social issues with social dimensions, as well as personal issues with personal dimensions."[44]

Moderates were always anxious to establish the authenticity of their general (and sometimes vague) declarations of Christian social concern in biblical terms. Like Henry, they acknowledged the exclusive authority of the Bible in the realm of ethics, and they were uncomfortable in the face of any movement outside this realm. They contended that increased social concern was right because the Bible, indeed Christianity itself, required "active opposition to social evil and positive efforts to ameliorate human woe."[45] Jesus taught this truth. So did the Old Testament. The full weight of scripture came down on the side of those urging social action, though this inescapable fact did not mean neglecting the central task of evangelism. The drive to lead men and women to Christ was as important as ever, but it was a mistake to proceed with that task in isolation from the scriptural goal of fighting social ills. Both were God's will. Both could operate together. Neither had to be sacrificed, and neither should be sacrificed.[46]

Moderates tended to be confident that increased Christian social responsibility posed few really serious problems for traditional evangelical practices, much less its faith or values. They had little sense that their emphasis required a revolution within evangelicalism. They had in mind less a fundamental change than a renewed emphasis on a withered part of the evangelical faith. To their more radical compatriots this analysis was naive. It was undoubtedly cautious, though that did not mean uncritical of mainstream evangelicalism. John Warwick Montgomery, among others, noted what more reform-oriented evangelicals were to discuss at length: the record of nineteenth-century evangelicals who were deeply involved in the controversial social issues of their age. The contrast with the record in his own time bothered him—and other moderates. They insisted that Jesus did not offer an example of withdrawal; his lesson was just the opposite, and evangelicals had to follow his example. If Jesus "did not remain aloof, or refuse to get involved, or hide away," how could anyone else?[47] To follow Jesus' example, modern evangelicals would have to stop being so concerned to achieve personal purity and so anxious to avoid the dangers of evil outside their secure worlds. They would have to examine their affection for rigid separatism with a critical perspective. They would have to reject their anti-intellectualism and their predilections for thinking that was "*shallow*" or even "*suppressive*" of a larger world of disagreement and conflict outside.[48] Pious cliches and in-group slogans would no longer substitute for serious thought in touch with the larger world. Only when evangelicalism held fast to its truths, while reaching out to this broader world of life and problems, could it fulfill Christ's double charge: to save souls and aid the suffering on earth.

Moderates worried about several specific issues of social significance.

Two were race and personal morality. Their views on race, like Henry's expressed the consensus among evangelical opinion leaders that Christianity prescribed racial equality. While they opposed self-indulgent hatred of racists, racists were wrong and society needed "a baptism of love" to move forward to a new and more just racial pattern.[49] John Anderson, for example, reported with considerable pride his efforts to get open housing legislation through the House of Representatives in the face of sometimes ugly opposition. He believed that a Christian had to have "a deep regard for human rights," and he believed he had fought for that ideal.[50] As other moderates explained, the state coercion involved in achieving racial equality was in this (exceptional) case absolutely necessary. Some people meant well, but without state action they rarely followed their often enunciated phrases of good will and good intentions.[51]

While moderates spoke with one voice about the evils of racism, they offered little in the way of detailed programs or policies to fight the evil. There was an abstract quality to their stance as there often was to Henry's. This was less true when they stepped on the more familiar ground of traditional evangelical social morality. They were specific in defending the nuclear family, objecting to easy divorce, opposing liberalized abortion, denouncing extramarital sex, and the like.[52] It was commonplace, moreover, to read more general denunciations of the decline of "traditional morality." The old verities of family, honesty, temperance, and the like, they charged, were in a state of near collapse in the United States. This fact was uniformly regretted. There was never a sense that something better might be evolving. Their frame of reference always compared the degenerated present with the better "past." While this analysis was partly a reflection of simple traditionalism, it also reflected a belief that scripture supported traditional values of personal ethics.[53]

Moderates assumed that state action promoted by evangelicals could help retard repeated violations of godly ethics. Such intervention was no substitute for faith in Jesus Christ, but it could assist by prohibiting abortions or forbidding casual divorce. In this way it inevitably aided in promoting the social good just as much as it did in combating racial injustice. Here again social concern and individual change should work together.

Yet these moderates were cautious. They were, as we know, determined that social concern not abolish evangelism among authentic Christians. They were also extremely uneasy about proposals for change which were not offered in a spirit of skepticism toward all the hidden objectives of such change—and all the earthly means to realize them. John Warwick Montgomery nicely explained this second sign of caution. Over and over he warned of the danger of sin and the folly of a sense of social action not infused with a chastened optimism. In this light Montgomery did not think Nazism was inexplicable. It was the creature of naive optimists, of Enlightenment liberalism. Weimar and Buchenwald are near each other in Germany; in symbolic terms this was no accident. Weimar was the home of Goethe, a significant figure in the German Enlightenment and a frank believer in the gospel of man rather than God. Such an illusion led to the horrors of Buchenwald. When men fail to see themselves as sinners they will attempt anything. But human limitations will block their way and stimulate their sinful natures to a passionate fury which will do great evil. Awareness of human limitations was a realistic doctrine which left fewer victims in its wake.[54]

Montgomery concluded that the same problem was often present in modern historical experience. In the heyday of optimism in the United States in the nineteenth century Americans were guilty of a similar blindness. Many Americans then had believed in themselves, and they left us an unfortunate legacy of smugness and insensitivity to the evil we did. More reading of Melville, Montgomery remarked, might have helped. Americans needed to discover that no one could build an Eden on this sinful earth without God's aid.[55]

Moderates' caution often took the form of an almost Niebuhrian realism. For example, these writers felt peace was a worthy goal to pursue, but they always reiterated their point that one had to be a "realist" and recognize what history illustrated. Peace was unlikely to arrive before Christ returned. The same point was made about democracy. Only a democracy grounded in the "reality" of human sin could possibly endure. Absurd "trust" in rulers or "the people" was a formula for disaster, not a hopeful ideal for democracy. It was a naivete which was doomed.[56]

Like their conservative brethren, moderates endlessly sounded the theme of human sin. It was obviously their touchstone. John Warwick Montgomery returned to his frequent invocation of sin's effects, for instance, in a review of Herbert Marcuse, the celebrated philosopher of the New Left. The fundamental error of his analysis, Montgomery wrote, was Marcuse's sanguine view of human nature. John Anderson shared Montgomery's belief. However much we all wanted a better society, we had to be realistic. To be a true Christian was to accept this fact, to be also a sophisticated Christian who knew that we cannot erect "that perfect society which we all seek."[57]

Stephen Monsma made the same point by recalling the miserable record of religious experimental communities in America. They began on a high note of hope, excitement, and great expectation. They ended, however, in a mire of defeat which starkly outlined the ominous reality of human evil. Elton Trueblood contended that a frank confrontation of human limitations had its fortunate side: it provided an honest basis to guide us as a practical people toward the limited changes which were possible.[58]

Much of the writing by these evangelicals is sophisticated and thoughtful, even in its almost ritualistic citation of evil. Stephen Monsma's discussion of evil and politics, as complex and many-sided a consideration as one finds in the evangelical literature, was a good illustration. Monsma exemplified another trait as dominant among these moderates as their caution: their affinity for balance. These intellectuals saw a world which contained several elements which could not be understood apart from a balance among them. On one level, this often meant a determination to note the reality of sin *and* hope in the human person and in human experience. This was Monsma's stance. On another, moderates agreed with Elton Trueblood, who insisted that social action was vital, but so was evangelism, and they must be balanced. On a third level they shared John B. Anderson's sentiment that one ought to get involved in politics but only in a balanced, "responsible" manner.[59]

Like Henry, moderates were suspicious of those who did not appreciate complexity and balance. Such enthusiasts were more likely to be irresponsible cheerleaders than thoughtful actors, more likely to be ideologues than hopeful realists working in a somewhat dark world for the light of Christ's kingdom. They rarely acknowledged that their focus on complexity and balance introduced a potent factor of conservatism into their outlook. They did not appreciate that the proponents of balance and complexity are always the advocates of prudence and likely to be committed in practice to the status quo or only the most "prudent" changes to it.

Their attitudes toward patriotism and the United States are a good case study. They shrank instinctively from any position which either celebrated frantic patriotism or lauded the arrival of a "post-American" era. Yet they fundamentally favored a "balance" and saw a "complexity" which tilted toward praising America and accepting the legitimacy of patriotism. They were genuinely sympathetic to their country and not at all eager to ridicule it or wish it a speedy end. They did not regard patriotism as embarrassing, and they certainly rejected the idea that Christianity foreclosed patriotism. At its best love of country was "a continuing and legitimate love affair with a set of principles, with a common vision of the good life, . . . not a forced conformity to a single party, faction, ideology. Nor is it blind loyalty to any group currently in power."[60] However, the days of simple loyalty were over. Nicholas Wolterstorff reflected a widespread opinion in his analysis in *The Reformed Journal*. He supported patriotism, but he admitted that the fervor of his patriotism had diluted. Events in the United States in the 1960s and 1970s had inexorably eroded a full-hearted loyalty, and in light of the world responsibility of Christians, patriotism was somewhat old-fashioned.[61]

John Warwick Montgomery addressed the connection between Christianity and America in several focused essays written in connection with the bicentennial year of 1976. He was disappointed that even in 1976 some people were not able to tell the difference between the United States and

"God's Country." He dismissed the American right wing's mistaken understanding of the founding fathers to be Christians as a sad example of the
thinking of those who naively linked patriotism and Christianity. Yet Montgomery was proud of the American Revolution. It was a special event, in
spite of the founding fathers' often dubious Christianity. It was an adventure in defense of self-government and a decisive rejection of both anarchy
and tyranny. It was also partly about freedom, which he felt was a value
Christians and Americans alike should endorse. It followed a moderate,
prudent path. It was a testimony to the proper Christian approach to politics, an essay in Christian balance and realism.[62]

The Revolution seemed further and further away to Montgomery and
others whose patriotism was no longer so fervent. They shared Henry's
unease over contemporary America and often, in fact, were sure that there
was something deeply wrong with America. They suspected that "there is
something fundamentally wrong in the country today."[63] This was not merely
a fashionable judgment by these evangelicals in the late 1960s; it persisted
among them during the 1970s in very good health. Many of the complaints
pointed to rampant selfishness as the cause. The moderates insisted that
the unpleasant truth was that America increasingly substituted materialism
for the Holy Spirit and self-centeredness for God. Crime, corruption, violence, and cheating were more popular than Jesus. Few of our institutions
worked, and some, such as capitalism, tended at times to encourage the
selfishness that plagued modern America.[64]

Others bemoaned the radical separation of the secular American from
any spiritual wellsprings. It was a great tragedy there were only a handful
of people in politics who, like Mark Hatfield, the senator from Oregon,
were prepared to take the spirit into the modern world. Few any longer
hoped for a Christian America, an idea which seemed to them to be "an-
tiquated" and "impractical."[65] Finally, there were those who acknowledged
that many of our modern problems were the product of errors made when
the nation faced outward. Pride and self-confidence in foreign affairs and
in war had cost much, as any person who had gone through the Vietnam
era knew. Such pride was not acceptable for Christians, of course, since it
denied sin. But some moderates concluded that perhaps the discovery of
America's limits, painful as it had been, would be a price worth paying if
it led to a lasting sense of those national limits.[66]

There was no sentiment for giving up on America—or its government.
Moderates expressed satisfaction with the American political process. They
still had confidence in what they viewed as a free government, based on a
contract among the people, in which all were morally equal and had a say
and which bound its institutions under law. Like Henry they raised no
question about the basic institutions of American democracy.[67] Yet all was
not well. John Anderson sounded a popular alarm when he acknowledged

that many were alienated from political life in the United States. He believed people had good cause for some of their feelings, though he felt they should shoulder some of the responsibility themselves. It was true that government was disappointing in America. It grew ever larger, interfering with more and more citizen liberties, while in practice it was inefficient and ineffective. No wonder there was so much frustration. Citizens, however, should not just sit around and complain. They should go out into American politics and government and change what they don't like.[68]

Another common complaint focused on how little our government followed the higher moral law. Anderson contended that the idea of government in the United States had always incorporated a belief in the guiding wisdom of divine law as the appropriate "test of whether a government is just and whether its institutions and policies serve the basic moral law."[69] He continued to urge the importance of principle in political life, but he well knew that principle did not rule in the era of Lyndon Johnson and Richard Nixon. While he sought, he said, to be one politician who did depend on God and who prayed to him daily, most did not even participate in such activities as the prayer breakfast movement. And even that, John W. Montgomery charged, was insubstantial and perfunctory, like the rest of "Washington Christianity."[70]

The alternative was not clear, but more often than not, moderates invoked a goal of "community." This was *the* fashionable concept among leaders of all persuasions in the fold in this era. Often its specifics were vague, and even its proponents welcomed it with extreme caution. This was true for many moderates. They agreed with Henry that community with others in one's church, local neighborhood, and even nation was valuable. Yet they resolutely insisted that the only type of community that was acceptable was one in which the individual existed as an autonomous, independent figure. The objective, as Elton Trueblood summarized, was to pursue individualism and community at the same time and to limit one's search for each by devotion to the other. No one seemed to think this would be a modest task. Their normal assumption was always that community and the individual were two objectives unlikely to fit well together, indeed more likely to conflict with each other than anything else. Evangelical moderates were often torn by their conviction that Christianity pointed them toward community while their equally innate American ideology directed them toward the individual. Yet they were not deeply torn, since they declared that God endorsed both. In practice many leaned more to one or another, while supporting both, in their practical means of reconciling what they often considered irreconcilable. Always they kept some kind of balance, however, true to the kind of thinking they admired.[71]

CONCLUSION

Moderates, like Carl Henry, did not have an easy row to hoe. They knew that suspicion of them lingered in the corners of the minds of more conservative members of their faith. While the rigor of conservative biblical commitment among moderates was substantial—and few dared to challenge it—the same could hardly be said of the political ideas of moderates like Henry or Montgomery. Some observers even within evangelicalism did not always take moderates like Henry very seriously as advocates of change. They were not adverse to noting that sometimes moderates were more prepared to defend social commitment in principle than to propose and act on imaginative social strategies to combat the problems they saw. One extremely influential conservative remembered with amusement that people like Henry could point to their turgid academic discourses suggesting social action, but they could rarely demonstrate any practical action they had taken to alleviate social problems.[72] From outside evangelicalism it is somewhat difficult, no matter what one's own political views, to assess these mostly Republican figures as anything but timid proponents of very modest change. But context matters. Against the traditional twentieth-century attitudes in their faith, the moderates were forces for a new mood.

Moreover, in the 1950s and 1960s Henry especially was a pioneer—often a lonely one. That reform-oriented evangelicals who were the "children" of the 1960s as well as Henry's "children" turned out to be far more numerous *and* far more reform-minded in later years than Henry dreamed was an irony about which Henry and his allies could only be ambivalent. They made his cause less lonely, but they also made it more willing to take action as well as more serious about changes which moderates were not willing to endorse. Henry's "children" did not consume him, but they did not always prove to be his followers either.

Chapter Six

REFORM-ORIENTED EVANGELICALS

CARL F. H. HENRY POINTED THE WAY, but the decisive opening to political and social diversity within evangelicalism came suddenly, driven by remarkable force and energy in the late 1960s. A wave of evangelicals announcing that to "work for God's will in American society is to work for change"[1] became yet one more evidence of the forces of change in that era which appeared everywhere in American society. These reform-minded souls did not, we know, carry the day, but they came to occupy a substantial place in the discourse of the 1970s, urging others as William Pannell put it, to experience "the sounds of the seventies."[2]

On the one hand, the movement was self-conscious. The reform-oriented evangelicals—sometimes called the young evangelicals, though this ignored a good many grey heads in their midst—saw themselves as a distinct group within the fold. On the other hand, they were diverse in religion, in personal background, and in political and social values. They also could and did respect many kinds of evangelicals, citing Carl F. H. Henry as their pioneer, welcoming Leighton Ford of the Billy Graham organization, and praising *The Post-American* (later *Sojourners*).[3] It was a loose movement, far more so than its skeptics sometimes recognized, and its participants tended to be delighted about its looseness, diversity, and openness.

Four distinct beliefs united reform-minded voices.

1. They agreed that they lived in a time of undoubted crisis and therefore they had much to do.[4] As George DeVries expressed the mood in *The Reformed Journal*, they were determined to speak prophetically.[5] Since it was a revolutionary period, there was a genuine need for commitment to social action to meet the huge demands of the age.[6] Timothy Smith contrasted the current sluggishness with the passion and purpose of those nineteenth-century evangelicals who undertook to fulfill the social demands

of their time. He urged that evangelicals drop their "fortress mentality" and their affection for personal taboos and commit themselves to a broader field of social action.[7] David O. Moberg articulated another theme when he declared that it was past time for evangelicals to realize that inaction was action, action which sustained the existent social evils.[8]

This first conviction was most vividly and firmly enunciated in the Chicago Declaration of 1973, produced at a Conference of Evangelicals for Social Concern, an organization formed by some reform-oriented intellectuals. Ronald J. Sider called the conference and the Declaration "An Historic Moment for Biblical Social Concern," and it certainly was that for the 1970s.[9] The Chicago Declaration was a surprisingly sharply worded document that caught the sense of crisis and urgency which some felt regarding the social duties of Christianity in their present age. It was premised on what one contributor to Sider's book on the Declaration called "our hope that Christian evangelicals will not become just a part of the show," but would instead choose "engagement."[10] A broad assortment of evangelical opinion leaders signed it. Many were clearly liberally minded, including David O. Moberg, Vernon Grounds, Paul Henry, and Richard Mouw. Others were more traditional though open to social change, such as Carl Henry. Still others were clearly quite radical in focus, as were, for example, John F. Alexander of *The Other Side* and Wes Michaelson and Jim Wallis of *The Post-American*.

The Chicago Declaration was partly a document of apology to God. It confessed that "we have not proclaimed or demonstrated his justice"[11]: "Although the Lord calls us to defend the social and economic rights of the poor and the oppressed, we have mostly remained silent,"[12] and therefore "we have not demonstrated the love of God to those suffering social abuses."[13] It was partly a critique of American life: we "must challenge the misplaced trust of the nation in economic and military might," and we were to accept the unpleasant fact that we lived in what was "an unjust American society."[14] Finally, it was partly a series of promises disguised as admonitions: "We must attack the materialism of our culture and the maldistribution of the nation's wealth and services,"[15] and we "must resist the temptation to make the nation and its institutions objects of near-religious loyalty."[16]

2. They insisted that many of the evils of the world were social and required social solutions. David O. Moberg was an able early expositor of this sociological analysis: "From a theological perspective, sin is the ultimate source of all social problems. In the immediate contemporary sense, however, the causes are often too complex to attribute directly to [individual] sin."[17] Moberg and others obviously did not deny the continuing reality of individual sin and the power of individual reformation for a minute. Yet they insisted that the gospel of individualism in analyzing problems and in

advancing toward a solution could no longer suffice by itself. To be sure, some reform-minded evangelicals remained concerned about traditional issues such as drinking alcohol or sexual deviation, but reform-oriented evangelicals increasingly proposed going beyond these personal problems, which required individual resolution, to add other, broader social problems and to advocate more community- or state-directed attempts to meet them. As Chapter Nine makes clear, the three problems evangelicals came to consider above all others were racial prejudice, world hunger, and human poverty. The biblical case for addressing them seemed overwhelming, from the exhortations of the Sermon on the Mount to far less well-known passages in the obscure book of Zephaniah.[18]

3. Reform-oriented evangelicals usually sought to avoid identification with either the evangelical mainstream and its conservatism or the radical "biblically oriented" wing of the evangelical world. They had a pronounced tendency, in fact, to fault most of their fellow Christians as sluggards when it came to social healing. Moberg reported sociological surveys which forced him to conclude that evangelical social concern was low. This was a general belief among the reform-minded, who felt they were swimming upstream all the way.[19] Robert Clouse, Robert Linder, and Richard Pierard charged that the "failure of much of evangelicalism to leap over the wall of individual piety and to demonstrate a capacity to criticize the secular order has stunted the gospel witness."[20] Vernon Grounds saw no point in denying the painful truth that "the history of the Christian Church is a history of opposition to change," and it "has been complacent, compliant, and compromising, an uncritical ally of whatever authority might happen to be in power."[21] They intended to transform this record, following Letha Scanzoni's reminder that in politics "Carl Henry has said, today the only heresy is Orthodoxy."[22]

But they were not entirely devoid of caution. They knew they faced the animus of many established figures, an opposition which often surfaced during the 1960s and 1970s. It was frustrating because, as they saw it, their opponents were political and social conservatives who misunderstood the Bible, often in the service of what was little more than self-interest. These critics rarely admitted how much they were moved by the force of their political disagreements, more often choosing the "misplaced battle lines" of the controversy over biblical inerrancy.

Reform-oriented advocates insisted that they were not in the slightest practicing or presaging any abandonment of Christianity. On the contrary, they believed that an evangelicalism devoted in part to social change would create a Christianity at last true to its biblical roots. They thought fighting poverty, racial injustice, hunger, and environmental abuses showed them to be far more in touch with the Bible than many of their politically conservative opponents.[23] Moreover, as David Moberg observed, the proponents of most reform also intended to continue the traditional task of seeking new souls for Christianity. There was a third path besides the traditional choices of *either* evangelism *or* the social gospel. One could, and should, pursue both, acknowledging that Jesus commanded the faithful Christian to do exactly that.[24]

On the other hand, many of the reform-minded felt a considerable lack of ease with such radical evangelicals as Jim Wallis, *The Post-American*, or later *Sojourners*. They could, like Mark Hatfield, quote them or even write for them, but there were reservations. Paul Henry said of the radicals that a certain natural affinity with them should not free them from criticism. They had an unattractive fondness for "rhetorical overkill" and tended to lash out in too many directions from too many extreme positions. It was hard for him to take entirely seriously people who—in the name of Christ—sweepingly dismissed almost all of Christianity, the American government, the middle classes, the military, and much more.[25]

In contrast to their radical brethren, most reform-oriented writers adopted an attitude they felt was far more positive. This was not at the expense of criticism, since those eager for reform were certainly uneasy with their society. It was positive, as they saw it, in two ways: in its confidence that much could be done through admittedly impaired present institutions and in its spirit of hope in the chance remaining in the United States to "live a life of creative and joyful simplicity."[26]

4. The reformers insisted on rediscovering the past of their faith in America which they trusted constituted a rich legacy of commitment to God's service in the world. Following the leadership of Donald Dayton, they sought to demonstrate that it was only in the twentieth century that social inactivity gained sway. This inattention, in fact, constituted "the great reversal," the repudiation of a past of social commitment which clearly fascinated many voices for change.[27] It received so much focus from the reform-oriented in the 1960s and 1970s partly as a sincere attempt to rediscover the "true" history of their faith. But it was also an obvious tactic in their campaign for a hearing. It allowed them to justify their social goals *within* their tradition and to claim that they were the representatives of the orthodox tradition. This meant that their arguments for social action did not have to be presented as revolutionary—which their proponents did not believe they were. Their argument came dressed in conservative clothes as a plea for evangelicals to affirm their past.

The center of attraction was the life of evangelicalism in the pre–Civil War period, especially in the North. This was an era in American life in which religious energy was high and the growth and ferment in American religion was enormous.[28] There were endless utopian experiments in the pre–Civil War decades and numerous campaigns for reform in all aspects of the life of the nation; much of that activity grew out of the religious energy of the age. It was, as Sydney Ahlstrom reported in his magisterial work on American religion, an age which saw the "High Tide of Humanitarian Reform" and the high tide of the Protestant church's connection with reform.[29]

It was in that age that much of American Protestantism moved toward a theology of Arminianism, a theology which stressed salvation as a matter between God and the individual sinner. This theology looked more toward the individual than toward creeds or institutions and provided a stimulus for individuals to change the world in the service of God. Another feature of pre– Civil War evangelicalism was its acceptance of postmillenialism, a doctrine that encouraged evangelicals to believe that Jesus gave Christians the solemn duty to struggle now in this world to realize his will, rather than simply to wait for his return.[30]

The various historians of and commentators on pre– Civil War evangelicalism agree that it did indeed support a mood of reform, but they disagree on what it was that evangelicals wanted to alter. Evangelicals who undertook to mobilize the past in the 1960s and 1970s tended to notice the extensive pre– Civil War willingness to help the poor and to provide all types of social welfare to assist the unfortunate. There also was some interest in pre– Civil War evangelical women and their greater role in the church.[31] Some enthusiastic students of the history of "evangelical feminism" drew the conclusion that contemporary supporters of a new role for women should take great encouragement from the pre– Civil War record. It was a time when feminists were numerous in the Christian church, a time when they played a major role in religious reform movements. It proved that evangelicalism need not always serve as a roadblock to change.[32] Less enthusiastic observers noted that the struggle against alcohol and for sabbatarianism was more important than the struggle for women's rights in the 1840s and 1850s.[33]

The major dispute, however, was over the role evangelicalism played within the movement to abolish slavery. Reform-oriented evangelicals were proud of what they considered the admirable record of their brothers and sisters of more than a hundred years before. The story of the founding of antislavery Oberlin College, the nationwide antislavery activity of Charles G. Finney, the leadership of others such as Theodore Weld, Orange Scott, and the Tappan brothers, participation in the underground railway, the founding of the Wesleyan Methodists in the 1840s over the slavery question, the split of other Protestant denominations over slavery, all received a good share of attention. Those events were an inspiring lesson for modern times.[34]

While there was a side of pre– Civil War evangelicalism involved with abolitionism, the record, in truth, was mixed, as some straightforward denominational histories make clear. Evangelicals rarely had much sympathy for slavery, but that was a different thing from active enlistment in the abolitionist cause. Clearly, most denominations shrank from such a radical step. As Timothy Smith convincingly argued, many found themselves caught between painful dilemmas when they came to the slavery issue. Even if they hated slavery they had to deal with the fact that many abolitionists were not Christians, while many slaveholders, after all, insisted they were devout Christians. Moreover, to push antislavery was to divide churches and potentially the United States itself, no light consequences foolishly undertaken. Finally, then as now there were weighty questions about the place of violence in change. Though some entertained the pleasant contrary illusion, slavery was not likely to disappear on its own.[35]

Outside historians do not exactly deny the existence of a pre– Civil War record of activism, though they do not always accord it much attention. Rather, historians often suggest that evangelicals were a people "so overadapted to their empire that they lost the critical note" contained within the Christian religion. They were far more conservative than some reform-oriented interpreters suggested. Even when evangelical reform energies were present, they were frequently directed toward altering individual practices, above all the consumption of alcohol. There was rarely evidence of a theory of the social order, of an awareness of its systemic weaknesses, or of any plans to reform it.[36]

Yet none of the qualifications and caveats discouraged contemporary reform-minded evangelicals from their conviction which was at least partly true, that in the pre– Civil War days American Protestantism had included many Christians busily engaged in social action, nor their belief that this model should guide their movement in the 1960s and 1970s. Another earlier and somehow truer evangelicalism stood in judgment on the contemporary church, and its judgment was devastating.[37]

The model retained some vigor as the nineteenth century proceeded. There were still many examples of evangelical philanthropy and stewardship. For instance, the Missouri-Lutherans conducted a remarkable welfare ministry in the second half of the nineteenth century, helping orphans, the sick, and the poor. Also of note were actions by northern Protestant (including some evangelical) churches in the Reconstruction era to assist southern blacks. Involvement in Indian life and education as well as, of course, the temperance movement were two other efforts made in the years after 1865.[38]

Yet there was an unmistakable shift of mood after the Civil War. There was what reform-minded evangelicals considered a loss of drive to manifest the full message of Jesus Christ. Historians also see in the post– Civil War age a proliferation of corruption and confusion, problems in which evangelicals displayed little social concern. Protestants of most persuasions supported the status quo, including the industrial revolution. The gospel did not speak to the rich, except in the muted tones of a vague Christian stewardship, and it certainly did not speak to the poor. Religion became increasingly oriented toward individual piety. There was a rise in the influence of Old School Presbyterianism which strongly affected a number of evangelical groups and which accented the importance of both a conservative religion and a conservative politics. The language of individual sin became increasingly dominant, with a corresponding chilling influence on social interest. There was also a sharp rise in premillenialism which encouraged waiting for Jesus' return as the only feasible means to deal with the great evils of the world. Even among the Quakers, well known for their zealous social activism, the years after 1865 marked a change. Their movement toward social amelioration quieted in the industrial age. The exception was, as always, the campaign for prohibition, which was at the top of the agenda for Quakers, as for other Protestants. In fact, reform-minded evangelicals and outside observers agree that by the later decades of the nineteenth century any reformist edge in evangelicalism was gone, except for temperance.[39]

It might be argued that the Social Gospel movement of the late nineteenth and early twentieth centuries preserved a reformist edge. The Social Gospel movement was an effort by some Protestant thinkers and leaders to address the problems of modern industrialism. It changed greatly during its active years. The movement eventually supplemented its early interest in labor problems by confronting a whole range of social and economic matters; it supplemented its early tendency toward an individualistic analysis of society by an increasingly social perspective; and it replaced its early affirmation of American institutions with some affection for socialist or near socialist ideas. In the end, the Social Gospel was one of the factors leading to the formation of the Federal Council of Churches of Christ in 1908, parent of the present National Council.

But all this activity involved few evangelical Protestants. They were hardly the proponents of the Social Gospel, either in the late nineteenth century or later. Not only did most evangelical opinion leaders repudiate the political and social views which increasingly dominated among Social Gospel proponents; they also shied away from the liberal theological tenets characteristic of many Social Gospellers. Conservative religion and conservative politics became their watchwords.[40]

While social concern declined among evangelicals in these years and there was a clear connection between evangelicals (and many other Protestants) and the establishment in American society, the change with the pre– Civil War period can be exaggerated.[41] Students of this era have also noted the emergence of the Church of the Nazarene and the Salvation Army in the United States as examples of the growth of biblical churches involved with the poor and disadvantaged in this era. In fact, a number of Protestant groups went into the slums seeking converts and continued there, providing succor to victims as they preached "salvation in the slums." Not just the Salvation Army, but many religious bodies established shelters, rescue missions, healing centers, homes for unwed mothers, Christmas aid programs, prison work programs, and the like.[42] Moreover, there was the continuing struggle for prohibition of alcohol which took enormous effort and in its way, along with the attempt to eliminate prostitution, was an effort to demonstrate "real concern for the outcasts of society."[43] So were the limited missions which such evangelical churches as the Reformed Church undertook to blacks and Indians.[44]

On the other hand, there was the effort of Billy Sunday, the enormously popular evangelist of the early 1900s. He both reflected and promoted the common mood of hostility to social action. He saw no solution to any social problem except in radical commitment to Christ. He did not see much wrong with America anyway, and he locked Christianity and patriotism in a tight embrace: "I think that Christianity and Patriotism are synonymous terms and hell and traitor are synonymous."[45] In contrast to Sunday, though, stood another well-known evangelical of the age, William Jennings Bryan, who worked for a very different evangelicalism. Bryan was extraordinarily active in reform campaigns of all sorts—besides his presidential efforts—from temperance to world peace. His famous nadir in Dayton, Tennessee, in the 1920s should not lead us to ignore the counterpoint he ordinarily formed to the increasing conservatism of evangelicalism.[46]

Historians of all stripes, however, agree that the 1920s was the final stop. Social activism became identified then with both radical social ideas and biblical apostasy. Enthusiasm for social activism also waned in the 1920s for another reason: the cause which had drawn evangelicals out of their churches and into action more than any other, the fight for temperance, seemed won. Prohibition became the law of the land.[47]

The Great Depression did stimulate renewed social awareness, and a reborn interest in the Social Gospel occurred among mainline Protestant churches. It cemented social concern as an integral part of modern, establishment Protestantism.[48] Yet fundamentalists and evangelicals trod another path. It was not until the late 1960s that new voices and new national forces were to lead to what reform-minded evangelicals had long hoped for: another Great Reversal. They sought to spur their fellows to act with the assurance that they were leading back to their faith's roots, not promoting heresy, but reviving a faith which could take seriously the mission to enable God's kingdom to come on earth. It would be a world in which, as Jonathan Blanchard, the founder of Wheaton College, put it long ago, "the law of God is the law of the land."

STYLES OF REFORM-MINDED EVANGELICALS

It would be impossible to reduce the rich and exciting diversity within the universe of reform-minded evangelicals any further. This is particularly true in regard to the difference in the *means* of pursuing change among the reformers. Two models stood out. One was political action, often favored by those whose background was in the Calvinist tradition, which had long accepted politics and the state. Paul Henry of Calvin College was noteworthy as a straightforward advocate of the efficacy and wisdom of making change through politics and government. Wesley Pippert emphasized that the Bible, especially the Old Testament, respected the political process: "The Bible is full of politics," he announced, and this was our signal.[49] Government and politics were hardly the exclusive answer for many reform-minded evangelicals, but they concurred that such means could lend invaluable help.[50]

The other means of witness was community, the realization of more loving, sharing relationships among Christians lived out in the context of daily life.[51] It was a basic assumption of many reformers that a community and a political focus did not necessarily have to conflict. It was a crucial assumption of the entire "new" evangelical network in the 1960s and 1970s. Insisting on the validity of community was precisely what set many radicals apart from their reform-oriented allies when it came time to identify the proper means of change. To accept politics and to call for community was, in their view, both to accept and to reject the world. Many reform-minded evangelicals well understood this fact, and this mixed strategy was as reasonable to them as it was problematic to a good number of radicals.

SENATOR MARK HATFIELD

A study of the thought and action of Mark Hatfield provides a concrete illustration of the political approach. Hatfield was by far the most famous exponent of reform-minded evangelicalism who zealously pursued — indeed, exemplified — the political route to witness. He was the most important and controversial evangelical in Washington in the 1960s and 1970s and remained so until he was joined by Jimmy Carter. To some he was a modern prophet, although he was by no means so well thought of by everyone.[52] Hatfield was very active in evangelical circles through his extensive publication and speaking schedule. He wrote numerous articles for Christian journals of many persuasions, and he authored widely discussed books, including *Not Quite So Simple* (1968), *Conflict and Conscience* (1971), and *Between a Rock and a Hard Place* (1976). Particularly in the early 1970s it seemed as if Hatfield was everywhere in the evangelical world. His clear and unequivocal voice was often heard.

Hatfield became known for his vigorous pursuit of a politics of love. He claimed that our common life as a people was declining because of "the vanishing of love and care for one another." Such an idea ensured he would be a controversial figure within evangelical precincts, especially when he insisted it meant rejection of the casual linkage of theological and political conservatism. He declared that "somehow, many Christians have assumed that faith places them in a mandatory alliance with the political status quo. But this is not the message of the Bible."[53]

Hatfield's early lack of enthusiasm for the Vietnam War and his subsequent open criticism of it brought him considerable evangelical notoriety. His criticism was unusual in evangelical—or Senate—circles in the late 1960s and early 1970s, and it is no wonder that Hatfield found this a trying time in his relations with numerous other evangelicals. Some denounced him at every opportunity as a near AntiChrist. Hatfield felt such criticisms. They did not deter him, but he was bothered by those who would not accept him as a "brother in Christ" just because they did not agree on Vietnam. Yet he declared he had little choice but to pursue his chosen path on Vietnam since it was a "deeper spiritual urging that compelled my actions."[54]

The pattern of opposition to Vietnam began early for Hatfield. By the mid-1960s he was in trouble with many evangelicals and Republicans for airing his doubts about Vietnam and for voting against President Johnson's Vietnam policies at the annual national governors' conferences—49–1 votes do focus attention on the single dissenter! Hatfield believed that we were hurting ourselves, indeed our souls, in Vietnam. How could we possibly bomb so many people so far from us in culture and experience, killing and hurting them for no apparent end? We could not make the Vietnamese people like their rulers by using our weapons of war against them. Vietnam needed social, economic, and political reforms, but these were measures *we* could not accomplish. In fact, our dominance of that sad nation had sharply increased its incapacity to take care of itself. In short, Hatfield's view was that our role in Vietnam was immoral and ineffective. He insisted that his and others' right to suggest such unpalatable conclusions must be inviolable. He ridiculed the idea that dissent hurt our troops in Vietnam. The best way to assist our troops was to protect them by bringing them home.

Hatfield sought to relieve the anguish of those in the United States most affected by our foolish and immoral war by advocating a far wider provision for conscientious objection than the Vietnam era law allowed. He insisted that those who went to jail, responsibly taking their punishment for disobeying the draft or other laws in opposing Vietnam, should receive a generous amnesty once the war was over. On the other hand, other draft evaders, such as those who left the country, did not enjoy Hatfield's approval. They were often weak and selfish, but even they deserved consideration on a case-by-case basis if that would help heal the pain and scars of Vietnam.[55]

Instead of praising American government and society and following America's leaders uncritically, Hatfield declared we should think of what America could be. There was much more each of us could do to advance our nation toward divine goals, especially the goal of a more loving society. Hatfield believed that this had long been the objective of many Americans, those who had constituted the noble and active religious side of American history that we too often ignored in our celebrations of civil religion, individualism, and material growth. What was needed, he thought, was a rebirth of the better part of our country's past: the deep hope that, under God, American Christians could go forward to do God's will and realize the law of love. Certainly Hatfield resented those for whom such hope metamorphosed into nothing more than a bland, conservative faith.[56]

Hatfield disliked the New Left's simple and messianic approach to change, but the unthinking substitution of civil religion for a truly Christian faith by so many other Americans also made him impatient. Civil religion represented a far too comfortable marriage of Christianity and the American government, when what we required was less civil religion and more "biblical faith."[57] Hatfield was dissatisfied over the status of the Christian religion in Richard Nixon's White House long before Watergate. He suspected that most of the religion at the White House was for show and the rest derived from a confusion of Christianity with the American presidency in general and Richard Nixon in particular. Hatfield questioned the wisdom of prayer breakfasts in the White House and, more boldly, the wisdom of Billy Graham's preaching for Richard Nixon there. While Hatfield was strongly convinced that American Christians needed prayer and fasting, he held that these were private acts and should not be confused with what he contemptuously described as "pious patriotism."[58]

Hatfield felt there was a full agenda of needs which Christians should actively tackle. In setting this agenda, he claimed simply to be following the Bible. Hatfield was undeniably a thoroughgoing evangelical, since for him the Bible was his genuine point of reference. His reading of the Bible was less consciously sociological perhaps, especially in his explanation of sin in the world around him, than the view of some of his reform-minded compatriots. The language of sociology was not his native tongue; he had been a law professor, not a sociologist. Yet his analysis acknowledged the reality of "social sin," that sin often appeared as social problems which required social analysis and, to some extent, collective treatment.

When Hatfield noted the numbers of poor and hungry on our planet the promptings of his biblical vision of love were expansive. He urged that Christians undertake a program "To Heal the World" with the eventual goal of fulfilling the "total needs" of mankind.[59] As we will see, he had specific proposals to make to accomplish this goal. But he also knew such a task required a profound effort from Christians to succeed in "the revolutionizing of our world—to the alleviating of human suffering and to the work of God on earth."[60]

The fact was, Hatfield claimed, that God demanded we manifest "a love for the poor and dispossessed." In God's mind, the poor and exploited were one with the rest of humanity. They were not inferior or lesser souls. As Paul had admonished, in Christ earthly distinctions melted away. We could not withdraw into a shell of property rights and forget social problems, at least not if we took seriously our Christian duty to remember that property was ours merely as stewards of God.[61]

He saw environmental issues also in this light. The entire environment around us was ours to use—and not abuse. It was on loan to us from God only so long as we treated it lovingly. We had no right to ignore "God's call to the stewardship of our environment."[62] Hatfield felt no automatic prejudice against economic development and had in fact promoted development for Oregon when he was that state's governor. But he did not think that his vigorous support of conservation was in conflict with that goal. Conservation and development were not mutually exclusive; development need not mean the destruction of the environment. Americans obviously did not take seriously God's command for stewardship since we allowed so much human and environmental degradation in America and around the world. In this Hatfield recognized some of the world's most shocking evidence of sin.[63]

Concerns for the environment, for the poor, and for the hungry were all aspects of the same divinely appointed task of human love, according to Hatfield. And in each case most Americans had an embarrassing record. We stood guilty before God for our affluent lifestyle which reflected so little genuine caring about others: "We should allow ourselves to feel uncomfortable about our wealth, our lifestyle, our diet, and all our subtle worship of affluence."[64]

This approach was not always well received. The reason was not the whisperings of inconsistency which occasionally surfaced later in the 1980s in the face of Hatfield's impressive Washington home or his direction of the fancy 1981 inauguration for Ronald Reagan. Rather, problems arose because it simply conflicted with the strong political views of a number of other evangelicals. For example, Christianity Today applauded Hatfield on the world hunger issue but it also voiced the reservations of those who were more conservative. It warned that Hatfield appeared to be enunciating the doctrine that everyone had "the right" to food. This, the magazine remarked, was neither Christian doctrine nor a practical doctrine for any person or nation to advance. As always, Christianity Today spoke for the mainstream. In 1976 the National Association of Evangelicals convention rejected a "right to food" resolution similar to Hatfield's.[65]

There is no evidence that Hatfield paid any more attention to ȯpposition to his food crusade than he did to opposition to his Vietnam stand. He just continued arguing that Christians had to feed the hungry. They had to do all they could, pray for the end of famines, contribute to organizations working in the field to ease the suffering, and fast—or at least reduce their meat consumption, since the American meat industry absorbed so many grains badly needed for export to other, sometimes starving, people. Hatfield believed much more was needed, however. Change had to come in basic economic policies and structures all over the world. He proposed adapting a new economics "to sustain humanity," one which would require sacrifice in both the East and the West. Rich nations had to organize to accomplish a drastic shift of money and other resources from their well-stocked larders to the poorer countries of the globe. Poor nations had to undertake comprehensive land reform, income redistribution, and new ventures in cooperatives and joint capital investment. Exactly how this revolution would occur was unclear, and Hatfield knew its chances were problematic.[66]

Hatfield saw his age as a time crying for bold action, and he emphasized the prophetic in his approach to politics and social life. He demanded that every Christian assume a "posture of servanthood" to God and man in politics. Christians were to challenge the state willingly when necessary. He felt we could live with conflict within and without the state, but not the "heresy today" which held that "the sphere of Caesar and God are equal, or that they can never make conflicting claims on the Christian."[67] Such a notion he considered a resignation to the status quo, which by no means had God's blessing. It is not surprising that his principal criticism of the Christian church in the United States was that it was insufficiently dedicated to fulfilling God's strictures upon us; it did not insist that our conscience come alive and serve God rather than the culture around us.[68]

There was scant doubt in Hatfield's mind about the reality of sin in the human race, including in himself, nor did he question the eventual reality of the relief of sin in the second coming. But such facts, and they were facts for Hatfield, did not imply any lesson to him about prophetic commitment in this age. No matter how sinful we were and no matter how short the time till the second coming, the responsibility to carry out God's will on earth lay heavily upon the Christian.[69]

Part of that responsibility, of course, involved winning souls to Christ. Hatfield was deeply evangelical and he had much confidence in the "transforming power" such conversions could have. But he always asserted that one could not take such conversions seriously until we saw if they had an impact on an individual's relationships with other people and the broader social community. If an individual or a church followed the "spirit of withdrawal" from the world, it was not a genuine convert. It had spurned the example of Jesus and failed to help improve the world. People would have to learn that genuine conversion and genuine Christianity must include social action. God's commands were too direct to risk any hesitation, just as the list of serious problems, from racial conflict to disparate incomes, weighed too heavily on the true Christian for him to depend on individual religious conversions without an explicit social commitment to overcome these concrete challenges.[70]

As an evangelical reformer in Washington, Hatfield appreciated the importance of government and politics as a means to encourage some of the changes he favored. He had long been clear that government had an important part to play in such matters as welfare and the management of the economy. On the other hand, Hatfield had his fears about politics and understood very well the traditional evangelical suspicion of politics and government. He perceived what our government and all governments could do to people. He knew from closer contact than most of its critics how much it could corrupt. He was convinced of the sad truth of "the essentially dehumanizing character of relationships in the political world."[71] His campaign to make the CIA stop developing and using contacts among American missionaries abroad was in this spirit. It was not just an attempt to enhance the credibility of American missionaries as they undertook their holy work, but also very much an attempt to free them from the sordid reach of political corruption.[72]

The corruption which Hatfield contended politics induced manifested itself in the abuse of power far more than in any other way. In Christian terms, that danger opened the way to the greatest sin: pride. Hatfield thought that the Bible, especially his reading of the Old Testament, eloquently warned against the abuse of power, the terrible plague of both rulers and citizens. He found similar warnings in the Book of Revelation, which interpreted politics and the state in a context of evildoing that rang true to Hatfield.[73]

But the possibility of the abuse of power posed a genuine difficulty for Hatfield in that he neither hated the state nor did he accept it only passively. On the contrary, Hatfield approved of the state and felt society needed positive political leadership. He hoped that in America these leaders would be Christians, since as such they might make a difference. But in any case, political leadership and the state were a necessity, even though always dangerous. This was his dilemma. He needed what he feared. We needed what we should fear.[74]

Watergate certainly accentuated Hatfield's dilemma. It led him to return again and again to the dangers intertwined with power. He increasingly faulted what he interpreted as the tradition that we worship the president in the United States. The American attitude toward the president bordered on idolatry, clearly no testament to the Christian faith. This attitude contributed to Nixon's flagrant abuse of presidential power, which Hatfield was early among evangelicals in denouncing.[75]

The problem, Hatfield thought, was that leaders, including American presidents, often thought they were "beyond the scope of transcendent judgment," a view every bit as blasphemous as our inclination to worship them.[76] No wonder they all too often shamelessly grasped for maximum power. The ideal leaders were creatures of quite a contrasting type: "The style of leadership that we can emulate is again seen in the person of the Lord. We must understand that leadership is not the problem of power, but rather the commitment to service."[77] This style would, he knew, require Americans to develop "a whole new understanding of leadership and power, one which is just the opposite of what our society would have us believe."[78] Hatfield had faith, though, that all Americans, including leaders, could learn the lesson of service rather than selfishness if they chose to do so.

It would not be easy and it would not happen quickly. In the meantime Hatfield suggested a number of institutional reforms to blunt the dangers of misuse of power. He favored separate elections for the president, vice-president, and some key members of the Cabinet; he proposed decentralizing private and public institutions, where possible, thus diffusing power; he urged increasing democracy within all institutions, thus providing ways to remove abusers of power; he favored a referendum on the key issue of the draft so that no authoritarian leader could institute it for *his* purposes without popular check. These objectives, once accomplished, he hoped would help tame future presidents who might create their own Watergates or Vietnams.[79]

Hatfield's attention to leaders did not for a moment mean that he thought they were somehow a class apart from ordinary mortals. Hatfield was too much an evangelical to suppose that. Leaders were not the only sinners — everyone was a sinner. That was why Hatfield refused to place all the blame for Watergate and other abuses of trust on particular leaders. Everyone shared the blame. He was sure that "the problem is not the system, but rather, the people themselves, and their values."[80] He held that the cliché was true: citizens got the government and the governors they deserved in light of their own values.[81]

Yet Hatfield did not let this judgment deter him from a long list of denunciations of American rulers. He was a Republican, after all, and it is not surprising that he disapproved of many leaders in addition to Nixon. He directed a good deal of criticism toward the bureaucrats who often run Washington. Their rules and regulations had created a new form of tyranny, the tyranny of centralized bureaucratic power which operated in silence. This bureaucracy had done little that was positive; in fact, it could do little that was positive. After all, government by itself could solve few really fundamental social problems. Hatfield was an evangelical who sought change, but not toward a state bureaucratic apparatus.[82]

The line Hatfield drew here was common for reform-minded evangelicals. It needs to be clear. On the one hand, the centralized bureaucratic and leadership structures of government had a disappointing record of *service* (though a sadly "impressive" record of restricting human freedom). On the other hand, government was important and bureaucrats were necessary. They could be a factor in fighting poverty and hunger, and should be. Yet they could not solve these problems alone by any means. Only a changed populace with the *assistance* of government, both acting far closer to God's teaching of servanthood, could master pressing social problems.

The criticism of centralism by Hatfield was a good example of the mix of attitudes in this former state official. Centralism limited human freedom and development. It did not allow people to decide for themselves on the moral and spiritual directions of their lives. He had considerable confidence that the average soul would be more creative and more sensitive if some massive public or private agency were not always at hand to guide him or her when a problem emerged. He was convinced that we could not be reminded often enough that no problem was ever solved without returning to individuals. It was individuals who had to change. Hatfield provided that government and laws could, and often should, assist in this task, but he did not want any enthusiasm for them to diminish a realistic understanding that they must work in concert with individuals or fail.[83]

Where individuals could not effect change on their own, Hatfield always felt that government should do all that it could on the local level first. Hatfield believed many people underestimated the possibilities of locally based change. Since it was closer to the people and to local needs, it was bound to be more humane and less bureaucratic than centralized structures ordinarily were. Only when individuals did not succeed alone and only when local political structures appeared overwhelmed should the larger state step in. Then its service should be used without apology. The central government was sometimes a great blessing—as long as it continued to work in cooperation with local governments and individuals and did not begin to show its potential arrogance of power.

The ultimate destination for a Christian was one which, according to Hatfield, neither laws nor great leaders nor individual heroics could reach. He aspired to Christian community, and neither statism nor nineteenth-century individualism were substitutes in his vision. He knew the 1960s and 1970s were no age of Christian community. There was little love. Yet with love among us much could alter for the better—in politics and elsewhere. Our directive was clear: "Embracing the power of love, we are to forsake the love of power." Only then could community flower.[84]

The question of government authority remained. No thoughtful writer who lived through the days of Vietnam and the New Left could avoid confronting this matter. What were the boundaries of required obedience to the state when it did not aid Christians on their pilgrimage and turned to evil? Hatfield made no effort to duck this controversial question. He affirmed that all Christians should pray for government officials and rulers.

But he resisted any biblical interpretations which bound all Christians to obey every ruler or rule. The most he would grant was that government as a general institution was divinely instituted. God was, in his judgment, no anarchist, but it was hardly appropriate either to saddle him with particular governments such as the Hitler regime.

Moreover, God established government, in Hatfield's understanding, to serve people. Seen in that light, God could hardly expect the citizen to obey in every instance. Even if some read the Bible differently, Hatfield did not find strict parallels between biblical citizen-state relationships and those of the modern era very plausible. There was, he was sure, quite a difference "between the Israelite's relationship to his or her rulers and the relationship of the Christian toward a secular modern state." We were used to more responsiveness—and properly so.[85]

Hatfield believed we were to judge in every case whether or not the authority of rulers was "rightful," whether it partook of God and respected his purposes, and whether government did or did not involve itself in activities which were God's. The ideal would be what Paul had in mind in Romans: a government under the aegis of God, dedicated to serving its citizens. Such a government would at all times undertake to do justice among its people, serving in all the ways it could to supplement individual and community efforts to realize God's will. The key word would always be service. Just as every Christian must serve others, so must government. Even the lowliest public servant had to remember that she or he was not there to exploit or condescend to the public. True love precluded such unchristian attitudes.[86]

When governors, or governments, consistently fall far short of the ideal, we should act. In making our judgments we were to be practical and not ask the unreasonable, while also showing considerable skepticism about the state. Hatfield thought that often evangelical Christians gave the state the benefit of the doubt. This was improper and led Christians to render "unto Caesar that which is God's" far too frequently. The Jesus Hatfield saw in the Gospels was hardly one who allowed the state such a margin. Jesus did not have much regard for the "wisdom and wishes of those holding power in society" and neither should we.[87]

All this sounded potentially radical, but it was not. For Hatfield, in fact, was extremely wary of lawbreaking for any reason. His commitment to lawful behavior was intense. He was not pleased with the actions of many Vietnam era protesters, who were too quick to launch campaigns of civil disobedience. Hatfield was very much the traditional evangelical on this score, uneasy about a too casual orientation toward lawbreaking.[88]

Part of the reason was that Hatfield feared the politics of dogmatism and certainty in all its forms. The ultimate wisdom of this point affected him when Hatfield visited Hiroshima in 1945. This visit profoundly impressed him and taught him the terror of undiluted conflict, of the pursuit of political goals at any and every cost, and the attractions of a more restrained, gentle, and nonviolent politics. But he thought this should not be a new discovery for Christians. It was the age-old Christian lesson, even in the Old Testament, not the least bloody of books in human history.[89]

Jesus Christ was an absolute, but beyond him there was little room in Hatfield's universe for dogmatism and certainty, and particularly not in political life. He thought there was a much greater need for openness, for listening, and for humility. The politics of gentleness was what Hatfield the Christian admired. This did not mean weakness in the service of God and man, but it did require greater change in the attitudes of citizens and politicians than we could imagine. It would lead to a politics focused on such matters as feeding the hungry, for humility and gentleness meant devotion to the concrete love of God's people. Hatfield really seemed to believe that as a Christian politician he had to take Christ's proclamation "such as you do to the least of them so do you also to me" seriously.

THE EXAMPLE OF THE CHURCH OF THE SAVIOR

Hatfield was the most prominent exponent of the (limited) value of politics for reform-oriented evangelicals. Another approach popular with them was their concentration on community building. Indeed, the exhortation to community pervades much of this literature, as does a constant criticism of American life for its romance with individual egoism and its sad repudiation of community.

However, most of the discussions of community were perfunctory, providing little illumination. They were overwhelmingly vague. Reform-minded evangelicals rarely defined, defended, or detailed community. But while the reformers offered little of substance in theory or detail when they affirmed community (unlike some radical evangelicals), they did sometimes offer as models communities which existed to exemplify the ideal. None received more praise in the 1960s than the Church of the Savior in Washington, D.C.

In the 1960s the "call to commitment" at the Church of the Savior in Washington, D.C., became well known among reflective evangelicals. It obtained fame as a community of reform-minded Christians — maybe radical evangelicals — where Christian ideals were not pure fancy. Long before the idea became fashionable, even before the later 1960s, this church practiced reform-oriented evangelicalism. It rejected using an imposing church building; it insisted on forging a strong community among its members (and restricted admission to only those who could meet its rigorous standards); and, of course, it practiced Christian service in its local environment.[90] It was serious about Christianity in the way that few churches or people were (or are).

Its seriousness appeared in many guises. For example, the Church of the Savior proclaimed that members of the church would find the cost of association high, and it demanded discipline from its members and would-be members. It did not approve of those for whom Christianity was merely a habit, an adornment, a diversion, or something to expose children to Sunday mornings. Another guise was even more to the point: their stress on creating a community of saints. While no one suggested that sainthood was easily obtainable on earth, there was a commitment to work as hard as possible to approximate that divine goal. This was what the corrupt world needed; it was the "world's deepest need." Such a dramatic demand was a remarkable idea to propose to Christians, except in an occasional sermon by a naive clergyman. Yet it was apparently meant to be taken seriously at the Church of the Savior.[91]

There was much, of course, about these goals which the reform-oriented could admire. Above all, they shared the conviction of the Church of the Savior that to serve Christ dramatic changes had to take place among Christians. To take up the cross meant to transform oneself and the world around one. As Elisabeth O'Connor, the chronicler of the Church of the Savior, put it, this task encompassed a twofold journey: there had to be both great inward change and great outward change. Again and again her theme was that the Church believed that one journey without the other was a trip with no successful end.

The inward journey implied more than that one had to be a formal Christian. It implied a continuing search for God's truth, revelation, and will. It also suggested that Christians, both as individuals and as group members, must grow toward closer communication with others and with God. Honest exploration of one's limits was also a duty one should pursue on one's journey. Faithful Christians had to know and live as if they knew that they were sinners, and they should forgive the sins of others.[92]

While the Christian focused on his inward journey, he could not forget the call to the outward world. Christians were to work to craft an equal and yet pluralistic community. There a love which respected each soul in his commonness and in his uniqueness was essential. A community combining pluralism and equality in this fashion was the only one which could fill the diverse but real human hungers which God had created. To do so service and change in the world were necessary, but only in a context sensitive to pluralism and one which knew that progress in the inner journey would show the way: "The outward journey is determined in part by the gifts discovered in the inward journey."[93]

There was also a feeling that necessary modesty must guide activity in the world. The reason had nothing to do with theories about unanticipated consequences, the dangers of revolution, or other similar worries. It rested, rather, on a hard-headed, pragmatic belief that one could accomplish the most in one's own neighborhood, or at least one's general geographic home. Here one could actually do something, rather than just send money or pass resolutions. The Church of the Savior worked to restore nearby houses, to help local kids without homes, to provide a coffee house ministry, to operate a place for those who needed mental help, and much more. There was little effort to solve world poverty or world hunger. But there was much effort to demonstrate a concrete social concern which any Christian could respect and which many did respect.[94]

Another church which received considerable publicity as an effort to witness to the goal of Christian community was the LaSalle Street Church in Chicago. In the late 1960s, under the dynamic leadership of Bill Leslie, the church decided it was not fulfilling Christ's admonition to witness and it must change. It became "a church that takes on trouble" as it learned to live the gospel of reform-oriented evangelicals that "doctrine and ethics both have an essential role in the life of a Christian."[95] The church reached out to assist the weak, the defeated, the young, the old, the poorly housed as it turned to "doing justice."[96]

While the Church of the Savior of Washington, D.C., and the LaSalle Street Church of Chicago were notable cases of reform-oriented values come down to earth, they were by no means the only ones. They were spearheads which their admirers hoped—but did not really expect—marked the future. Few could match their record, but their example did awaken many churches to the need to act as Christ did to succor the needy.

Chapter Seven

THE RADICALS

BEYOND REFORM-MINDED EVANGELICALS, beyond Hatfield, beyond the new history, and beyond the activist church lay another territory. It was a terrain which self-styled radicals within the faith occupied beginning in the late 1960s. It was the creation more of Jim Wallis and the magazine he edited, *Sojourners* (earlier *The Post-American*), than of anyone else—unless it was President Johnson and the Vietnam War.

It was not until the 1970s that it became clear that there was a growing number of radicals within the evangelical movement who had to be taken seriously. A few voices had become transformed, as Wallis expressed it at the time of the declaration of principles by Evangelicals for Social Action in 1973, into a chorus determined to adhere to an authentic and radical biblical truth.[1] The lines separating the radicals from reform-minded brethren are not always easy to draw, though this chapter attempts to draw them when necessary, but Jim Wallis provided a good summary of the origins of evangelical radicalism when he characterized what created *The Post-American*: "Alienation and hope were two things that brought us together from the beginning."[2] Alienation in particular loomed large, and continues to do so, among evangelical radicals. As one sympathetic observer remarked, what really distinguished *The Post-American* and another sometimes radical evangelical publication, *The Other Side*, from *Christianity Today* and the evangelical mainstream was not only their refusal to celebrate America and to link it to the eternal gospel of Jesus, but also their almost Manichean belief that America and the gospel were in nearly irreconcilable opposition. This attitude led Jim Wallis to criticize even Carl F. H. Henry, the patron saint of reform-oriented evangelists. Whatever Henry's service and virtues, Wallis said, one had to note that he still represented the past, the naive and dangerous evangelical trust in American power. Only a radical break and a turn to God and the power of his word were acceptable.[3]

Another side of radical alienation was a specific attitude toward the

Bible. The standard radical position was that only the radicals were totally committed to the Bible because only they were prepared to face its social side seriously. In this sense, radicals eagerly supported "a return to the Bible" and confidently cited chapter and verse to sustain their claim that Paul and Jesus and others in scripture provided impeccable scriptural support for social action. Radicals also affirmed their biblical credentials by claiming that they alone had the tenacity to try and live its gospel. They did not just talk—they acted. As John F. Alexander, the editor of *The Other Side*, put it: "The central issue about the Bible is whether we live it. Theories of inspiration are nothing compared to obedience."[4] This assertion, widely shared among radicals, suggested distrust for those eager to sustain an "inerrant" scripture above all else. As Wallis observed, the fact was that many Bible-believing and Bible-living "young evangelists" were not willing to endorse complete inerrancy claims.[5] Donald Dayton directly attacked Howard Lindsell in *The Other Side* for what Dayton considered his sad fixation on a single view of scripture and his wasted efforts on a "wrong front."[6] So much energy went into quibbling about a few passages, John F. Alexander contended, while so little went into living out the vast remainder of the Bible. It was a bitter shame.[7] Moreover, the cult of inerrancy could, and too often did, lead to admiration for Christians who dismissed reflective learning and ridiculed broader culture. It could encourage, Virginia Mollenkott found, constant invocations of dogma, with such absurd results as judging works of art by their propaganda value and what Mollenkott termed the "poor taste in many evangelical churches—for the sickly sweet art on church bulletins and for the sanctified crooning of certain church soloists as well as for trite, unrealistic poetry."[8]

Alienation from the dark side of America and from mainstream evangelicalism were common themes. But did the radicals in the late 1960s and thereafter really differ *in values* from their conservative brethren? Perhaps the only, if important, genuine points of separation lay in their perception of America and their means of following the Bible. Beneath the clamor of disagreement was there a base of unity which was, in its way, more significant than the noisy public disagreements? Put another way, the question was just how radical these evangelical activists and writers really were within the larger movement.[9] The answer, we shall see, is that they were very radical, not only within evangelicalism but also in American society as a whole. They were in sharp disagreement with the conservative mainstream at the most basic level. The values which radicals saw in the Bible simply were not the same values that mainstream conservative evangelicals perceived. Community and service were not the same as individualism, patriotism, and capitalism. Moreover, the doctrine of hope, the other side of the radical temper, also suggested that the gap between the radicals and the mainstream was much more than a matter of varying perceptions of the worth of Americans or evangelicalism. Hope for radicals meant not only hope in God's love and God's grace but also hope in what God's people could do. They could comprehend a good deal of his will for themselves and then take steps to live the life he commanded. In a life of simple community which spurned violence, materialism, and hate, they could go far toward realizing the hope of God's people. They could live radically in their faith in an often fallen world.

In our exploration of radical evangelical thought from the late 1960s to the middle 1970s, we will examine many of the torrent of books which poured forth in enthusiastic advocacy of this new world. We will also pay close attention to certain journals which were centrally involved in the movement during the ten years from 1967 to 1976. There were a number to choose from, some of which, such as the feminist journals *Daughters of Sarah* and *Radix*, were relative latecomers.[10] Two journals were the most important and the most widely read: *The Other Side* and *Sojourners*.

The Other Side first appeared in 1965. Its founder was Fred Alexander and it is now edited by his son, John F. Alexander, and others. Its name originally was *Freedom Now*, and in its first years it focused on the black civil rights struggles. In the late 1960s and on into the middle 1970s it never followed an inflexible radical position, though its general focus leaned that way. It always presented a number of points of view, not only Jim Wallis's but also Harold Lindsell's. Over time its editorials by John F. Alexander grew increasingly radical, and Alexander emerged as an unmistakable radical voice.[11]

The Post-American (later *Sojourners*) was more coherent, but also less open to other perspectives, from its beginning in 1971. Consequently, it was more often than not understood as *the* organ of radical evangelical thought in the 1970s. We shall use it more than any other source as we draw the picture of this segment of the evangelical intellectual community. Many of *Sojourners'* original writers and publishers were young ex-divinity students, often from Trinity Evangelical Divinity School (near Chicago), who felt a call to establish a community to publish a magazine speaking to their Christian concerns. They announced in the first issue that they were radicals: "We require radical transformation, a new understanding of society and ourselves. As the analysis of our dilemma must be radical so must our solutions."[12] In the fashionable language of the Left of those now receding days, *The Post-American* proclaimed its goal to be "a gospel of liberation" and declared itself prepared to articulate "the ethical implications of that gospel, by working for peace, justice and freedom," sure that "our strength will never lie in bureaucratic structures but in the dedication of people willing to organize locally."[13]

Three years later, in late 1974, Jim Wallis evaluated *The Post-American*. It had succeeded as an enterprise, as a prophetic voice; as a result it would expand its number of contributors and plunge into a broader range of issues. Yet its focus would remain; it would "continue to explore the implications of the historic confession 'Jesus is Lord'." That still meant that the "social and political order will be evaluated biblically and the major cultural assumptions upon which it is based will be contrasted with the priorities of the Kingdom of God."[14]

Wallis did point to one change without quite naming it: *The Post-American* had increasingly shifted from its original interest in "liberation" toward "community." As Wallis stated: "A major focus will center on the church as a new community."[15] This was concretely manifested in 1975 when Wallis announced that *The Post-American* community had chosen for its permanent home a poor, largely black area in Washington, D. C., in order to instantiate their ideal of a biblical Christian community where it would really count.[16]

This courageous move coincided with another change announced in the next issue of 1975: *The Post-American* was to become *Sojourners*. Jim Wallis explained that the title *Sojourners* caught the spirit of their community better. It expressed the reality of those who sought to live radically as a community faithful to Christ. Such a community was necessarily the story of the alienated, the strangers, the sojourners. *The Post-American* was a name too narrow for the community vision which *Sojourners* endorsed by 1975. Both titles signified a certain alienation from the world, but *Sojourners* stood for something more. It stood for hope also, for a community of radical believers, alienated but not lost, seeking to travel as a group on God's path for humans on earth, rather than merely to proclaim their "liberation" and their determination to be "post-American."[17]

THE COMMUNITY

The measure of the radical evangelicals was their overwhelming focus on Christian community. This, they believed, set them apart from the conservatives, who in their opinion were obsessed with individual liberty, and from the moderately reform-minded evangelicals, for whom, the radicals suspected, community was only one somewhat tepidly held value among an ill-digested collection of norms. Radicals self-consciously posed their allegiance to community against what they took to be the evangelical as well as the broader American intellectual tradition. For them community was a value proclaimed by God as the central mode of life for his people on earth, which both church and culture in the United States shockingly flaunted. They proposed to rediscover the radical message of Christ called community, to reintroduce what John Howard Yoder called "the *messianic* community."[18]

The radical evangelicals repeatedly invoked the ideal of community.

Their conviction was strong that every Christian had to have "a common life, the life of a people more than the life of individuals."[19] There must be community—*koinonia* was the often used Greek word—a condition in which human solidarity under God comes before the self. Surely, Virginia Mollenkott contended, "loving, decent human relationships are the acid test of whether or not a man is really born again," and community was the place to test the commitment.[20] This did not mean the individual would disappear. In true community, they argued, the "uniqueness of each member is preserved and cherished but each fully lays down his life in service of others."[21]

The radicals based their community vision on scripture as they read it. As we know, the radicals refused to agree with their critics and concede that they were somehow less than biblical. On the contrary, they were stern in their assessments of other evangelicals, who did not appear to them to be devoted to the teachings of the Bible when it came to community. It was not, however, a matter of textual exegesis so much as it was living the word, taking up Jesus' cross, as John Howard Yoder put it. The biblical fact was, as another radical saw it, that Jesus "calls men and women to a complete change of heart and mind," and that had to be demonstrated in biblical community, a model of a common, sharing, and loving life.[22] This route was "not for all men," said Yoder, but it was the way the early Christians lived, Diane MacDonald suggested, as we could all see from reading the Book of Acts.[23] This was a point made by numerous others, including a Spanish Jesuit whom *Sojourners* called on to argue the case that Jesus and the new Christians "proposed to create a new society whose essence was community."[24]

There was considerable discussion of what early Christians had in mind by community. Virgil Vogt, among others, noted with approval that the first Christians *shared everything* they owned and produced with each other. They were not socialists in our sense of that word, but they were devoted to the idea that what they had as individual persons was not theirs but God's and therefore should be used by the group as *needed*. They had a kind of socialism of consumption.[25]

Early Christians were a model for the realization of Christian community, radicals often believed, because they reflected another characteristic of a living community: the determination to stand as a Christian witness. Christian community in the 1960s and early 1970s had to be "witness to the new social order of the kingdom in the midst of the old," as Jim Wallis put it, just as the first Christians proposed.[26] Clark Pinnock insisted that the witness meant a visible church community, one that reached Paul's ideal as a community acting as a discernible "physical body."[27] James Jones and Art Gish similarly insisted that the witness must be concrete, in the world, and the unmistakable "first fruits of the new order."[28]

John Howard Yoder stressed the potential loneliness of such a true witness. He accepted the view that "the morality of the New Testament is a minority morality, and the same will be the case whenever the Christian church lives in genuine missionary nonconformity."[29] The witness would also be, as Jim Wallis said, prophetic, "motivated by the ethical imperative, acting in prophetic judgment upon the prevailing patterns—political, economic, social and moral—of American life."[30] Winning over the enemies in the world in the short run was hardly important for such a community. Its life of prophetic witness—as a functioning alternative to the world—would be what mattered. This was exactly what made sense to Jim Wallis. Victory for the "movemental church" was far away by Wallis's calculations—but that did not really matter.[31]

A genuine community, radicals often felt, would be like a household which was extended to a larger but still personal group. The metaphor of Dave and Neta Jackson, the community as extended family, encompassed the social focus and concern which radicals wanted. It also suggested the intimacy they often sought in community. Art Gish spoke for many when he specified that community involved close, human commitment, not casual anarchism. It must exist as a disciplined and authoritative relationship for all its members, and it should be self-governed by collective participatory decision making among equals.[32]

Finally, the community that radical evangelicals yearned for had to reach out. It had to be open to other communities, other worlds, and other persuasions. It should seek to construct bridges between communities, building toward a world which might one day be known as "A Community of Communities." This aspiration explained, for instance, why Jim Wallis was delighted at contacts which emerged between some charismatics and some radicals in the middle 1970s. Here was the process of reaching across barriers to encourage community.[33]

Over and over the radicals proclaimed that community was their goal and to achieve it would be to make a revolution. As Jim Wallis declared, "the making of community is essentially a revolutionary act."[34] As Gordon Cosby believed, "to build a faith community . . . that's the revolutionary act."[35] To work for this goal was to demand a great deal from a Christian. Radicals felt this was only as it should be. Too often the Christian church settled for far too little. After all, as Wes Michaelson of *Sojourners* claimed, God required Christians to strive to become a community of holy people. We were to be, Wallis asserted, a people of God. Nothing less was enough.

And such a community was not impossible. Radical evangelicals often cited the community embodied by the Church of the Savior in Washington, D.C., as an enduring example of their idea. The Koinonia Community of Georgia also occasioned comment, as did a number of experiments in Christian community tried in the late 1960s or early 1970s. The most discussed witness of all was Sojourners Fellowship of Washington, D.C. More than any other group it symbolized the aspirations of many for community, and it drew attention as an inevitable result. Obviously it also attracted notice because it published first *The Post-American* and then *Sojourners* —and because *Sojourners* decided to display the vicissitudes of its witness to all its readers. *Sojourners* laid before its public the joys, fears, successes, and failures of its experiment in community in what proved to be an attractive and convincing way to illuminate its witness. *Sojourners* sometimes did come alive as a community, not just as a magazine.[36]

All this enthusiasm in theory and practice for community among radicals had its critics, sometimes friendly and sometimes not. Friendly voices warned that *caution* had to be exercised in seeking community. Community, they warned, was an elusive goal, not a fruit ready to be plucked from a convenient and generous bough. It was not likely to be a product of any one structure, but rather of a spirit; that made it all the harder to mold. Certainly it was, as James Jones suggested, impossible to approach mechanically: "Beware of the one who comes to you with a blueprint under his arm."[37] *Sojourners* carried a series of articles beginning in 1976 (at the end of our period) by Graham Pulkingham which spoke to the challenges of establishing Christian community in as optimistic but "realistic" language as anyone could wish. His message too was the admonition that structures cannot breed communities. An authentic "church family" must come first, and that required Christians who had drastically transformed their lives. Even a community of transformed Christians would not quickly—or permanently—blossom. Living together in community, Pulkingham sternly lectured, is often painfully arduous. It should never be confused with a romantic experience of ethereal joy. Even for the unmarried person the commitment it required and the intense interactions it promoted were a harsh test of commitment. For a married couple, people with multiple obligations, it could be even more cruel in its demands. There should be no starry-eyed mistake. After all, most communities fail, Pulkingham frankly told his readers, and those that lived tended to metamorphose into something far different from their original stirring vision.

Another, and even more controversial, part of Pulkingham's insight was his judgment that Christian communities needed to face the issue of leadership. It was attractive for some Christian communitarians to believe they could sweep aside that question in the midst of glorious affirmations of community. But without leadership Pulkingham doubted that any community could last. This did not mean he had a pattern or structure of leadership to suggest; he did not. Yet he was convinced that every community needed leaders to assist in speaking to individual needs lovingly *and* to speak to a group when it lost its vision and forgot that it had to partake of the "grace of God" and nothing else. Pulkingham knew the dangers of leadership and the need to hold dear the duty to be "a servant of the whole community," but he also felt called to focus attention on the costs of the absence of able internal help.[38]

THE NEW MAN AND THE NEW WOMAN

The other side of community as a central goal of radical evangelicals was the ideal of the reborn individual living in Christian community. A new individual and a new community went together. Neither could be achieved without the other. Each prophet of this new man and woman described the goal slightly differently, some calling for "a new man," others "a revolutionary man," still others "the Christian model." The terms did not matter. What did matter was the strong emphasis on a transformed person walking in God's light and living in one of his communities.[39] Radicals were absolutely sure that such a new creature would have to be dedicated, prepared to leave behind "little cosy nests," and eager to start taking risks. He or she would also have to accept the costs of being an outsider: "The call of Christ comes clear and strong: Stand with me in true nonconformity outside the city."[40] Radicals assumed, perhaps with some satisfaction, that "to be a Christian is to be an extremist."[41] It was not unusual to read that true conscience-directed Christians existed *only* among those who are in conflict with the established order."[42]

The new person was to live, not just endorse, the new life. He or she was to live it in the spirit of love. This love had to respect the power of sin in others (a doctrine of limits) and in oneself (a doctrine of humility). It had to reach out to change others, but it had to extend the hand of help and reconciliation also.[43]

There was also a great deal of stress on the importance of radical discipline and obedience to God. This characteristic was necessary for a new person dedicated to loving God and others in community. God's undeniable mandate for "obedience to Christ" and for a scripturally grounded discipleship as a manifestation of obedience appeared repeatedly in the writings of the radicals. That meant applying the word of God to all aspects of life in faithful witness. It meant accepting the loving discipline of one's Christian community. It meant being prepared for the act of "laying down lives," were that act necessary. It meant realizing that "the worship of God and the assigning of ultimate value to his kingdom become a radical act, a political threat."[44] Above all, as numerous writers argued in The Post-American, it meant being alienated from one's culture and country. One observer underlined what he took to be the inevitable truth, that "Gospel Christians" (as opposed to "Caesar Christians") necessarily were estranged from the world around them.[45] The "call" and the "quest" for discipleship required, Jim Wallis frequently admonished, breaking away from the institutions, values, and practices of the reigning order.[46] As Gordon Cosby stated, this alienation could not be passive. A choice had to be made, and more than a gentle withdrawal was necessary. True loyalty to Jesus imposed on every Christian the responsibility "to debunk every other power."[47] This was the teaching of Romans 12:2: "Do not be conformed to this world but be transformed by the renewal of your mind."[48]

The radicals expected the new person in Christ to live a simple life as he or she served God in community. Some of the concern for a simple life derived from the belief that a less cluttered, less busy, and less materialistic existence would bring substantial liberation from the world and a chance to serve God. Art Gish contended that this need have nothing to do with asceticism, which he believed was hardly Jesus' teaching: "It is important that as we give up things, we do it not out of a mere sense of duty or with a feeling of superiority, but in a spirit of celebration. . . . Simplicity is liberation."[49] Others, such as Clark Pinnock, were more directly focused on the evils of materialism and the need to adopt a simple life as a rebellion against the reign of things. This concern could become mundane, as it did at times in 1974 and 1975 when *The Post-American* gave detailed home-makers' advice about such matters as how to make the remnants of soap bars useful or, under the title "Eat That Garbage," how to recycle sour milk and lemon and orange rinds. Radical evangelicals called for simplicity in life most often, however, because of the ecological crisis and the worldwide poverty and hunger of our age. Wes Michaelson rejected President Carter's energy plans because he claimed they did nothing to cut down on America's costly (to others) life-style. Others agreed that people must pledge to cut back before the world was obliterated.[50]

On this issue, however, there was dissent. Evangelicals in *The Other Side* frequently endorsed the popular, if often vague, goal of a simple life for the new man, but there were also rumblings of dissatisfaction with this emphasis. How relevant was such a goal for the genuinely poor around the world? Did such a goal speak to their needs, much less their desires? John F. Alexander revealed the hidden skepticism when he attacked the ecology movement as "of concern mostly to comfortable whites." What a difference there was between the poor who were desperate to break away from their poverty and the Christian who had suddenly discovered ecology and the simple life. Were they speaking to each other? Could they?[51]

Finally, radicals strongly advised their new man to walk what Clark Pinnock termed "second mile life style." If we were truly Christ's disciples, committed to "offer him our bodies as a living sacrifice," we had to show it in a willingness to aid God's other creatures, to go the extra mile for them, to be "willing to be last, to serve."[52] A new life-style which did not include this service was the same old, selfish way, not a demonstration of true rebirth. There could be no compromise. One had to act and speak out: "Silence is complicity—collaboration with the existing world system. Conformity to the world's values and support of the status quo are incompatible with a New Testament Christian witness."[53]

Radical evangelicals regarded the plight of the poor and the conditions that resulted in their poverty as their own most serious concerns. They constituted the most urgent area for Christian witness, outranking ecological concerns and even questions of war and peace. The radicals were determined to make the sacrifices required by such a concern a litmus test of service to Christ. They felt that only those who were prepared to sacrifice for others could honestly look themselves in the mirror and call themselves followers of Christ. What better way was there to serve than by assisting the poor? Christ cared for them, the radicals said, and so must we.

There were several basic observations about the mission to the poor which they declared every new man must accept. Obviously, they insisted that service to the poor was God's unmistakable *command*. John F. Alexander, editor of *The Other Side*, which campaigned as much or more for a witness to the poor as *Sojourners* did, contended that "being tender-hearted" was a solemn duty from God. The poor, the hungry, and the oppressed needed to be fed, and God wanted Christians to do it. This responsibility, Alexander stressed, was not something new and by no means the Christian response to a current American fad. Concern for the hungry and impoverished was a permanent and ongoing Christian mandate and had been for two millennia. Jim Wallis delivered the same message in *Sojourners*. So did others. We were to love the dispossessed—and even our enemies—because God loved them and ordered us to do so. Disciples follow their master.[54]

The radical evangelicals went even further. They believed they should *identify* with the poor and be one with them. In their version of scripture, Jesus did not just urge aid for the poor; he expected Christians to be among the poor in a profound sense. Too often they were falsely cast as evil or horrible beings. The truth was that God "exalts the poor and the oppressed."[55] Gordon Cosby reminded his readers that Jesus had just such an intense identification with the poor.[56] John F. Alexander agreed, quoting Luke 6:20: "Blessed are you poor." There was no doubt in his mind that "the poor are in a sense God's chosen people."[57] This claim was always backed up with numerous other citations from the Gospels, especially from Luke, the radical evangelicals' favorite Gospel, since it dealt most with the situation of the poor and powerless.[58]

The reverse side of the need to *identify* with the poor and to recognize their special status in Jesus' eyes was the unremitting hostility which the radicals contended Jesus showed toward the privileged and which they themselves expressed even more frequently and vigorously. Robert Sabath argued that the New Testament warned against accumulation of wealth. John F. Alexander in *The Other Side* was fond of quoting Luke 6:24 on any available occasion: "But woe to you that are rich." He and others offered numerous other scriptural declarations which they interpreted to the same effect. Like Sabath, Alexander did not agree that the Old Testament was any safer ground for the wealthy than was the New Testament, where Jesus' strategy was clearly "offense to the mighty." *The Post-American* and *Sojourners* made the same interpretations and breathed the same fire of antagonism toward the rich and powerful.[59]

But what did radical evangelicals think they should actually do to change things, to act concretely as new people witnessing to the poor? John F. Alexander complained that this was exactly the question that should be asked, but too rarely was. There was much talk, he said, but little action. So much of the failure of evangelicals, despite their words, came down to a failure of the will. For Alexander that meant a failure to demonstrate commitment to Jesus Christ. Though few wanted that truth put so starkly, he saw no other conclusion as honest.[60]

There were a number of radicals who proposed to work through politics to deal with poverty. Whether the issue was poverty or war or any number of other questions, they claimed that the Bible was intensely "political." It had a great many things to say which were unmistakably relevant to public problems and were intended to be so. At the same time, William Stringfellow, among others, warned that no one should confuse the Bible with one political ideology or another. It was not a book of ideology and should not be thought one. Nor was it a book of practical political advice. That it spoke to public ethical and political concerns was not at all the same thing as providing a general political ideology or pragmatic policy solutions.[61]

Evangelicals who looked to politics and government to help with poverty rarely went so far as to endorse socialism or drastic income equality, though they sometimes expressed admiration for foreign nations who moved in these directions. More often their program called for a substantial expansion of the welfare state *and* a transferal of part of America's wealth to the Third World. Both objectives would, of course, have involved a greatly increased state role in the economy and substantial intranational and international economic redistribution. Radicals commonly pursued such ideas, but never without important provisos. These revealed the deep reservations about politics characteristic of radical evangelicals—as characteristic of them in their way as of conservative writers. Those who sometimes looked to politics did so only with the understanding that government *without* spiritual energy and perspective would not succeed. Bureaucrats and dollars could hardly solve poverty. A spiritual dimension was absolutely crucial. As John F. Alexander put the same thought, Washington was not the center of power in the world and never would be. God was. Washington without God was helpless.[62]

Alexander also expressed another common uneasiness about the route of politics and government when he claimed that "by itself a program of gradual reform through political compromise is terribly inadequate."[63] This judgment underlined the radicals' impatience with compromise and the impure politics which they thought corrupted pluralism in America. It was not right to accept the lesser of two evils and go home satisfied. This belief partly explained why *The Post-American* continually faulted the American political process as a never-ending story of disappointment. The 1972 election produced what it saw as the dreadful Richard Nixon, who *The Post-American* thought was wrong on all the issues from poverty at home to the enduring but unendurable Vietnam abroad. To be sure, politics also produced George McGovern, whom *The Post-American* treated very well. But it also produced his crushing defeat. According to Jim Wallis, when Nixon left the scene politics did not improve in any measurable way. Ford proved "there is not much new in the new regime."[64] He pardoned Nixon and brought a Rockefeller in to run things. It was politics as usual. Carter met no better fate, a result foreshadowed during the 1976 election, as Jim Wallis ridiculed the idea that change could come from elections. The entire apparatus basically existed to thwart change—and it was notably successful in this function. Wes Michaelson liked this kind of analysis and applied it to the presidency itself, an institution which he thought should be completely demythologized. Worship of the president had to stop and so did the focus on what the president—or would-be presidents—said in answer to one or another trivial question. What mattered was whether there were any aspirants for presidential power who wanted it in order to aid others through principled actions.[65] Radical evangelicals insisted that change could come only "when principled people take stands on moral issues."[66] If "to be a Christian is to be a radical," then it followed that John Alexander was correct when he proclaimed "the inadequacy of moderation."[67]

Radicalness explained the other reason why politics was so suspect. If drastic changes were required to defeat poverty, how was it possible that much good could come by political means? Frequently the radical answer was that it was not possible. The state might be a requisite agency, but ordinary politics would never bring it into play to end poverty, or to stop foreign wars, or to take any other conclusive measures. Despite denials, many believed, as John F. Alexander put it in *The Other Side*, that as they became more radical they had to become less political. The changes they sought were so basic and their priorities of repentance and discipleship were so consuming that routine politics was often irrelevant.[68] After all, as William Stringfellow declared, the real politics had to be "to live as Jerusalem, the holy nation, amidst Babylon," while remembering all the time Robert Sabath's popular view that there was room in the scriptures for seeing the realm of government and politics infested with the lackeys of Satan doing his "hindering" deeds.[69]

This was unquestionably the attitude of John Howard Yoder, who rarely missed an opportunity to denounce the political process in the United States. It was an insubstantial world, basically non-Christian, teeming with illusions such as the absurd idea that voting could alter the harsh relationship between the few with power and the many without it. Politics deserved all the suspicion we felt toward it.[70]

The suspicion of politics accounted for the pervasive focus in these writings on nonviolent action as the best means, when necessary, to force the state to follow God's light. Radicals rejected violence, and indeed, pacifism received a warm (though not completely unopposed) hearing. Opposition to violence was intense because (1) the Jesus they knew was opposed to violence; (2) radicals sought the conversion of sinners, not their destruction; and (3) they thought violence denied the sacred personhood of every individual.[71]

More controversial in the 1970s was the increasing interest by some radicals in the so-called Anabaptist position, which critics professed to see as a withdrawal into communities of the faithful at the expense of any political action at all. There was no doubt that such radical intellectuals as Clark Pinnock, Jim Wallis, and John Howard Yoder increasingly looked to witnessing communities above all else. They, as Clark Pinnock described them, would function just as the radical Anabaptists of the sixteenth century had functioned, as a radical alternative to the world as it existed and to politics as people knew it.[72]

Some criticism of the "overemphasis" on this approach even came from sympathetic observers. For example, John Alexander of *The Other Side* contended that the implication of the Anabaptism among some of his fellow radicals was withdrawal from the day-to-day struggle for the poor and other causes in which Christians must fight. While we know Alexander was no unqualified enthusiast for working through politics himself, he couldn't see much point in complete withdrawal either. He noted, pointedly, that radical black evangelicals did not applaud Wallis's views. Their needs were too pressing to wait for the triumphs of alternative communities of witness.

Wallis and his allies always denied that a commitment to building alternative communities required them to avoid politics and to spurn government action. They could—and they did—operate on more than one front, although Wallis contended that "we must enter the political process only when the spiritual and moral issues at stake demand our involvement."[73] John Howard Yoder argued that withdrawal was manifestly unbiblical, and he did not want to be identified with any such movement.[74] But neither he nor Wallis denied for a minute their belief that politics could never do what a Christian community of witness could do for new persons or for service to the poor. Sojourners Fellowship in Washington was, indeed, Wallis's (and others') best evidence. In the shadow of power stood poverty and in that poverty dwelt Sojourners Fellowship, a community that concretely demonstrated God's way far better than the billions of antipoverty dollars which, in the end, did so little. Still, *Sojourners* gave a good deal of space to Clark Pinnock's thorough attempt to create a theology for "public discipleship." Pinnock opposed those who sought to reduce religion or theology to a private world of piety or to personal existential dilemmas. He contended that the Bible also had something else in mind for the faithful Christian. What was needed was a tough-minded commitment to work from a community under God toward social justice and full human liberation.[75]

There was a strengthened sense in the 1970s of the importance of a pastoral as well as prophetic mission for radical evangelicals. There was also a tough conviction that exclusive preoccupation with "great issues" must not eclipse loving and sharing in community. But few radical evangelicals thought Christian community was separate from such issues. At its best it was, on the contrary, an eloquent demonstration answer to them, a witness of the directions Christians must take. It was far from a retreat. It could only seem so to the tepid spirit of those who did not understand that there would be no resolution to the crises of the modern day within the current system. A witnessing Christian community was a break with the established order. It was, Wallis and his friends believed, a revolutionary act.[76]

Another area which attracted the energies of *The Post-American* and *Sojourners* in its quest for a socially relevant individual in the 1970s was the cause of women's liberation. We consider this issue from many evangelical perspectives in Chapter Ten. It is important to underline here how vigorously *The Post-American* (and *The Other Side*) opened their pages in the 1970s to evangelical feminism. The new man was to be joined by the new woman, both in service to Christ.

Some of the feminist writings resembled Lucille Sider Dayton's attempt to ground the case for woman's liberation in the Bible. She contended that Jesus (not Paul or the Old Testament) was the proper starting point. He was, in fact, a great liberator, in Dayton's view. She also wanted to distinguish time-bound and eternal principles in the Bible. By this means she dismissed many of Paul's specific injunctions regarding the inferior place of women. Dayton's view was echoed by many other radical evangelicals. Both her insistence that a women's movement had to proceed in a biblical framework to follow a model of effective and ethical discipleship and her conviction that the Bible, on balance, provided generous support for women's liberation won wide approval among radical evangelicals. As Jim Wallis argued, unless evangelicals recognized that "their" struggle in this and other cases was really "our" own, then little progress toward understanding and realizing the meaning of liberation could take place.[77]

CHURCH AND STATE

It was in the light of their overwhelming dedication to community and a new human person that radical evangelicals judged their church and their nation. Their assessments were critical and, some said, self-righteous. The most bitter criticism fell on the church, especially the evangelical church. It is obvious that radicals expected so much more from their religious home than they got in the late 1960s and 1970s. Writers in *Sojourners* favored the concept of captivity to describe the condition of the American church. If the U.S. church was, as they said, "held captive," the really unfortunate aspect of its captivity was that it would not proclaim prophetic truth. It would not proclaim the truth to the world—nor to the faithful. The "captivity of the church is also a captivity of the life of the professing Christian community and its members. . . . [T]he people of the church have sacrificed the vision."[78]

Jim Wallis also complained about the weakness of church community. There was, he thought, far too much stress on selfish individualism in the church and far too much denial of the Christian truth of community. What were emphasized, he said, were the "easy belief and simple formulas" which the church used to "conceal the cost of discipleship." The modern church had sold out. Instead of stressing community and the new person, it chose to call "many to belief, but few to obedience."[79] The common evangelical assertion that the "modern church is so respectable" rang completely true in his ears.[80] There could be only one question: is each of us to be "a follower of *established Christianity* or a practitioner of *biblical faith*?"[81]

This stark division had wide appeal, and became, not surprisingly, staple fare at *The Post-American* and *The Other Side*. John F. Alexander expressed it clearly in an essay detailing his great sympathies with the young turks in the evangelical movement. He refused to consider himself an evangelical in any establishment sense. In contrast to fundamentalists, establishment evangelicals "lacked guts." They simply would not take on the world, or at least its manifold evils, in the name of Christ. Mainstream leaders never did anything radical—and biblical—like that. They were always so "sane," he observed, "so well adjusted to the world order, and so intent on getting better adjusted to it that they felt no conflict with it." Honest evangelicals knew they faced the problem of how to "keep their integrity before the powerful," but Alexander believed too few gave any evidence of realizing this fact. They were usually too busy making no waves and hobnobbing with those in power.[82]

Alexander knew his words were not likely to be palatable. But he admired radical evangelicals and agreed that here they were right; one should "tell it like it is."[83] Jim Wallis felt the same way. He knew he offended people by his continued references to the evangelical captivity and his comparison of the United States to Babylon. That was regrettable but unavoidable. He agreed with others that it was past time evangelicals ceased identifying the United States with the world Christ sought. They should change their outlook drastically: "No longer can our Christian message be a defender of racism, a missionary of imperialism, a chaplain of militarism, and a champion of capitalism. We must conform our lives to the life-giving Gospel of Christ, to challenge the life-destroying institutions and forces of Babylon."[84]

Yet Wallis argued that the evangelical churches should not be abandoned as relics of the past—far from it. They should be conquered for the biblical Jesus. Breaking their nexus with the American order was an achievable first step. Christians could appeal to those seeking real change again by remembering that Christianity was in part a transcendent religion. As Dennis MacDonald wrote in *The Post-American*, transcendence should give support to every radical Christian, reminding him that Christ was not an American and foretelling the coming of a new and better order. It would give him the same perspective as Jesus and the prophets, who had sought to bring to sinful societies the sense that the pattern of ordinary lives and God's wishes for his people were far apart. To reduce the gap, believers would have to cut their corrupting ties with the world around them.[85]

If, as Clark Pinnock claimed, the institutional church in the United States was a counterrevolutionary apologist for the status quo and thus not genuinely Christian, then it was true that the church was as sick as the society around it. The question which followed was always the same: could the evangelicals break from their captivity? Jim Wallis shared the confidence of many others when he defended the possibilities of the radical evangelical movement. It could raise consciousness, and it would. It could help the church stand for Christ in concrete human experience rather than serve as a mere appendage of the ongoing order. This hope did not imply an easy victory, nor a quick one. But the optimistic sense that it could be done pulsated throughout radical writings.[86]

What else could a renewed evangelical movement, or church, do? Certainly there was a need for the development of a social action movement. Once Christians cut their moorings to the present cultural order, they were to struggle for substantive changes. It would not be easy; after all, growing up a Christian, one author remarked in *The Other Side*, was embarrassing. Evangelicals had offered little creative thinking or action about the crises of modern social life. Often they let them pass in silence: "My Lai, the Cambodian invasion, Kent State, and the Christmas bombing [1972] all passed without evangelical comment."[87] One student of *Christianity Today*'s record suggested it had little to offer on social action because *Christianity Today* spoke for an evangelical establishment that did not want to confront or even acknowledge evil in America or its policies. He charged that *Christianity Today* accepted voluntary segregation as perfectly biblical until the 1970s, long after the nation itself had decided that the practice was unacceptable. He also noted that *Christianity Today* faithfully backed the bloody twists and turns of our government's Vietnam policy till the bitter end.[88]

It is fair to observe that the radical evangelicals did not take very seriously conservative evangelical suggestions that concentrating on the conversion of individual souls was a better way of improving the social order. Radicals generally thought such personal healing had too little connection with structural healing in society. To many radicals, the usual evangelical emphasis on conversion was in practice an excuse for avoiding social commitment.[89]

Radicals thought there was much to hope for in the many voices in the fold who cried out for social action. The theme was omnipresent and it lasted long after the New Left was gone. One good illustration which fairly represented all was the effort of William Pannell and other faithful blacks who were particularly eager for all evangelicals to demonstrate social concern. He repeated the widespread assertion that the record was—and had long been—miserable. It was time to reverse that pattern, a goal that could be achieved.[90] The formation of the Evangelicals For Social Action in the 1970s was in part an attempt to establish that goal as a corporate, ongoing objective. Its continuation showed at least some commitment to the goal was there, even though achieving it would long be a struggle.[91]

Another task for a reborn church had to be escaping from the preoccupation with communism, what Jim Stenzel called the "Anti-Communist Captivity of the Church." Radical evangelicals proposed to lay down the anticommunist passion of post–World War II intellectuals. *Sojourners* undertook to attack the signs of what they considered the anticommunist obsession that lingered on in the 1970s. They attacked Bill Bright and his Christian Freedom Foundation as a front for the ultrapatriotic, anticommunist far right. That Bill Bright was a powerful and influential evangelical did not bother them in the slightest. He just was one more of the noxious links between evangelicalism and the present order, social irresponsibility, and the fetish of anticommunism.[92]

Another mission involved recapturing the past of the evangelical church from its conservative expositors. While less effort went into this cause among the radicals than among the more moderate reform-oriented evangelicals, the results were likely to be more dramatic. This was particularly true of Donald Dayton's hard-hitting version of nineteenth-century evangelical roots in America which first appeared in *The Post-American* in the early 1970s. He portrayed much of the past world of his faith as unmistakably radical—a world where social change and personal piety went together. He complained that modern-day evangelicals rarely understood this reality. He noted that modern versions of the story of the great evangelist, Charles G. Finney, had a suspicious tendency to leave out his reforming side. They transformed Finney from an evangelist seeking new souls for Christ *and* reforms in a sinful society into a one-dimensional figure serviceable for contemporary conservative interests. He reported that there was a striking contrast between Wheaton College then and now. Wheaton, a center of mainstream evangelicalism today, home of the Graham Center and near *Christianity Today*, was once a hotbed of reformist sentiment. The founders, father and son Blanchard, had a vision of evangelicalism when they established Wheaton which involved vigorous commitment to social action, including active participation in the antislavery struggle.[93]

Despite the mood of hope for the evangelical church or the movement which sustained many radical evangelicals as the New Left days faded and the 1970s unfolded, there were times of discouragement. Progress often was slow. The appearance of anticommunist crusaders like Bill Bright was disheartening. For radicals, 1972 was an especially bad election year. Many of them were committed to George McGovern and against Nixon—whom they saw as a warmonger, a racist, and a potential (or actual) despot. It was a terrible defeat, Clark Pinnock said, and one which suggested that things were sliding backward in evangelical circles. Art Gish, equally unhappy, asked what lesson there was to be learned. The answer, he said, was to learn to speak out more clearly, to witness more effectively, to be the Christian community which convinces.[94]

The radicals' criticism of the evangelical church resembled the treatment a wayward suitor might receive. The criticism was fierce, but it was in a context of love and of determination to fight for its soul. The intensely and coldly negative reaction to America and its state was very different. The radical evangelicals treated America—as they knew it—as the past, a bad past, and they shed few tears for it.

The problem with America was not only that it lacked community, a fact so obvious to the radical evangelicals that it scarcely required comment. That fact was only one sign among many that encouraged William Stringfellow, a frequent critic of America in *Sojourners*, to declare that there was no hope for the United States. Indeed, America now stood for the fall: "The nation *is* fallen. . . . America is a demonic principality."[95] Its day was done, though it did not follow for Stringfellow that there was no hope *in* America. The very fact that the sun was setting on the old American nation gave hope for the most exciting prospect of all, the emergence of a biblical hope for a biblical people. Right now, however, Stringfellow proclaimed, we were in a time of "emergent contemporary American totalitarianism."[96] To be sure, Stringfellow observed, ours was not to be the same as Nazi totalitarianism. Our form was less direct, but hardly less insidious as "technological methodism" more and more conquered us.[97] It was apparent that Jacques Ellul, the much admired French evangelical, and his *The Technological Society* had had a great impact on Stringfellow as well as on other radical evangelicals. The view of the state as a near totalitarian engine fueled by technological control was quite common. Jim Wallis, for example, argued the same point, as did Bill Pannell in a slightly more modest and distinctly less technologically-oriented presentation. As he looked at the Nixon years he saw a profound "lawlessness" in the state that made him shudder with fear. Government actions in Vietnam, in treating dissenters, in dealing with the media all frightened him deeply: "The time has come for Americans to face up to the real threat to our fundamental freedoms, the attack on these rights in the name of law and order by the Justice Department. . . . [T]he experiment called democracy may very well be over."[98]

Nixon left, but the fears remained. The justice department was less often under fire in *Sojourners*, but technological totalitarianism remained a wrenching problem. So did the alleged moral emptiness and decadence in the United States. Stringfellow pounded away at this other image of America, as Babylon, and how it showed its true colors in our selfishness, our hardness of heart, our supine weakness before the powers that ruled for the forces of property rather than people. By far the worst and most widespread poverty in America was our "moral poverty." One sign of this spiritual impoverishment was materialism, and the radical evangelicals saw it everywhere. Another was America's capitalist economy and the competitive, selfish values they insisted it inculcated.[99]

A concerted assault on the civil religion in America and the entire tradition of national patriotism which was bound up with that civil religion was also very much in evidence. The radicals were determined to understand America in terms of the Bible and "*not* to construe the Bible Americanly." To some, civil religion in America was a disgusting example of the yoking of religion to the interests of an immoral, even fallen, society. Bob Sabath contended that the United States was increasingly like ancient Rome. Leaders used religious language to justify sagging nationalism and political greed. Nixon was an obvious example, not to be dismissed as an isolated and irrelevant case.[100]

One cover of *The Post-American* had a cartoon of Nixon on its cover with the caption reading "god is an American and Nixon is his prophet."[101] Jim Wallis frequently denounced Nixon and his "self-righteous American piety which even takes on a certain religious mystique" as having little to do with the religion and spirit of Jesus. Instead, he believed "that national self-righteousness is aggressive, dominant, arrogant and an imperial spirit."[102]

As one commentator in *The Post-American* declared, there could be no truck, in the end, with any civil religion. It built a false community at best. The church devoted to prophecy and true community should always reject the fashionable values of every society, including ours, and it certainly had no biblical mandate to melt into any nation's state religion.[103]

THE OUTER WORLD

The radicals were extremely interested in the broader world. They were delighted that they had escaped what they saw as the narrow parochialism of too many evangelicals, a parochialism that had warped evangelical vision in the present as in the past. According to the radical evangelicals, biblical Christians' loyalties knew no provincial boundaries. Yet the global world outside of church and nation was also disappointing to many radicals. It hardly resembled a community, nor were there encouraging signs that its transformation was on the horizon.

There were a number of international problems which radical writers took seriously over the years. A few examples give a sense of their wide reach and the tenor of their arguments. The Vietnam War and, after that, the possibility of other wars were very much on the agenda. This book discusses the full range of evangelical opinions on the Vietnam War in Chapter Eleven, but the Vietnam War was too important in the emergence of the new and sometimes radical evangelical movement in the late 1960s to ignore altogether here. *The Post-American* in particular crusaded against the Vietnam War. Its editors claimed that it was a racist war against Third World peoples; that it was a practice ground for the U.S. military; above all, that it served American corporate economic interests bent on continuing to exploit underdeveloped nations: "The Gospel says it is wrong to kill for profit and power; that is what's going on in Vietnam."[104] It was a murderous, evil affair which no Christian, they believed, could stomach. None of the tricks of the war, such as the emphasis on "remote" killing by bombing, changed in a positive way the ghastly reality of the moral crime that the war involved. Bombing was very much still war; it left terrible death and destruction in its wake. None of the other tactics of Johnson or, above all, Nixon fooled the radicals: "Vietnamization, pacification, protective reaction, are just the rhetorical cover for the determination of the Nixon administration to prop up a corrupt military dictatorship at the cost of slaughtering thousands of innocent lives and destroying the fabric of an entire society."[105]

After Vietnam, the fear of war continued to concern *Sojourners*. Unlike some individual radicals, it never unambiguously endorsed pacifism, but it did place the sin of war high on its list of evils. Its pages carried frequent expressions of alarm over the possibility of nuclear war, the building of nuclear weapons, and the possession of a nuclear arsenal. It issued urgent calls for action toward disarmament. It insisted that "every Christian community and congregation must struggle to find meaningful, consistent ways of acting against present nuclear policies."[106]

Radical evangelicals also were very interested in America's relations with the Third World in general. *The Post-American* and later *Sojourners* indignantly chided America for its "exploitation" and "oppression" of the Third World, which the Vietnam War, it thought, illustrated most poignantly. America's business interests, complemented by our rapacious consumer society, had created a terrifying "invisible empire" over much of the world. It was routine for Jim Wallis to claim that the United States thus was directly responsible for much of the world's oppression. Moreover, the world noted our "oppressive" record at home. John Perkins observed that Christianity was not succeeding on the African continent before the onslaught of communism. It was too identified with a West, especially a United States, perceived to be oppressive at home. We had to change at home, to tame capitalism and deal seriously with our own poor, before we could be taken seriously in the Third World.[107] John F. Alexander agreed in an editorial in *The Other Side*. We needed to look to America to cut back on our profligate living here. We needed to activate our government to block those elements in America who used the Third World for exploitation. We also had a Christian responsibility to send substantial financial aid abroad.[108]

AGENDA FOR A BIBLICAL PEOPLE

No single work could catch all the dynamics and nuances of the radical case in the years of the late 1960s and the middle 1970s. There were too many voices working through too many events and too many controversies. But if any work could speak for all it would be the book *Agenda for a Biblical People*, published in 1976. The author was Jim Wallis, former member of the Students for a Democratic Society, ex-divinity student, cofounder of *The Post-American* and *Sojourners*, and leading radical evangelical.[109] His *Agenda for a Biblical People* was a late statement, but that is an advantage, for it well describes the stance of Wallis and so many others in the year of the evangelical, 1976. It paints a world and a vision almost as far from Jimmy Carter as from *Christianity Today*.

Wallis described his *Agenda for a Biblical People* as "more than anything else, a sort of tract."[110] This was hardly true of a book that had a considerable argument and its share of complexities. But while the book was not simple-minded or merely a collection of rhetorical shouts, Wallis did design his book as a call to action, a call written directly to Christians to win them to his Christianity. He did not see his book as a collection of reflections, a testament to philosophy, or a breakthrough in theology. It was none of these, certainly, though it was much more than an ordinary tract.

Wallis's book, like all of his thought and action, was written under the imposing shadow of Vietnam. Although the Vietnam War was long over when *Agenda for a Biblical People* appeared, Wallis repeatedly returned to the war. He reminded his readers once again that he and the larger movement of radical evangelicals were indisputably children of the late 1960s and of the conflict over Vietnam. That would always be the context for him and his generation, the "historical occasion for a renewal of biblical faith."[111]

For Wallis the nurturing which that context provided inevitably presented every Christian with an enduring and unpleasant choice, as stark as it was straightforward: "What matters most today is whether one is a supporter of establishment Christianity or a practitioner of biblical faith."[112] There was no middle ground, as we know, in this dualistic world, especially given Wallis's conviction that the scriptures told the story of how "biblical faith overturned established religion."[113]

What exactly did Wallis believe the biblical faith to be? What was its message which set it so far apart from ordinary Christianity? It did not put forth "a new theology or value system."[114] Instead, it proclaimed the permanent truth that Christians must rediscover "the radical Christ of the New Testament" and the biblical "message of change; we are continually in need of being transformed."[115] The thrust of the Bible was toward a "revolutionary mission" and was necessarily "subversive."[116] Wallis's biblical faith involved a determined commitment to undertake the arduous, radical evangelical road, the "pilgrimage of discipleship," the ministry of servanthood, and the choice of "obedience." Repentance for individual and national sins was also crucial.[117]

These commandments were not always formulated in precise terms, but they became clear when they were coupled with Wallis's withering attacks on the larger world. Those attacks continually absorbed him and indicate how much of Wallis's thought was the thought of opposition — although an opposition which clarified the truth he loved in the Bible, truth he asserted "we have suppressed."[118]

Wallis said that real Christians must accept the fact that the world is against them and that they will be among the few struggling to keep free of its dark clutches. The good Christian church must, he said, "accept its minority status in a hostile world."[119] But Wallis did not see this tense situation as an entirely negative reality — a most important point. Having an "adversary relationship to the world" was a *blessing* for the Christian, and Wallis believed that the committed Christian *needed* such a relationship. The tethers of the world's corruption could be cut in no other way.[120]

When Wallis looked for the forces that were the most dangerous, he returned again and again to the Christian church and America. On Wallis's

Agenda for a Biblical People, as on so many other radical agendas, as we know, was a new church—and prolonged denunciations of the old one. Wallis raised three primary criticisms. First, he bitterly dismissed ordinary Christianity as "a religion of accommodation and conformity."[121] It worshipped the world, not God. This was true of all types of Christianity and very much included his own: the tarnished "evangelism of conformity."[122] He felt there was simply no question: "Our churches are now, in most every instance, bearing the marks of a paralyzing conformity to the world."[123] Wallis asserted that church conformity to elite and ruling elements in American society was as egregious as it was disgusting. Vietnam proved this fact, he felt, in the most unpleasant of ways, revealing "a church captive and morally impotent."[124] The time was long past when the church's false trust in the goodness of the world's power and institutions could be tolerated.[125]

Second, Wallis objected to the heavy element of individualism which Christianity in America reflected. Typical churches did not incarnate the body of Christ. They were "little more than voluntary associations of autonomous individuals."[126] Moreover, the church's unending celebration of the individual not only violated the community ethic of Christianity, according to Wallis, but it also "carries the danger of making salvation into just another commodity that can be consumed for personal fulfillment and self-interest."[127]

Finally, and not insignificantly, Wallis disliked American Christianity because he felt it was secular at its core, whatever its liturgy and however many crosses it had in its buildings. Liberal Protestantism, in particular, he clearly believed to be what Carlyle said of Unitarianism: "a reminiscence of a religion." Wallis had a Bible-believing background and, no matter what his critics said, he held to that legacy. In fact, as we have seen, he contended that his own version of biblical Christianity was the most biblical of all. His frame of reference remained biblical authenticity, in any case, and such a deeply evangelical approach to Christianity was bound to have little use for the world of liberal Protestantism where the Bible had receded from view almost as fast as church membership declined.[128]

Of course, Wallis had little use for the American state either. Its religion continued to be America. Nor did he respect "The American Empire," which he felt was repressing multitudes all over the world.[129] Since, as he sincerely believed, "America is a fallen nation" and since "the fall is the principal political and spiritual fact of America," the best advice that could be given was the "need for a disloyal opposition."[130] This opposition, in turning aside from the fallen world, had to do better in building new forms of life. To do so it had to understand what Wallis took for granted: "I have no confidence that the vision and power for new human values and relationships can be generated from the present system or from its ideological opponents."[131]

The old battles were dead. Like so many other young radicals, Wallis acted very much like a new man, claiming with considerable confidence that he was part of a "prophetic minority."[132] That minority, Wallis declared, must become "incarnational," must build the Christian truth into the "daily realities of the believer's life in the world."[133] It would be difficult to accomplish that goal; Wallis's approach was ethically rigorous to say the least. There could be no backsliding or halfway measures, since "one's life rather than one's doctrine is the best test of faithfulness to Scripture."[134]

Incarnation, Wallis proclaimed, might be revealed in Christian lives in many ways. But he thought the crucial testing ground would be the daily life of community. He underlined the centrality of community on all occasions and he always had in mind one's particular "local community of faith" in which he expected every Christian to participate. Action in and through community would "make change and hope visible," would be the incarnation every Christian had to live. These incarnated communities, Wallis hoped, would always act with love in their hearts and use nonviolent action when they had to move firmly against the regnant powers. Under no circumstances did they have a right to proceed differently than Jesus had proceeded; force and violence were the way of death.[135]

The result would be a special group of people worshipping and living "according to the gifts of the Spirit."[136] "The servant community is the gathered style of biblical people. It is the style of those who live as sojourners in the land, and it is the way that God has so mightily used a faithful people in history and will use them again in our own day."[137]

CONCLUSION

Wallis's *Agenda for a Biblical People* was somewhat more emphatic, or strident, than some other radicals' views. But it was also more coherent, disciplined, and pointed. It was a vision. It should be clear that this vision went far beyond disputing with mainstream evangelicals over America's relative faults or other evangelicals' inconsistencies between their faith and their practice. Their base was the same, to be sure; the Bible and the God revealed there were what mattered to all evangelicals. Yet the Bible Wallis and other radicals read was simply not the same Bible presented in *Christianity Today*. At least with regard to politics and the social order, the gap was profound. At issue was a decisive difference in values, in what Christ taught. The radicals renounced what they took to be the political gospel of both the mainstream evangelical and the ordinary American: patriotism, individualism, capitalism. They affirmed another world, above all the committed and witnessing life of Christian community. They insisted that they must live their values in radical discipleship.

They were, to be sure, evangelical Christian radicals, not radicals by one or another secular definition of radicalism. They were not, for example, Marxists, or even (usually) democratic socialists. Yet their criticisms, their values, and their commitment to them clearly made them radicals within evangelicalism; their criticism of the United States, its values and institutions, made them radicals in the broader framework of intellectual life in America; and, finally, their values of community and service made them (in their view) the only genuine radical alternative available in the modern world. They spoke truth to power, confident that only truth could accomplish the conversion of power to truth.

Chapter Eight

MECHANISMS FOR CHANGE

BY THE LATE 1960s, many evangelicals agreed that sweeping change was needed. This view continued into the 1970s, with its proponents endorsing drastic change both in human individuals and, less often, in human societies. The evangelical advocates of change knew there was a vast, awesome gap between Christ's admonition to do his will and be perfect and their own highly imperfect individual behavior as well as the imperfect social institutions around them.

The model was Jesus and his early followers. While some informed evangelicals insisted that "frequent references to Jesus as a great nonconformist or revolutionary are . . . patently untrue and grossly misleading, wholly misrepresenting the attitude and behavior . . . of Jesus,"[1] the mood of the late 1960s which lasted into the 1970s most often portrayed Jesus and the early Christians as proponents of drastic change. Evangelicals rarely meant to suggest that Jesus was a violent "first-century Che Guevara," but they did understand and accept Leighton Ford's identification with "Christ who is the true revolutionary."[2] They did approve of *Christianity Today's* image of Christ as "The Liberator." They did support Bill Bright's conclusion that in Jesus' spirit we need "revolutionists for Christ."[3] They often shared Vernon Ground's aspiration: "We ought to be spiritual subversives, duplicating the redemptive radicalism of those first-century Christians who were condemned for turning the world upside down."[4]

Clearly, what their repeated endorsements of drastic change meant in concrete terms varied enormously among individual thinkers. We know there was no common pattern. We should also realize that the widespread use of language calling for extensive change can be misleading when it is not coupled with the other side of evangelical discussions of the desired extent of change. In their discussions of change, evangelicals stressed both sweeping change *and* the wisdom of *limits* to change. There was always a large element of caution in the evangelical air even in the excited times of the late 1960s which rang with cries for revolutionary change. The spirit of caution spoke in familiar terms: God and his purposes mattered more than anything else; there would be no human utopia. For those, like Paul Henry, who were enthusiastic about the efficacy of political action, it still followed that politics must always be tempered as a method. Politics inevitably involved a mixture of good and evil, and this fact of life would not alter just because more Christians became active. Moreover, only a fool could seriously propose that even if one knew the nature of God's ultimate wishes it would be an easy, or possible, assignment to incarnate them in society. Political decisions were too complex and too contingent for that kind of simple deductive transfer.[5]

Evangelical voices also united, as Robert Culver put it, on the impossibility of political utopia: "A Christian view of civil government must always steadily and consistently hold to the fact that human society is a society of fallen beings under the just judgment of God. The perfection of society cannot be either promised or attained, and it is not the purpose of civil government to do so."[6] Harold Lindsell insisted that "men should not be led to think there will ever be a warless world or a race of men who are well fed, well educated, and undivided." Christ told us we "would have tribulation" and no "social engineers could overcome that fact and make us perfected men."[7]

This conclusion was especially attractive to conservatives, but it would be a serious error to believe that the doctrine of limited means and limited ends was theirs alone. Moderate and even radical evangelicals shared this perspective, even if they believed more change was possible than conservatives did. They understood full well that a belief in utopia, however reached, "imples that the Kingdom of God can come inside history."[8] Such a view was utterly false.

It was in this context that evangelicals evaluated the New Left. *Christianity Today* led the way in the campaign against the New Left, but it had many allies. The critics contended that the New Left offered too little rational analysis about the goals it sought *or* the proper means to obtain them. Its rampant emotionalism and cult of action were no fitting substitute. Herbert Marcuse and others like him, high priests of New Left culture, were "flaming rationalists" "in comparison to others in the movement," but even these intellectual models were disturbingly irrational.[9] Evangelicals urged citizens to observe the situation on radical campuses where "irrational revolutionists" worked their wills. Everywhere one looked at the campus world in the late 1960s one saw the results of irrationalism, especially the violence and coercion by which the minority ruthlessly imposed its will and promoted nihilism and an inchoate enthusiasm for violent revolution.[10] The tragedy of Harvard College, Columbia University, and the University of Wisconsin, where the disorganized mania of emotional change existed with little check, was disgraceful. It was an overwhelming lesson, L. Nelson Bell warned: "It Can Happen Here." Christians, he said, cannot permit such nonsense and remain true to their twofold biblical mission to stand for "gentleness and love" while they "back those who could maintain law and order."[11] Love, piety, and individual change could not easily integrate into the New Left.[12]

Yet the New Left had a surprising number of tempered admirers among evangelicals. There was praise for the New Left because it exposed the materialism of America: "This youth protest is more right than wrong. A society which dedicates its existence to Wall Street, to the mercenary objectives of labor unions, to the giant financial profits of giant business corporations . . . is bent on achieving self-destruction. The youth protest knows that the authentic life of the individual and of society does not consist in the abundance of things possessed."[13] Others lauded the New Left for its opposition to the Vietnam War, its rejection of racism, its alarm over technology, its enthusiasm for community and a participatory polity, its sympathy for experience, its activation of conscience both within the church and within the larger society, its (sometimes) optimistic expectations for people, for society, and for the future: "They dared to hope."[14]

Most of the time the excitement and support for the New Left was chastened, even among its more ardent evangelical admirers. Calvin Linton, for instance, gladly acknowledged that the youth of New Left days had "sensed the bankruptcy of the philosophy of materialism, technology, machines and statistics."[15] What they had not done was offer much by way of a substitute—and certainly nothing that was recognizably Christian. Clark Pinnock observed in *The Post-American* that the New Left was a comprehensible and serious response to important moral problems, but it was a secular response which could not pretend to offer much by way of solutions. It lacked moral depth. Moreover, Stephen Monsma and Art Gish both contended that the New Left overdid its optimism regarding human beings. Of course, we all had to recognize wisely the social dimensions of evil. But the New Left and every Christian who agreed with it were foolish when they did not see that the ultimate roots of evil lay in individual sin. No theory of change dared ignore this awesome reality.[16]

Above all, the critics focused on the means that the New Left employed, means which to many seemed shockingly violent in a way that dishonored its proponents and flagrantly denied Christianity. The consequence in part, however, was a determined evangelical effort to think through just what means of change were appropriate for Christians.[17] Once again, this time on the issue of the appropriate mechanisms to alter the world, it was an exciting time in the evangelical arena—controversy abounded, consensus disappeared, and diversity grew.

INDIVIDUAL REFORMATION

The traditional conservative view was that the way to change the world was to change individuals. People who discovered the truth of Jesus Christ and applied it to their lives inevitably created a better environment for all of God's creatures. L. Nelson Bell, longtime columnist for *Christianity Today*, declared that "many of us are convinced that it is impossible to reform the social order apart from the personal; if anyone is in Christ, he is a new creation; the old has passed away, behold, the new has come."[18]

Many of those who stressed individual means of change recognized that one-time conversion experiences were hardly enough. There was an ongoing need for individual growth "in the Lord." This usually led to considerable support for individual prayer as a concrete means for continual growth as a Christian person. Prayer was a vital force for the redemption of individuals.[19] Others of a similar persuasion insisted that walking "in the Spirit" was the answer, not laws which have "*never* produced holy living and . . . never will."[20] "Misbehavior is not primarily the result of our environment; it's a problem of the heart";[21] God could transform those born again in him and accomplish "extraordinary things" through them.[22] Even many less conservative voices argued that this was the only route to change, citing Paul's agreement in his famous statement in 2 Corinthians 5:17, "If any one is in Christ, he is a new creation."

Some evangelicals, such as Carl Henry, expressed impatience with churches or individuals when their "sole preoccupation is private saintliness, preaching 'Christ crucified' in absolute isolation," but that did not mean that such individual actions as prayer were of no use.[23] Paul Rees suggested that piety and prayer *could* have great impact to work change. Whether it did or not depended on whether prayer built empathy and was thus actually a form of engagement or whether it was an "escape from social concern and initiative."[24] More conservative defenders of prayer did not believe it was an escape. They shared Bell's conviction that it was practical and indeed extremely so. Only prayer spoke to the human heart, "the heart of the problem" for any change. It did appeal to God, and he was the fount from which any and every change had to come.[25]

Traditionalists also worried a good deal about the tempting snare for those who forgot that change must come through individual discovery of Jesus Christ: the Social Gospel. To conservatives, the Social Gospel's greatest fallacy was its urge to solve social problems above all else, an attitude which was utterly unacceptable from their understanding of Christianity. The first priority must be the saving of souls for Jesus Christ. L. Nelson Bell warned that one must "beware" of those who became so excited about social problems that they forgot their first duty. Moreover, there was the danger of overcommitment to the world. Complete devotion to changing the world was in its way just as much of a surrender to this world as was the most unyielding mood of status quo conservatism. It was another reason why the Social Gospel was best understood as an "old serpent."[26]

Cynics often suggested that mainstream emphasis on individual change was little more than a cover for the status quo. Individual reformation did little in the larger world, and "prayer isn't very nourishing food" for the hungry of the globe.[27] There were evangelicals who undoubtedly knew full well that focusing on individual means had deeply conservative implications for society as a whole, but they insisted that there was no choice for one who would follow scripture. The more sensitive allowed that there were limitations to the amount of social impact that resulted through individual transformations, though they were often tart enough to observe that the actual social impact involved in the widespread *verbalizations* of the wisdom of other means of change (backed up by absolutely no action in most cases) was even smaller. Moreover, conservatives underlined their common belief that concentration on individual means to alter society could *not* be taken to mean that no efforts by Christians, singly or in ad hoc groups, need be undertaken. This was a false, unchristian position. Christians had to demonstrate in "personal practice" their new life, or their continuing reborn life, by loving God and his children.[28]

Critics remained skeptical. They said that such admonitions were always (suspiciously) vague. But proponents of individual paths to change were not deterred. They had the ear of many evangelicals and evangelical-fundamentalists and they produced an unending stream of arguments for their point of view right through the late 1960s and early 1970s, the supposed age of enthusiasm for institutional and social means of change in evangelicalism. The most frequent approach was to recount often simple and always pointed stories of changed people who changed the environment around them in prison camps, on the back streets of New York or Minneapolis, or on the country music circuit. Sometimes the authors of these accounts had truly remarkable tales of transformations to tell, as they preached their message that "the heart of the Gospel is change. It is transformation. It is being born again to a new life."[29]

Numerous examples of this literature were written in the 1960s, especially by evangelical-fundamentalists like the Wilkersons. Among the classic books were *The Cross and the Switchblade* (1963), by David Wilkerson; *Parents on Trial: Why Kids Go Wrong—Or Right* (1967), by David Wilkerson with Claire Cox; and *The Gutter and the Ghetto* (1969), by Don Wilkerson and Herm Wiskopf. The Wilkersons recounted the story of their work among drug-damaged minority youth in New York City. These stories were surprisingly blunt, with a good deal of narrative texture, and they focused on the sometimes dramatic life-changing decisions which brought the authors to their remarkable work and which led others to change also. They were realistic, but also optimistic, and they were very much a testament to the power of religious conversion in individual lives.

Al Palmquist told a more recent tale in the same mode in *Miracle at City Hall* (1974). Palmquist, a graduate of the Wilkerson Teen Challenge, started out as a cop in Minneapolis concerned with drugs among teenagers and went on to provide an entire set of social services within a Christian framework; homes for boys and girls, a coffee house ministry, and more in several locations in the upper Midwest.[30]

Another Wilkerson-influenced work in the same genre, Nicky Cruz's *The Corruptors*, concentrated on a sweeping condemnation of the evils of the modern world—the devils of the modern age. It was a summary of a popular view. It offered blistering attacks on pornography, alcohol, homosexuality, drugs, and materialism, and it defended "the straights and the squares" over the "drug addicts, the revolutionists, the protestors, the crooks."[31] The goal of Cruz, the Wilkersons, and others was to point the way for those who wanted to transform their lives, but were far away from the world of "the straights and the squares." The way was through the transforming word of Jesus Christ.[32]

Escape from the drug culture was the favorite topic of books recounting conversion in desperate circumstances. Sometimes the motif was escape from drugs in the ghetto, as in John Gimenez's *Up Tight*. Sometimes it was escape from drugs in the colleges of the late 1960s, as in George Edwards's *Crawling Out*.[33] On the other hand, despite the enormous importance of the Vietnam War in the late 1960s and early 1970s, there were few books reporting remarkable acts of individual change through individual conversions in the setting of that ugly war.

It was not a war which led many to God, but there were evangelicals who wrote of men who discovered a strengthened faith while in military hospitals or in prisoner-of-war camps.[34] A number of versions of life in the North Vietnamese prisoner camps told how under such adverse conditions some men rediscovered God and how this deeply altered their lives. The best of these works was *In the Presence of Mine Enemies 1965–1973* by Howard and Phyllis Rutledge. It not only presented a graphic account of the inspiration prisoner Howard Rutledge found in a renewed appreciation of God but also dealt with how his wife coped at home and how much she learned to depend on God. Both changed greatly as individuals and both made their presence felt around them in a better life.[35]

Clearly all this literature was intensely concerned with change and animated by the conviction that change was, with the grace of God, possible even in the most uncongenial environments, whether ghetto neighborhoods or prisoner-of-war camps. The literature focused on individual struggle, and it took for granted that change which really took command of one had to be individually motivated and reach into the deepest parts of one's being. It was something only an individual could do, though one changed individual working with a soul eager for salvation could offer great aid to society. From the point of view of its authors, this literature was a story that affirmed the individual. What people could do, how remarkably they could recover from low depths, was a testimony to the human spirit—when blessed by God.

There was also a good deal of failure to report. After all, these writers felt that sin was also very much present in the world. Sheer selfishness was responsible for many of the disappointments. At other times the culprits were more specific, such as immoral sex and free-flowing but destructive drug trafficking; sometimes the sin was less obvious, such as the dangerous effects of "lonesomeness."[36] The identified causes were many, some individual and some social, though the latter invariably led back to individual weaknesses. In the more traditional language which some of these works used, the devil worked in many ways. However he operated, though, these writers did not hold him responsible for individuals' sin. He tempted people, but they were responsible for what they did. Neither society, parents, nor schools were very often the scapegoats; this, for example, was the tough message of John Gimenez's *Up Tight*. David Wilkerson, on the other hand, while stressing individual responsibility, argued that the youth he dealt with were often the product of neglectful and far too permissive parents.[37]

How did these evangelicals and fundamentalists propose that individuals accomplish the change they should seek? Of course, their contention was that people had to rediscover God and bring this resource to bear in their fight to change. The common view was that "there's very little we humans can do to change ourselves or others. . . . [All we can do is] bring our hearts and minds to God."[38] We had to change, but we had to have God's help. The answer was to "trust God" and his Bible, to pray to him, and to watch his miracles happen. Again and again, the point was made: "Not by might, nor by power, but by my Spirit, saith the Lord of hosts."[39]

A life of earthly service under God's guidance and sovereignty had much appeal as a second means to fight evil. It included the service to prisoners, to the sick, to the confused, to the addicted. It included love of our friends and especially one's family. Serving love aimed to help people as individuals in God's universe, of course, and it was a widespread evangelical conviction that it could do so only when it was a firm love prepared to discipline; love without discipline was not only ineffective, it was not really love, only its weak appearance. Loving discipline, then, under God, at home and in all aspects of life was crucial to defeating the devil, to routing evil.[40]

If politics or the action of the state have not appeared as important means to produce individual change among these popular writers, this reflects no oversight. These books by and large ignored the politician and the bureaucrat. They judged government and politics largely irrelevant, not capable of providing any basic answers or of genuinely inspiring or altering any soul. Government and politics could not defeat evil. They may not have been totally useless in effecting change, but to interpose them between the influence of God and his servants who lived lives of disciplined love and those who needed or wanted to change was a pointless waste of time.

A good case in point was how to deal with drug addicts. The lack of success of government programs for them was well known. Some of the most powerful and fascinating stories in evangelical literature reported how some had escaped, assisted in their victory by godly men and women, prepared to give their all in love backed up with a demanding regimen of self-denial — exactly the strategy which book after book claimed would prevent drug addiction in the first place. No change could be greater than escape from drug addiction, and the answer proffered in this apolitical literature was far removed from the sociological cliches and fashionable answers of the believers in political change or social revolution.[41]

The Jesus Movement

A second example of the continuing importance of the case for individual reformation as the appropriate Christian path of change was the influence of the Jesus movement — and mainstream reactions to it — in the years around 1970. The Jesus movement arose just as the most intense New Left sentiment waned among many youth. It attracted a large, but never precisely counted, number of young people. Some were former political radicals and so-called hippies; many others were straight young people who expressed dissatisfaction with conventional Christian structures and worship. The Jesus movement emphasized deep commitment to Jesus, enthusiastic, outspoken worship of him, active proselytizing, and the value of Christian community. It displayed little interest in — often considerable hostility to — traditional forms of the Christian church.[42] Most members of the highly informal "movement" supported a dramatic reinstitution of the Christian experience to produce genuine Christians and to achieve genuine Christian community. They saw themselves as actively seeking change, but they carefully stated their conviction that authentic transformation was something individual — being "born again" in the faith of Jesus Christ.

Many mainstream evangelicals welcomed these obviously apolitical young Christians. They were turning to what counted, Jesus, and acknowledging the only type of change that worked, individual change. Some found their "zeal and love in true community" particularly inspiring. *Christianity Today* and Billy Graham enthusiastically endorsed the Jesus movement.[43]

All was not praise, however, even among those highly prejudiced in the movement's favor. *Christianity Today* tempered its endorsement by worrying that the Jesus people did not take *teaching* the basics of the faith seriously enough, substituting affirmation for doctrine. A few evangelicals were extremely critical. Marlin Van Elderen, for example, dismissed them in *The Reformed Journal* as "a new extremism . . . that worships a Jesus from whom most of us shy away constitutionally, a hip Jesus of the cheap-grace quick fix, the easy answer."[44] His judgment was unusually harsh, but there is little doubt that the Jesus movement stimulated uneasiness. While no one failed to note their "searing indictment of a desiccated hidebound institutional church,"[45] there was no unanimous sentiment that the fault lay entirely with the established churches. Even if one wanted drastic change, proceeding through established forms was a good way to go. There was much to be said, at the least, for keeping the lines open between the regular churches and the Jesus people. The benefits could be substantial. The ordinary Christian could be challenged to consider Christ's teachings far more seriously, and perhaps undertake genuine personal change. On the other hand, the Jesus movement might learn the value of institutions. It might abandon its belief that the Bible could be easily understood. It might also remember that reason must be joined to experience to provide Christianity with the mooring and perspective it required.[46]

Reform-minded evangelicals went further. They chastised the Jesus people for viewing change in such a "conservative" way. They focused very much on individual change and lacked a social focus and a social theory of change. To critics that meant that in the end they stepped away from social problems except as they could be mastered in individual terms. No wonder the Jesus people were a bitter disappointment. Here was a movement within the fold which knew that Christ demanded drastic change and which insisted on it. Yet it was a movement which saw change in deeply apolitical ways.

A typical expression of the Jesus movement was Jerry Halliday's *Spaced Out and Gathered In* (1972). Halliday overflowed with love of Jesus in a style characteristic of the movement. His energy of affirmation overwhelmed everything else. His book's celebration of "the Jesus experience" showed much more interest in "Progress to Groove On" and a determination to "Let the Son Shine In" than anything even vaguely hinting of creed, much less theology. Halliday claimed that "All We Really Need Is Love!"[47] The only apparent counterindication was his praise of Francis Schaeffer — "he's one hip dude, believe me" — but there was reason to doubt his affinity with Schaeffer since he misspelled Schaeffer's name consistently and never discussed anything for which Schaeffer and L'Abri stood. Moreover, Halliday reflected the mood of alienation from organized religion. He excitedly assured his readers that the world he experienced was not conventional Christianity. The Jesus movement "isn't churchianity at all."[48]

At first glance Halliday was somewhat political. His Jesus told people to change the world, and Halliday intended to follow that admonition. He explicitly talked in the language of revolution and claimed he shared much of the perspective of the New Left. But it is clear these sentiments had meaning only within the special language employed in the Jesus movement. They did indeed represent a call for great change—but not by political or social action. We could not meet the problems of the world, Halliday argued, by "hate," which he saw as the style of the New Left. Satan preying on human vulnerability caused them to use his methods to enact their well-intentioned change. Our task was to fight the devil on all fronts. What one needed to do was to get in tune with Jesus and not go around tearing things down. In the end, Halliday and the Jesus movement generally were another affirmation of the individual route to change.[49]

Hopes by some "new" evangelicals that the long-time evangelical romance with individual reformation as the principal means of change would cool proved premature in the 1960s and 1970s. It was, as one leading conservative spokesman observed, too simple to suggest that changed Christians would somehow produce a changed world with no complications.[50] But belief that Christians must pursue this route in hope and in faith remained strong and powerful. For many evangelicals it was the only true biblical way.

INSTITUTIONAL REFORMATION

Stress on individual change as the appropriate means reflected not only a traditional American antipathy to institutions but also a significant tradition in Protestantism that had always feared the grip of institutions, creations of this world. Yet there has never been consensus within evangelicalism on a single approach to change, nor on the noninstitutional approach as a correct one. Moreover, in the 1960s and early 1970s theologies which always had greatly respected institutional activity, the tradition of Calvinism, for example, received reinforcement from the reform-minded evangelicals' belief that genuine social change required greater power and planning than that which could be generated by individuals acting alone.

Government and Politics

Thoughtful evangelicals fully explored the role of government as an agency of change in the 1960s and 1970s. They were part of a culture in which faith and then disillusionment in government were both dominant attitudes within one fifteen-year period. Evangelical sentiments about the state derived in part from the usual pragmatic estimates as to its efficacy either in general or in specific instances. But they also originated in prior biases toward government. There were numerous shadings of opinion, and nothing like a single perspective existed. Many evangelicals accented God's support of government. As Robert Culver noted, it was biblical doctrine that "all governments derive their power from God," and it was he who "directs the rise of nations and their course in history."[51] This was the message of Romans 13. It did not mean that God approved of all governments, for, after all, he could and did bring down governments when he chose to, but it did imply that government was part of God's plan. It might not always be the appropriate means of change, but it ought to be respected and ordinarily obeyed.[52]

It was usually agreed that Christians were to be followers of Jesus first and citizens second. Some writers took satisfaction in noting that this fact had often produced conflict with the state in the past. The usual emphasis lay in simply reminding all evangelicals that "the Christian citizen has obligations to *both* Church and state. His ultimate allegiance, however, belongs to God."[53] It included reminders to rulers that they "are responsible to God" and that, as Robert Culver phrased it, "doctrinaire democratic theory is no less unscriptural than divine right monarchy"; the truth was that "God alone has sovereign rights."[54] Yet it would be misleading to suppose that representatives of the mainstream thought that the average citizen would face any choice between God and his or her government. God was first, of course, but it was only under the most rare circumstances that a person would have to make the terrible choice between his God and his government.

Especially among conservatives, evangelical commentators spent much more effort acquainting lay Christians with their responsibility to obey their divinely ordained government. The age of the 1960s and early 1970s obviously was not an era of confidence in government authority—it was often just the contrary. But evangelicals insisted that the Bible demanded confidence in government. Over and over they cited the stern, clear command of Paul in Romans 13:1–7 which begins: "Let every person be subject to the governing authorities. For there is no authority except from God, and those that exist have been instituted by God." Other passages made the same point. For example, Titus 3:1:"Remind them to be submissive to rulers and authorities, to be obedient . . ."; 1 Timothy 2:1: "I urge that supplications, prayers, intercessions, and thanksgivings be made for kings and all who are in high positions, that we may lead a quiet and peaceable life, godly and respectful"; 2 Peter 2:10: "And especially those who indulge in the lust of defiling passion and despise authority. Bold and wilful, they are not afraid to revile the glorious ones. . . ." These and other texts represented an overwhelming case for Christian citizens to serve established government with loyalty and faithfulness. No one denied that the limit of such allegiance came when government pushed beyond God's ordinances, but many evangelicals felt they should concentrate their attention in the rebellious 1960s and 1970s on the importance of obeying and respecting government.[55]

This emphasis, which fit so well with one side of the conservative mainstream, was scarcely a new idea in evangelical political thinking. It was a routine doctrine. While evangelicals had long taught that "Caesar has no right to touch my conscience," their principal preachment was that the "Christian above all men should be in quiet subjection to constituted authority" and usually "never mind if [rulers] are bad ones."[56] If government did demand what was God's, the Christian was to submit passively, for "no one can decline submission to government."[57] Altogether, the typical conclusion was: "Let us love and cherish government and reject the way" of the rebel.[58]

Robert Culver, among others, skillfully defended the scriptural basis of these traditional conclusions. To him the evidence was everywhere. Jesus always showed respect for and faithfulness to his political rulers. Paul did the same by holding on to his Roman citizenship and the rights it obtained. His citizenship was essential to his self-definition.[59]

Radical evangelicals had somewhat similar views regarding government legitimacy and its role in God's plan. They acknowledged, if sometimes rather reluctantly, that the state had a scripturally sanctioned justification in God's universe. They usually rushed on, however, and argued that the fact government had a legitimate place did not mean anyone should give it "uncritical and blind obedience" — the radical impression of many fawning evangelicals. Demanding respect and one's rights from rulers on the one hand and pushing them to serve the public good on the other were more appropriate Christian responses.[60]

Moreover, as Bob Sabath, a writer for *Sojourners*, pointed out, there was also the Book of Revelation. That is, there was another biblical tradition, one which did not propose political revolution, but did call on Christians to view the state with the most profound suspicion. Was it not the territory of Satan? Were not its officials and bureaucrats the minions of Satan? If so, there could be little respect for government, and Christians would have to learn again that they could be God's servants only in the style of the "alien, pilgrim, prophet — a counter cultural community of outsiders."[61] This was the conclusion of Jim Wallis of *Sojourners* as well. And it was the claim of John Howard Yoder, who declared that the Christian community should trumpet the good news that Jesus had already defeated such forces, institutions, and elements of power. Jesus was the triumph over the devil — and the devil among us.[62]

In this view government and politics daily posed potentially serious threats to the achievement of Christian community. God ordained government, to be sure, but his Bible showed us its reality as an earthly institution which, by definition, rarely served him and was commonly led by sinful persons alienated from him. It was an area which would never be fertile for the maturing of Christian fruit.[63]

The usual view that God had ordained government because human sin required it suggested the most widespread evangelical definition of its proper function. Almost all evangelical commentators considered government's appropriate minimum task to be the imposition and maintenance of basic order in society. The old Pauline and Augustinian definitions of government's task remained strong. The restraint of obvious disorders and of violations of the public peace was the province of government. To the minds of many conservatives, government should do little else. To defend the divine institution, authority, and necessity of government did not mean to celebrate the American welfare state. They saw no biblical warrant, not even human sin, for a state with the vast purposes and enormous size of our own. Nor was there a warrant derived from human sin. Our government had mushroomed into an institution of such disturbing size and influence that everything else, including the church and the individual Christian, was diminished. No wonder there was considerable unease, first, over its potential to destroy other biblically sanctioned institutions and, second, over its growth as the result of the illusion that government and politics were somehow the means to God's kingdom.

Conservative evangelicals generally recognized that government had grown so much, and the reliance on politics had deepened for many groups, because of a widespread belief that somehow government was the appropriate mechanism to promote social change. Most of those who read scripture's defense of government concluded, however, that it was usually a poor instrument for social change. From their perspective this was correct because, while God established government, he did so only because we were sinners. There was, after all, no government in the Garden of Eden. A government established on human sin had as its major task the maintenance of order. To ask it to do more was to ask it to alter what brought it into existence: sin. And the constant refrain was that government could not defeat sin.

What followed, as we know, was that mainstream conservatives were unhappy at the idea that government and politics were the way to relieve social evils and enhance social welfare. Conservatives such as Harold O. J. Brown and moderates such as Carl F. H. Henry charged that dependence on the state for welfare was an unbiblical usurpation of a role God assigned to the individual and the family. It would end eventually with the affirmation of socialism and the denial of God. *Christianity Today* reiterated the usual theme that God rather than any "secular agency" was the route

to human welfare, but it also spoke in terms of ordinary American conservatism. It was "sick" of throwing money and laws at an attempt to
achieve human welfare; that attempt just did not work.[64]

Fundamentalist conservatives usually felt even more strongly on this
matter. Their leaders often complained bitterly about the modern state.
They asked what was wrong with private families and private property or
with the profit motive and free enterprise? The Bible unmistakably endorsed private property. The eighth commandment stood against liberalism
and socialism and for capitalism; after all, state dominance over property
and wealth was really stealing. Ephesians 4:28 agreed: "Let the thief no
longer steal, but rather let him labor, doing honest work with his hands,
so that he may be able to give to those in need." Common sense made the
same observation, reminding us that "Big Government means little men."[65]

Far more commonly, evangelical writers often felt that government and
politics were not the appropriate mechanisms with which to enforce their
particular moral values. As Carl F. H. Henry said, "the Christian view of
society does not require forcing the fruits of regeneration upon unregenerate men."[66] Others felt the same way: "Government should maximize
. . . freedom, not force even the loftiest of moral standards on to anyone."[67]
More conservative evangelicals were sympathetic to the same proposition.
Christianity Today was appalled at the "open licentiousness" of the modern
age, but it concluded that this terrible reality should not fool anyone into
adopting what it characterized as the error of legalism as a means to resolve
the situation.[68]

A case study of the reluctance of evangelical thinkers to summon the
state to institute their values is not hard to find. Their attitude toward state-
enforced prayers in the schools is a good case in point. Despite the situation
today, leading evangelicals did *not* favor a constitutional amendment re-
quiring school prayers at the time those prayers were banned, and many
still do not. Billy Graham did, but he did not in this instance reflect the
opinion of most thoughtful voices. Carl Henry, for example, frequently
spoke out against a prayer amendment, contending that required prayers
did little good and accepting the separation of church and state doctrine
which led the Supreme Court to declare them unconstitutional. He shared
Christianity Today's perspective that forced prayer was hardly the means
to assist religious life. But Henry was not happy about some versions of the
church-state wall which appeared to put all matters connected with the
state in a *secular* mold. As a result, he favored teaching the Bible and
allowing a place for religion in the public schools.

Evangelical resistance to government ties did not constitute an absolute
prohibition of state assistance for evangelical morality. John Warwick Montgomery proposed that the test of involvement be "demonstrable social necessity."[69] When "demonstrable social necessity" existed was an open

question to which different people gave alternative answers. It was an obviously imprecise term. We know most evangelical writers did not think prayer in the schools could meet the test. We know they were not united either in favor of laws against pornography. The one exception, and it is a large one, was the question of abortion. As we know, there was a deep belief that the state must prohibit, if not abortion, at least any state funding for it. It was a "demonstrable social necessity" since it was, in their opinion, a matter of life and death.[70]

Despite the pervasive feeling that government and politics were ordinarily not appropriate instruments for advancing personal morality and the considerable sentiment for restricting their province to matters of law and order, there were other views. In the 1960s and 1970s there was a tremendous revival of interest among reform-minded evangelicals of the Calvinist view that government and politics could have a good many positive uses for the Christian. Several Calvinist evangelicals ran for and were elected to political office. In the 1970s Stephen Monsma won election to the Michigan state senate and Paul Henry won election to the Michigan House of Representatives. One was a Democrat, the other a Republican, but both were from Grand Rapids and were former Calvin College faculty members. Paul Henry, like Monsma, was an articulate supporter of the legitimacy of using government and politics. He read Romans 13 as a message for everyone that God had created the state as a gift in order to serve a variety of useful purposes. He thought that to have the negative view of the state and politics which characterized most evangelicals was to be unbiblical and pessimistic. If politics offended people, the answer was for them to get involved and change things.[71] Robert Linder argued that willfully ignoring the political dimension in life was really just another statement of the fact that "too many so-called Christians are not really concerned about anyone but themselves."[72] Wesley Pippert thought the existence of evangelical Christians in government such as Senator Hatfield proved that government and politics could be a noble activity.[73]

Most of the reform-minded evangelicals who were determined to follow Paul Henry and Carl F. H. Henry and develop "a positive attitude toward the state" wanted to employ the state to attack such problems as poverty, hunger, and the environmental and energy crises. They were convinced, as so many of their more conservative evangelical brethren were not, that government could help in these areas a great deal. Stephen Monsma stated that he had "a commitment to an active, interventionist, humane politics," and he proposed that the state get involved in a major way in the health care business. David O. Moberg was especially concerned about the poor and the need for active welfare programs. Robert Linder also wanted evangelicals to discover what federal and state programs could do to assist the poor and to get busy in support of them.[74]

Linder contended that even if one did not share this goal evangelicals had to recognize the enormous role government and politics played and they had to get involved. Christians who airily ignored them also ignored the lessons of Nazi Germany, where Christians kept themselves pure and did not deign to touch the mess. The result was that they did not commit the weight of their witness to stop unquestioned evil. Stephen Monsma agreed with Linder. He too believed that those who stayed out of politics were really too pessimistic either about change or about human beings or both. There were things we could do, Monsma contended, and therefore we ought to act. We needed to realize that politics and government could make a difference. It would not necessarily be for the good, but there were risks to take on the side of hope.[75]

Richard Pierard and Robert Linder reviewed all the negative arguments and still came down on the side of seeing the benefits of government and politics. They recognized the Christian view that said all activities of the world were evil and we ought to abstain as much as possible. They appreciated the opinion that held politics and government to be too dirty for Christians. They knew the belief that all evangelicals ought to devote themselves exclusively to winning souls for Jesus. And they were fully acquainted with evangelical skeptics who doubted that political and government action could ever do much, if any, good. Nonetheless, they proclaimed that politics was a legitimate and needed realm of human activity. It might not, it would not, solve all human problems, but it was one weapon in the arsenal which hard-pressed modern man should employ for God's work.[76]

While some shrank from politics because it was bound to involve compromise, or corruption, others developed a "realistic" analysis of government and politics. Not only did Paul Henry, for example, urge the importance of the state in God's universe, but he also strongly advocated educating evangelicals about government and politics. They were not pure forms of activity but no such pure forms existed. Of course they involved conflict and compromise. Of course they dealt with complicated issues and with people who had mixed motives. This was simply the way of people and the world. It could not be circumvented, and evangelicals had to overcome their prejudices and use the state *as it was* for their purposes.[77]

The Church

While evangelicals expressed no consensus on the exact line between church and state, separation of the two institutions continued to be a popular and well-established norm among the faithful in the 1960s and 1970s. Yet by the late 1960s a number of activists in the fold began to urge clergy and

laity in churches to be a force for social and political change. There was no
need, said Paul Henry, to pay attention to those who warned of the dangers
of politics for the church. The church was necessarily involved with politics
in the most intimate fashion. There simply was no escape. Even utter silence
on political questions was a political statement of approval or at least ac-
quiescence.[78] Indeed, more than a few evangelicals charged that the silence
which churches too often chose was no accident. Either it was a kind of
irresponsible cowardice or it was part of a political strategy of supporting
the status quo while hiding behind declarations of noninvolvement. This
was the tragic "cost of silence," as Peggy Herbert saw it in *The Post-American*. Churches and leaders, citing separation of church and state, opted to
avoid controversy, knowing full well that this act put them on the side of
the ongoing order.[79]

David O. Moberg spoke for those who expected the church to be a
vigorous agent of social change. It should assume its task boldly: "When
a church is made a fortress protecting itself from evil, it can easily forget
it has a ministry as an army to go forth and conquer evil in the name of
Jesus Christ."[80] As another evangelical put it: "The church is under biblical
constraint, living in the world, to speak to the world in concrete terms."[81]
This duty might include, in the words of Paul Henry, that the "pulpit . . .
must . . . be supported as a place to speak courageously on social and
political issues."[82] The clergy and the church were to address the great
questions as the church learned in practice to share its money and its love
with the broader society. Of course there were dangers. Of course there
would be mistakes. The church "will speak irresponsibly on occasion; that
is inevitable because it is a divine-*human* instrument."[83] Moberg noted,
however, that there were a good many dangers also from the church *not*
getting involved. The greatest, of course, was egregious neglect of God's
will. Our task was to try to see that "on earth" "thy will be done," and an
inactive or timid church hardly acted to realize this divine responsibility.[84]

Those who were comfortable with the church being in politics, busy
taking stands and promoting change, were rarely advocates of participation
alone. They were almost always convinced that the Christian church had
to complement "prayerful participation" with "worshipful contemplation,
which offers spiritual re-creation." For the Spirit must guide every Christian
and every Christian church. Even as it went out in the world, so it must
also return home for growth.[85]

The zest for the church as an instrument for social change characterized the moderately reform-oriented and, especially, radical evangelicals.
But it was not characteristic of them alone. While many evangelical fundamentalists denounced activist churchmen and their "traitorous activities"
and declared that the focus of the local church must be "souls saved, converts baptized, spiritual growth," not the "social gospel, human betterment"

movements, and "the graveyard of social salvation and do-goodism of all kinds,"[86] not everyone did. Some evangelical fundamentalists who wanted nothing to do with the building of a "world socialist order" believed that all Christians had a warm heart and had to display a ready willingness to aid in ameliorating problems of "social structure and welfare." They knew that evangelicals could do much better both as individual Christians and in the Church of Christ and they urged them on.[87]

Most enthusiasm for church involvement in social action offended the tastes of typical evangelical spokesmen. Carl Henry was sympathetic, for example, but he could not muster anything more than ambivalence. It was only right for the church to affirm publicly the great norms of social and political life which the scriptures established. The church had a sacred "witness to the social order" that it dared not forsake. The miserable record of southern churches on race made the embarrassing reluctance of churches to fulfill their duty all too clear to Henry—and it also made the duty all the more pressing. Those who worried about costs did not impress Henry: "The Christian church is not revolutionary, . . . yet . . . the church . . . [must remain] ready to proclaim and ready to be martyred."[88]

Henry, however, was a good deal more cautious than radicals in what he wanted and expected from the church. Any church had to be modest. It had no business viewing "itself the conscience of the State, or the pulse-beat of the body politic." To do so was "directly merging its interests with those of the world."[89] Similar caution was appropriate for would-be crusaders among the clergy. Most of the time they were well-advised to urge political participation, to provide discussion, and to promote prayer—and to do no more.[90]

Billy Graham and Sherwood Wirt reached a similar conclusion. Churches and clergy should be careful in what they said. If they believed they were called to speak out, they should do so, but only where Christians *knew* what was right and only on the essential moral issues at stake (as opposed to all the political details). In general, moderate evangelicals thought, the individual Christian should be the actor for change, not the church or its clergy. When the church and its ministers did act, though, they were to work through their local community rather than through grand pronouncements overflowing with high-flown plans which painted church leaders as "modern social engineers."[91]

Conservatives were far more adamantly opposed to church involvement in most cases. Their belief that the "church has no business in politics" was a combination of several factors. First, they often were against any agency agitating for change—they were conservative about American institutions in general. Second, they did not perceive any scriptural warrant for the church to rush in on political or social matters. Third, they thought that noninstitutional, individual change was the only kind that God mandated and the only variety which could succeed. Fourth, they profoundly distrusted clergy (such as the Berrigans) when they became active in political or social causes.[92]

Militant opponents of church involvement came back again and again to their dissatisfaction with activist clergy, a feeling which surveys of evangelicals in those years showed to be widespread. Laity did not want their clergy picketing on social and political issues. Seventy-two percent of them stated they would be upset if their minister went on the picket lines, while only 29 percent thought the ministry of Martin Luther King was an odyssey in making Christianity relevant.[93] These judgments harmonized well with numerous evangelical spokesmen, who pursued clerical activists with unceasing and strident attacks. Billy Graham faulted clergy who "have become angry with the world and are determined to use violence to change the social structure of society."[94] L. Nelson Bell lashed out at activist clerics, including evangelicals. Over and over he asserted that their taste for social concern inevitably—and obviously—eclipsed their first sacred vocation, saving souls for Christ. Bell hoped that lay displeasure with such errant preachers would manifest itself and halt the transformation of churches into social action agencies. *Christianity Today* also joined the spirit of denunciation of "The Church's Defection from a Divine Mission" or "Putting First Things Second."[95]

Christianity Today declared that the question was: "Who speaks for the church?" Did liberal ministers, who confused the Bible with left-wing politics? Or were the genuine spokesmen the authentic interpreters of the Bible, those who knew that it was not a Social Gospel handbook?[96] The standard view was that "when evangelism becomes politics, it is no longer the Gospel of Christ's Kingdom."[97] The scriptures the conservatives read spoke of the folly of belief in easy stratagems, of the wisdom of trust in God, the duty to obey him, and the responsibility to live a life of patience and meekness."[98]

A fifth part of the conservative case against the activist church was their suspicion that it would lead to a "seduction of the Church" by the world of social causes. Less conservative spokesmen had the opposite fear. They worried that the church was already too much seduced by the world it lived in, too comfortable to undertake what Wallace Henley characterized as "the risk of conflict" with a sinful world. It was not likely to take even the first step which sometimes generated conflict, "the risk of presence," of witness. Such an engagement did not abandon seeking souls for Christ or such private (but powerful) means of change like prayer. What it did mean was a willingness to mobilize the church of Christ on occasion to show some of the caring social energy at home that it manifested in inexhaustible supply in foreign missions.[99]

As the argument ran its course, George Marsden asked: "Did Success

Spoil American Protestantism?" Like others, Marsden surveyed the historical record of Protestantism in America and concluded that it was marred by cultural conformity regarding morality, political ideas, and anti-intellectualism. The awkward answer to his query was "yes." More moderate voices like that of Carl Henry were not so sure what the answer to Marsden's question was, but they were acutely aware of the problem of cultural captivity. Indeed, the question might be put, Who was held captive? Those who were proponents of a clergy and a church wary of the realm of political and social action or those who sought an engaged evangelical clergy and activist churches? Or both?[100]

THE COMMUNITY OF BELIEVERS

As we know, a conviction that communities of Christians witnessing for Christ was perhaps the best route for reformation was widespread among many more radical evangelicals. They did not tend to view this approach as "institutional" in the sense that the church or the state are institutions, but clearly it was in contrast to the traditional emphasis on individual reformation. It was not a popular alternative within the movement as a whole, especially because of its intense collectivist and putative withdrawal sides, but no idea received more discussion or sparked more controversy.

This position, which we know stressed that living according to God's will in community and aiding people there and in one's local area was important, proved attractive to some thinkers from groups like the Mennonites, who had long favored such a stance but whose relationship to the larger evangelical fellowship had also long been problematic. It came into prominence, however, only when in the early 1970s it proved increasingly attractive to the Sojourners fellowship and others of its persuasion. Disappointed by the results of organized social change in the late 1960s, some radicals discovered a new way to be witnessing Christians: local communities, of which the Sojourners fellowship was by far the most famous.

It is not hard to find radical evangelicals who were alarmed with the possibilities of political and cultural "seduction" and the urgent need to avoid it. They were convinced that the history of Christianity was an embarrassing tale of "preaching one thing, but living in a manner" which indicated Christians did not believe their own words. Radicals declared that it was time to believe Christ's words (as they understood them) and boldly turn away from the "seduction" of wealth, of nationalism, of war, and much more. Those who wrote in *Sojourners* spoke directly in the same idiom, suggesting for example that the Anabaptist model of creating a countercultural community as a means to change was attractive, or that a crucial lesson from the Vietnam debacle for Christians had to be a determination to spurn the status quo and remain "pure from evil."[101]

There was a tendency to reject political elections as an ineffective mechanism of change. Conventional politics failed, Jim Wallis argued, and only a life of principled witness could have an impact on politicians or anyone else. Wallis, Wes Michaelson, and others also argued that only a person of spiritual commitment, rooted in Christian community, could move into politics and make any impact. Politics could not be separated from a personal spiritual orientation, which was why the witness of a Christian community was in the highest sense of the word a profound, if unorthodox, political act.[102]

The Other Side was also a forum for those who contended that "withdrawal" was God's will. They always posed the question sharply: How could a deep witness to Christ do anything but lead away from the world's institutions, given their profound and necessary entanglement with evil?[103] The editor of *The Other Side*, John F. Alexander, understood the impulse that led in this direction. He agreed on "the inadequacy of moderation," and he proclaimed that God, not Washington, was the center of power.[104] But Alexander wanted to go no further than his declaration that "*by itself* a program of gradual reform through political compromise is terribly inadequate."[105] He was no proponent of the abandonment of politics.

The center of the controversy was John Howard Yoder and his writings, especially his book *The Politics of Jesus* (1972). Yoder was one of the most sophisticated and sensitive "biblical" writers in the late 1960s and 1970s. There are many facets to his rather complex argument on this issue. His view was not nearly as free from ambiguity and hesitation as it sometimes appeared in the hands of its critics. Yoder did boldly defend Christian withdrawal from politics and the state in order to build Christian community. He denied that the individual could deal with the world in a loving Christian manner without community; those who expected the "individual to be the bridge between grace and structure" were naive. Yet even Yoder did not ordinarily spurn a role for conventional political action. Once a Christian was a successful member of a Christian community, free of the pragmatic style of politics in the larger world, then he could *return* — reenter the Cave — to play a role in politics if it was appropriate. And it was appropriate, unless Christians faced a polity of hopeless corruption and evil. Even then an almost hermetic withdrawal was not to be a routine choice nor an easy one. It could be a moral one, however, and Yoder's readers were hardly to be blamed if they drew the conclusion that he favored such a choice in our time.[106]

Yoder's position received full and sympathetic treatment in *Sojourners*, and he attracted admirers like Dale Brown, whose book *The Christian Revolutionary* praised Yoder warmly because Yoder cast away the Zealot (violent political revolution) role for the contemporary Christian and yet did not completely embrace the Essene (total withdrawal) model either.

Brown agreed that Christians must pay great attention to creating a "prophetic community of hope" wherever they were. There and only there could freedom be nurtured, "freedom *from* basic self-centeredness so that one is free *for* others."[107] At the same time the Christian could not, like the Essenes, simply withdraw into the special community and wait. There was much to do in the broader world, even the political world. But priorities were crucial. God was first, the base of Christian community second, and only after these came politics.[108]

The well of sympathy for the community of "withdrawal" was not deep. Richard Mouw, for example, questioned Yoder from the more widely shared Calvinist perspective. Yoder's affinity for withdrawal represented to him a kind of politics which most evangelical thinkers always feared, the politics of perfection. Yoder made much of the fact that governments fell far short of God's will and politicians rarely achieved God's goodness. Mouw contended that this was self-evident. Meanwhile problems remained which the state could address, if not solve, which the "purity" of withdrawal simply abandoned to others, others who were unlikely to do better if uninfluenced by Christians. Mouw spoke for the majority who believed that politics was not evil but a kind of damaged good. He spoke for a Christian world which could never be a new earth, only this tarnished world which offered only the efforts of ordinary Christian men and women, fallible institutions, the example of Jesus' cross of service, and ultimate hope in Jesus.[109] Stephen Charles Mott made somewhat similar points in the Calvinist *Reformed Journal*. Jesus did not abandon everything and retreat to community, nor should Christians do so today. The world, and its structures, were there and we were to make the best of them. Yoder had some insight, but he was ultimately a quitter. He did not propose to fight for the world. Mott proposed to continue the struggle "to conform the world to the will of God, even if it does need the caution that can come from listening to the perspective of Yoder."[110]

For Yoder and at least some other radicals in the 1970s this was no response at all. It did not reflect the example of Jesus as they understood it. Jesus knew the sharp limits of politics and the disaster of compromise with it. He did not turn to the state as his means of change and he did not advocate that others do so. His moral demands were and would remain far too great for the compromised contours of politics.

OTHER MEANS OF REFORMATION

While most of the discussion by evangelicals about change concentrated on the relative biblical legitimacy and ordinary practicality of individual and institutional procedures, there were other dimensions. In an age in which violence caught Americans at home and abroad, there was necessarily a good deal of reflection on violence as a path to change—as well as on nonviolent alternatives. These considerations continued in the 1970s.

Almost all reflections on this issue began with the image of a peaceable Jesus. It did not imply, as we will see, that all evangelicals rejected violent revolution, or the violence of wars like Vietnam. Far from it. It did mean that they identified with a Jesus who they knew was uncomfortable with physical force and coercion. In this context there was widespread and spirited rejection of the so-called Brandon thesis. Samuel Brandon published a book, *Jesus and the Zealots* (1967), which advanced a strongly argued hypothesis that Jesus' ideas and behavior were close to those of the Zealot party in Palestine in his age and that he was no meek-hearted soul opposed to violence or coercion. The Zealots were Jewish revolutionaries committed to the violent overthrow of their Roman rulers and the establishment of a national religious state in Palestine. They were undoubtedly involved in the eventual Jewish uprising against Rome which began in 66A.D. A good illustration of the specifics of the dispute was the acrimony over the meaning of John 2:13–22, Jesus' famous use of the whip in the synagogue. Brandon and his followers suggested that a Jesus swinging a whip was hardly the peaceable Jesus. Diverse evangelical commentators disagreed. They emphasized that the whip was really just a collection of reeds which Jesus used only to drive *animals* out of the temple. It was not an example of Jesus employing violence when dealing with other people. There were no such examples. Jesus was devoted to a "suffering love," and neither the Zealots nor any other violent group could claim him as a member.[111]

The considerable uneasiness over violence appeared in many guises in many hands. Condemnation of protest violence was frequent. Many critics declared that it showed little respect for constituted authority and was inadequate in solving actual problems. But condemnation of violence was often notably selective. For example, *Christianity Today* in the late 1960s frequently objected to violent activities by blacks and New Left activists and manifested an obvious distaste for "sedition and insurrection."[112] At the same time, there were few words of condemnation for police violence or for the violence of Vietnam. On the other hand, some evangelical protestors of the violence of Vietnam were not necessarily known for their denunciations of the violence that poisoned some protests against the Vietnam War in the 1960s.[113]

A particularly sensitive and probing critic of violence was Vernon Grounds, in his *Revolution and the Christian Faith* (1971). Grounds was uncomfortable with the political Left's affinity for supporting violent revolutions while piously condemning violence in Vietnam. He demanded consistency and pointedly observed that "there is no Biblical sanction for a lifestyle of violent, political revolution."[114] Moreover, he noted that violence in a revolutionary cause would be a risk of enormous proportions which would in every case exact high costs. He knew that revolutions by their nature were not easily disciplined and could roar out of control with a terrifying speed. This was, indeed, one of the several aspects of revolution and its accompanying violence which he judged to be sadly predictable. Another was the fact that no matter what expectations people had it was quite impossible to expect a revolution "without atrocities and reprisals," just as it was absurd to be "naively" sanguine that once started violence rapidly "tends to decelerate." Revolution and violence promised "the considerable risk of anarchy succeeded by tyranny."[115]

Yet evangelicals could justify violence. Consider the case of revolution. In this instance, reluctant defenders included people exactly like Vernon Grounds who ordinarily undertook to draw the case against violent revolution. They justified violence when governments usurped the place and rights of God (though not for "mere" political grievances, no matter how extreme). For example, many evangelicals concluded that opposing the Nazis on this ground was perfectly legitimate and, indeed, mandatory. The Nazis swept aside not only legitimate government but also all aspects of God's civilized order.[116] Vernon Grounds illustrated the reluctant justification of the necessity of violent revolution in extreme circumstances which many evangelicals accepted. He supposed that everyone realized that "loyalty to the Bible may lead to the barricades," since "repressive power . . . must be broken—in the name of love, freedom, justice, and God—by the counter-violence of revolution."[117] But caution was always essential.

The message was similar even among "the activists" within evangelicalism who accepted the necessity of violence in the situation of war. Evangelicals generally believed that God expected them to fight when necessary for values he approved. There were few enthusiastic evangelical militarists, but it was a common conviction that the fallen nature of man required realism about war as a human instrument; that "just wars" — admittedly a slippery and dangerous category which was understood to mean "defensive" wars — were legitimate; and that God approved just wars in the Bible. The Old Testament established the principle which Jesus' acceptance of death fully confirmed, that God gave the power of the sword to the state to provide protection, and we must acknowledge it. While the New Testament did not show God overtly sanctioning wars, the Old Testament evidence on this count could not be brushed away. Nor could Jesus' extremely high praise for a soldier, praise which did not hint that he should cease to do his job.[118]

The view that war was part of God's plan as punishment for sin was not dead among evangelicals either. Vernard Eller advanced this possibility as he dismissed the hope that politics or social change could end war. When God decided to end wars, only then would they cease to be part of human experience. At the same time, though, Eller felt as ambivalent as most evangelical writers did about war—actually, more so. In his mind, Jesus prescribed a Holy War, but one that had nothing to do with arms and troops. Jesus wanted us to wage the contest that really counted, the contest for human souls through "loving service and defenseless suffering." Moreover, Eller wondered with Isaiah whether or not there ever had been a war just enough to have received a blessing from God; he doubted it.[119]

Similar suspicions permeated the thought of many in the late 1960s and early 1970s. They were not the dominant view, but the rise to public notice of an articulate evangelical minority who were pacifists—or nearly so—was a major development, one which spawned intense debate among thoughtful evangelicals.[120] A commitment to pacifism was an article of faith with the radicals, which was a crucial reason why they could *not* join hands with those in the New Left or in North Vietnam whose policy objectives they often admired. Violence was wrong and war was wrong and it did not matter who indulged in it. Sometimes authors explicitly identified themselves with pacifism and rebuked those who supported war and conscription, claiming "conscription and war are obscene and blasphemous in God's sight."[121] Few of the evangelicals who opposed war, whether they overtly called themselves pacifists or not, operated outside a scriptural context. They always turned to what they held to be the overwhelming biblical authority against war. They granted that the Old Testament was hardly fertile territory for them, but Jesus' teachings about brotherly love, turning the other cheek, returning not evil for evil, and the fate of those who lived by the sword persuaded them of the peaceable Jesus. They also accented what they took to be the dismal record of war as a means of change. People like Art Gish and Bill Lane pressed the idea that Vietnam should constitute an indelible lesson in the permanent immorality and futility of military violence.[122]

John Howard Yoder was a prominent spokesman in making the case for pacifism, skillfully representing the peace church side of the radical evangelical movement. His status as an evangelical was dubious in the view of *Christianity Today*, but he was obviously welcome at *Sojourners*. He systematically studied pacifism and isolated a number of kinds of pacifism in his several fruitful analyses. But his major goal was normative rather than analytic. His objective was to convince others that God commanded pacifism, a view most evangelicals did not support.[123] *Sojourners* was so sympathetic with this position that it rarely expended effort to argue it. Its focus, instead, was on how to hurt the machines of war at home. At one time, for example, it gave considerable attention to tax resistance and allowed its pages to be used by those with one scheme or another to avoid war taxes while paying for the needs of peace and legitimate order.[124]

In this context it is predictable that there was sympathy among some evangelical writers for the moral viability of nonviolent action, including civil disobedience, as a means of change. They usually believed that "the rejection of violence of any kind is the theme of New Testament proclamation from beginning to end,"[125] while feeling strongly committed to accomplishing social and political changes. The result was their conclusion that civil disobedience and other forms of nonviolent pressure for change were perfectly appropriate for good Christians.[126] This sometimes went far among radicals, extending even to calls for a politics of noncooperation with the "powers that be," what one enthusiast called "Prophetic Resistance."[127] John Howard Yoder supported such moves during the Vietnam War, explaining why "I Don't Pay All My Income Tax."[128]

Dale Brown in his *The Christian Revolutionary* energetically supported Yoder's position. Brown wanted nothing to do with those who snugly coexisted with the established powers. "To be a Christian is to be a radical," Brown kept insisting. Nonviolent action was the key mechanism for change, and, like many others who used it, Brown wanted only to avoid violence, not necessarily conflict. Nonviolent pressure should have a sting and an ability to expose contradictions, to force people to *think*. Reconciliation was part of the Christian ministry, but where there was no confrontation first there could be no meaningful reconciliation.[129]

Not all evangelicals shared Brown's enthusiasm for nonviolent confrontation, however — far from it. The broader evangelical intellectual community was uneasy with the more ardent celebrants of nonviolent action. L. Nelson Bell spoke out in *Christianity Today* in the late 1960s denouncing those who were indulging themselves in civil disobedience. The ugly truth that such self-righteous protestors did not want to face was that they were tearing the country apart over the issues of race and the Vietnam War. How could anyone regard such a severe consequence as appropriate or moral? Much of the time the editors of *Christianity Today* were similarly upset, and we know they had more than a few critical words to say about both radical demonstrators and the New Left. The editors recognized that such nonviolent tactics had a great impact and challenged their use in those situations in which *Christianity Today* did not approve of the goals being sought. Its basic question was, is it appropriate to use such extreme tactics in disputes involving nothing more than conflict over policies? Not surprisingly, since the magazine did not share the policy goals of 1960s protestors, it did not think so.

Christianity Today, however, did not reject nonviolent action in all cases. It could approve violence, but with reservations, so it was hardly likely to reject a mechanism of change that it felt was, where practical, clearly preferable to violence. The magazine clearly indicated that is supported civil disobedience in the service of God's commandments when they clashed with the state. Civil disobedience was a moral response, even if the record of the so-called civil disobedients often infuriated *Christianity To-*

day. God took precedence over Caesar, and when the state contradicted that principle, certainly nonviolent responses were far more Christian than violent ones.[130]

Most of the time, of course, *Christianity Today* did not think it made good practical or biblical sense for Christians to ally themselves too closely with nonviolence or nonviolent action as the sole means of change. It hoped that for Christians other routes, from prayer to politics, could serve to bring about change, and *Christianity Today* remained close to the Calvinist tradition of political thought, accepting the unfortunate necessity of violence in the world and rejecting pacifism.

Chapter Nine

SOCIAL CONCERNS

BETTER THAN ANYONE ELSE, George Marsden has carefully recounted the path which led evangelicals and fundamentalists to turn against social action in the late nineteenth and early twentieth century. His book *Fundamentalism and American Culture* (1980) demonstrates how many strands contributed to that rejection of social action and led instead to the twentieth-century tradition: the evangelical call to concentrate on individual salvation, repentence, and regeneration, and to avoid anything hinting of the Social Gospel.

We know these attitudes persisted throughout evangelicalism in the 1960s and 1970s. L. Nelson Bell articulated the traditional judgments well: "Are there poor and needy around you? Then for God's sake and for his Glory, do what you can to help. . . . But above and beyond all this, give them the Bread of Life and tell them of the One."[1] Another conservative approach stressed that social concern was possible and important, but *only* through the mechanism of individual regeneration and healing. This was the route to transformation of society. W. A. Criswell, leader of Dallas's largest Southern Baptist church, exemplified a third conservative approach. Criswell simply chose to ignore the question of social concerns, even to the point of excluding personal charity. When he asked "What To Do Until Jesus Comes Back?" his answers included evangelizing, promoting foreign missions, praying, and warning people about hell. They did not call for much, if any, social commitment.[2]

But Criswell's attitude was unusual. There were few parts of the evangelical fold which were not sensitive in the 1960s and 1970s to an increase in social reform energies. Harold Lindsell, another leader of conservative evangelicals, was quick to affirm that while the first and primary duty of the church was to preach the "good news" of Jesus Christ, Christians also were to "reach out to help men everywhere."[3] Conservative evangelical publishing houses issued books which discussed "the church's social re-

169

sponsibilities" and "the Christian and social action" and called Christians to join to assist the poor and others in need.[4] They declared that the "social ministry" was necessarily important as the realm in which "God's people express their conviction of being a new kind of community."[5] Indeed, Martin Scharlemann went so far as to claim, "Our trust in Him can express itself only in terms of solidarity with human need."[6] These orthodox works often opposed most civil disobedience, denounced many of the other tactics of more activist evangelicals and other Americans, and were impatient with "excessive breast-beatings" and "morose activity."[7] But an insistence that both Christian people and Christian churches must rally to confront the human problems of society was the message of many of these works.[8]

There were, as we know, a host of voices within evangelical circles calling for the opening of minds and hearts to the social issues around them. Paul B. Henry called for evangelicals to admit that "twentieth-century evangelicalism has failed in the tasks of giving social and political expression to its commitment to Christ."[9] John Warwick Montgomery deplored what he called a "blind spot" in evangelical attitudes toward social change.[10] David O. Moberg argued that it was "a sin not to be concerned about the needs of suffering mankind,"[11] while Richard Mouw warned that God watched everyone, and he would take account of "who it was that fed the hungry, clothed the naked and visited the prisoners."[12] Ronald J. Sider insisted that the Bible taught that both evangelism and social action were vital and both must go together. Others agreed that it was past time for those who claimed to follow the scriptures to "concentrate exclusively on personal conversion and personal morality."[13] The scriptures required a wider field of mission. Everywhere evangelical thinkers proclaimed: *"Let us follow Jesus . . . in His loving service to those in need."*[14] John W. Montgomery, who was no radical, summarized the mood: "If you know what Christianity *is*, you know immediately and by definition that it demands of its adherents active opposition to social evil and positive efforts to ameliorate human woe."[15]

This chapter addresses the revival of social concern concretely by exploring evangelical thought on three issues with which it grappled seriously: race relations, world hunger, and human poverty. Succeeding chapters look at others, including women's liberation, abortion, and the Vietnam War. Concentrating on specific issues is the best way to obtain a sense of the overall directions, specific concerns, and balance of opinions that characterized evangelical approaches to social concern in the years from the New Left to Carter.

RACE RELATIONS

The impact on evangelical thought of the racial upheavals and the racial change in the United States in the 1960s was enormous. Perhaps the most dramatic effect was the emergence of articulate blacks within the precincts of the evangelical faith who pointedly probed how their branch of Christianity had followed, or failed to follow, the Bible's unequivocal teaching of equal dignity among all races.

The new black writers charged that the record of their evangelical Christianity on race was shameful. Many white spokesmen agreed that the situation was "dismal." It was common to read such uncomfortably frank proclamations as, "We deplore the historic involvement of the church in America with racism."[16] And when the record did not show open racism, some complained, it justified accusations that evangelical churches preferred to ignore blacks and not even attempt to make them converts.[17] It was asserted that Sunday at eleven o'clock was the most segregated hour in America. The tendency of white churches to flee to the suburbs came under scrutiny. Some concluded that evangelicals should accept the harsh evaluation that their witness on race was shockingly far from the genuine Christianity of the New Testament. Change was the only alternative to the terrible judgment that Christ might pronounce upon this record of failure.

Christianity Today criticized racism, yet some blamed it as a chief agent of those who would ignore—or even justify—racism. For example, in 1973 *The Post-American* carried an angry assault on the publication, accusing it of following a typically conservative policy of "benign neglect" regarding the racial situation, hoping blacks would go away. Moreover, *The Post-American* claimed, whenever racial conflict did occur, *Christianity Today*'s racist tendencies shifted from latent to overt status. That magazine always exonerated the police no matter who started trouble or how many black victims there were.[18]

Blacks reported on the experiences of blacks in evangelical colleges, where pious assurances of racial equality, when they even existed, turned out to mean little. One writer recounted the absurd situation at one institution in which the administration permitted the handful of black students to organize a Black Students' Union only so long as its members promised to stay completely clear of race problems. The situation was most serious in more separatist and fundamentalist institutions. One of the sharpest contrasts in the 1960s between mainstream evangelicalism and the fundamentalist fringe was apparent in their stances on social matters. Fundamentalists usually did not respond to the racial upheavals of the 1960s. Critics within and without evangelicalism suggest that fundamentalists were not involved partly because they were ambivalent about social action at best and partly because they harbored more than a little racism: "an element of racism courses through the Fundamentalist movement."[19] It does not take an arduous search to find writers of fundamentalist persuasion who lent credence to this indictment. One defender of Bob Jones University's segregation policies denied that "racial segregation is an evil thing *per se*."[20]

He observed that it was integration that was the evil if, as was usually the case, it led to intermarriage. He also indignantly dismissed as false and absurd assertions that the Bible prescribed universal brotherhood. There was no scriptural warrant for any such claim. Those who believed to the contrary were playing into the hands of the communists, if they were not already communists.[21]

Such opinions were given little sanction, however, by other fundamentalists such as Billy James Hargis. While he knew that the news media constantly typed him as a segregationist, he considered such a label demonstrably false and malicious in intent. Hargis defended the possibility that any person could become a Christian, and he assumed that all Christians were one in Jesus Christ. He felt that blacks and whites had to work together as humans and as Christians, and he accepted no racial dogmas which flouted this position.

On the other hand, Hargis was hardly sympathetic to the widespread black unhappiness, much less the racial confrontations, of the 1960s and early 1970s. He advised blacks that they would do well to stop complaining, assess their tremendous opportunities in the United States, and take advantage of them. Nor was there any point in bewailing slavery, which was properly long dead. Yet, Hargis explained, it had in its time served a purpose. It had taken uncivilized blacks and introduced them to Western culture — a priceless gift![22]

There were some black voices which had positive experiences to recount about white evangelicals and race. There was consistent praise for Billy Graham and his organization; Graham had been a pioneer, and blacks knew it. And some observers, like William Pannell, knew well enough that the lamentable record could hardly be judged apart from the larger society's actions. Evangelical racism necessarily "reflects these majority values."[23] Yet the discontent was deep. Some black and white evangelicals were "broken-hearted at the callousness and hypocrisy" of their faith and their churches on race. Others indignantly attacked racism not only in the evangelical movement as a whole but also that which dwelt within most individual white evangelicals.[24]

White Opinion

There is no question that evangelical resistance to racial change, especially in the South, was often substantial. Yet the message of white thinkers within the fold was almost unanimous in affirming the religious truth of racial equality and in faulting the questionable accomplishments in this area by many evangelicals. Surveys showed that clergy of all religious views, including evangelicals, agreed that civil rights were important and that the churches had done too little on their behalf. While theologically conservative clergy were more likely to attribute the plight of blacks to black irresponsibility, most conservatives firmly rejected this theory. It was clear that evangelical clergy were often in advance of a good portion of their laity on racial questions. This was even truer of evangelical writings in the years from the New Left to Carter.

The consensus in favor of racial equality was impressive. So was the corresponding denunciation of practicing racial prejudice, denigrating a race, labeling it inferior, and discriminating against its members. It was all but impossible to uncover a spokesman who did not declare his complete opposition to racial prejudice. The list of those who went out of their way and "opposed any form of racism" or who stated it as their firm conviction that "prejudice is sin" was lengthy. Skeptics wondered how free evangelical opinion leaders were of racism, and at least one prominent figure did not hesitate to admit that, while he strongly opposed racism, he was hardly free of racist feelings. His honesty in no way diminished his membership in the consensus. In a way it enhanced his membership and made it a more authentic choice.

It is a measure of the sweep of this consensus that there was so little attention to the biblical basis for racial equality. Over and over commentators asserted that God created all people and all races as part of one family, and he required all men and women to love every person just as Christ did.[25] They tended to think that the relevant question was not whether racism was legitimate, but how it could be abolished in American society. A systematic treatment of the scriptural foundations for emphatic rejection of racism like Thomas O. Figart's *A Biblical Perspective on the Race Problem* (1973) was somewhat unusual. But its scholarly analysis of biblical texts endorsed the general opinion in a reflective and detailed fashion. It argued that God made no racial distinction in his creation of the first man and woman. It demolished the old racist claim that his curse on Ham referred to the black race. It explored the reality of slavery in Old Testament times, observing that there was no slavery "in the beginning," and argued that slavery had to be understood and judged for what it was, an institution founded in sin, not divine approval. Figart's treatment of the New Testament was sensitive in its recognition that it contained unattractive tensions between peoples (e.g., the Jews and the Samaritans). But, as Figart expounded the teachings of Jesus, they did "militate against slavery" and against all ethnic and racial distinctions. Figart concluded that God held all men and women, of whatever background, as one in sin and one in God's love.[26]

To be sure, there was a ritualistic, if sincere, quality to many of the statements which formed the consensus. It was rare to read remarks like Virginia Mollenkott's self-accusation that "I am guilty. I admit my guilt," or "I am ashamed of what my race has done to yours." It was equally rare to read of an evangelical like Mollenkott who quit her all-white church for an integrated one as a witness to her beliefs.[27] Clearly it was one thing to declare against racism and quite another to do anything, however modest, about it.

Skeptics suggested that most evangelical spokesmen really did not care, despite their mild protestations. As always, the critics suggested that conservatives opposed racism with no energy because they did not want much change of any kind. These suspicions transcended evangelical party lines. For instance, Francis Schaeffer, as we know, explicitly affirmed his and others' failures in the community regarding race relations. He insisted that evangelicals must do better, not toward the goal of racial tolerance, but toward the goal of a world in which race mattered not at all.[28] John F. Alexander, editor of *The Other Side*, achieved a reputation on racial questions which exceeded that of most others. His unequivocal assertions that if you do not attempt to understand and empathize with the black experience "you do not follow Christ" were notable, but his disavowal of the goal of integration received even more notice. In touch with radical black ideas of the late 1960s, Alexander believed that white and black cultures were so deeply different and divided from each other that in the immediate future both should go their separate ways. Black power was to be a fact of life. Whites could and should aid blacks on black terms, but beyond that Christians could do little other than accept black power.[29]

Consider the case of *Christianity Today*. The magazine often discussed racial questions in the 1960s and 1970s. In so doing it faithfully reflected the increasing interest in race among evangelical writers. Amidst the multitude of positions, white and black, formal and substantive, conservative and radical, it sought to carve out a somewhat complex middle road, which did appear to be representative of widespread white opinion.

Christianity Today repeatedly endorsed racial equality and racial integration. Its testimonials to these objectives were, in fact, so frequent that it is unfair to question its earnestness. The periodical attacked myths about blacks — such as the fanciful "curse of Ham" — which purported to establish or justify an inferior role for another race. It was sharply critical of white churches, clergy, and laity who did not hold out the hand of Christian welcome to blacks.[30] It carried articles probing deep into the race issue, even exploring the "Psychology of Racism." It sympathetically reported official evangelical efforts to curb racism. It consistently followed the principle that communication among the races was absolutely vital, and it improved that communication among its evangelical readers by providing extensive coverage of events within black churches, by covering the activities of leading black evangelicals, and by highlighting black advances within largely white denominations, such as the election of a black to the presidency of the American Baptist Convention in 1969.[31] Moreover, this interest and concern, highest in the late 1960s, did not disappear in the

Christianity Today of the 1970s. As late as January 1976, the periodical devoted a full issue to blacks in America.

Of course, not a few black evangelicals faulted many of their white brothers and sisters, asserting that their focus on race was only abstract. They charged that the dominant impulse of opposition to racism was not matched by any commitment to specific programs to help blacks in their concrete situation, the only possible way to turn support for equality into a living witness. This charge was not true of *Christianity Today*. The magazine frequently called for public and private action to assist blacks in meeting and mastering the problems they faced, especially in urban ghettos. One of its most memorable reports was a news story in 1969 describing the situation in Memphis, Tennessee, one year after the murder of Martin Luther King, Jr. The account by William Willoughby was an eloquent appeal for whites to act to assist blacks in their daily lives. It was also a searing condemnation of white neglect of fellow humans in Memphis and a stinging rebuke of the hypocrisy which could allow white churches to fight alcohol by any and all means and then plead that individual salvation was the only path to aid blacks. Finally, *Christianity Today* itself could take an acerbic stance toward those evangelicals who were interested more in denunciations than in solving problems. Those who, for instance, dwelt on the sins and provocations of Angela Davis should better spend their time aiding talented young blacks.[32]

Yet there were some puzzling anomalies. For example, the magazine editorialized in 1968 that the Internal Revenue Service ought not to challenge Bob Jones University's tax exempt status, even though the institution manifestly engaged in racial discrimination. *Christianity Today* asserted that religion must be given the greatest possible margin of freedom. In this case, of course, the religion of Bob Jones University was appallingly in error. Yet the danger of state intervention, of putting the state over even false religion, was too great even for the just cause of racial equality. Religious freedom must come first.[33] Moreover, *Christianity Today* sometimes pandered to the anxieties of many thoughtful souls who were deeply frightened by black riots and crusades in the 1960s, frequently denouncing urban upheavals in hyperbolic and alarmist terms. The reasons were several. *Christianity Today* complained that ghetto violence showed that some blacks were far too much under the sway of the dominant ethos of materialism. The "American Negro has learned from the American white—victim of materialistic hallucinations that he has become—that fullness of life is to be sought especially in an abundance of possessions." The American government, especially during the Johnson years, was partly at fault. It encouraged both races to believe in its Great Society "which so easily deteriorates into the idea of fulfillment of human wants by political handout."[34] So did Martin Luther King. A reviewer in *Christianity Today* panned King's *Where Do We Go From Here?* in part because it overemphasized a better economic life for blacks. Conservative evangelicals insisted that acknowledgment of sin and the search for personal redemption were also crucial. Why did King not emphasize them?

Christianity Today complained also that blacks were too militant, often too violent. The magazine fiercely denounced ghetto riots and insisted that all people had to reject the alluring language of violence and hate as foreign to Christianity. Its horror over domestic insurrections explained its extremely negative reaction to the effort of James Forman and others to wring substantial sums from white churches in "reparations" for past injustices to blacks. Forman's activities received extensive—and very hostile—treatment during their height in 1969. *Christianity Today* charged that whatever Forman got was won by pressure and implicit threats of violence, not by Christian love. It was hypocritical for churches to give in that way, just as it was profoundly immoral. The magazine noted that it did not suspect that Forman would spend the money in worse ways than the many churches did now. Nor was Forman wrong to suggest that American churches had their sins to carry for their past treatment of blacks. But giving must be in the spirit of Christ which—in this situation anyway—*Christianity Today* declared could have no connection with force.[35]

The magazine did not think any better of the behavior of people who should know better. Martin Luther King practiced a kind of "nonviolent" militancy that skated close to violence and was shocking in a Christian. It was one thing to criticize ghetto upheavals and quite another to attack King, who in symbol and act stood for the civil rights revolution. Inevitably this raised doubts among many even within evangelicalism as to what extent *Christianity Today* was really committed to the fight against racism.[36]

The response of *Christianity Today* was that a kind of balance had to be struck. There was a need for justice and succor for the blacks in America. There was also a need for law and order. Both goals must be sought at once and the accomplishment of each depended on the achievement of the other. *Christianity Today* refused to align itself with the racists or the cold-hearted who thought they could ignore black needs, but it insisted that there could be no cooperation with those black forces who sought to advance through violence.[37]

This belief accounted in part for *Christianity Today*'s opposition and considerable overreaction to the small Black Panther movement. They condemned it as a violent movement in word and potentially in deed, but harbored another objection as well. Black Panthers favored black power, which in all its alternative forms meant black control of black lives. *Christianity Today* denounced every suggestion that even hinted of black power. To accept black power was to renounce the goal of an integrated and functionally color blind society, which they felt Christians must defend in theory and practice. When American black athletes gave black power salutes during the playing of the Star Spangled Banner at the 1968 Olympics, *Christianity Today* tried to avoid moral indignation, but it was clearly alarmed. It had no more sympathy for the appearance of some black clergy promoting so-called "black theology." Harold Kuhn asked skeptically: "Does Theology Come in Colors?" He did not see how there could be but one God and one faith. Both black power and white prejudice were forms of unchristian racism. Both denied the loving, unitary truth of Christianity.[38]

Black Voices

What made the issue of race so alive in evangelical debates was not just the impact of the larger culture where struggles over racial justice and equality raged through the late 1960s and into the 1970s. Also important was the emergence of a cohort black spokesman within evangelicalism. It was itself a sign of dramatic change in a movement whose public face was overwhelmingly white.

The most prominent spokesman for the new black presence in evangelicalism was Tom Skinner, a Baptist minister and prolific writer, whose articles appeared everywhere in the evangelical world in the 1960s and 1970s and whose books received respectful attention. Skinner had worked with Billy Graham after a long climb out of a troubled, gang-filled adolescence. Also a sometime team chaplain to the Washington Redskins football squad, he eventually founded Tom Skinner Associates, an evangelistic and social help organization. He was, like Graham, very much the evangelist preacher who had a message of the utmost urgency to deliver.[39]

Skinner was always a source of controversy from the start of his ministry in Harlem, where he soon came into conflict with fellow black clergy. Many of them did not impress him favorably—to say the least. They wanted him to spend the bulk of his time on fund-raising, and it became clear to him that much of Christianity in Harlem as practiced by too many black clergy consisted of little more than scheming to get money—sometimes to buy sexual favors. No wonder he concluded bitterly that too often "the churches have become a racket."[40] No wonder he found a profound "hostility toward the Gospel of Jesus Christ" in too many black churches.[41]

As he came into contact with white churches, Skinner applied critical judgments to them, including white evangelical churches. They proved time and again that they were racist, a condition hardly compatible with the teaching of Christ. They also proved that they had trouble accepting a black evangelical who cared about social action, supported the small Evangelicals for McGovern Committee in 1972, and dared to use evangelical airwaves to fault Americans for their racism. Skinner had personal proof of discrimination. He was excluded from some Christian radio programs because he was frank about racism in the United States.[42]

Skinner frankly addressed the condition of blacks and the relations between blacks and whites. On the one hand, he defended the full right of blacks to equal, integrated treatment with whites. This included a bold discussion of a subject rarely mentioned by evangelical writers, intermarriage. While most blacks were not interested in intermarriage, Skinner said, scripture did not forbid it, and if two people of different races felt it was God's will that they marry, of course they should. On the other hand, Skinner was much caught up with the black power mood of the late 1960s and early 1970s. He was quite sympathetic to the idea of black power so lamented by *Christianity Today* and many other white voices in the evangelical fold. Skinner argued at some length that to be a follower of Jesus it was not necessary to give up being a self-conscious and even proud black. But on the subject of power, Skinner stressed that the salient question in every situation was how it was used. White power, black power, all power needed to be employed in a framework of service to Jesus Christ. Then and only then did power serve the good.[43]

Of all the evangelical writers of his time, Skinner was among the most telling in his criticism of America. Christianity and patriotism had become embarrassingly connected in the United States. Christians had "wrapped God up in the American flag, and we honestly believe that Jesus is the founder of the American system, president of the New York Stock Exchange, chairman of the Joint Chiefs of Staff."[44] The United States also was a place where materialism ruled all else. It was a land with—he observed with racism especially in mind—a *"corrupt heritage,"* where things were manifestly falling apart. Altogether, Skinner concluded, "we are living in a very sick society."[45]

The answer, according to Skinner, was faith in and service of Jesus Christ. In a time in America when "the number one issue in our Society is whether we can pull off living with each other," he felt there was no other possibility.[46] He wanted a Jesus who first of all preached the truth of personal salvation and repentance, conditions of belief that were crucial to him. He sincerely believed: "I don't have to struggle for human dignity anymore. Christ has given me true dignity."[47] Skinner's Jesus also taught community. Skinner felt he had a Christian responsibility to work on behalf of community in local churches, in the evangelical fold, and between and among the races. But he felt his special responsibility was to black men and women.[48] Finally, Skinner's Christ urged active efforts to alleviate social conditions for all humankind: "It is impossible to be committed to Jesus Christ and not have social responsibility."[49] This truth could hardly be denied. The Christ Skinner knew commanded it, but there was also a practical reason: "We can't go to a man who hasn't eaten for four days and try to tell him about the bread of life."[50]

Skinner argued that going out into the world to serve God and man would include using (and even breaking) laws to seek justice, but he believed with all evangelicals that laws alone were not enough. Money was not enough either. Nor was education. They could all help, but none of them alone or in combination was enough. Skinner did not advocate any "utopian" solutions to human problems, for they consistently overlooked the permanence of sin. Nor did he display any warmth toward non-Christian black radicals such as Malcolm X; they obviously did not understand that without Jesus no real change could occur. Yet Skinner eagerly and repeatedly defended Martin Luther King, Jr., and his militant efforts to assist blacks, and he did so in an evangelical environment that was, to say the least, frosty. It was Skinner's opinion that the real Jesus was not a white middle class conservative evangelical. He was a "tough radical Jesus." Skinner assumed this Jesus would share Skinner's unhappiness about racial and economic inequalities in America as well as his determination to erase them. He also was sure that Jesus was not a puritanical God with a sour face and a forbidding word constantly on his lips. Nor was he the "proper" suburban evangelical confused into thinking the length of one's skirt or hair mattered to salvation. Surely, Skinner suggested, God wanted everyone to enjoy life and not feel "hemmed in."[51]

Other Black Voices

While Skinner was the most important black voice to emerge, he was not the only one and not for everyone the most respected one. Among other blacks who spoke were William Bentley, John Perkins, William Pannell, and Columbus Salley. John Perkins, for example, was an impressive and eloquent articulator of the southern black experience with white tyranny. He reported the struggles of numerous blacks, including himself and other participants in his Voice of Calvary ministry in the 1960s, with a power and directness that is stirring and effective. His book *Let Justice Roll Down* lamented white evangelicals' ignorance of black problems and the tragic absence of Christian civil rights activists. Evangelicals too often did not realize that they must witness for the entire gospel, including its concern for dignity and justice for the weak and lowly. To do that they would have to put aside their racial prejudices and open themselves to the actual conditions experienced by blacks in Mississippi in those years: the humiliations, the fears, the beatings and burnings. They would also have to turn aside from their abstract opposition to concrete tactics such as economic boycotts or their avoidance of plausible alternatives to racist and exploitative economic structures such as economic cooperatives.[52]

Probably the most open forum for black writers was *The Other Side*. From its beginning, it was primarily concerned with racial questions, and when it broadened its focus, it did not forget its original intent. It also elicited black opinion on other matters in addition to race. *Christianity Today* or *The Post-American* did not entirely ignore the rise of black evangelical voices, but their pages featured black writers far less frequently. *Christianity Today* was not exactly a natural forum for black evangelical spokesmen in large part because black evangelicals often favored substantial, and often radical, social action. *The Post-American* and later *Sojourners*, though eventually located in a black section in Washington, D.C., was so interested in local witness and a variety of national and international issues that it never served as an explicit outlet for black evangelicals — at least compared with *The Other Side*. Black evangelicals such as John Perkins did, however, find its pages hospitable on occasion.

Many black evangelical critics sharply attacked the United States and its treatment of blacks. It was not unusual for the United States to be described as a "sick" and "lost" nation, because "for the Negro the American dream was still just that."[53] These writers were convinced that to be black in America meant to be "inferior" and to be treated too often in an inferior manner. Blacks found even white allies for the struggle for black advancement often disappointing. Whites, especially in the late 1960s, tended to be far too worried about riots. They allowed themselves to get sidetracked into denouncing demonstrations or riots when they should be fighting prejudice and its conditions. The reason was often hidden prejudice. One black went so far as to declare that he preferred the communists to Americans. The communists were at least frank in their advocacy of evil, while so many Americans disguised — often from themselves — the pervasive racism which infected them and our culture.[54]

Black critics rarely came to a gentler assessment of the white evangelical movement. Evangelicalism talked too much about the Spirit without perceiving that for blacks, the most basic needs for human survival and decency still had to be met. Many black writers did certainly identify with the evangelical tradition and believed that many black churches had long been within it. But this fact only made what they took to be the too reluctant, even grudging, evangelical response to black needs in the 1960s all the more frustrating. They thought evangelicals surely should have been at the forefront of the black cause, while instead they turned out to be much more responsive to a tainted, even racist, white culture than to their fellow evangelicals.[55]

Perhaps the most debated question among black writers in the late 1960s and beyond was the explosive matter of "black power." Some black evangelicals were open supporters of black power or black "development" rather than integration. They rarely thought in terms of ultimate separatism, since as Christians they were necessarily committed to a religion of one God and one company of the faithful, but there was a real sense that blacks needed to work together now, often on the local level, to advance their race. Columbus Salley's angry, young voice expressed in *Your God is Too White* was a determined example. To him Christianity too often had meant white power and black oppression. Whites could help by repenting and acting to defeat racism on every front. Blacks could help themselves. They had to discover the "true Christianity" not ruined by whites as well as what black self-help and self-determination, black power, could do. They should employ every means possible to wrest a dignified life for blacks from the hard ground of a white society.[56]

Along with black power there was a corresponding interest in black theology. In practice this often meant respectful consideration for the non-evangelical black theologian James H. Cone, whose work was the most influential. Black theologies usually depicted a God highly sympathetic to black needs (as defined by one black or another) and one clearly the product of black experience in the United States. He was often a God focused on this world, a God devoted to blacks, a God of justice determined that blacks should receive their due. He was almost always a God angry at established institutions, including the established Christian church. But evangelical interest in black theology was always qualified, even in the heyday of black power. As William Bentley observed, black evangelicals needed to be careful and remember that black theology approached God by way of the black experience. Congenial as this might be for many blacks, it was not really an appropriate strategy for evangelicals. A Christian, including every black Christian, must operate in an opposite manner. He must start with *God* and approach the black experience from him. God was the center and should always remain so.[57]

Some blacks—as well as many whites—believed that the dilemma posed by black consciousness need not be as harsh as some of its more zealous proponents thought, that it should be possible to respect black culture and still work toward an integrated church.[58] Somehow—it was often not clear exactly how—concern for black integrity and advancement need not lead to a further division of the races, so contrary to God's vision. Black evangelical writers, in the main, struggled to discover how they could reach this road of compromise and illuminate it for others. Yet doubt lingered, especially in the late 1960s, as did a mood of black militance.[59]

HUNGER

If race was the classic issue of social concern for the 1960s among evangelical writers, hunger was the dominant issue in the early and middle 1970s. The famines which afflicted Africa in the early 1970s sensitized many evangelicals to world hunger. So, from another side, did the much discussed explosion of world population.[60]

Those concerned about hunger included many conservatives. For example, *Christianity Today* reported the grim facts of hunger from around the world and demanded that Americans become active in the struggle to repulse the "Spectre of World Hunger."[61] At the same time, however, many conservatives were disturbed that assorted reform-minded evangelicals were pressing to alleviate world hunger in extreme haste, with little or no mention of saving souls. There were almost as many conservative expressions of anxiety about this lapse as there were exhortations to aid the hungry. It was important to feed the hungry, L. Nelson Bell said, but the *first* responsibility of Christians was to bring the life-saving message of Jesus. *Christianity Today* agreed and reminded evangelicals that scripture held religious skepticism to be a more "heinous sin" than social injustice. After all, the magazine editorialized, there are several forms of hunger: some people were physically hungry, but more were spiritually hungry. Christians must meet both kinds of hunger. Ignoring spiritual hunger in all the excitement about world famines and exploding population was just another example of the shocking conquest of Christianity by the world.[62]

Another aspect of the social concern for global hunger gave pause to *Christianity Today* as well as the National Association of Evangelicals. Some evangelicals, especially Senator Mark Hatfield, went too far by declaring everyone had a "right" to have food. As we know, *Christianity Today* praised Hatfield's involvement in the crusade to assist the hungry, but it was not prepared to endorse any "right" to food. In its opinion this notion reflected faith in statism and hinted at socialism while it ignored the duty of every individual. Every person had a responsibility to make an effort to feed himself and his family; the notion of a "right" to food downgraded this individual duty.[63]

Aside from these conservative reservations, however, a great deal of evangelical attention in the earlier 1970s was focused on the importance of meeting the problem and included a great many varied, specific means to address the vast need.[64] Evangelicals preferred churches and church-related organizations as the best vehicle to tackle world hunger. This was a logical choice, and one they were comfortable with. It was also an area in which evangelicals, sometimes in cooperation with others, could boast of significant accomplishment. The leading example was W. Stanley Mooneyham and World Vision. Mooneyham was a widely admired evangelical and World Vision was an aggressive evangelical organization devoted to raising and spending money to combat hunger.

Mooneyham talked to his fellow Christians in frank terms which, coming from nonevangelical sources, might not have received the kind of hearing he got in *Christianity Today* and elsewhere. Mooneyham did not think the American record toward a hungry world was impressive. Part of the blame fell to ignorance, especially of the heart. People often read about world hunger needs, but Mooneyham believed it was urgently necessary to "emotionalize" the issue in order to stir them to action. Part of the trouble was the failure of our rulers and the political institutions they presided over. They desperately needed a "conscience." Part fell to churches who did so little. Part fell to the kind of Christians who indulged in declarations that the end was near and blithely avoided the suffering of their fellow creatures. Part fell to the cruel "lifeboat theory," the tough-minded view that there were (or soon would be) just too many people in the world for available resources and food. Hard choices would have to be made. Not everyone could get in the lifeboat if anyone was going to survive, and those who made scant effort to save themselves would have to be abandoned. Mooneyham judged this idea to be both repulsively anti-Christian and absolutely futile in practice. The world would live or die together, and no people or nation would be allowed to have any special consideration.[65]

Mooneyham breathed a confidence which was steely and determined rather than naive. He knew the hunger situation too intimately to offer his readers any easy reassurance. The effort that lay ahead was enormous. Yet the world's hungry could be fed. The challenge was not to raise production, nor was it a matter of inventing a miraculous technology. The real issue was the present pattern of distribution of food in the world. Global patterns were shockingly unequal, violating the Christian principle of respect for each of God's children. Elites and masses, especially in rich nations, had to reexamine their lifestyles and their priorities in order to defeat hunger. Mooneyham knew they could and, optimist that he was, he thought they might. His was, indeed, a "world vision."[66]

Mooneyham well understood, however, that vague expressions of good will were not enough. He stressed the responsibility of dedicated Christians to give of their financial resources. Giving had to be serious and involve surrendering our "unrestrained pursuit of superaffluence," not just dropping a few stray coins in Christmas charity boxes.[67] More radical evangelicals identified with John Perkins's belief that "if we can just learn how to get our wealth to the poor we will have treasures in heaven and a lot less worries on earth."[68] Some asserted that the hungry could be helped a great deal also if people would simply cut down, even sacrifice, in the amount of their own eating. Why did Americans have to eat so much? Why did they have to eat so much meat? Why not consider "kicking the Meat and Potatoes Habit"? Why not begin to take vegetarianism seriously? Why not start fasting on occasion? A simpler diet, a smaller diet, the renewal of the ancient Christian practice of fasting, all these were objectives Christian evangelicals began to propose to fight hunger by disciplining their own hunger.[69]

Many writers had high confidence that the hunger issue was one about which Christians really could do something, both as individuals and organized in church groups. This may explain why this was an area of evangelical social concern where the arguments over the role of the state were not as bitter as they often were when the issue was poverty. The fact was, however, that state aid was important, too—and leading representatives of the hunger crusade knew it. Stanley Mooneyham of World Vision warned that government assistance was vital. Individual efforts were laudatory, but hunger in the world required more than the ministrations of private charity. We needed tough public policy decisions not only to plan national and international economic development but also to channel large sums of foreign aid from the United States (and other wealthy nations) to the Third World. The embarrassing fact that we as a nation gave precious little had to change—soon. What we did as a nation through our government for Europe after World War II established an impressive model which we failed miserably to emulate in the 1960s and 1970s as we overlooked the Third World. Christians knew they had to work hand in hand with government to win the godly battle against world hunger.[70]

Far less often were evangelical voices raised to suggest that the hunger crisis could best be solved by structural changes in both domestic social and economic orders or in their international counterparts. Occasionally someone, like George DeVries, Jr., in *The Reformed Journal*, implied that the problems had many of its roots in class and privilege patterns which would not easily yield to exhortations to Christian benevolence.[71] But with some exceptions, Mark Hatfield, for example, most evangelicals involved in the hunger concern were not radical regarding Western institutions nor interested in sweeping structural changes. Indeed, that was one of the most important, and possibly most attractive, aspects of the hunger issue for evangelicals. It was a vehicle, a sincere and purposeful vehicle, for those evangelicals who wanted to participate in the new mood of social concern but had no intention of supporting radical, not to say revolutionary, schemes. Hunger was always an important issue—and usually a safe one. The radical evangelicals turned to another world, the world of socio-economic relations, the world of social justice.

THE POOR AND THE RICH

Race and then hunger were the most popular manifestations of evangelical social concern through the 1960s and the 1970s. However, they did not monopolize the agenda of social concerns. The condition of the poor and the moral status of the rich often shared a spot on the agenda. There was no single period when the disparity between rich and poor dominated as the single most important issue, but questions about economic relations were repeatedly raised and discussed. No consensus emerged, but there can be no question that there was intense argument. It was an issue that increasingly mattered in the 1960s and 1970s.

Often evangelical writers confronted the issue of the rich and the poor in the Christian framework of sympathy and the importance of universal love. The central, overused word was compassion. Everyone from Billy Graham to Jim Wallis spoke of the poor—and often the rich—in terms of compassion. It was sincere enough, but skeptics often wondered if it was worth much. A vague, sincere "concern" did no good. It was a pleasant, if sometimes condescending, attitude, but not a practical program to change things.

Yet the widespread evangelical unity on this, among other, responses had significance. No programs or strategies would succeed *without* an enveloping spirit, in this case a spirit of compassion. To be sure, some evangelicals conceived of compassion as traditional Christian stewardship, those better off helping the disadvantaged, while others understood compassion to involve an existential solidarity with the oppressed. All, however, proceeded in the common belief that to reach the poor and aid them required the special spirit of compassion.[72]

At the same time, the years from the New Left to Carter's election saw an explosion of evangelical literature complaining in Christian terms about economic inequalities, a good deal of it as venomous regarding the rich as it was sympathetic to the poor. A great proportion of the writing on this subject took the form of the expression of biblically based moral outrage, hardly what one would expect from "conservative" evangelicals.

Yet it would be misleading to imply that the protest over the poor's condition was identical in emphasis and in tenor across the spectrum of evangelical political perspectives. Distinctions must be made, but only with care, for there was anxiety everywhere. After all, poverty threatened its victims with the loss of their sacred personhood.[73] Conservatives raised their voices, too; they knew "the abominable conditions in slums of Western capitalist societies."[74] They knew that even in the Old Testament the poor were special: "neither things nor statistics, they are persons and families."[75]

Not surprisingly, the edge became sharper among more reform-minded evangelicals. General denunciations of "the materialism of our culture" were frequent.[76] So were sometimes blistering critiques of the "maldistribution of the nation's wealth and services."[77] Moreover, from a world perspective, the shoe pinched even tighter. We were the world's rich. Did we realize that? Did we really want justice?[78]

Only in this context may we turn to the radicals' hostility to the rich and their denunciations of the fate of the impoverished. Their judgments were not completely unusual, although they were more central to the Christianity espoused by the radicals. The radicals were indeed more sweeping

in the changes they proposed, and they were far harsher in their arraign-
ment of the rich. This latter point is especially noteworthy. It is one thing
to bewail the condition of the poor and to acknowledge its evil from a
biblical vision, but it is quite another to blame the rich, and often merci-
lessly. It is even one thing to talk of the maldistribution of wealth within
the United States or between America and much of the rest of the world
and quite another to crusade against the rich and exalt the poor. Francis
Schaeffer and Paul Henry, for instance, cared about the poor. But they did
not reiterate again and again that the Bible teaches us to distrust the rich,
or quote repeatedly from Luke 6:24: "But woe to you that are rich." They
were not likely to say that "the poor are . . . God's chosen people." The
sense of class judgment and conflict which tinctured radical writings was
missing. But radicals writing in journals such as *The Other Side* or *Sojourners* did not hesitate. Paul and the Old Testament invoked the same absolute
truth, that God cared for the poor and condemned the rich. They asserted
that it was not possible to muddy this stern message if one would be a
biblical Christian.[79]

Probably the most widespread framework within which to act even
among some of the angriest evangelicals, was to emphasize that wealth and
property were legitimate only if seen as a trust from God and employed for
all people with that understanding in mind. Socialism or capitalism were
not Christian frameworks so much as secular dogmas. From this perspective, poor people were a testimony to the failure of humans to respect that
common trust. They were a tragic illustration of the failure of community
among men and between God and men. No wonder a "revolution is needed
in our thinking about money and possessions."[80]

Proponents of this view were often critical of Christians or others who
were so confused as to think "that the purpose of man's existence is to
acquire wealth and property and to do as he pleases with it."[81] Such people
were ignorant of the Bible. They did not realize that the Old Testament
taught that God's people had to exercise the stewardship of property. The
New Testament also urged stewardship, not least by the example of the
behavior of the early Christians. They knew their goods were part of God's
bounty and that every Christian had a solemn responsibility to remember
this truth when it was time to collect for the poor, provide for widows, or
share common food.[82]

Another way of making the same point was to stress the specific standard of *use*. Those who looked on property in this perspective contended
that the scriptures did not necessarily constitute an argument against private property or even against the existence of the wealthy. The crucial
question was how property or riches were employed. Did they serve the
"common good"? Did they work toward the alleviation of poverty? If they
did, then Jesus' ethical imperatives were alive and the "ruinous preoccu-

pation" with possessions which corrupted both the grasping materialist and many of his socialist opponents would be overcome.[83]

All of these considerations of the rich and poor and private property fell short of a direct attack on capitalism and the principle of private ownership. To be sure, some evangelicals, whether they spoke in the language of anger, or of compassion, or of community, or of use, suggested positions which were not notably sympathetic to capitalism; they sometimes even appeared to be intentionally cool to capitalism. Attitudes varied widely, however, and most of those who were critical were so mostly by indirection. Direct attacks on private property, or on capitalism as an economic system, were hardly the fashion, no matter how much the poor were on the agenda of social concern for evangelicals in the 1960s and 1970s. This is an important feature of the outlook of evangelical thinkers which would not make much sense to Marxists and others of a leftwing political disposition in the broader intellectual world. Yet most evangelical voices just did not believe that there was an irreconcilable conflict between the reduction of poverty and the existence of a privately owned economic system.

A few writers did attack capitalism outright. The problem, they said, was always the same. Capitalism by its *inherent* nature celebrated selfish, individual goals. It was *necessarily* devoted to private goal satisfaction, not public needs, such as overcoming poverty. It therefore denied the inherent dignity of man. The issue, they said, was straightforward: how to change "our free enterprise culture, which upholds the profit motive as its chief virtue (as opposed to the service motive of Christian ethics)."[84] Critics felt Jesus demonstrated this sad truth not so much in eternal parables as in the more powerful lesson of action. For, as John 2:13–25 showed, Jesus drove out the capitalists from his temple. Surely this was the model for all Christians who would make the entire world a temple to God.[85]

What distinguished these radicals, such as John Alexander of *The Other Side*, was their conviction that advocating compassion meant little in concrete terms unless one *directly* confronted the fact (as they saw it) that a capitalist economy stood permanently in the road blocking this ideal. Not to oppose this economic system was to avoid reality and to waste much effort uttering pieties which in the end would not assist the poor much.[86]

We should not conclude, however, that the anticapitalist remnant were somehow in love with state socialism. Many favored a drastic expansion of government to direct the economy and develop the welfare state. But the state could not substitute for a deeper and more pervasive concern for the community, and socialism could not substitute for genuine compassion and Christian stewardship. State socialism lacked the spirit of Christian love and community, and without these no change could really come to end capitalism or aid the poor.

The Defense

Supporters of capitalism within the ranks of evangelicals found the 1960s and 1970s trying times. At home opponents of capitalism blossomed in ever greater numbers and sometimes, as in the New Left era, too often went unanswered. Abroad the communist enemy continued its slow, but inexorable march. Everywhere the assertion was that procapitalists were cruel and uncaring exploiters. Evangelicals strongly for capitalism, however, insisted they were committed to aiding the disadvantaged poor. This was part of their Christian duty. They were, however, annoyed and frustrated by what they considered to be the hostile atmosphere that faced private property and the larger capitalist system both within and without evangelical ranks. Harold O. J. Brown and L. Nelson Bell bewailed any efforts, from ruinous taxation schemes to proposals for a guaranteed income, which seemed to them more calculated to hurt the propertied than to relieve the impoverished. They felt as *Christianity Today* did that capitalism was not flawless, but it was time for its defenders to speak up and note its many advantages.[87]

Conservatives complained that critics of capitalism always assumed that concern for the poor and support for capitalism were irreconcilable. They vehemently denied this contention. The truth was the opposite: "Capitalism combined with Christian stewardship can do more good for more men than any other economic system" because capitalism was so enormously productive.[88] It provided opportunities for all. To be sure, it could not automatically help those struck down by life's tragedies and should not relieve those who chose the way of "indolence." But turning to the state to fight poverty was an absurdity. Statism interfered with free enterprise and inevitably came to generate poverty, not eliminate it.[89]

Conservatives also insisted that scripture hardly proposed crushing capitalism. As Harold O. J. Brown remarked, nowhere in the New Testament could any denunciation of the principle of private property be discovered.[90] Robert Culver combed both the Old and New Testaments to locate all the reported animus to capitalism or private property. He claimed to find nothing. In the Old Testament even the "prophets were not advocates of social and economic leveling."[91] Jesus was no enemy of private property or the rich either; he "had no poor man's prejudices against the well-to-do and the privileges accompanying wealth and property ownership."[92] The opposite was more nearly true: "Capitalism is more consistent with the principles of the Word of God than any other system of economics."[93]

CONCLUSION

As one reads the voluminous literature which poured forth in these years from evangelical writers one realizes that the later 1960s and early 1970s was an era of unmistakable renaissance in social concern. Probably nothing like it had existed in the evangelical world since before the Civil War. To be sure, even within the movement critics were sometimes skeptical of this renaissance. They pointed to its strength in intellectual circles, but challenged whether it permeated deeply into the rank and file. They suggested that it was likely to be a short-lived phenomenon, a creature of the broader culture's upheavals, rather than the sign of a genuine change of heart.

Other skeptics both within and without evangelicalism noted with disapproval the concentration on hunger as a fashionable issue of social concern. Was it not a "safe" issue, one which did not threaten the United States and one which (at least for the naive) could be pursued without challenging any structures of the world order? Even poverty was no better, the critics said, in that too often evangelicals gingerly skirted any dangerous terrain touching on the existing order as they proposed their lame or nonexistent solutions. In short, the doubters suggested that the turn to social action meant little when all was said and done. The effort to revive social concern never got away from vague and lifeless sentiments and approaches which, in fact, fitted comfortably, even snugly, within the paradigms of the American liberal capitalist order.[94]

That the renewed interest in social responsibilities within evangelicalism was more prevalent among critics and "opinion leaders" than much of the laity appears to be true. But that it could not advance further in the 1980s and beyond is a conclusion which critics draw more confidently than they have any reason to do. They are expressing a suspicion about evangelicals which would never have predicted the rise of interest in social concern in the late 1960s. On the other hand, suggestions that world hunger is somehow a "safe" issue make a certain sense. So does the evangelical response, however, that no issue could possibly be more important for those who care about people. That the evangelical interest in poverty produced few advocates of radical solutions is true, but that does not necessarily mean that the evangelical response was a failure. No other response has proven to be a fully effective way to battle poverty either. In any case, secular radical critics often seem to fasten on mainstream evangelical proposals as the only evangelical responses to poverty. For better or for worse, other evangelical ideas were much more radical, did raise serious questions about the rich and even about capitalist structures, and could hardly be called rationalizations of liberal capitalism.

There was, in fact, a great change of attitudes about social issues in the late 1960s and early 1970s. The new pattern of evangelical thought did not fit the dogma of secular left-wing thinkers (or of right-wing conservatives either). But, at least within its own world, a significant portion of informed evangelical opinion underwent a metamorphosis toward a greater social awareness and social caring. The racially disadvantaged, the hungry, and the poor were rediscovered once again as children of God.

Chapter Ten

THE FAMILY UNDER ATTACK

THERE WERE MANY SIGNS that evangelical writers in the years from the New Left to Carter continued to stress the absolute importance of traditional values such as family, marriage, conservative sexual standards, and antifeminism. While some observers in the middle 1970s suggested that behavior in the movement was changing with regard to divorce, premarital sex, and profanity,[1] evangelical writers did not reflect this reputed trend. It was here, more than anywhere else, that mainstream conservative views were firm—and widely shared. There were divisions, especially on the subject of women's liberation, but overall there was considerable unity.

It should be pointed out that evangelical interest in issues such as the family, sexual mores, and women's liberation was enormous. All one has to do is know the slightest thing about evangelical participation in crusades against abortion to recognize this fact. The curious fact is that both evangelicals and their critics ordinarily did not see their interest and involvement in these questions as the expression of substantial social commitment. Surely, to accept the claim that these were private issues was an error, since issues like the family, abortion, or the status of women are questions of vast significance for any commonweal. No amount of polemical claims that they are, or ought to be, "private" matters alters this reality. Evangelical conservatives often confused the issue by claiming their concern was to defend the private family and Christian norms against the larger, public, secular world. This view tended to obscure the fact that the issues were inevitably public with great public consequences. From this perspective even the most conservative evangelicals had a long and continuing record of willingness to take "public" action, at least when it came to their fight for the values of "private" life.

Certainly, devotion to the family was the core value in evangelical writing in the 1960s and early 1970s. Evangelicals united in insisting that the family must remain central in every Christian's life. Marriage and family received the utmost respect. They were sacred relationships, truly "God's 'super' structure," as one popular account put it.[2] Attacks on the nuclear family invariably elicited spirited counterattacks. Criticism of divorce was often sharp, though the rules limiting it were not as rigid as they once had been. The usual view was that divorce was evil because it was unbiblical and because it struck at the family. But it could be accepted in some cases, as could remarriage. Some writers justified divorce in the case of adultery, though opinion was not unanimous as to how to interpret New Testament injunctions on this point. One suggestion was that the Bible provided two different sets of rules, one for marriages between two believers, and one for marriages between a believer and a nonbeliever or marriages between two nonbelievers. Partners in the first were not really expected to divorce or remarry. But almost all approaches to divorce had as their objective the preservation of the family, while granting that "there are times when divorce is preferable to an unhappy marriage."[3]

Similarly rejected was the sexual "revolution" of the 1960s and the 1970s. Figures such as Harold Lindsell frequently summoned people to "the battle of the flesh," to defeat soul-destroying sexual libertinism. Only fools ignored the obvious reality that "sex is an explosive and powerful force" which could ruin much good when it gained irrational mastery over us.[4] The Bible had to be our guide in sexual life—and the Bible taught that only sex within marriage was moral. Again and again evangelicals cited the many biblical passages condemning adultery. Many were equally adamant in opposing premarital sex. The contraceptive could not set the Bible aside. In mixing the sexes in dormitories, colleges shamefully promoted premarital sex. Everywhere evangelical spokesmen resisted pressures to modify conservative sexual norms. They were in full accord with L. Nelson Bell's conviction that "to lower standards of morality can only be described as Satanic."[5]

Proponents of the "new morality" argued that it gave greater range to human love. But few evangelical thinkers were disposed to separate love from law, and they denied that Jesus had favored such a separation. Love and law together were the only road to the moral life under God. Moreover, some evangelicals wondered if the "new morality" which left ethical decisions to individuals in concrete circumstances—the famous situation ethics—was not a harsher, more demanding ethic for the conscientious (though it was no ethic at all for the weak). Law, especially God's law, provided a substitute for the substantial burdens of personal choice and responsibility imposed by situation ethics on the thoughtful person while at the same time offering rules for those who were defenseless before sin without them.[6]

It is interesting to note at the same time that the gospel of sexual enthusiasm so pervasive in American culture in the 1970s bounded into evangelicalism also. There were a surprising number of books like Dwight

Harvey Small's *Christian: Celebrate Your Sexuality* (1974) whose attitude toward sex was far from puritanical. To be sure, these popular works kept away from the "new morality" and saw sex as legitimate only within the bonds of marriage. What made them so unusual, however, was their downright excitement about sex within marriage. They highly lauded sex for recreation, sex for renewal, and sex for love as well as sex for procreation. They happily linked sex and joy. By this view, a Christian marriage was to have much room for sex as every couple sought "one flesh, one spirit, one love" and gained "a sense of well-being, complete identity, joy unbounded, perfect mutuality" through sex. Such a relationship could only be positive, providing the married couple saw themselves as celebrants under God. Christians knew that God stood over marriage and he would judge their life as married lovers.[7]

Other books, such as Tim and Beverly LaHaye's *The Act of Marriage* (1976), offered explicit advice on the techniques of lovemaking. This represented a substantial change in the spirit of evangelical books on sex even over the 1960s. To be sure, its treatment was entirely within a Christian perspective (or at least one Christian perspective), and no sexual "immorality" received encouragement. Nonetheless, the book suggested an enthusiasm for sex and a recognition that how one performed the sex act was essential to fulfillment sexually. It was undoubtedly a revealing sign of the times that the LaHaye book received the designation by *Christianity Today* as one of the "25 choice evangelical books of 1976."[8]

Perhaps more typical were popular books like the now well-known Anita Bryant's *Amazing Grace* (1971). This work was a quietly told account of the Bryant family life and, like so much other evangelical writing, a hymn to the virtues of such a family-centered lifestyle. In such books politics and the state were far, far away. Domestic "bliss" and tales of miracles and near miracles predominated. As Anita Bryant saw it, for example, since she was a child of divorced parents, the success of her family life was almost a miracle. From her husband's dramatic conversion experience the night before their wedding to the survival of their twins born two and a half months premature, Bryant saw a confirmation of God's love and blessing for her and the family as God's community.[9]

While more intellectual writers stayed away from the simple-mindedly hortatory approaches to Christian sex or Christian family life, they were as deeply devoted to the sacredness of the family and ineluctably involved with the realms of sex and family life in the modern age. Four issues in particular stirred the most controversy: pornography, abortion, homosexuality, and women's liberation. Each was something of a honey pot, at least in the sense of attracting endless comment and controversy. Certainly each was a passionate matter for many of the most thoughtful writers in the

1960s and early 1970s. This chapter considers evangelical opinion on all four, examining the fourth, women's liberation, in the greatest detail. It was, at least in the 1970s, the most divisive within evangelicalism of the four, and it provides some fascinating insights into the structure of evangelical thought in recent times.

PORNOGRAPHY

Contrary to what some outside observers might expect of pornography, abortion, homosexuality, and women's liberation, pornography was the least worrisome topic for many evangelical spokesmen. It is hard to find evidence of an obsession with pornography. It simply did not rank with either abortion or women's liberation as a topic of significance. Yet it was still on the agenda as part of the war on all fronts for a Christian understanding of family and sex.

Evangelical writers on pornography indignantly denied the assertion that pornography was an elusive concept which escaped definition. Nobody could escape doing something about the problem by using such a flimsy excuse. The most thoughtful definitions suggested that pornography was the treatment of human sexuality in ways that insulted and degraded the human spirit. By this view no one should confuse pornography with sexual excitement, nor with obscenity, which might include such things as violence. The usual focus, clearly, was sexual behavior which took vulgar and dehumanizing forms.[10]

There was little discussion of whether pornography was bad or not, simply because the question did not merit discussion. Opinion was also unanimous that pornography did affect people. All sexual behavior—and the existence and promotion of pornography is sexual behavior—necessarily affected society. Pornography hurt the family. It separated sex from love. It created fantasy worlds which misrepresented the tender and complex world of sexual interaction. It destroyed the rights of privacy in its leering, public displays.

While some social scientists dismissed the idea that pornography had these social consequences, evangelicals were rarely impressed. They did not worship the gods of social science. They felt that social scientists who thought pornography did not have such effects were naive and contradicted obvious common sense. Meanwhile, pornography's corruption grew and grew. The media was saturated with it—from television, to movies, to *Playboy*, to the secular sex manuals which turned a divinely-instituted aspect of life into mere technique.[11]

Sentiment about what to do to curb pornography was mixed. On the one hand there were calls by the National Association of Evangelicals,

Christianity Today, and others to take stern measures, to pass and enforce laws to eliminate pornography from the streets and the media. This was the dominant position.[12] These demands depended on three arguments. Proponents held that no one could believe in complete secular freedom, not at least if they had a firm commitment to God's word as their first priority. Thus, pornographers had no inherent right to hawk their wares. Second, they asserted that freedom should be abridged when, in cases like pornography, there could be no question of its corrupting and anti-Christian impact. People had a perfect right, they felt, to pursue God's conception of the common good and not to allow scare talk about the dangers of censorship to deter them. Censoring political liberty was one thing. Censoring pornography was different; it was in fact a duty if one would be faithful to God. Third, it was agreed that enforcing laws against pornography would hardly eliminate it altogether; still, proponents of action contended that there should be laws which tried and which thereby set standards for public morality.[13]

Yet the issue of censorship did raise its head again and again. Not everyone was prepared to move in a direction which unquestionably sanctioned censorship. For this reason, all along some evangelical voices were not willing to enlist in the crusade. Others wondered if pornography and politics could really be distinguished. In some left-wing publications they were inextricably mixed, so that to censor pornography would be to censor their politics. By 1975 even *Christianity Today* acknowledged that a middle ground was desirable. It desired to counteract pornography but not at the risk of damaging free speech in religion or politics.[14]

The truth was that evangelicals thought pornography was evil and sentiment for eliminating it was strong, but it was a secondary issue, one which over time did not seem quite as simple as it once did to sweep away without cost. Richard J. Mouw illustrated this mood in an article he wrote in *The Reformed Journal.* He declared that his coreligionists should fight for their sexual values in society, and they had to have the right to advance these values through schools, churches, and the like. But that did not mean that an elaborate series of laws to regulate sex and sexual messages was a good idea. Mouw reached the conclusion that laws could not replace what Christians must do themselves in their own lives.[15]

Occasionally there were evangelicals, often radicals, who went even further. John F. Alexander of *The Other Side*, for example, shared the widespread opinion that pornography was repulsive, yet he displayed no interest whatsoever in endeavoring to stamp it out. For him the question was one of priorities. Such problems as poverty or racism were far, far more serious in their human and social costs, and Christians should direct their attention to them.[16]

ABORTION

Argument over abortion has, of course, been one of the most controversial and heart-rending disputes touching family and personal life in the past fifteen years. Even churches famous for their liberalism have found themselves in painful disagreement over when, if ever, abortion might be justified. It is no surprise that evangelical thinkers were often involved with this question nor that they were extremely hostile to what Lewis Smedes in *The Reformed Journal* called "the abortion epidemic." One of the interesting ironies of the vigorous opposition to abortion which characterized most writers was that it linked evangelicals with the Roman Catholic "pro-life" forces. It was a rare issue indeed which could stimulate such unity and lead them to say warm things about Roman Catholicism. Abortion was, however, very much such an issue. The struggle was intense and any allies were welcome.[17]

Another irony was that consideration of the biblical teaching on abortion did not provide the firm basis for certainty which usually undergirds any evangelical stance. The problem was that evangelical interpreters, who had their hearts in the right place, just could not and did not find an overwhelming case against abortion in the Bible. They could and did argue that abortion was against the Christian tradition, assuming that abortion was murder. But there was precious little specific discussion of abortion, no matter how remote or small in the scriptures. Scant explicit biblical guidance was available.[18]

Nothing whatsoever was in the New Testament about abortion. The Old Testament was more forthcoming, but not exactly in the hoped-for directions. Scholars often noted that it did "not equate the fetus with living persons." To be sure, the Old Testament placed great value on the fetus and thus viewed abortion as a serious activity, not lightly undertaken. Yet God did not describe the fetus as a being with a soul in the Old Testament (Leviticus 24:18), and killing the fetus was not a capital offense in Mosaic Law (Exodus 21:22–24). Nevertheless, interpreters suggested that the ancient biblical understanding was that God was still involved with the fetus from the moment of conception. It may not yet have been a person, but it was of God and thus sacred.[19]

The main evangelical argument against abortion held that abortion was murder. That the Bible was at best not clear as to whether or not the fetus had a soul and was a person was not the issue. What mattered was the pervasive evangelical conviction that the fetus *was a person or was to become a person.* If it was, to eliminate it was to commit the sin of killing.[20] This belief explained the unquestionable tide of antiabortion opinion. The movement demanded legal action to interfere with some or all abortions. It pointed to biblical passages (such as Jeremiah 1:5, Isaiah 49:5, and Psalms

139:14— 16) which observers thought could be arguments against abortion.[21] Evangelical writers railed at the Burger Court which they saw as a profoundly evil force for permitting, indeed encouraging, abortions. The Supreme Court in this instance was shockingly antireligious. As Harold Lindsell phrased it, the Supreme Court "stands on the side of paganism against Christianity"[22] in its abortion decision. How could anyone who was religious possibly tolerate abortion or institutions which indulged it, since it was "homicide, for it terminated a genuine human life."[23]

   Christianity Today was a determined opponent of abortion. It did not hesitate to provide the most forceful arguments in opposition, including a disturbing description of an actual abortion by a shocked witness. Articles in the magazine demanded to know if in all the shouting about the mother's rights, there was any care for the fetus's rights.[24] Again, the assumption was that the fetus was a person, or nearly so, and therefore had both rights and the glorious love of God. Finally, the poignant question was raised as to whether human beings had the right to control life. Evangelical writers insisted this awesome power lay outside the proper purview of humankind and was God's domain. Abortion was an attempt of the most obvious sort to interfere in that domain and was thus a remarkably impious act.[25]

   The arguments varied, but the cry for government action to reverse the tide of abortions was constant. Pluralism and freedom were words, evangelicals suggested, which could be used to deflect the faithful from their righteous purpose. They must not be permitted to do so. One writer argued that "freedom of choice" was a slogan which in this case was a trap. Freedom had great resonance, but it could not and should not exceed God's limits. Abortion was far more evil than would be the reduced freedom necessary to curtail it.[26]

   The truth of these judgments did not, as Nancy Barcus remarked, relieve people from their responsibility to concentrate on serious arguments. They should avoid the wild and sometimes utterly irrational rhetoric which "pro-life" as well as "pro-choice" elements were all too capable of generating. Most of the writing on abortion within evangelicalism met this test quite well. Polemics surged through the public debate, of course, but despite strong feelings, they were not the order of the day in evangelical outlets.[27]

   The explanation does not lie in the calm that can prevail among people who are of one mind. Argument among evangelicals was common, though there were few thoroughgoing supporters of unrestricted abortion. Some writers did reject the idea of the "right-to-life" amendment to the United States Constitution, because they were uncomfortable at such a blatant attempt to impose their morality on a vast and divided citizenry. On the other hand, it is revealing of the depth of antiabortion sentiment that Senator Mark Hatfield, a reform-oriented evangelical, was a proud cosponsor of the "Right-to-Life" amendment.

Some evangelicals questioned whether or not efforts to regulate or ban abortion by statute were not usurpations of God's prerogative. There was also speculation that legal prohibition of abortions was not likely to succeed. Abortions would always go on no matter what the law said. Some defended the possible legitimacy of abortions in the cases of rape or incest, others in cases where the health of the mother was at stake. Even the most hard-line opponents of abortion knew that concern for life had to include concern for the life of the mother, too.[28]

There were very few evangelical writers in the 1960s and early 1970s who went any further toward a liberal or permissive stand on abortion. The Bible may not have been completely clear, but their Christianity was: human life (or its potentiality) was a gift of God, and abortion was ordinarily a terrible sin.

HOMOSEXUALITY

Homosexuality represented a different situation. Biblical interpretations played both more and less of a role in evangelical discussions of this question than they did regarding abortion. There was no ambiguity about biblical teaching on homosexuality. Both the Old Testament (Leviticus 18:22 and 20:13, Genesis 19:5–9, and Judges 19:22–28) and the New Testament (1 Timothy 1:9, 1 Corinthians 6:9, and Romans 1:27) condemned homosexuality in unequivocal terms. The Bible's teaching was so clear that it did not need the elaborate and sometimes dubious essays in textual exegesis which accompanied too many evangelical reflections on abortion. Thus in discussing homosexuality, writers analyzed the Bible less even as they cited it often in their arguments. Its ready ban on homsexuality made it a handy weapon among people who took it seriously as the word of God.

Through the middle 1970s there was, however, little sign that a crusading attitude toward homosexuality existed. Anita Bryant had not yet emerged as the firebrand opponent of equal rights for homosexuals. The bulk of evangelical writings on homosexuality condemned it, of course, in firm terms. They completely opposed any concessions to homosexuality, such as the idea of homosexual marriage, which they thought contravened the Bible and threatened the traditional family. Harold Lindsell was a typical, if unusually important, voice who asked how evangelicals dared turn away the unmistakable biblical teachings on homosexuality. His *Christianity Today* frequently insisted that those clear teachings must be upheld in both articles and editorials.[29]

A second position softened the usual militancy. One version declared that homosexuality was immoral, but sought to carve a distinction between condemning the homosexual person, an attitude which could be cruel, and the more important and defensible task of resisting homosexual activity, where possible. Another view accepted the practice of homosexuality in private. It was unbiblical and thus ultimately wrong, but no law could get at such private behavior, and Christians must simply accept its inevitability in a sinful world.[30]

A third opinion granted the biblical unacceptability of homosexuality, but insisted that there needed to be far more human love and far less hostility shown to gay people. Like everyone else, homosexuals were God's creatures and they deserved the tender ministering to which all people responded. There were degrees of sympathy here, some observers noting that homosexuality certainly should be forgiven, others going much further and directly attacking "homophobia" and praising the worth of love and friendship in all its forms. This last view did not quite involve an outright repudiation of biblical instruction about homosexuality. It was, rather, an effort to emphasize one part of the Bible, Christ's love for all, over the biblical passages which expressed sharp animus toward homosexuals.[31]

This third position, however, was not the characteristic disposition among writers within evangelicalism on homosexuality. The usual unanimity was hardly surprising in light of the Bible's pointed judgment on homosexual behavior.

WOMEN'S LIBERATION

The rise of a movement toward women's liberation throughout American society in the 1970s was no small phenomenon, as we all know. As was so often the case, evangelical thought did not proceed in isolation from the larger world. Evangelical advocates of new roles for women in the 1970s attacked dominant conservative attitudes as they undertook a vigorous (and, in terms of recent evangelical tradition, a revolutionary) defense of the equality of women in society. They were often met with shock. Most of these evangelical voices were women, who by this very fact of gender modified the intellectual milieu of evangelicalism which in the 1960s was almost entirely the terrain of men. Female names began to dot the journals and book lists; some of these women appeared radical and all of them were controversial. They found their principal outlets in books and periodicals. *Sojourners* was notably open to them, but their view of the world obtained a wide hearing in all sorts of publications. Among these advocates of a new role for women were Lucille Sider Dayton, Nancy Hardesty, Virginia Mollenkott, and Letha Scanzoni, but there were many others as a tide of women's liberation arguments suddenly flooded into evangelicalism in the 1970s. Their names were often hardly known outside of the evangelical world and certainly not in the broader world of women's liberation. But in their environment they were pioneers.

Evangelicals arguing for women's liberation were hardly timid in their approach. They were often strongly committed, and they knew they had to overcome the lack of sympathy pervasive in their religious community.[32] This resistance was true even among male evangelicals who were open to change in other areas of life. Nancy Hardesty testified that there was much opposition to the formulation and declaration of a "proper" stand on women among reform-minded activists at a landmark meeting in Chicago in 1973. All that was accomplished was agreement on what she saw as a limp plank which said: "We call on both men and women to practice mutual submission and active discipleship."[33] Yet this hesitation among otherwise change-minded male evangelicals was nothing compared to the resistance which feminists encountered when they faced conservatives. Evangelical feminists were appalled at those who seemed to believe that "self-abasement" of women was somehow an appropriate Christian doctrine for the 1970s. Surely, argued Letha Scanzoni, there was some tragic misunderstanding of God's teaching. He prescribed service toward God, toward one's spouse, and in all aspects of life, but he did not single out women to slave under the rule of men in some fixed, cosmic chain of being. His plan was for every soul, whether male or female, to serve "out of the fullness of one's own uniqueness."[34] After all, how fundamental was the gap between the sexes? Most of the differences as they applied to social roles, Scanzoni maintained, were learned. She looked to a new diversity of lifestyles and choices tied together by a core of Christian faith to replace old sexual stereotypes.[35]

Change-minded evangelical women believed there had to be significant alteration in the situation of women everywhere. It was common to argue that the spreading desire by women to achieve their full potential as humans was an inescapable fact and that this trend could not be halted by any old-fashioned prejudice, especially since it was progress in the light of God. It represented a dramatic moment in human history, women discovering their personhood in God's universe, something God would applaud.[36]

In the hands of a more utopian vision, such as that advanced by Virginia Mollenkott, the great change promised by a Christianity which broke the shackles of tradition was an advance toward genuine community. This ideal was a Christian world where the struggle between the sexes was over and full equality was achieved in the context of a loving, mutualistic, godly community. It would be a world in which power and ugly contests over power were muted, if not absent. Truly transformed men and truly liberated women would leave this world of power and self-aggrandizement behind, and we would have crossed the bridge "from machismo to mutuality."[37]

In two areas in particular the new mood urged change. First, the pattern of the sexes in marriage needed transformation. Letha Scanzoni argued that an authentic Christian marriage was one of loving equality under God's loving grace. Even those passages in Paul's letters (such as Ephesians 5:21–25) that evangelicals sometimes read to sanction the husband's authority over his wife, she and others read to teach God's authority over both and to command both to have great love for each other as they loved their Lord.[38]

A second area that called for change was in the role of women in the church. While there were somewhat different traditions regarding women in the ministry and other aspects of church life within the many branches of evangelicalism, evangelical feminists were unanimous in complaining that women had an astonishingly small place in their religion. They believed that embarrassing fact should be altered quickly. As Virginia Mollenkott declared, full participation by women in their church was the goal. Some advocated ordination of women and invoked Christ's idea of the priesthood of all believers and the absence of any distinctions in a proper Christianity to justify excluding women. Others objected to what they felt was a foolish waste of female talents and energies, a waste which ignored the fact that God had taken up the cross for all people.[39]

These writers within the evangelical movement who were supportive of women's liberation knew they would get nowhere unless they addressed the principal charge against them. They did not have to pay much attention when their opponents ridiculed their aspirations as no more than a dangerous cultural faddism creeping into the church. But they had to react differently when their critics asserted that their common touchstone, the Bible stood against their hopes and would always do so. Conservatives claimed that supporters of women's liberation within Christianity would have to choose whether or not they were prepared to follow a biblical Christianity. They could have their women's liberation, but not while they claimed to be Bible-believing men and women.

Evangelical supporters of women's liberation, in fact, turned to the Bible as every evangelical did. What they found there, however, was a study in contrast to what their critics supposed was there. They usually built their case on one or more of the following parts of the Bible:

(1) *Jesus' teachings in the Gospels.* Evangelical feminists uniformly contended that Jesus' new covenant was the highest moment of inspiration for women in the Bible. He treated women equally and was by far the best friend—fittingly—women might find in the entire Bible. As Judith Sanderson proclaimed, his attitude was "revolutionary" since he saw women as persons with full human dignity and worth. *Sojourners* even announced that Jesus had been a feminist. His teachings and his life, they declared, wiped out the cultural legacy of inferiority which the Jews transmitted to women. He broke through the Jewish traditionalist environment.[40] Letha

Scanzoni summed up this Jesus: Jesus "does not suggest that the woman is weak and easily deceived. He does not forbid her to study theology or teach his word. He does not blame her for the first sin or remind her that men will rule over her because of it. Rather he treats all daughters of Eve as persons created and re-created in his image and likeness."[41]

(2) Paul. No enthusiast of women's liberation within evangelicalism could possibly stop with the gospel of Jesus. No matter how much they might believe with Virginia Mollenkott that "the *vast preponderance* of biblical evidence points toward an idea of human unity and egalitarian harmony in the body of Christ,"[42] they all knew they had to confront their critics on the critics' strongest biblical ground, the early church and especially the Pauline epistles. As Nancy Hardesty remarked in *Sojourners*, the Bible had to be faced in all its dimensions.[43]

The fact was that conventional conservative opinion had long held women to be secondary to men in church, in marriage, and in most other aspects of life on the basis of New Testament passages from Paul in particular. Paul's teachings, therefore, were a crucial battleground. Evangelical feminists did not always express a great deal of respect for Paul's notions regarding women. One argued that, as "a man socialized in a very chauvinistic society, naturally Paul would believe in the inferiority of women."[44] A more popular way to confront Paul, employed by such figures as Virginia Mollenkott and Lucille Sider Dayton, attempted to distinguish the portions of Paul's writings which were the word of God and those which were no more than cultural artifacts of the first century A.D. The latter, of course, turned out to be the passages which one evangelical labeled "Paul's Bad News for Women." This approach was intensely controversial since it implied a denial of biblical inerrancy. But feminist determination to "de-absolutize the biblical culture" was strong.[45] Mollenkott said that surely Paul and others' "specific comments about women in local first-century congregations" could not reasonably be confused with "God's norm for all places and times."[46] She offered as evidence the fact that in different books of the Bible Paul enunciated contrasting dicta regarding women. For example, his First Epistle to Timothy states that women may not play much of a role in the church while 1 Corinthians provides that they may.

Lucille Sider Dayton put the same point in another manner. She observed that few evangelicals took seriously the admonition in 1 Thessalonians 5:26 to greet all with a kiss or that of 1 Corinthians 11:5 that women must pray with their heads covered. Everyone routinely made a distinction between the time-bound instructions of the New Testament and those that were eternal. This was sensible and natural and should be extended to include New Testament observations about women's proper place. Another observer made the same point and remarked wryly that there was scant respect for Paul's repeated endorsement of chastity among the same people who considered his sentiments about women so sacrosanct.[47]

Feminist evangelicals also felt it appropriate to contrast Paul's declarations with the more binding illumination offered by Christ.[48] By this test Paul's assertions that women ought to keep quiet in church or his command that they ought to obey their husbands took on a new light. Clearly they were not in accord with Jesus as these feminists knew him, the Jesus who swept away all distinctions and united as one all who loved and followed him.

Some reform-minded souls less critical of Paul suggested that there were other sides of him which both conservative and feminist evangelicals should recall. Galatians 3:28 was the key passage: "There is neither Jew nor Greek, slave or freeman, male or female, for all are one in Jesus Christ." But there were others, such as 1 Corinthians 11:11–12: "Nevertheless, in the Lord woman is not independent of man nor man of women; for as woman was made from man, so man is now born of woman. And all things are from God." Paul, by this account, then, sometimes emerged as an ally of evangelical women's liberation, faithfully promoting Christ's belief that we are all one in God and denying that any inequalities were ultimately legitimate or important in God's eyes.[49]

(3) The early church. Another tack was to examine the record of women's participation in the early church, especially that of the first century A.D. Letha Scanzoni and Virginia Mollenkott followed this path at times. Scanzoni concluded that the biblical record revealed that women acted "fully and equally with men" in early Christianity, even though Paul and some other males were all too busily involved in "maintaining the cultural status quo."[50] Virginia Mollenkott cited the service and importance of Priscilla as an example. Both women evangelicals felt that the story of women in the early church was a proud one, and they set out to rectify appalling evangelical ignorance of it.[51]

(4) The Old Testament. The most unyielding ground for feminist evangelicals was not Paul's writings, and certainly not the experience of the early church, but the Old Testament. Conservatives used it along with Paul's epistles to buttress their arguments. Virginia Mollenkott claimed that the Old Testament was not entirely barren of aid for the feminist cause, but it was hard going. Judy Alexander in *The Other Side* contended that the basic question was whether women were people or not, and she felt the Old Testament offered some hope of a proper answer. She observed that the Bible described women as a "helper" from the beginning in Genesis 2, while fifteen other times the Bible used the same word for God, a fact she chose to interpret as a dramatic confirmation of God's estimation of woman's personhood.[52] This was, however, an unusual judgment about the meaning of the Old Testament. More often feminists admitted that, on balance, the

Old Testament was hardly supportive of an image of a God or a godly culture congenial to equality for women.[53]

Of course, much of the reflection about the will of God as it was revealed in the Old Testament focused on the book of Genesis. Opponents of a changed situation for women gave attention to the early chapters of this book on the ground that there, they said, God unmistakably indicated his basic position: man was created first, woman was created from man and for man, and woman was the cause of the first sin. Evangelical feminists routinely denied these interpretations of Genesis. They contended that the order in which man and woman were created had as little significance as the fact that woman was produced from the rib of man. Both proved nothing about God's intentions.[54]

The most controversial work on the appropriate role for women published by an evangelical in the 1970s acknowledged the importance of Genesis and focused almost entirely on this crucial topic of the Old Testament. This was Paul K. Jewett's *Man as Male and Female* published in 1975. Jewett insisted that a close reading of Genesis showed that God created both men *and* women in his image. Thus man—or humankind—was properly understood as a generic term in Genesis and meant both "*male and female.*"[55] God did not, therefore, form woman in man's image with the implication of female inferiority. That Jewish culture lost sight of this fact of basic equality under God which Genesis taught was unfortunate, though it hardly surprised Jewett given the strength of Jewish culture. That Paul often followed his Jewish culture was also no surprise, though Jewett was impressed with Paul's occasional ability to advance beyond his cultural limitations as in Galatians 3:28: "There is neither male nor female; for you are all one in Christ Jesus." That passage proved that Paul could sometimes understand God's wisdom as it was delineated in Genesis. Indeed, Jewett suggests, Galatians 3:28 was the "Magna Carta of Humanity" which could not be ignored by those unprepared for equal marriage, women as clergy, and the sacred Christian goal "to live as man *and* woman in a true partnership of life."[56] This was what the Bible was all about, Jewett proclaimed, its truth from Genesis to Paul, very much including the word of Jesus.[57]

The Resistance to Women's Liberation

The number of articles and books in evangelical publications in the 1970s proposing changes in the life of women was enormous. The emergence of a determined group of evangelicals, usually women, committed to altering what they considered to be evangelical and, more broadly, American attitudes toward women was important. It was a remarkable chapter in the recent history of evangelical thought in the United States as well as a part of a nationwide transformation of attitudes toward women. But this flood of evangelical feminist argument, as we know, hardly went unchallenged. Far from it. The very magnitude of the flood was a good measure of the problem which confronted supporters of the women's movement. The fact is that neither the traditional evangelical attitudes nor the bulk of intellectual opinion among evangelicals in the 1970s proved congenial to women's liberation. Even among many moderate and even radical evangelicals there was a tendency to do little more than endorse the milder assertions of evangelical feminists and move on to topics of greater interest, or of greater comfort.

The argument was fierce. Many of the most articulate voices *for* the traditional perspective were female. The debate within evangelicalism on the proper role for women was largely an argument among women. To be sure, there were negative judgments about feminism by significant male figures. Billy Graham disapproved of women's liberation, and his wife explained that her philosophy was that she should be a homemaker devoted to serving her husband.[58] John W. Montgomery agreed with Graham. He expressed his delight that his wife was on the right track and had not "fallen for" the women's movement.[59] Bert Block insisted in *The Reformed Journal* that only a fully subordinated wife, subordinated to God but also to her husband, approached God's ideal. And so it went.[60]

Harold Lindsell and his *Christianity Today* in the early 1970s was far less antagonistic than these—and other—male evangelicals, but he was inclined to the critical side in the controversy. Lindsell attacked the women's liberation movement because its partisans "have sold out to license" and rank selfishness, caring only about their "rights" and not surprisingly numbering few Christians among their leaders.[61] However, he also called for equal treatment of women in all aspects of church life and granted the obvious: "There are no sections in heaven marked off 'For Men Only.' "[62] *Christianity Today* asserted that the church needed to encourage women to be active and to get involved in religious boards and religious periodicals.[63] At the same time Lindsell did not support measures designed to push women ahead only because they were women or because women had not received fair consideration in the past. Merit, not sex, must be the grounds of advancement.[64] Lindsell's outlook was consistent with *Christianity Today*'s approach to all problems of this type, including race. Individual worth within an integrated world should be all that counts; all other considerations, present and past, should melt away as we became a common humanity.

The acid test of *Christianity Today*, perhaps, was its stand on the Equal Rights Amendment. It first endorsed the amendment unequivocally in 1971, no doubt ruffling a great many evangelical feathers. This step was a less radical move than it seemed later, not only because at first the E.R.A. was popular in the country at large but also because it marked no conversion to feminism or women's liberation by *Christianity Today*. It was rather an acknowledgment that in Jesus Christ there is "neither male nor female." Yet it is equally significant that *Christianity Today* soon began backing away from its endorsement. While it did not withdraw its 1971 stance, it tilted in that direction as evangelical campaigns against the E.R.A. gained steam. For example, in a 1973 editorial, the editors warned that the E.R.A. might allow homosexual marriages or the sharing of toilets by men and women, a standard charge of the more extreme opponents of E.R.A.[65] There was clearly no longer much enthusiasm left by the middle 1970s at a *Christianity Today* which had never been a natural home for evangelical feminists and their cause.

Women led the way in the assault on the feminist movement. Women evangelical writers balked particularly at altering what they held to be divinely instituted leadership for men in marriage. Ephesians 5:22 ("Wives be subject to your husbands") was repeatedly cited to sustain the traditional assumption that God had unmistakably established the wife's role to be that of a loyal and subordinate helper to her husband. To deny this teaching, traditionalists observed, was to confess apostasy from the Bible. Of course, as Robert Culver remarked, God's will here was as apparent to the typical woman as it was to the traditionalist man. "Feminism and legal emancipation have not been able to persuade her out of it."[66]

Conservative women evangelicals such as Maxine Hancock suggested that the entire Bible provided instruction that women were to demonstrate "submission" in all matters, from sex to spirit. To be sure, no Christian marriage could work, they contended, unless both husband and wife were submissive to God, but that did not change what they took to be the duty of wifely obedience within marriage. Hancock appealed to women to be honest. "Let's face it: we have a desire for 'husbanding'—for someone big enough and strong enough to be more than just a partner, someone to take the leadership of the home in every essential way."[67] What upset her was the diminishing number of men able to play this divinely approved role. There were too many weak and passive husbands—and consequently too many disastrous marriages.[68]

The ancient refrain "love, honor, and obey" continued to be of great salience to many writers. Some stressed submission by women in marriage, assuring them that they need not fear this status since God had ordered men to love them. Others saw the matter in a more complex light. One suggested that obedience and hierarchy did not precisely catch the spirit of Paul's divinely ordained rules for relations among the sexes in marriage. The truth was that God favored equality for all people before him. Men and women were equal—and would always be equal—but equal should not be confused with sameness. God had assigned each a unique function. The station and role of the woman within marriage was to assist her husband, not to be the leader. The man, then, was to be superior within the marriage, though not before God.[69]

Gladys Hunt highlighted this popular position among authors who were opposed to the feminist mood in her book *Ms. Means Myself.* For Hunt as for others feminism was a selfish denial of God's creation of women for a sacred mission. Women had been given "an almost intuitive understanding of situations and people's feelings" and "a special sensitivity to the needs of others" for a purpose.[70] Their ministry was to apply this sensitivity to their husbands and children. Serving others in the family context developed women's deepest natures and fulfilled God's teleological plan for them. Hunt contended that most women knew this was what marriage should be. Those who jumped on the bandwagon of feminism were irresponsible and attempting to deny their nature as women. Often feminists were unhappy, Hunt suspected, but they usually had no idea why they were unhappy. "The confusion and tragedy of the contemporary Women's Lib movement is that women are being led to think that children, housework, or the confines of marriage are the cause of their personal frustration when the root cause lies deeply within their own personhood."[71]

Of course, other conservatives also looked to motherhood and service in the family as women's divine vocation. At times in the early 1970s it seemed to some that "mother" was on the way to becoming a "dirty word." But traditional evangelicals protested that motherhood had God's full sanction. Only the devil hated the word "mother." There was widespread belief that most (if not all) women were unusually qualified to be mothers, that "mothering" had to be done and therefore it should be done by those created partly for this purpose and by those who alone had the basic natural talent. Moreover, women who spurned motherhood were widely assumed to be missing not only a divinely established and natural experience, but a special and memorable human experience.[72]

Elizabeth Elliot's *Let Me Be a Woman* (1976) was typical of a spate of evangelical books by women which wholeheartedly agreed on these matters. God made woman, Elliot argued, to be "a helper," and that was what women had to be. "The woman was created from and for the man."[73] The man who Elliot thought should eventually matter to a woman was, of course, the husband, who was "to initiate, command, and dominate."[74] Women were to give all they had in life, not indulge themselves in their egoistic desires. The service they could perform in assisting their husband was, once again, to be effective, loving mothers for the children: "motherhood . . . is the essence of womanhood."[75] While Elliot knew that feminists would accuse her of denigrating women over against men, she did not agree. She did not insult women in pointing out to them God's way and their way to happiness. On the other hand, similar accusations that she did not favor equality did not bother her, since "Equality Is Not a Christian

Ideal" and "it is the nature of the woman to submit."[76] To her such statements would seem strange or infuriating only to individuals who did not know the natural difference between men and women. "Women can and ought to be judged by the criteria of femininity" and nothing else.[77]

Given their conception of the proper place of women within marriage, it will hardly occasion surprise that traditionalists did not want women in the ranks of the clergy. Men were to head God's house too. Women commentators were often especially emphatic on this score. Their judgment was that scripture did not provide for women clergy. How could this indication of God's will be casually overturned by a current fashion? Women could and should be active in the church. They were needed. Yet ordination for women was inappropriate.[78]

In this climate of opinion it was not hard to locate writers who stoutly rejected all efforts to adopt the Equal Rights Amendment. The doctrine of rights was just too selfish as well as too egalitarian for many traditional evangelicals. Women's goal of service could not be helped by the E.R.A. To build a home for her family was a godly act of love and duty, far away from the realm of rights.[79]

These conclusions were supported by the two most prominent assaults on women's liberation from within the evangelical fold in the 1970s, the critique of Edith Schaeffer and of Larry Christenson, in his enormously popular *The Christian Family* (1975). Schaeffer felt sorry for women who spurned the sacred institution of the family and the calling to serve as a mother and housewife. Women's liberation should not mislead women, Schaeffer warned. It could not substitute for family. Moreover, women had to make family work: "Who can make the family a career? The natural person provided with the attributes for that is the woman."[80] Females working outside the home who had children at the same time were neglecting them as well as the larger ideal of family. No woman should fool herself into thinking otherwise.[81]

Christenson designed his energetic and hard-hitting book as a defense of the patriarchal model of male domination in marriage and family life. He made no apologies for his views. God's commands, he was convinced, sanctified this arrangement. Efforts to modify it or to destroy it were sinful blows struck at God. His book contained a long list of injunctions such as "Wives, rejoice in your husband's authority over you! Be subject to him in all things. It is your special privilege to live under the protection of his authority."[82] To be sure, Christenson had demanding standards for husbands also. They were to respect their wives; they were to express great care for them; they were to sacrifice for them and their families; and they were to exercise their God-given authority with great humility. A family was to be a community, and it had no substitute for love among its members.[83]

The Case of Marabel Morgan

No writings on women created more popular controversy in the middle 1970s than did those by Marabel Morgan, especially her book *The Total Woman* (1973). She spoke in religious language, in part, but her book had no prominent church figures promoting it at the start. At the usual, sedate evangelical bookstore it was at first not easily available. That changed soon enough in the face of the enormous demand for *The Total Woman* and Morgan's own claims to be in the evangelical mold.[84] *Christianity Today* not only carried advertisements for her book, but presented an interview with her in which her remarks were treated with full seriousness. Certainly no evangelical could avoid the fact that Morgan claimed to be an active ally, even if not exactly a comfortable one. Like evangelicals, Morgan insisted that marriage could work best only if it were based on Jesus—whom she called the "power Source." She declared that her advice to women was always grounded in the Bible; she was convinced that she had articulated the word of God, a word which spoke above all of the importance of devotion to Jesus, the only answer in life.[85]

Morgan rarely was specific about where the Bible supported her ideas and she never entered the controversies over biblical interpretations regarding the proper roles for men and women. It is not insignificant that the first book in *The Total Woman's* bibliography was Dale Carnegie's *How To Win Friends and Influence People* and not the Bible. Her discussion was far more specific when it came to the techniques of total womanhood than it was in establishing that they had any genuine connection with the scriptures. Moreover, Morgan was completely antagonistic to any aspect of women's liberation. Morgan's book was really for the woman, or perhaps especially the man, for whom the question was completely closed. For the most part Morgan dealt with hints for the unliberated Christian woman, not the relative worth of, or the biblical case for, women's liberation.

These hints had a relation to each other, and together they formed a kind of strategy or approach which might be termed an ethic. Many within and without evangelicalism have bitterly denounced it, of course, but Morgan did not propose an easy or soft ethic. It was in its way the furthest thing from a permissive ethic. It was a program which Morgan knew to be demanding even as she proposed that every woman follow it. It required a woman to be prepared, above all, to give on a regular, indeed constant, basis. Morgan's image of a woman in *The Total Woman* was partly biological; giving was her nature.[86] It was also partly biblical: "It is more blessed to give than to receive."[87] The truth was, she thought, that if women gave they would be happy and have their deep need to be loved fulfilled. The road to love was not through self, but rather through caring for husband and family, a frequent theme in much evangelical literature on women. The form of caring which Morgan thought mattered most to men was admiration. She claimed that men crave admiration more than anything else, and therefore they want a wife who would genuinely, enthusiastically, and endlessly admire them—in all ways. Such admiration, famously, was intended very much to be directed to men's bodies and sexual natures.[88]

But lavishly expressed admiration for one's husband was not enough. Every woman was to make clear, according to the formulas of *The Total Woman*, just how grateful she was to her husband for his support. Every wife was to accept her spouse completely and recognize that "a man's home is his castle. . . . He should feel free in the privacy of his own castle, free to do what he wants." She should adapt those qualities in herself which were not congruent with him.[89] Morgan granted in *The Total Woman* that this would demand a considerable amount of calculated submission by the properly admiring and loving wife toward her husband. There was, however, no other road than a submissive and home-oriented existence for a woman who would be happy and fulfilled. She might work outside the home, but Morgan did not really think this was a good idea even when the home remained first on the wife's agenda. Morgan obviously doubted that it would be easy to do two things at once and do both of them well.[90]

It was in this context that her enthusiasm for sex, that feature of her book that was the most apparent source of uneasiness among some evangelicals, emerged. She believed that men liked attractive women and she was certain that "every man needs excitement and high adventure at home."[91] The best means to provide that was to endeavor to give him "Super Sex," and Morgan had many suggestions how that might be done.[92] To be sure, her unabashed enthusiasm for sex was only part of her program for women. They were not to present themselves entirely as self-conscious sex objects. To Marabel Morgan, former beauty queen and former staffer for Campus Crusade for Christ, the "high adventure" of active sex within marriage was part of a broader framework in which it was a matter of faith that "only when a woman surrenders her life to her husband, reveres and worships him, and is willing to serve him, [does she become] really beautiful to him. She becomes a priceless jewel, the glory of femininity, his queen."[93]

Morgan was an extremist. Her focus on sex was exaggerated even in a time in which some evangelical Christians "rediscovered" sex and sometimes read evangelical works which discussed sexual techniques. Her tenuous links with the Bible and her complete approval of women who were totally in submission to their husbands were also not entirely popular. There was something unmistakably vulgar and crass about her opinions which many evangelical intellectuals did not approve. She was hardly in touch with the understated style of most evangelicals.

Yet Morgan faithfully reflected one (albeit somewhat sensationalized) part of the intense controversy over the proper position of women in America in the 1970s. More central were proponents of biblical feminism such as Nancy Hardesty and Virginia Mollenkott. They were taken far more seriously and written about a good deal more. We may guess that their appearance was much more historic in the evolution of evangelical social thought in America.

But evangelical feminists have not carried the field. They entered the lists — and they continue to do so. By 1975 they had organized an active Evangelical Women's Caucus under the direction of Lucille Sider Dayton and also the journal *Daughters of Sarah*, but there is little evidence that they have won over evangelicalism to feminism.[94] Even among more intellectual evangelicals, as among other Americans, there are other opinions and other values.

Chapter Eleven

EVANGELICAL CHRISTIANITY, COMMUNISM, AND VIETNAM

EVANGELICAL WRITERS REJECTED COMMUNISM every bit as thoroughly and unanimously as one would expect. A few voices expressed interest in "liberation theology," but they were muted and rarely attracted to the forms which built on Marxism. The most important question about the relation of evangelicalism and Marxism and communism in the 1960s and early 1970s was the depth of evangelical concern over them. There were those in the movement who were more alarmed at the existence or threat of communist practice and Marxist theory than at any other danger. This was most true of the most conservative fundamentalist evangelicals who continued to live up to their long-standing reputation for strident anticommunism in the 1960s and 1970s. The contest with communism was significant for them long after many others had banked the fires of the Cold War. Fundamentalists had gained the most attention for their zealousness in the 1950s when Carl McIntire cooperated with Senator Joseph McCarthy and identified Methodist bishops who were "soft on Communism," or Billy James Hargis set up his Bible Balloon Project, sending 50,000 balloons containing selected Bible passages sailing to Eastern Europe. Yet their campaign went on even when the publicity largely stopped. Their only real, if fleeting, moments of notoriety in recent history were Carl McIntire's March for Victory during the Vietnam War, which did attract thousands of the faithful in 1971, and his later public denunciation of President Nixon's popular trip to Communist China.[1]

There was no doubt among these men that communism was a total evil, some said satanic in origin. After all, communism challenged Christianity itself as well as the best of the libertarian and constitutional tradition of America. Communism was on the march everywhere and no one was prepared to stop it. America was on the retreat before Communism, and we had to rally if we were to reverse our sagging fortunes.[2]

213

The extremists felt increasingly lonely in their concern. Hargis sensed that in the 1970s no one—or at least too few—understood the danger in our country. The evil had spread: "Our country is sick, and the weakness is Communist infiltration."[3] The Kennedys, ever a favorite target, alive or dead, did not help. Martin Luther King, Jr., with his "nonviolent" agitations, did not help either. Certainly the National Council of Churches, compromised by its ultraliberal and procommunist politics, did not. Nor did Billy Graham, who was unwilling to denounce all anti-Vietnam demonstrators with sufficient vigor and who failed to see Vietnam as Armageddon.

Carl McIntire once again zeroed in on Graham. He was not only faint-hearted, in McIntire's opinion, in reacting to communism; he was down-right soft on communism. Graham's eagerness to visit communist nations was McIntire's acid test, one which Graham, of course, failed to pass. Hargis concentrated on the role that liberals in all aspects of American life played as the chief factor in communist advances at home and abroad. Liberalism and communism were intimately connected, since liberalism was really "Marxist liberalism."[4] Liberalism like socialism like rock music like dope were "all the different faces of the world-wide movement of Satan to enslave the world."[5]

Where else could one turn? Not the United Nations, certainly, because communist dupes were already well in control of that body. Not the United States government. It was honeycombed with socialists and liberals who proposed to substitute government rules and edicts for God. Not the radicals in the land, who were always stirring the pot "to push their own brand of politics at the expense of religious truths."[6] Certainly not the campus revolutionaries since what they did had its origins in the "diabolical hand of communism": "I don't hesitate to say Communists are behind every single campus revolt without exception."[7] All roads were blocked. All roads, that is, but the road of Christ. The American Christians, the real ones, knew this fact and they would travel on not in expectation of early victory, but certain of ultimate triumph over demonic communism. The final hour approached. It would be a great day for Christians and a terrible day for their opponents.[8]

These views were not solely characteristic of rather isolated figures such as McIntire and Hargis. Many other conservatives shared them, if not their proponents' sometimes overzealous language. For example, it was the opinion of Harold Lindsell that communism was very much on the march, that it infested the New Left and had a surprising amount of indirect influence on radical evangelicals. Christianity Today was always alert to what it saw as the communist danger. Bill Bright of the Campus Crusade for Christ clearly feared the advances of communism and worked to provide Christian resistance. The list could easily go on, although it does not justify the assertion in Sojourners that anticommunism obsessed the evangelical community and that there was an "Anti-Communist Captivity of the Church."⁹

The truth was something quite different. Overall, concern with communism was hardly at the heart of evangelical political thinking in the 1960s and 1970s. In no way did communism, even in the darker days of Vietnam, conquer or dominate the evangelical imagination. Fear never became paranoia.

This fact is one more sign of the diversity of political attitudes which emerged in the faith. Conservative opinion was now no longer so significant, and right-wing anticommunism went out of style (if not out of existence). There was, however, a good deal of discussion of communism and Marxism. It may not have been at the top of the agenda by any means, but it was definitely on the agenda, as it had to be in that age of our involvement with Vietnam. No consideration of evangelical political thinking may avoid probing three sides of their concern. First, there was much reflection on Marxism as a philosophy, and there were frequent attempts to refute or deny its premises and values. Second, there was much consideration of the actions of communist movements in assorted parts of the world. In some evangelical quarters there was a kind of watch of communism abroad year after year. Finally, there was Vietnam. No issue, no struggle, no country, no contact with communists produced more agony within evangelicalism — and none produced anything like the flood of words about that controversy. Vietnam was the locus of evangelical division over communism.

MARXISM

One might not have expected reflective meditations on Marxism in evangelical intellectual discourse. Unbending hostility toward communism hardly leads to an objective exploration of Marxism as a philosophy. Yet Marxism was a subject of some fascination among a number of evangelical thinkers, and not all of that interest derived from a desire to register complaints against what they universally agreed was a false doctrine. The explanation for this interest had to do with evangelical recognition that Marxism in theory (and communism in practice) was an ominous threat to Christianity. If interest was sometimes analytical, though mostly normative, the source lay in the common, though not universal, assumption that error needed to be comprehended in theory as well as practice.

Interested evangelicals argued the case against Marxism vigorously. They proceeded from a level of understanding of Marxist writings which was sometimes sophisticated, though there was rarely evidence of any in-depth mastery of the corpus of Marx's work. Some of the approaches did not get beyond simply citing selected quotations from Marx, but often they were more elaborate. One evangelical writer even discussed the post– World

War II Marxist-existentialist, Merleau-Ponty. More often, the evangelical authors spent less time reporting what Marx or Marxists said than discussing basic Marxist doctrine.[10]

The evangelical commentators directed most of their attention by far to Marx's self-proclaimed atheism and Marxism's active encouragement of atheism. It was eminently logical for evangelical writers to concentrate on these facts, though it may seem surprising to secular intellectuals. The usual debates between Marxists and their opponents do not focus on this issue. But a religious perspective was always preeminent in the evangelical assessment of Marxism, and it was only natural that no aspect of Marxism would cause greater discontent among evangelicals than its open allegiance to atheism.

The evangelical writers insisted on the centrality of atheism to Marxism. Without atheism, they wrote, there would be no Marxism. Their Marx was determined to destroy religion and replace it with a world which was frankly "atheistic and godless." This was why, above all, so many objected to the fashion among some Christians of "liberal" persuasions of pursuing Marxist-Christian dialogues. They asked what was the use unless Marxism metamorphosed into a world view that abandoned its animus toward religion? If it would not, and clearly it would not, then why bother with dialogue? What good could come of a dialogue with a perspective which denied from the start what all true Christians must believe, the reality and glory of God?[11]

Atheism, some also charged, meant a commitment to materialism, which few Marxists sought to deny. A materialist world presented a horrifying vision to evangelicals. It blotted out the realm of the spirit and the soul and described men and women as mere phenomena of matter. They lost their intangible, but very special, essence. Materialism in its Marxist incarnation reduced human action, thought, culture, and institutions, in the end, to mere phenomena of economic matter, of economic systems. Human agency greatly diminished in significance and the special spiritual spark that distinguished every individual disappeared as well. Moreover, such a materialist view of the world encouraged the triumph of relativism. It made all claims to truth into creations of the brute facts of economic structures, and therefore abandoned us to a relativist outlook that was already far too widespread. It promoted an utter collapse of traditional morality based on absolute standards.[12]

If Marxism utterly failed to comprehend the spiritual side of reality, and represented a sadly partial view of the universe, it likewise failed to understand the sinful aspect of existence. Evangelical thinkers complained that Marxism just did not appreciate the dimensions and dynamics of human fallibility. This made Marxism a dangerous doctrine, promising what it could never deliver, making it likely to deliver only disaster. Marxism necessarily "promised too much" because it overlooked "sinful man." Over and over evangelicals, even those writing in *Sojourners*, made the same claim. Marxism was inadequate because it "underestimates sin's depths."[13]

Evangelical thinkers held Marxism doubly at fault. It was at fault because it entertained the idea of "the perfectibility of human behavior"[14] and because it went further by holding that this idea was actually true. This self-confidence was simply another statement of Marxist overestimation of human ability and promise. The proper remedy for such a double error was a healthy appreciation of sin.[15]

Even those attracted to the concern in Marxism for social justice — and there were some — were uncomfortable with Marxism's silence on the sin of power. Marxism might confront such problems as greed and economic and social injustice, at least in theory, but it did not touch "the primal struggle for power and control pervading Marxism and capitalism alike."[16] No matter how much Marxism spoke to the abuse of wealth and property, if it did not address power in all forms, no matter who held it, it remained isolated from the real world of sin. It was necessarily inadequate.[17]

The idea that Marxism was flawed by its inattention to the inescapable fact of sin was, some evangelical writers thought, revealed in yet another way. Class struggle was a central part of Marxist dogma. Class struggle was obviously about selfish, sinful group activity, to express its essence in non-Marxist vocabulary, and Marxists really believed in its eventual demise in history. The error here, their critics suggested, was that even when they did catch a glimpse of this form of "sin," they fell into their illusion that people could abolish it. Harold O. J. Brown called this hope preposterous: "Class struggle cannot bring the millennium, but it could bring back barbarism."[18] Escaping evil would not be as easy as Marxists thought. It would not come by struggle among classes or the destruction of one or another set of social conditions. Nor could it arrive ushered in on the wings of a supposedly ideal class like the proletariat, actually or potentially exempted from sin.[19]

The great difficulty here, as several observers saw it, was that a humanist heresy motivated Marx. He believed, they insisted, not only that men and women could make their way out of a condition of sin, but also that they could do it themselves, by collective human action as part of a revolutionary movement. Evangelical commentators asserted that this was quite impossible, something that Marx as a historian should have understood. There was no such escape on earth, and certainly none without the active care and involvement of God. One sought to hope in God rather than in inevitably sinful humans.[20]

Of course, the evangelicals sometimes noted with dismay that Marxists respected people on the basis of their class. While the working class were or could be impressive beings, the middle and upper classes were not. Marxist hatred for the rich was, to say the least, suspicious in such alleged admirers of humanity. It was also frightening in its passion. Christianity cared for all human souls, or at least it had a mission to do so, since God loved everyone, rich or poor. They were all equal in his sight. God—and not some historical utopia—was the end of the class struggle.[21]

From these writers' view, the point went beyond the inconsistencies in Marxist class hatred or the Marxist unwillingness to accept the limits sin placed on their dreams. Placing the human person at the center of the universe and defining the ideal world as one in which men and women on their own achieved (one version of) human perfection were the truly fundamental Marxist errors. Such assumptions amounted to "absolutizing human activity." The Christian could accept only one absolute, and that was God, just as the Christian knew that only God could save anyone. All hope rested in him.[22]

Evangelical thinkers often criticized Marx for other reasons. Some of the more conservative objected to Marx's affection for economic and social equality. They argued that Jesus' concern for all souls did not mean he favored a leveling down of everyone to the same economic or social level. His mission was to save souls, not legislate earthly laws, institutions, or practices. Others complained about Marx's supposed determinism and lauded Christianity, which they saw as committed to the reality and importance of human choice. Few of these commentators knew much about the humanistic Marx who some Western Marxists liked, the Marx who was open to human action and honored its major role in history. It did not matter, though, because no version of Marx could sanctify choice to the extent which these Christians considered essential for a moral world.[23]

Some objected to Marxism because of what they took to be the inaccuracy of its extensive historical claims. Evangelical detractors thought it was ironic that a doctrine which proclaimed its reliance on history proved to be so manifestly poor as a predictor of history. Almost a century had passed since Marx's death, but there had been no collapse of the middle classes, no final crisis of capitalism, and no Marxist revolutions in the West.[24] As a result, some proposed to call Marxism not a philosophy or a science, but a sign of the end, or a temporary Christian heresy, or a temporary outbreak of demonic energy which happened from time to time in history. Evangelical views of the place of Marxism in human history differed, but there was no disagreement that the true teaching of history was that at the second coming Jesus and not Marx would be triumphant.[25]

Yet there was a considerable lack of ease among informed critics of Marxism at its movement toward respectability in the larger culture—and even in evangelicalism. They believed the arguments against it were strong and convincing, but were pained that not everyone respected this truth. Evangelical writers on the subject found especially frustrating the attraction Marx had had for many intellectuals in the past twenty-five years in the

West and in the Third World. They complained (accurately enough) that Marxism and communism got extensive analysis in major public and private universities and colleges in the United States, not to mention Western Europe, while the Christian religion often received scant mention and never seemed to merit the approval sometimes accorded Marxism.[26] They were also well aware of the growth of the "theology of liberation" in Christianity in the 1960s and 1970s. They knew that many Third World Christian theorists, especially in Latin America, saw many similarities in Christianity and Marxism, including a stress on human liberation that included liberation from poverty, injustice, and exploitation and an emphasis on vigorous (and not always peaceful) action to achieve these goals. Evangelicals usually repudiated any claims of Christian and Marxist congruence for reasons which we have already noted, most of all, perhaps, because of Marx's frank avowal of atheism.[27] There were sympathetic students of the theology of liberation, radical evangelicals impatient with the mainstream's tendency to rationalize the status quo, but they rarely accepted liberation theology completely. Marx's *Capital* was hardly the Bible.[28]

THE COMMUNIST MOVEMENT

Evangelical treatment of communism as a factor in actual world political life was harsh. Many discussions of communism were "scarcely above the level of propaganda," a fact which is a good guide to the general disposition of those who wrote on the subject.[29] They may well have been an unrepresentative group, since they probably were unusually conservative compared to the mainstream of thoughtful evangelicals, based on other remarks which often accompanied their denunciations of communism. Yet no evangelicals, whatever their political disposition, showed any respect for communist practice. Condemnation was universal and routine. It was common to view communism as a deadly (and all too effective) enemy to Christianity, to the United States, and to all those "who give allegiance to justice and freedom."[30] The most frequent characterization of communism, especially among more conservative spokesmen, was self-consciously simple and direct. It was evil, and in that light, nothing more need be said about it.

Some evangelical comment on communism proceeded in less sweeping terms and focused on the status of communism in particular countries — especially as it inhibited or tolerated the progress of the Christian church. Once again, the conservative mainstream led the way in reporting on communism in particular nations, though it was not alone. Not surprisingly, conditions in Russia stimulated more comment than did the situation in any other communist center. *Christianity Today* followed developments regarding the Christian church in Russia closely throughout the 1960s and later.[31] There were also a number of books produced for American audiences with titles such as *Christians Under the Hammer and Sickle* (1972) and *Miracle in Moscow* (1975). These volumes reported the persecution of Christian Protestants in the U.S.S.R. in detail. They often contained accounts of secret meetings, Bible smuggling, illegal religious activity, and an entire underground world struggling to survive the relentless opposition of Soviet authorities. These often firsthand accounts were rarely political in the sense of explicitly spelling out the political lesson of the evil of communist government, but this was an obvious secondary theme of them all.[32] When they were political in an overt manner, it was to warn Americans of the colossus that atheistic, communist Russia was—and of its threat: "Americans . . . do not take the rise of atheistic Russia seriously. They do not see that when godlessness is married to enormous military strength and driven by a mania of historical destiny to conquer the world, the result is chaos for all."[33]

Their more important primary theme was the story of Christians who survived persecution and did not bow before the terror of the Soviet form of politics. The "miracle" of the persistence and growth of Christianity in the U.S.S.R. was real, and it should surprise no one that some evangelicals found it inspiring that the church somehow prospered in the corners of a hostile Russian world.[34] The writings of the faithful did not exude a false confidence of imminent triumph in Russia. Not at all. There was a continuing sense that the contest in Russia was hard and would continue to be so far into the future. But there was also an excitement over the tenacity of Christians in such a hostile world.

Christianity Today did not offer a warm embrace to those East European countries where the religious climate for Christians was notably better than it was in Russia, although the magazine did note their generally better conditions for Christians.[35] Evangelical discussion about Communist China started from the premise that Christianity no longer existed there. It was with this fact in mind that several writers disagreed with right-wing opinion and welcomed Nixon's initiatives with China. They felt that communication with China was the only chance Christianity would have to break into what had never proved to be a fertile mission field. Only through the gradual reduction of barriers between China and the West could Christianity begin edging through the bamboo curtain. Some told Nixon that he ought to suggest to Chinese leaders a relaxation of restrictions on religious freedom. They did not cheer him when he obviously failed to do so.[36]

Evangelicals gave little or no consideration to the progress of communism in Africa. The days of worry over Marxist penetration there lay in the future. There was, however, some attention given to communist movements in Latin and South America. Cuba got as little praise as one would expect. Even *Sojourners* carried an unfavorable assessment of a revolution which promoted education and health but paid no respect to the idea of human political rights. *Christianity Today's* coverage of Chile was distinctly hostile to the Allende regime and happy at its demise.[37]

The question, at least for *Christianity Today* and those of its persuasion, was always the same: What was the record of communism in its dealings with Christian churches and Christian peoples? The answer varied to some extent from regime to regime, but nowhere was it satisfactory. Communism in practice, like Marxism in theory, was a path of failure.

VIETNAM

The Vietnam War best captured the dynamics and ambiguities of evangelical attitudes toward Marxism and communism. Evangelicals had much to say on this topic from the 1960s through the termination of United States involvement in 1974 and the subsequent "fall" of South Vietnam. Like all of us in those years they were deeply involved in the Vietnam War.

Evangelical writing about the war took two forms. One was a familiar enough fascination with the progress of Christianity in war-torn Vietnam while the second dealt with the war more directly and with the American role in it; these two approaches were not always separated. Most discussions of Christianity in Vietnam inevitably concerned Protestant missionaries there, rather than the dominant Roman Catholic church. Some of what was expressed was a persistent belief, especially in *Christianity Today*, that Protestant Christianity was making enormous gains among the Vietnamese people. At moments, indeed, there was an excited sense that Vietnam perfectly exemplified what a joyful Christian revival should look like. Rarely did anyone broach the subject of the part which the American presence played in creating the alleged revival. One reviewer in *Christianity Today* was virtually alone in suspecting that crusading American anticommunist missionaries endangered not only themselves but also Christianity (which should know no nation) in Vietnam.[38]

That there was little self-consciousness about the intermingling of strident anticommunism and missionary endeavors for Christianity is not startling in retrospect because evangelical writers often saw the two causes as part of the same struggle. Most thoughtful evangelicals were firm supporters of the Vietnam War, some to the very end.[39] Division eventually appeared, however, and it tore at the evangelical fabric much as it tore at the larger American nation. The new socially concerned, and sometimes radical, evangelicals were by the late 1960s more often than not hostile critics of the conflict in Vietnam. In the evangelical fold as elsewhere in America Vietnam reaped a bitter harvest which included more than irreplaceable lives and lost treasure.

Through the late 1960s references to the Vietnam War in evangelical

books and periodicals were almost always favorable. Sometimes they endorsed the war in the name of anticommunism and the defense of human
liberty.[40] Sometimes they included denunciations of opponents of the war,
such as Harold O. J. Brown's attack on those doves who actively protested
the war. Brown spoke for those who were angry because "the domestic
agitation for peace in Vietnam at any price has played into the hands of
our external enemies."[41] What criticism there was of the war focused on
the unwillingness of the Johnson administration to "go for victory," as
Harold John Ockenga urged in a 1968 report on Vietnam.[42]

Few influential figures in the evangelical world of the 1960s broke
rank. Carl F. H. Henry was an exception, of course. Henry was a long-time
supporter of the war, but he observed with mounting unease the growing
consequences of the commitment to Vietnam. He saw the growing division
in the country, and he worried about it.[43] Mark Hatfield was the first prominent evangelical voice to raise persistent and pointed doubts about Vietnam, and he received vituperative criticism for doing so. We have already
considered his evolution on Vietnam and its results in Chapter Six. Hatfield's transformation was a gradual phenomenon, though his opposition
was in the open long before the publication of his book, *Conflict and
Conscience*, in 1971.[44]

During the late 1960s there was an occasional editorial in *Christianity
Today* urging that evangelicals, like other citizens, should not support or
oppose the war lightly. Everyone had an awesome responsibility to study
the issues carefully and to ask if his or her own prejudices corresponded
with God's commands. But the magazine's usual attitude toward Vietnam
betrayed no caution in those days. For example, an editorial in 1968 attacked those who counseled compromise with or retreat from our communist opponents in Vietnam. We had to pursue the war vigorously because
the United States and "Communist tyranny" were locked in a struggle which
we could not and should not avoid. We had to stand up to the "power-
hungry world-wide conspiracy" of communism, and in the 1960s Vietnam
was the decisive battleground.[45]

As late as 1969, *Christianity Today*, under Harold Lindsell's editorship,
was clear that in its judgment our participation in the Vietnam War was a
commitment that must be honored. Growing national sentiment for a withdrawal from Vietnam did not affect opinion at *Christianity Today*, where
the idea of quitting seemed "tragic." Yet there was no hiding the fact that
national discontent over the Vietnam War had begun to affect this respected
periodical. It issued calls for prayer. It requested that President Nixon at
least listen to the cries, the pleas of the millions of dissenters. It demanded
that Vice-President Agnew be quiet and stop fanning the flames of passion
and disunity. It conceded that for *Christianity Today*, as for everybody else,
the war had dragged on far too long.[46]

During this period of the first Nixon presidency (1969 to 1972), the ardor for the war cooled dramatically among evangelicals, but there was no complementary shift to an antiwar position. *Christianity Today* reflected the mainstream and took the road of supporting Richard Nixon and his alleged policy of achieving "peace with honor." The magazine spoke for the considerable body of evangelicals who proposed to support Nixon and hope for the best. This was the constant theme of *Christianity Today* editorials. Give Nixon a chance, they said, and they supported every move he made from his Vietnamization plan to his cease-fires. This stance sharpened during the 1972 presidential election, when McGovern criticized Nixon on Vietnam. *Christianity Today* urged that "all Americans, and especially Christians, should stand by the President, even if they think his policy is mistaken," at least until the election returns were in. This was the stance of Harold Lindsell, and he remained faithful to it until the Vietnam War was over for America and painful post-Vietnam reappraisals began.[47]

By the early 1970s there were few well-recognized evangelical voices who were any longer leading a charge to fight on in Vietnam. Those days were suddenly over. Yet even as enthusiasm for the Vietnam War visibly eroded, many evangelicals, like *Christianity Today*, remained steadfast in their bitter judgments of those who had sought to end the war. This was an enduring sentiment. It continued a long and active tradition of widespread evangelical animus toward dissenters on Vietnam who turned out to be right—but not loved. *Christianity Today*, as so often, addressed the general mood. It had long attacked clergy who were dissenters. For example, its editorials in 1967 repeatedly criticized protesting ministers and priests. They were hypocrites who opposed violence in Vietnam, but were violent themselves when they promoted social change at home. They may have claimed to pursue "nonviolent" methods, but they had a way of stimulating violence and justifying it when it broke out among "disadvantaged" people. Their actions in opposition to the Vietnam War undoubtedly assisted the communists and might be seen as treasonable. Certainly, they lacked judgment. In later years there were angry denunciations of priests who damaged the Washington office of Dow Chemical, the maker of napalm, and theology students at Boston University who held a memorial service for Ho Chi Minh.

Clergy were not the only ones at fault, however, in that age in which so many people protested the Vietnam War. *Christianity Today* admonished participants in one mass peace march in Washington, D.C., to direct their protests to the Communists in Hanoi. It vehemently denounced entertainer Eartha Kitt for daring to object to the Vietnam War while she was at the White House. It recommended to three congressmen who tried to get arrested in a war protest demonstration what it considered to be a far more admirable model the record of a member of the House from Florida who had answered 2,242 roll calls in a row.[48]

By the early 1970s, of course, *Christianity Today* hardly represented all shades of opinion on Vietnam or anything else. The repudiation of the war had spread among evangelical intellectuals, especially younger ones, as it had elsewhere in society. The split in America finally came home to evangelicalism. The most important single fruit of that division was the founding of *The Post-American*, as we know, and the emergence of articulate voices who castigated both the Vietnam War and the long-time evangelical apologia for it. While *The Post-American* was too "extreme" for many thoughtful people within the evangelical world, it did accurately catch the spirit of disenchantment and impatience which many younger evangelical writers felt in the early 1970s.

Writers in *The Post-American* unequivocally denounced the war. They contended it was a product of the unchristian and unbiblical notion that it was all right "to kill for profit and power."[49] They suggested that the war had a great deal to do with the efforts of American elites to pursue their objectives—sometimes described as "the development of S.E. Asian economy in accordance with American corporate and military interests"—whatever the cost to others.[50] The cover of one issue of the magazine had lines of grave markers on it, lest anyone not realize how serious these costs were, or forget the war's "slaughtering thousands of innocent lives and destroying the basis of an entire society."[51] *The Post-American* proclaimed that the solution to Vietnam was a prompt withdrawal by the United States. In its first issue in the fall of 1971, the periodical published "A Joint Treaty of Peace Between the People of the U.S., South Vietnam and North Vietnam" providing for exactly this solution.[52]

Of course, the end did come for the United States in Vietnam. *Christianity Today* greeted the final steps toward ending the years of involvement with detachment and passivity. Its editorials during the years from 1973 to 1975 were bland, lacking much indication of a clear will or message. It had nothing profound to say. Clearly, its editors experienced a certain disgust at how the war had ended, a process that increased their respect for neither South Vietnam nor the United States. Neither nation proved to have backbone in the end. Yet, like a number of well-known evangelicals surveyed for a report in its pages, *Christianity Today* favored binding up the wounds and looking to the future. It hoped that American citizens would learn to depend on the Christian faith, their only certain and trustworthy support. The immediate tasks included assisting the Vietnamese refugees. *Christianity Today* dutifully urged its readers to shoulder their part of the burden, despite the fact that many of the refugees were not Christians and most of those who were Christians were Roman Catholics. Aside from dealing with refugee problems, however, and the expression of pious wishes that evangelical Christians and Christian institutions left behind in Vietnam would prosper, *Christianity Today* set its face away from Vietnam as an era that was past.[53]

At no time, however, did the magazine suggest that apologies were in order to anyone regarding the Vietnam imbroglio. It manifested none of the guilt feelings which some evangelicals expressed. When evangelical Congressman John B. Anderson stated that Vietnam was a ghastly error for which he, among so many others, had to share the responsibility, the evangelical mainstream did not agree. *Christianity Today* offered only silence to such declarations. Silence and a determination to move on to other worlds without guilt or regret was its policy. After all, it was not evangelicals (in general) who failed in Vietnam, but American leaders and the will of the American people.[54]

On the other hand, *The Post-American* and later *Sojourners* constantly returned to Vietnam. They insisted that Vietnam was nothing which could — or should — be forgotten. Jim Wallis claimed we needed to remember Vietnam and learn from it no matter how much the lesson hurt. Otherwise, biblical Americans, both as Christians and as participants in our nation, would soon repeat their roles in the heinous crimes Wallis thought Vietnam symbolized.

Wallis did not mince words. He argued that the major truth about the horror of Vietnam was that American imperialism caused it. Our imperialism had its origins in our undemocratic political and economic institutions and their tendency to take advantage of people at home and abroad whenever they could get away with it. It also had roots in the casual irresponsibility of Americans, who seemed all too prepared to justify exploitation when it took place in far away places such as Vietnam. Finally, Wallis placed a good share of the blame on the ugly reality of white racism in his native land. As he put it, the "cultural genocide inflicted upon the Vietnamese people is tragically consistent with America's historic treatment of racial minorities."[55]

Radicals, including Wallis, had many unflattering things to say about the American church, too, for its alliance with American nationalism, a nationalism which eventually trapped our country in Vietnam. Writer after writer in *The Post-American* indicted all elements of American Christendom for their tardy discovery of Vietnam and their belated (when it existed at all) record of opposition to that terrible war.[56]

Moreover, when the war did end, writers in *Sojourners* worried that the United States had scarcely become wiser as the result of experience. Our national pride, ever dangerous and always unchristian, remained intact. The old arrogance endured. Vietnam demonstrated its folly, but few cared. It was strangely true that "rarely in the history of war have the victors remained so vanquished and the defeated so haughty."[57]

CONCLUSIONS

After 1974 concerns with the philosophy of Marxism, the advance of communism, and the legacy of the Vietnam War did not disappear from evangelical writings. But there is no doubt that interest in them dimmed. Marxism and communism were still enemies, and dangerous ones. Yet after Vietnam it was no longer clear how evangelical Christians should proceed to meet the threat. Moreover, domestic issues quickly came to the fore, above all the Watergate affair and the 1976 presidential election.

Chapter Twelve

CONCLUSION: FROM WATERGATE TO CARTER

THE EVENTS OF THE YEARS 1973 to 1976 brought politics into painful prominence not only in America at large but also among evangelicals. Once again, events in the larger culture set the agenda for evangelical writers on politics and society. Watergate eventually convulsed evangelical opinion and led to some sustained reflections on America three-quarters of the way through the twentieth century. But Watergate did not permanently depress most thoughtful evangelicals — nor were they usually willing to see its significance as a tale of the decline of America in our time. The 1976 election followed the low point of 1974 and Watergate. The year 1976 found evangelicals themselves courted by press and politicians as never before. It was also the year in which one of their own was elected president of the United States. No wonder many evangelicals remained convinced that America — and even American politics — contained hope as well as failure.

WATERGATE

The Watergate crisis exploded over a nation which shortly before had chosen Richard M. Nixon to be president in the landslide election of 1972. There were divisions among evangelical intellectuals over the 1972 presidential race, but there seems little doubt that the great majority backed Nixon in his contest with McGovern. Even for many reform-minded evangelicals McGovern represented an untested and excessively radical alternative. Nixon was a Republican and he was also far closer to the evangelical mainstream than McGovern was. Indeed, even as the events of 1973 and 1974 unfolded inexorably toward the termination of the Nixon presidency, *Christianity Today* sometimes contained references that suggested its reluctance to abandon the Nixon it and others had for so long supported. For example, early in the Watergate hearings *Christianity Today* complained

227

that important legislative business was being neglected while Congress involved itself in a witch hunt that trod upon certain individuals' rights.[1]

Overall, however, *Christianity Today* took quite a different tack as Watergate unfolded, one which illustrates the pervasiveness of Nixon's loss of legitimacy among evangelicals in his last year or two as president. *Christianity Today* called for a full report on the Watergate affair and insisted that evidence implicating Nixon in dirty political activities, if it existed, be fully aired. Later, editorials denouncing the shame of Watergate appeared, coupled with firm if as yet somewhat naive requests that the guilty be brought to justice.[2]

The style of the Nixon and the other Watergate conspirators damaged their reputation among evangelicals as much as their more serious deeds. Their proclivity for vulgar and profane language hurt them among evangelicals, for whom personal piety often mattered a great deal. Nixon suffered in this regard because he had crafted such a false image of pietism, which many evangelicals had believed.[3]

Christianity Today was hardly among the first to declare that there was enough evidence for impeachment, but it did insist that Nixon had to be far more forthcoming than he ever was willing to be in 1973 and then 1974. This was its "message to the President." Eventually, of course, such calls became pointless, but spokesmen like John Anderson and *Christianity Today* remained anxious to get at the entire truth. Perhaps this reflected a lingering hope that somehow Nixon would turn out not to be guilty of obstruction of justice, although even that hope was eventually abandoned. The tone of Watergate articles in *Christianity Today* in 1974 increasingly suggested that Nixon was guilty and favored proceeding with the impeachment and removal process in service of the full truth.[4]

When it was all over, *Christianity Today* placed the seal of mainstream respectability on the demise of its one-time ally Richard Nixon and his entire administration. From "Spiro Agnew, whose 'law and order' mentality was grossly at variance with his personal practices," to Richard Nixon, whose "guilt was established beyond reasonable doubt," a disastrous era had ended.[5] All the old Nixon voices fell silent. His once powerful evangelical front melted away.

How clear this was became apparent when Gerald Ford pardoned Nixon. Evangelical leaders had warmly received Ford when he stepped into the presidency. His professed religious leanings, his son studying for the ministry in an orthodox seminary, and his contacts with Midwest evangelical circles all stood him in good stead. Yet his decision to pardon Nixon received sharp criticism. *Christianity Today* did not approve, and it editorialized in opposition. To let Nixon go without punishment did not seem at all appropriate, even though he had never admitted his guilt. To deny pardon to one who maintained his innocence while offering it to one who confessed his guilt was not inconsistent. If the magazine was to maintain its credibility, it had to condemn the pardon, since it had always advocated individual responsibility in the world, though it was prepared to relax that rigorous ethic before the repentant. A pardon simply was not right for a man who had not confessed his sins. Writing in *Christianity Today*, Harold Kuhn worried about the pardon from another angle. He questioned how one could support a pardon for Nixon and yet oppose one for draft evaders. Since he, like others at *Christianity Today*, was not prepared to pardon Vietnam evaders, justifying a pardon for Nixon posed a serious problem.[6]

Another voice which joined the chorus of disapproval was that of Carl Henry. In his opinion the pardon was inappropriate because it confused two important but quite different realms: justice and mercy. Henry believed that politics in its legal dimension should properly focus on matters of order and must therefore employ punishment as much as the Christian virtue of mercy. The realm of mercy, especially if it dominated politics, obscured God's expectations that the political order achieve justice. To be consistent, that same logic had to apply to Richard Nixon.[7]

John B. Anderson complained that evangelicals and their spokesmen were often among the last to understand and condemn Watergate. This fact, he thought, was shameful.[8] Billy Graham, of course, obtained a kind of notoriety as a durable apologist for Nixon and skeptic about the ignominy of Watergate, but he too eventually changed his mind about the Watergate episode.[9] Graham's views and those of others like him were not really surprising. Their political instincts were conservative and they were in the habit of affirming that what the United States' leaders did we should follow. Moreover, a good number had been eager defenders of Richard Nixon for many years.

On the other hand, evangelicals were able to explain Nixon's disappointing behavior and incorporate it into their world view because of the doctrine of universal sin. Nixon's activities came as a shock, but in the long run many knew that they were all too conceivable. Evangelicals contended that believing Christians should learn the lesson again that the frailties and vulnerabilities of rulers were always real. Sin often dominated men of power and influence now as in the past; its stain was never eradicated. Watergate was only one more chapter in this long-running story. At the same time, evangelicals pointed out that sin is universal. We were to express humility in the face of our own sin, even as we criticized the world of the Nixon White House. The lesson was not only, they insisted, about sin in high places. It was about the prevalence of sin, in high places and in low places, sin which was everywhere and which had to be fought everywhere.[10]

It is obvious that these discussions of Watergate were intensely moralistic. One consequence was that when they focused on rulers and the political process, they reiterated the need for more moral leaders. All evangelicals took for granted that all leaders would have their weaknesses, but most believed that much could be accomplished by leaders determined to act with a fresh style of heightened moral sensitivity. Our leaders needed to be concerned to tell the truth and to respect the importance of proper means in politics. Evangelical thinkers more and more argued for the rejection of an immoral and disastrous concentration on achievement of ends at all costs. Nixon and the Nixon White House were indicted for having had precious little concern with ethical means.[11]

Perhaps the most poignant transformation was that of Nixon's evangelical pastor at Key Biscayne, Florida, a man who described himself at one time as having a "deep love for President Nixon." He discovered in his experience with Nixon how false and unethical politicians could be. He spoke to Nixon about Watergate, and Nixon gave him private assurances that he was doing all he could to bring justice in the Watergate mess. This act, he later learned, to his dismay, was sheer duplicity. Nixon had lied to him, and the president's former minister said so in frank language which *Christianity Today* reported.[12]

Watergate conceivably could have stimulated serious reservations about government or the rulers of government among conservative evangelical thinkers. It might have led away from Romans 13, the standard text of many evangelicals about governors, with its stress on divine establishment of government and the importance of obedience. It might have turned evangelicals more toward the Book of Revelation, permeated with disappointment and disgust with states and their masters. Some more radical evangelicals moved in this direction. For them Watergate was another, albeit important, impetus toward the rejection of business as usual in America as the evangelical mainstream defined it. Most, however, remained convinced that the enduring lessons of Watergate had more to do with the universality of sin and the need for more moral leadership.

Those who were more critical concluded that Watergate suggested how easy it was for those in political power to worship power rather than God. They said the real issue was one of idolatry. They charged that too many people, including rulers and their staffs, were so devoted to holding or seeking power that they placed it above all else. They shunted God aside every bit as much as they rejected ethical dealings. The critics also suggested that sometimes government or its leaders were tempted to confuse themselves with our nation, with the United States. They contended that one should put one's faith in no such false gods. No leader and no country was a proper locus for faith—only Jesus was.

This was a truth, critics said, which the church as well as individuals had to absorb. The church, indeed, had turned out to be an institution which found it all too convenient to ignore the transgressions of Nixon and other Watergate culprits for a long time. Nixon and his cohorts had easily been able to "use" God, the churches, and the supposedly godly for their own political purposes.[13] Occasionally strong words of almost sneering disappointment appeared in print. Said *The Other Side*: "Later, even as the scandals broke . . . establishment evangelicals flocked to East Room worship services at Richard Nixon's whited sepulchre."[14] More muted complaints, such as those which implied Billy Graham had been too available for Nixon's purposes, also appeared in evangelical writing about Watergate. There was considerable awareness that nonevangelicals enjoyed denigrating evangelicalism because Graham and a vague evangelical piety were associated with the Nixon White House where Watergate took place. Evangelicals tried to meet such accusations with vigorous if rather defensive arguments. They claimed that the Watergate cast of characters and the White House prayer group were generally two separate sets of people, and one could hardly be blamed for the other. They also pointed out that there had been much less religion at the Nixon White House than most people realized. Only one in every six Sundays saw a worship service at the White House. Moreover, during all the years Nixon was in the White House Graham in fact had presided over only three Sunday services.[15]

Whether or not the individual Christian or the church as a whole learned humility and the limits of rulers (and all people) before sin, there was a widespread suspicion among evangelical writers that the presidency and the state would come down to earth as the result of Watergate. They would now be viewed as ordinary institutions occupied by human beings whose power deserved to be watched and distrusted.[16] This was a prospect that evangelicals welcomed. The radicals at the *Post-American* were one example. They undoubtedly experienced some glee in Nixon's downfall and not a little self-righteousness at the demise of the figure they had so often and so bitterly denounced during the brief existence of the *Post-American*. However, the radicals certainly argued that no one could fairly transfer all the blame to Nixon for what were *the general sins of America*. They particularly accused Americans of idolatry, asserting that what the United States had to discover from the Watergate affair was the danger of idolatry and the glory of Christ.[17]

Jim Wallis did not see the lesson of Watergate, however, to be the need for more moral presidents. Its teaching, he believed, was far deeper. Watergate exposed the state itself for the evil thing it was. Wallis, indeed, reflected the mood of the Book of Revelation and urged his readers to perceive that a radical loss of faith in the state, not just Nixon, nor the presidency, was what we needed today. From such a loss of faith, he hoped, could come a rebirth of Christian citizenship and with it a growth of Christian community. Perhaps now people would turn away from the state to their responsibilities to do God's will. Perhaps now people would care about the suffering and injustice in the world. To be sure, people could not do it entirely alone; often they would need the state, but the only state worthy of respect would be one responsible to Christian citizens who demanded leaders prepared to do righteousness. Quoting the 1973 Declaration of Evangelical Social Concern, Wallis stated: "We acknowledge our Christian responsibilities of citizenship. Therefore we must challenge the misplaced trust of the nation in economic and military might. . . . We proclaim no new gospel, but the Gospel of our Lord Jesus Christ. . . . By this declaration, we endorse no political ideology or party, but call our nation's leaders and people to that righteousness which exalts a nation."[18]

Wallis sought a radical birth of "biblical" people, but most evangelicals drew another conclusion from Watergate, that America needed less a new birth than a reaffirmation of the biblical absolutes among a once faithful people. Watergate was one more tale of our decline as a Christian people, degenerating from belief in absolute moral truth to situation ethics. This was by far the most discussed and most widely shared opinion about Watergate; it proved that situation ethics encouraged sin and it proved that traditional, absolute Christian ethics were desperately required for modern times.

SITUATION ETHICS

From the first, situation ethics emerged as the leading culprit in Watergate according to the analyses of many evangelical thinkers. It had part of its origin in the argument of Jeb Stuart Magruder, a minor Watergate figure, that he went wrong because he had absorbed too much corrupting situation ethics in college from the liberal Yale chaplain, William Sloan Coffin. His explanation appealed to many evangelical commentators who saw it not only as the best guide to the tragedy of Watergate, but also as a sound guide to the broader dangers which constantly threaten to envelop us all in this modern age.[19]

Criticism of situation ethics under one name or another had long been a staple of evangelical ethics. By the middle 1960s it was common. L. Nelson Bell, for instance, denounced situation ethics as a "morality" which justified altering rules to fit one's own individual convenience as particular circumstances changed. It was really no morality at all, for it had no respect for universal, absolute truths, and no respect for any divine truth above and beyond us and our particular life dilemmas.[20]

In the 1960s and 1970s a number of evangelicals published books and articles attacking situationalism. Among the best were works by Erwin Lutzer and John Warwick Montgomery. The observations they made were heard again and again in the evangelical critique of situationalism before and during the crucial Watergate years of 1973 and 1974. Montgomery, for instance, dismissed situation ethics' claim to have its own universal standard, love. His judgment, which coincided with that of others, was that the concept of love was hopelessly vague and left one without much practical guidance. Its incredible vagueness as a universal ensured that anybody could do anything and claim that in their situation it was an act of love.[21] The Bible, on the other hand, Lutzer declared, offered rules which everyone required in life. After all, biblical love was not situational and sentimental; in the Bible "love is *defined* as obedience to law," and it is valid only when it *"fulfills* the law."[22]

Montgomery knew that situation ethics necessarily focused on individual action. The result was bound to promote growing distrust among people. After all, he insisted, we base common moral life on mutual agreements. We have to be able to trust that others will keep their word no matter what the situational vagaries are. He fully understood that the promoters of situation ethics argued that responding to circumstances in moral matters was far more important than worrying about longer term social effects such as the potential decline of the essential social cement of trust. He felt they were foolish and wrong, and he suggested that everyone would be wiser to acknowledge their sins and seek God's forgiveness rather than waste time inventing excuses for violating God's absolutes.[23]

Finally, evangelical writers like Lutzer and Montgomery shared the suspicion that such a human-centered and potentially selfish morality as situation ethics would inevitably move in the wrong directions. Lutzer was bothered by the situationalists' frequent tendency to justify things by good intentions, as if feeling love in a situation could justify anything or everything in that context. Both Lutzer and Montgomery, on the other hand, were uncomfortable with the frequent link between situation ethics and a crude utilitarianism. Situationalism could rationalize all sorts of acts in the name of the greater good of "love" and similar banalities. This was a doctrine suitable for communists, some asserted, or for any unscrupulous person seeking to have his way. Transcendental rootedness was a far better approach to life, Lutzer protested. Surely we had had enough sin starting with the first transgression of Adam and Eve, which Lutzer predictably saw as a product of situation ethics.[24]

Skeptics suggested that Montgomery, like other moral absolutists, was rigid and confused, but Montgomery insisted that this was a false accusation. Montgomery was not so naive as to think that in moral life choices would not sometimes have to be made among absolutes. The point was not that choices could be avoided. Rankings might be necessary, but whenever this was true, one had to do it knowing it was a choice which involved sin. To rank one absolute over another was a sin and required us to pray for forgiveness. Certainly we had to lie sometimes, Montgomery conceded, but what counted was whether we knew that the lie was evil and whether we confessed it. This was not to imply that good intentions mattered. They did not. Self-consciousness and confession did matter, however, and the crucial issue was whether we did the best we could to realize our absolute ethics, while granting our necessary shortfalls as humans and requesting divine forgiveness for them.[25]

Watergate and Richard Nixon fitted into the evangelical condemnation of situation ethics as a perfect, if painful, case study. Watergate was a tale about people who operated on a man-based ethic, who thought that the ends could justify the means, who did not confess their sins, and who should be a permanent lesson to all of us of the terrible potential of situation morality. Yet it was not they alone who were guilty. We were all responsible. We were all part of a permissive, indulgent time when even versions of Christianity such as a "reformed" Catholicism and a liberal Protestantism had abandoned ethical verities in order to dance to the tunes of the modern age. Whatever the standards of the contemporary era, evangelicals insisted that Christ rejected situation ethics and so must we. It was morally wrong in this as in every age. And it always failed.[26]

According to *Christianity Today* it was no accident that so many well-educated Americans had fallen victim in the disgrace of Watergate. Contemporary education was partly at fault. It did not try to save anybody from the snare of situation ethics and at such elite universities as Yale seemed rather to encourage such a foolish course. Nixon's own considerable advanced education had not prevented "his commitment to situation ethics." On the contrary, he was an appalling lesson in a failed moral education. It was time for a different approach, time for an education in eternal rights and wrongs.[27]

THE VIEW FROM WITHIN

The evangelical analysis of Watergate came at least partly from those who had been within the White House as well as from without. At least two evangelicals who for one reason or another played a role in the White House during the Nixon years offered their judgments on what happened, just as so many other Watergate insiders did. Charles Colson's best-selling book *Born Again* was obviously the most well-known example. Another was Wallace Henley's *The White House Mystique*, a thoughtful essay by a minor White House denizen of the Nixon era.

Most evangelical reviewers of Colson's book lauded it as an edifying story of confession and conversion, and it got warm reviews, though not all its notices were favorable. A review in *The Other Side* predictably, if not entirely accurately, faulted Colson. *Born Again* was described as a tale of conversion to Christ which left out commitment to social action.[28] Colson's emphasis did lie heavily on the importance of finding or refinding Jesus Christ. This discovery resulted, Colson felt, in a dramatic transformation in his life. He believed that the entire experience exposed him to a new model of human relationships exemplified in the aid and comfort of caring Christians who assisted him as he proceeded toward becoming "born again" and toward his new life. He learned that all human relationships did not have to replicate those of the Nixon White House. There was another path besides the cold, ruthless, instrumental road.[29]

Of course, evangelical escapees from the world of the Nixon White House judged that one of their chief lessons to report was the continuing truth that human beings were all too capable of sin. They concluded that Watergate was a tragic example of the enduring hold of sin over human beings and thus human history. They doubted that prosecutions of Watergate figures would end the threat of similar sin in the future. What it might do was remind people once again that rulers and followers alike could not and would not easily escape sin. There was a need for perpetual vigilance. This need applied to everyone, but especially to those in political office. Power was such a corrosive, corrupting force. Colson confessed that "*Hubris* became the mark of the Nixon man because *hubris* was the quality Nixon admired most."[30] Henley frankly described his book as a tale of how a Christian could swiftly "yield to the temptations of power."[31]

How quickly the allure of power could overwhelm all other influences was a reiterated theme. A politician's sense of pride, his heady sense of self-importance, could sweep away restraints and make possible the Nixon White House, where "God could be worshipped in the East Room on Sunday, and lies be told in the press room on Monday."[32] This atmosphere explained the famous "fortress mentality" which overwhelmed the Nixon White House's sense of reality and "plunged us across the moral divide."[33] The fatal White House "infection" was "DED (Dissent Equals Disloyalty)." It led to conformity and not to Christianity.[34]

Another lesson that evangelical participants in the Nixon White House felt they learned was the wisdom of viewing leaders skeptically even beyond their human proclivities toward sin. They repeatedly admitted that they had gotten too far involved in Richard Nixon, especially Richard Nixon as president of the United States. They believed too much in him and what they thought were his idealistic goals, and they did not acknowledge his weaknesses. "Presidential mysticism" proved to be too much. It was a rare person, like Wallace Henley, who could break out of the corrupting spell and flee the fortress. He resigned after the 1972 election and turned back to his God.[35] Colson also turned to God, of course, but only after he was forced out of the White House by Richard Nixon. And, despite all, *Born Again* contained no unequivocal rejection of Richard Nixon as president. What did disappear was Colson's "awe" of Nixon. Colson discovered that Nixon was a human being. He also came to see that he had allowed himself to become a cipher. Both Nixon and Colson, he thought, had been corrupted.[36]

There were other lessons too: the lesson that obedience to law was vital in a world in which human persons were so vulnerable to sin; the lesson that citizens must be active in order to control their community affairs and prevent Watergates of the future; the lesson that all public institutions had real limits.[37] Colson, for instance, conceded that before Watergate he had been a statist because he believed he could use the state to get the goals he sought. After Watergate he styled himself a Jeffersonian, disappointed with the state and often fearful of it. This conclusion derived also from his subsequent experience with the federal prison system. It was, he declared, a "debilitating, demoralizing, depressing, oppressive" world, which was hardly conducive to helping people trod the straight and narrow in the future.[38] Colson turned after his release to working on a prison ministry, attempting to assist the rejects of society. Despite his critics' suspicions, he left Watergate and prison with a new truth in his Christianity, which impelled him to act differently in the conduct of his life.

When all was said and done, Colson felt he had learned the truth that Watergate taught them all: "Going into the White House without a granite-like set of convictions was like sailing into a hurricane without a rudder!"[39] There were and there had to be absolute standards. Colson was convinced that he had survived the entire experience, but how many other people could expect to get through life in permissive America with the aid of a phoenix-like rebirth? Could America itself make its way in the years ahead? Colson and other evangelicals remained confident that the answer was "yes," but only if we turned to Jesus Christ.

TOWARD JIMMY CARTER

Watergate and the decline of American ethical standards that it symbolized were discouraging, however, to many evangelical voices in the 1970s, just as the racism and the disorder of the late 1960s had been. Yet discouragement did not yield to pessimism. One of the reasons was the rising evidence of evangelical impact on political life. Nixon's successor, Gerald Ford, eagerly courted evangelical opinion and declared that, though an Episcopalian, he was an evangelical. Moreover, within two years an unquestioned evangelical, Jimmy Carter, received the presidential nomination of the Democratic party. These were signs that evangelical views and attitudes were reaching broader elements of the American culture. Other signs were evident in the gathering momentum of crusades against abortion and homosexuality, which had substantial evangelical support and leadership. Evangelicals were now a force to be reckoned with. Their long isolation in the American polity was over.

The nomination of Southern Baptist Carter and would-be evangelical Ford for the presidency was the most striking event. It was reinforced by both candidates' unvarnished and uninhibited struggle for the evangelical vote. The election contest of 1976 also showed the spreading political diversity within the faith, a diversity encouraged by the cross-pressures set up for normally Republican evangelicals by the fact that the more obviously evangelical candidate was a Democrat. Carter was particularly popular among reform-oriented evangelicals and resolutely opposed by the conservative leaders of the mainstream. Yet Carter did unusually well in garnering voters as a Democrat among his coreligionists, and he cut substantially into the Republican vote among ordinary members of the fold. He got about 40 percent of the vote of evangelicals, a far better showing for a Democratic presidential candidate than in any election since 1964. He ran especially well (not surprisingly) among fellow Southern Baptists, but he did well elsewhere also. For example, he got one-third of the vote of students at Wheaton College, a key center of modern evangelicalism, a much better showing than most recent Democratic nominees for president had gotten among that student body.[40]

Christianity Today reflected the new situation rather clearly. Chapter Two observed the magazine's cautious tradition of sympathy for Republican nominees for president. The same sympathies were evident again in 1976, but in a muted context stressing neutrality. Four discernible features made up this influential magazine's 1976 election coverage:

1. The magazine treated neither candidate harshly or unfairly. It gave Ford a warm press from the beginning of his presidency through the 1976 campaign. The periodical often praised Ford's personal openness and lauded many other sides of his life. *Christianity Today* covered Carter in a far more restrained manner. He rarely received enthusiastic praise to compare with Ford's. On the other hand, while Carter's *Playboy* interview and some prominent evangelicals' angry reactions to it were reported on several occasions, the magazine also took note of Ford's smoking, drinking, and dancing and the fact that some evangelicals were uncomfortable over his indulgence in these activities.[41]

2. The magazine gave a good deal of attention to Ford's evangelical connections *and* to his determined courting of evangelicals. News stories appeared recording Ford's Sunday brunch for religious athletes, his speech at the 1976 National Association of Evangelicals Convention in Washington, and his campaign stop at the national meeting of the Southern Baptist Convention in a fashion which could only assist Ford with *Christianity Today*'s readers. In fact, after the *Playboy* interview became known, *Christianity Today* clearly showed more respect for Ford's religious life than Carter's.[42]

3. Overall, the magazine's discussions on the issues carefully avoided

almost all overt side-taking. Yet, if one reads them closely in the context of the times, a distinct message emerges. *Christianity Today*'s argument was that evangelicals should not vote for someone just because he was an evangelical or the member of an important evangelical denomination. That was no way to select a president. The proper direction, instead, was to look at what policies a candidate would promote. This contention was an indirect, but hardly hidden, argument against the appeal of Carter, especially since *Christianity Today* defined the central issue of 1976 as whether or not the United States needed more equality or whether we ought to show more consideration for "earned and legitimate privilege."[43] Any reader of *Christianity Today* knew what its answer to this question was and why Gerald Ford was therefore the better candidate.

4. Just before the election, editor Harold Lindsell announced that *Christianity Today* would remain neutral on the contest. Compared to 1972, the magazine's campaign coverage did in fact remain neutral. Lindsell supported Ford, but even within his family there were Carter votes. Evangelicals were seriously divided. Consensus was gone. Or, as Lindsell put it, "so many of the saints who agree with me about religious matters seem to be so ornery, so obtuse, so recalcitrant — in other words, so opposed to my political opinions."[44]

But the dominant mood at *Christianity Today* was not so genial after Ford lost. The sober, even somber first issue after the election made that clear. Lindsell did not congratulate the winner. He spent his time instead insisting that Carter should keep in mind that he had set a high standard for himself and now he had to fulfill it. And what of the defeated Ford? The lead section of the postelection editorial focused on him and how impressive he was, how much he had given America, and how much he would be missed in the presidency.[45]

Christianity Today gave a considerable amount of space to the campaign. Many other evangelical publications steered away from the 1976 election. This was true of journals as diverse as the radical *The Other Side* and the intellectual *The Reformed Journal*. *The Reformed Journal* had criticized the Ford administration before the election season was in full swing for being short on leadership.[46] But 1976 saw no such articles, with one significant exception. Nicholas Wolterstorff published an essay on "Carter's Religion" which was one of the most thoughtful and least polemical dissertations on that now (and then) overworked subject. It was his conviction that Carter's religion was sincere, and he reminded his readers that for Carter that was bound to imply a commitment to keeping church and state separate. Nonetheless, he thought it was an intriguing question what the dynamic was — and would be — in Carter between his faith and his "progressive politics." Was he an evangelical Protestant who had moved on to liberal politics? Or was he both a political liberal and an evangelical "side by side"? The latter would indeed be a sign of a mighty change in the world of evangelicalism.[47]

On the other hand, *Sojourners* was intensely interested in the 1976 election. It provided an opportunity for numerous radicals to issue anti-system, anti-institutional, and antipolitical declarations. Jim Wallis scoffed at the electoral process as no more than window dressing designed to deck out the status quo.[48] Wes Michaelson, who had earlier proposed an attempt to construct a "responsible" theology of power and communicate effectively with presidential candidates, had no respect for the 1976 presidential candidates, and he did not propose to communicate with them. He had obvious contempt for Jimmy Carter, who received no other support from other quarters at *Sojourners*. Ford was even worse than Carter, who was at least a moderate, reform-oriented evangelical. But Carter was clearly no radical. Michaelson dismissed him brutally as "a shallow self-righteous smiling messiah who would be King."[49] The entire electoral pageant was disgusting, he thought, because it consisted of one candidate after another promising that somehow America might escape the fall. It was all so foolish.[50] William Stringfellow took a different tack. He was interested in the election, but he felt a candidate like Jimmy Carter needed to know that elections did not determine the real governors of the United States. Beyond political leaders lay a "second government" of corporate, technological, and military groups. He wanted their existence brought into the light and their behavior under the law.[51] There were other approaches also; none speculated about electoral odds or probed the campaign dynamics; all were decidedly skeptical of the entire process.

While neither *Christianity Today* nor *Sojourners* joined the Carter bandwagon, there were several campaign books generated from the evangelical world which reflected the excitement Carter attracted from a considerable number of the faithful. Howard Norton and Bob Slosser's *The Miracle of Jimmy Carter* was the most unreservedly enthusiastic. As its title suggests, this book was immodest in its claims for Carter, but it was an intriguing (though hardly intellectual) attempt to present Carter as an impressive expression of the evangelical culture. The book celebrated his life, his family, and his thoughts with a heavy religious emphasis and in a pietistic style. By its light the most significant dimension of Jimmy Carter was his religious faith and his religious experience. He was a true Christian who knew his Bible just as any good evangelical should.[52]

Also sympathetic, but far more restrained and thoughtful, was David Kucharsky's *The Mind and Spirit of Jimmy Carter*. Kucharsky identified Carter's intellectualism as one of the things that was much in his fellow evangelical's favor. Kucharsky, like others, was well aware of the "historic bad blood between the modern intelligentsia and the Puritans from whom evangelicals derive much of their outlook."[53] He regretted the anti-intellectual reputation of evangelicals, which they too often proved valid by their own behavior. He thought Carter could reverse that. He "has drawn the attention and admiration of evangelicals who chafed under an impression that one had to turn off his or her brain to be a Christian."[54] Kucharsky also liked the fact that Carter seemed determined to link religious and public service activities. Carter in this portrait spoke for the "new evangelicals" (though not radicals) and reflected a historic opening within the faith, "giving civil responsibilities their rightful place on the spiritual agenda."[55] Kucharsky's Carter stood for "hope for the pious, for the impatient, and for those who think America has already seen its best days."[56] Yet Kucharsky judged that Carter moved with a proper caution. Like Reinhold Niebuhr, Carter appreciated the sinful nature of the world and the formidable barrier it posed to miraculous transformations.[57]

Kucharsky recognized that Carter did not have a smooth road to the heart of many evangelicals. No matter how many reform-minded moderates there were, a host of others felt deep unease over Carter's politics: "In the evangelical community the chief anxiety over Carter is that his liberal ideology will result in the loss of liberty."[58]

The classic campaign book was Carter's own *Why Not the Best?* An evangelical house, Broadman, first published it in 1975, but during the campaign Bantam produced another edition. Compared to *The Miracle of Jimmy Carter* or to Kucharsky's *Carter, Why Not the Best?* skirted religion. It was surprisingly innocent of religious pieties, lectures, or affirmations. Yet the message was there. Carter presented himself as a candidate who was an evangelical Christian imbued with a sense of Christian vocation. Carter saw himself as a reborn evangelical, reborn in Christ and reborn in active social commitment and service.[59] He expressed his own identification with the themes of reform-minded evangelicals without using their language. In fact, he gave no evidence in the forum of his popular autobiography that he was aware of the divisions within his faith in recent years about the role of social commitment, or that he had read works by leading proponents of a more socially active evangelicalism. But there is no doubt that his sense of vocation in public service and in seeking means to help others was an example of concrete witness in the "new" mood.

Carter in his time was as much the sign of emergence of a new world of diversity and sympathy toward change within his religious tradition as he was the sign of the emergence of that tradition in the larger culture and politics of the United States. Evangelicalism had grown in another way than sheer size. It had become diverse and did not seem likely to offer soon again a monolithic political or social message—or to agree on the merits of one of its own when he ran for president.

CONCLUSION

Two facts stand out about the political and social thought among evangelicals in the 1960s and 1970s. The first is the persistence of a large place for conservative voices within the fold. The second is the rise of political and social diversity as new thinking and new evangelical minds had their impact. Much of the story we have described and analyzed was an account of two dialectics: between an eroding, but still vigorous, mainstream and a changing larger world; and between a still strong conservativism and a variety of more dissatisfied tendencies within evangelicalism. Everywhere in America in the late 1960s consensus slipped away only to be replaced in the 1970s by a world of factions, sometimes warring, sometimes coexisting. Evangelicalism was no exception.

Political and socio-economic conservatism, as we know, hardly died among evangelical laity and clergy in the 1960s and 1970s. *Christianity Today* spoke for this cause and helpful and sophisticated allies like Robert Culver provided support. Proceeding from a shared understanding of a scripture they believed to be true, they suspected the growing state, deplored the moral license which corrupted more and more people, and decried the gains of communism.

They diverged, often with love, from less conservative evangelicals such as Carl F. H. Henry, John Warwick Montgomery, and John B. Anderson. The divergences were matters of degree, though significant nonetheless. Moderates like Henry sought a faith more prepared to embrace social commitment and to oppose racism, pollution, and other evils of the day. Yet Henry and those of his general persuasion were often in the rhythms of the older conservative traditions. This was clear enough in contrast to the "new evangelicals" of the 1960s and 1970s who had no intention of preserving the conservative tones and substance of traditional evangelicalism's approach to politics. Paul Henry, Stephen Monsma, David Moberg, and others ignored the recent evangelical consensus on social and political issues and strove to revive the old pattern of a century and more ago of a believing church which was prepared to enter public arenas in search of changes in government, economics, the environment, and human relations. While they were no political revolutionaries with a taste for violence, they did propose change and they brought diversity to a once united realm of pietistic conservatism.

Far less numerous but no less articulate were the radical evangelicals. John B. Alexander of *The Other Side*, Jim Wallis and Wes Michaelson of *The Post-American*, and John Howard Yoder, among others, sought a drastic break with evangelical attitudes and practices in the realms of politics and society. Their goal was a community centered in Christ, and their conviction was that neither the American state nor the Christian church had proved hospitable arenas in which their new world could prosper.

Even as conservative voices remained healthy and strong, the new diversity matured and flourished. By the late 1970s writers and thinkers who saw themselves as evangelical or biblical could and did express a wide collection of political, economic, and social ideas. As yet it was an open question how much the diversity of political and social opinions among evangelical intellectuals which was the fruit of the 1960s and early 1970s penetrated to the average Southern Baptist or evangelical Presbyterian. Data was as scarce as opinions were plentiful. Nor was it clear that the developments of the late 1960s would continue with undiminished strength into the 1980s. The conflicting indicators cast doubt on every conclusion. Evangelicals for Social Action was very much alive by the end of the 1970s, *Sojourners* and *The Other Side* were busy publishing to significant audiences, and the chief figures of moderate and radical evangelicalism were as active as ever. Yet the number of books on social action and social responsibility coming from the evangelical presses slowed, and there was, at the least, no doubt that by the end of the 1970s the forces of political diversity—and change—within evangelicalism were stabilized in place and no longer spreading.

Perhaps the explanation lay in the diminution of urgency for change in the larger American culture (including among intellectuals) well before the end of the decade of the 1970s. After all, one of the findings of this study is how closely evangelicalism in recent decades interacts with the broader American society. Evangelical writers are no longer isolated from our society and, increasingly, do not want to be. They are aware of and they participate in contemporary dialogues and disputes about political and social affairs. Moreover, they are increasingly insistent that their voices be heard.

Undoubtedly the forces of change in American society in the late 1960s, the racial and Vietnam struggles, plunged many thoughtful evangelicals into the then boiling cauldron of America. It is also plausible to suggest that from these experiences came the diversity of political and social attitudes that was the legacy of that troubled era to the evangelical world of the 1970s. What is also clear, however, is that evangelicals were hardly passive forces which political turmoil and intellectual fashion in the larger society impressed to its patterns. Conservatism hardly collapsed among evangelical thinkers; what is remarkable is that it held on so robustly in contrast to its far less vigorous status in American intellectual culture as a whole even in these days of "the new conservatives." Moreover, many of the *directions* in which evangelicals went in seeking change were not those of the larger society. Perhaps one may say that the revival of interest in community paralleled a certain era of New Left thought, but it was quite another creature in evangelical hands. To be sure, evangelicalism itself produced many models of genuine community, some of them specific and some vague, but they all were built in a frame of religious faith and love that was qualitatively different from the once fashionable calls for community from the Left. Moreover, the search for evangelical community has survived as a rallying cry when the appeals of the New Left often seem ghosts from the past.

The force of the Bible in evangelical political thought remains extremely strong. The Bible serves many purposes in the diversity of evangelical political thought, seeming to support everything from laissez-faire to communitarian socialism and much in between, and many leading evangelical thinkers unmistakably apply it with one eye on the texts and one eye on contemporary culture. Yet the Bible still counts enormously. As it proves, however, to offer a home to more and more diverse social and political views, one wonders whether evangelical agreement on matters of faith (insofar as it still exists) will long last. The ultimate question about the rise of diversity among politically sensitive evangelicals is whether this is a sign of growth or of the loss of a common faith. All signs suggest growth, but it seems certain that it will be growth in a tradition called "evangelicalism" in which diversity about faith may follow diversity about political and social ideals. Evangelical intellectuals increasingly join American life—and so does their Bible. The price of growth—and rising influence—is likely to be the further rise of pluralism. Many reflective evangelicals will welcome this result. For others it will be a bleak tragedy.[60]

AFTERWORD

BY NOW IT MAY SEEM a long time since the historic 1976 election of a moderate evangelical to the presidency. Jimmy Carter is no longer president, decisively rejected by his electorate, including a strong majority of evangelicals. His replacement is another evangelical, less orthodox in tradition or self-conscious theology, but much more in tune with the politically conservative evangelical mainstream. Moreover, to outsiders anyway, the forces of political conservatism seem to be stronger than ever within the precincts of evangelical and fundamentalist Christianity. The rise of the Moral Majority and Jerry Falwell come instantly to mind; so does Christian Voice, the Religious Roundtable, and many other groups, causes, and controversies. Naturally, one wants to ask, What happened to all the evangelical political diversity that was the political and social fruit of the age from the New Left to Carter?

Of course, it is too soon to be sure of the meaning of the upsurge of conservative voices in recent years, to trace all their origins, to measure their influence, or to predict their staying power. No one should deny them as part of the map of American religion. But a good case can be made that the popular press has turned from ignoring evangelical and fundamentalist Christians, as it did until a few years ago, to singling them out, especially those who are politically conservative.

There is no doubt that this study shows that the mainstream of evangelicalism remained conservative in many ways during the 1960s and early 1970s. That has not changed today. But at the same time evangelicalism has not enlisted fully in the more *radical* of the conservative movements of our age; for example, the attitude toward Jerry Falwell by many evangelicals, including Billy Graham, has been cool, as Falwell knows too well. There is an unmistakable radical edge to groups like the Moral Majority which has not caught on even among conservative evangelical leaders. This

can be seen by reading any issue of *Christianity Today*. It reports on the
Moral Majority, but it does not endorse or praise it. It reports it as a
relevant, but somehow "other" phenomenon.

Moreover, all that diversity which this study claimed as a characteristic
of evangelical political thought is very much alive. Hatfield, for instance,
is still in the Senate, causing trouble for President Reagan in his current
position as chair of the Senate Finance Committee. John Anderson entered
presidential politics in 1980 and turned out to be exactly the kind of moderately liberal political animal this study sees him as. *Sojourners* publishes
to an ever wider (but hardly exclusively evangelical) audience, and its main
voice, Jim Wallis, is much sought after on the lecture circuit. This evangelical diversity may be ignored by the national press, but it lives on, now
in a sense more secure than ever; for it is now a fact of evangelical life,
well-established and, indeed, taken for granted.

Second, the most important thrust for "Christian conservative" change
has not come from the world of mainstream evangelicalism. It has support
there, though usually in a more tempered mood. But its stronghold lies
elsewhere, in fundamentalism. As Chapter One argues, the lines of division
are not always clear between evangelicalism and fundamentalism, but they
are there. And it is hardly a well-kept secret among biblically conservative
Christians that it is the fundamentalists who have most rallied to the Moral
Majority. After all, as Rev. Jerry Falwell never hesitates to state emphati-
cally, he is a fundamentalist, and this is, as he knows, a fact of real significance. Even in the age from the New Left to the election of Carter, as we
know, it was in the more fundamentalist side of conservative Christianity
that the greatest alienation from American politics existed; now this side
has become organized, often with sympathy from an evangelical mainstream always politically conservative. But the evangelical mainstream is
not the source of fundamentalist politics. Within evangelicalism as a whole,
the gift of the 1960s and early 1970s, political diversity, flourishes.

What the long run will bring, obviously, is beyond our certain judgment. It is not, however, implausible to suggest that it will see continued
diversity among biblical Christians when they turn to politics and economics. Perhaps one approach to the Moral Majority is to see it not only as a
reaction against the secular forces in America but also as a reaction against
liberal forces in its own evangelical fold. From this view, the Moral Majority
is an acknowledgement of the diversity which this book describes. Moreover, and ironically, now that the wave of the Moral Majority appears to
have crested, it may become just another evidence of the pluralism which
characterizes evangelicalism and fundamentalism today. Each age brings a
new emphasis: the New Left era brought us radical evangelicals; the con-

temporary period, the Moral Majority. But no single strain of evangelical political thought triumphs among biblical Christians, and several coexist as part of a world in which believing Christians do not agree on the teachings of Christ and the Bible about man and society.

NOTES

ABBREVIATIONS

CT —*Christianity Today*
OS —*The Other Side*
PA —*The Post-American*
RJ —*The Reformed Journal*
S —*Sojourners*

PREFACE

1. Donald Dayton, "Updating the 'Young Evangelicals,' " *OS*, Jan. 1979, pp. 28– 33.

CHAPTER ONE

1. See Albert J. Menendez, *Religion at the Polls* (Philadelphia: Westminster Press, 1977) for a detailed discussion of Carter's relative showing among evangelicals.
2. Donald G. Bloesch, *The Evangelical Renaissance* (Grand Rapids, Mich.: Eerdmans, 1973), pp. 13– 18; Martin E. Marty, *A Nation of Behavers* (Chicago: University of Chicago Press, 1976), p. 92.
3. Carl F. H. Henry, *New Strides of Faith* (Chicago: Moody Press, 1972), p. 17.
4. David Kucharsky, *The Mind and Spirit of Jimmy Carter* (New York: Harper & Row, 1976), p. 43.
5. James M. Boice, *The Sermon on the Mount* (Grand Rapids, Mich.: Zondervan, 1972), p. 85; Bloesch, *Renaissance*, pp. 57 and 28; Bernard L. Ramm, *The Evangelical Heritage* (Waco, Tex.: Word, 1973), p. 59; John Woodbridge, "On Evangelicals" (edited interview), *Voices of Trinity Evangelical Divinity School*, 4, No. 2 (1978), 6.
6. Richard Quebedeaux, *The Worldly Evangelicals* (New York: Harper & Row, 1978), pp. 87 and 154; Ronald Wells, "The Bible Alone?," *RJ*, Nov. 1975, pp. 4– 6.
7. Quebedeaux, *Worldly*, p. 21; Kucharsky, *Carter*, p. 50.
8. Virginia R. Mollenkott, *Adamant and Stone Chips* (Waco, Tex.: Word, 1967), p. 27; Richard J. Mouw, "On Scholarship and Discipleship," *RJ*, Jan. 1975, p. 7.
9. Ramm, *Heritage*, chap. 8, pp. 61, 23– 26, 117– 20, 70– 71.
10. Paul L. Holmen, "Contemporary Evangelical Faith: An Assessment and Critique," in

The Evangelicals, rev. ed., ed. David Wells and John D. Woodbridge (Grand Rapids, Mich.: Baker, 1975), p. 89.

11. Donald W. Dayton, "The Social and Political Conservatism of Modern American Evangelicalism," *Union Seminary Quarterly Review*, 32 (1977), 77–78; Richard J. Mouw, *Political Evangelism* (Grand Rapids, Mich.: Eerdmans, 1973), pp. 27–28.

12. Martin E. Marty, *Righteous Empire* (New York: Dial Press, 1970), chap. 17.

13. H. Richard Niebuhr, *The Kingdom of God in America* (Hamden, Conn.: Shoe String Press, 1956).

14. Jeffrey K. Hadden, *The Gathering Storm in the Churches* (Garden City, N.Y.: Doubleday, 1969), pp. 74–75 and 82; Menendez, *Polls*.

15. *Time*, Dec. 26, 1977, p. 54.

16. Richard Quebedeaux, *The Young Evangelicals: Revolution in Orthodoxy* (New York: Harper & Row, 1974), pp. 69–72; Gerald T. Sheppard, "Biblical Hermeneutics: The Academic Language of Evangelical Identity," *Union Seminary Quarterly Review*, 32 (1977), 87–88.

17. Robert Webber, *Common Roots* (Grand Rapids, Mich.: Zondervan, 1978).

18. Sydney Ahlstrom, *A Religious History of the American People* (New Haven, Conn.: Yale University Press, 1972), p. 952.

19. Quebedeaux, *Worldly*, p. 3; Kucharsky, *Carter*, p. 49.

20. Letter to author by David O. Moberg.

21. Quebedeaux, *Worldly*, p. 43.

22. Ibid., pp. 46–51; Marty, *Behavers*, chap. 5; Wells and Woodbridge, eds., *Evangelicals*, chap. 2.

23. Woodbridge, "On Evangelicals," p. 6.

24. Conversation with David Cook.

25. Woodbridge, "On Evangelicals," pp. 6–7.

26. George W. Dollar, *A History of Fundamentalism in America* (Greenville, S.C.: Bob Jones University Press, 1973), front cover and p. 3; Paul Carter, *The Decline and Revival of the Social Gospel: Social and Political Liberalism in American Protestant Churches, 1920–1940* (Ithaca, N.Y.: Cornell University Press, 1954), p. 50; Lowell D. Streiker and Gerald S. Strober, *Religion and the New Majority: Billy Graham, Middle America, and the Politics of the 1970's* (New York: Association, 1972), p. 93; Ernest R. Sandeen, *The Roots of Fundamentalism* (Chicago: University of Chicago Press, 1970), pp. 114–31 and xiii.

27. Paul Carter, "The Fundamentalist Defense of the Faith," in *Change and Continuity in Twentieth-Century America: The 1920's*, ed. John Braeman et al. (Columbus: Ohio State University Press, 1968), pp. 192–94.

28. Streiker and Strober, *Majority*, p. 93; Dollar, *Fundamentalism*, pp. 95–96; Carter, *Decline*, pp. 51–52; Sandeen, *Fundamentalism*, chap. 8.

29. Marty, *Empire*, chap. 20.

30. George M. Marsden, "From Fundamentalism to Evangelicalism, A Historical Analysis," in *Evangelicals*, ed. Wells and Woodbridge, pp. 146–48; Ahlstrom, *People*, p. 958; also see Erling Jorstad, *The Politics of Doomsday: Fundamentalists of the Far Right* (Nashville: Abingdon, 1970).

31. "Editorial: The Great Contender," *CT*, July 3, 1970, pp. 25–26.

32. Dollar, *Fundamentalism*, pp. 208 and 213–14.

33. Edward G. Plowman, "The Rise and Fall of Billy James," *CT*, Jan. 13, 1976, pp. 42–43; Jorstad, *Far Right*; Billy James Hargis, *Why I Fight for a Christian America* (Nashville: Thomas Nelson, 1974), pp. 25, 18, 17, and chap. 1.

34. Edward G. Plowman and Arthur H. Matthews, "Bicentennial Blessings," *CT*, Aug. 6, 1976, pp. 38–39; Edward G. Plowman, "News: McIntire's Melange," *CT*, May 7, 1971, pp. 36–37; see also *CT*, Dec. 7, 1973, pp. 29–30.

35. Dollar, *Fundamentalism*, pp. 288–89.

36. Ibid., pp. 252–53.

37. Ibid., p. 253.

38. Ibid., p. 194; Carl McIntire, *Outside the Gate* (Collingswood, N.J.: Christian Beacon Press, 1967), p. 246 and chaps. 22 and 20.

39. Jorstad, *Far Right*, pp. 43–44; McIntire, *Gate*, pp. 59–61, 173, and 126, and chaps. 9 and 10.

40. Gary K. Clabaugh, *Thunder on the Right: The Protestant Fundamentalists* (Chicago: Nelson-Hall, 1974), chap. 6; "ACCC: No Longer Doing Its Founder's Will," *CT*, Nov. 21, 1969, p. 41; see also Jorstad, *Far Right*.

41. McIntire, *Gate*, p. 322.

42. Clabaugh, *Thunder*, p. 126; William E. Pannell, *My Friend, The Enemy* (Waco, Tex.: Word, 1975), p. 50; Marty, *Behavers*, pp. 93ff.; Carter, *Decline*, pp. 57–58.

43. H. Crosby Englizian, "History and Polemic," *CT*, Jan. 17, 1975, p. 28.

44. Quebedeaux, *Evangelicals*, p. 13; Marty, *Behavers*, p. 101.

45. Carl F. H. Henry, *Evangelicals in Search of Identity* (Waco, Tex.: Word, 1976), pp. 30–31; "News: Bob Jones," *CT*, February 2, 1968, pp. 50–51; Pannell, *Enemy*, p. 53; William R. Harrison, "Is Hargis's Crusade Christian?" *CT*, August 16, 1968, pp. 38–40; Mark Hatfield, "Foreword" in John Harold Redekop, *The American Far Right: A Case Study of Billy James Hargis and Christian Crusade* (Grand Rapids, Mich.: Eerdmans, 1968).

46. Richard Quebedeaux, *The New Charismatics* (Garden City, N.Y.: Doubleday, 1976), chap. 5 and p. 68; conversation with Richard Martin.

47. Quebedeaux, *Charismatics*, pp. 28–30 and chap. 5; Ramm, *Heritage*, p. 14.

48. Don Danielson, "Charismatic Renewal and Social Concern," *PA*, 4, No. 2 (1975); Jim Wallis, "The Spirit in the Church," *PA*, 4, No. 2 (1975); Robert Sabath, *PA*, 4, No. 2 (1975); see Larry Christenson, *Social Action: Jesus Style* (Minneapolis: Dimension Books, 1976), chap. 3, pp. 39, 80–81, 101–2, 99, 92, 83–85.

49. Conversation with Richard Martin.

50. E.g., see Robert Webber and Donald Bloesch, *The Other Orthodox Evangelicals* (Nashville: Thomas Nelson, 1978).

51. J. Milton Yinger, *The Scientific Study of Religion* (New York: Macmillan, 1970), pp. 223 and 89, chap. 6.

52. Ibid., pp. 334 and 455–56; J. Milton Yinger, *Sociology Looks at Religion* (New York: Macmillan, 1961), p. 136.

53. Yinger, *Scientific Study*, pp. 490 and 275–78.

54. Ibid., pp. 299 and 533–35; Yinger, *Sociology*, pp. 36–37, 109, and 184.

55. Robert Bellah, "American Civil Religion in the 1970's," in *American Civil Religion*, ed. Russell E. Richey and Donald G. Jones (New York: Harper & Row, 1974), p. 257; Robert N. Bellah, *The Broken Covenant: American Civil Religion in Time of Trial* (New York: Seabury, 1975), p. 3, chap. 2; Robert Bellah, "Civil Religion in America," in Richey and Jones, eds., *Religion*, chap. 2.

56. Will Herberg, "America's Civil Religion," in Richey and Jones, eds., *Religion*, chap. 4; Sidney Mead, "The Nation with the Soul of a Church," in Richey and Jones, eds., *Religion*, chap. 3; Russell E. Richey and Donald G. Jones, "The Civil Religion Debate," in Richey and Jones, eds., *Religion*, chap. 1.

57. Bellah, "American Civil Religion," p. 263; Bellah, *Broken Covenant*, p. 158.

58. Robert N. Bellah, *Beyond Belief* (New York: Harper & Row, 1970), introduction, pp. 227, 252–53; Bellah, *Broken Covenant*, pp. xiv, xv.

59. Bellah, *Broken Covenant*, p. xiv; Bellah, *Beyond Belief*, p. 246. Bellah's personal feeling about religion was hardly calculated to lead to an interest in the evangelical explosion.

He reported that in his own development he had left both Marxism and traditional religion behind him, each no more than one stop on life's way. He frequently repeated his assertion that traditional Christianity was the past. However, a few years after his most discussed work on civil religion, he published an article, "The Role of Preaching in a Corrupt Republic," in *Christianity and Crisis* (Dec. 25, 1978), which suggested in Christian language that he was something of a Christian. He has kindly stated to me his current position as follows: "I am not currently a member of any church and so in an important sense not only sociologically but theologically not a Christian. On the other hand, . . . particularly in the context of the secular university, I do feel that I am in some sense a Christian" (letter to author, March 29, 1979).

60. Harvey G. Cox, " 'The New Breed' — American Churches: Sources of Social Activism in American Religion," in *Religion in America*, ed. William G. McLoughlin and Robert N. Bellah (Boston: Houghton-Mifflin, 1968), pp. 368–83.

61. Byran Wilson, "Religion and the Churches in Contemporary America," in McLoughlin and Bellah, eds., *Religion*, pp. 73–110.

62. William G. McLoughlin, "Is There a Third Force in Christendom?," in McLoughlin and Bellah, eds., *Religion*, pp. 42–72.

63. Frederick Sontag and John K. Roth, *The American Religious Experience* (New York: Harper & Row, 1972), p. 380.

64. Ibid., p. 339.

65. Ibid., pp. 123, 350, 276, 350, 259; chaps. 6, 7, 8.

66. McLoughlin and Bellah, eds., *Religion*; Jacob Needleman, *The New Religions* (Garden City, N.Y.: Doubleday, 1970); Robert Greenfield, *The Spiritual Supermarket* (New York: Saturday Review Press, 1975).

67. Luther P. Gerlach, "Pentecostalism: Revolutionary or Counter-Revolutionary?" in *Religious Movements in Contemporary America*, ed. Irving Zaretsky and Mark Leone (Princeton: Princeton University Press, 1974), pp. 669ff.

68. E.g., Zaretsky and Leone, eds., *Movements*, xxxv, xxvi.

69. Virginia Hine, "The Deprivation and Disorganization Theories of Social Movements," in Zaretsky and Leone, eds., *Movements*, pp. 646–61; John F. Wilson, "The Historical Study of Marginal American Religious Movements," in Zaretsky and Leone, eds., *Movements*, p. 608; Yinger, *Scientific Study*, pp. 275–78; Bryan Wilson, *Patterns of Sectarianism* (London: Heinemann, 1967), pp. 27–29.

70. E. Mansell Pattison, "Ideological Support for the Marginal Middle Class: Faith Healing and Glossolalia," in Zaretsky and Leone, eds., *Movements*, pp. 418–55.

71. Carter, "Fundamentalist Defense," pp. 185, 179.

72. Ibid., pp. 212–13.

CHAPTER TWO

1. "The Choice," *CT*, Mar. 29, 1968, p. 40.

2. Harold Lindsell, *CT*, Aug. 25, 1972.

3. Harold Lindsell, *The Battle for the Bible* (Grand Rapids, Mich.: Zondervan, 1976), p. 70.

4. Harold Lindsell, "The Crisis of the Church," *CT*, Sept. 11, 1970, pp. 4–6.

5. Harold Lindsell, "Whither Southern Baptists," *CT*, Apr. 24, 1970; Lindsell, *Bible*, p. 116 and chaps. 4–6.

6. Harold Lindsell, "Think on These Things," *OS*, Mar.-Apr. 1975, pp. 17–19.

7. Lindsell, *Bible*, pp. 117–21.

8. Ibid., p. 210; Carl F. H. Henry, "Review of *Battle for the Bible*," *The New Review of Books and Religion*, Sept. 1976, p. 98.

9. Lindsell, *Bible*, p. 139.
10. Ibid., p. 203.
11. Harold Lindsell, *The World, the Flesh, and the Devil* (Washington: Canon Press, 1973), p. vii; Harold Lindsell, "Sex, SIECUS, and the Schools," *CT*, Jan. 30, 1970, pp. 10–13.
12. Lindsell, "Things," *OS*, pp. 20–21.
13. Harold Lindsell, *CT*, Mar. 3, 1972; Harold Lindsell, *CT*, July 7, 1972; Lindsell, "Things," *OS*, p. 18.
14. Lindsell, "Things," *OS*, p. 18.
15. Ibid.
16. E.g., ibid., pp. 18–19.
17. Lindsell, *Devil*, p. 39.
18. Lindsell, "Things," *OS*, p. 19.
19. Harold Lindsell, "Lausanne 74: An Appraisal," *CT*, Sept. 13, 1974, p. 25; Lindsell, "Things," *OS*, p. 19; Lindsell, *Devil*, pp. 139–41.
20. Stressed to me by Dave Cook.
21. A point made to me by several interviewees.
22. Carl F. H. Henry, "Man in Modern Focus," *CT*, Mar. 16, 1973, pp. 24–25; Howard W. Ferrin, "Skinner's Utopia vs. Jesus' Kingdom," *CT*, Sept. 29, 1972, pp. 8–10.
23. "Editor's Comments: The W.C.C. and Socialism," *CT*, May 26, 1967, 15–16; "Editorial," *CT*, Aug. 8, 1975, p. 29.
24. "Editorial," *CT*, Nov. 10, 1972, pp. 38–39; see also Dennis F. Kinlaw, "Of Equal Opportunity and of the Bureaucratic Intrusions," *CT*, Nov. 5, 1976, pp. 16–18; G. C. Berkouwer, *CT*, Feb. 4, 1972, pp. 37–38; "Editorial: Insecure Security," *CT*, July 28, 1972, pp. 23–24.
25. "Rendering Unto Caesar," *CT*, July 3, 1970, pp. 32–33; "Slacks Split Clergy," *CT*, Jan. 18, 1974, pp. 45–46; Kenneth G. Elzinga, "The Demise of Capitalism and the Christian's Response," *CT*, July 7, 1972, pp. 12–16.
26. "Editorial: We Are Sick," *CT*, Sept. 29, 1967, p. 34.
27. L. Nelson Bell, "The Cheated Generation," *CT*, Aug. 1, 1969, pp. 29–30; L. Nelson Bell, "Changeless," *CT*, Jan. 16, 1970, pp. 22–23.
28. William Sanford Lasor, "Law and Order," *CT*, Jan. 30, 1970, pp. 13–14; "The Ugly Spirit of Mobbism," *CT*, May 24, 1968, pp. 26–27; "Editorial," *CT*, Apr. 28, 1972, pp. 24–25.
29. Roger Bennett, "The New Propriety," *CT*, June 23, 1972, p. 20; Robert J. Bartel, "Campus Tensions and Evangelical Response," *CT*, June 6, 1969, pp. 12–15.
30. Richard N. Ady, "D. B. Cooper, What Are You?" *CT*, Apr. 14, 1972; J. Edgar Hoover, "A Morality for Violence," *CT*, Apr. 28, 1972, pp. 8–13; J. Edgar Hoover, "The Interval Between," *CT*, Dec. 19, 1969, pp. 3–5.
31. Russ Walton, *One Nation Under God* (Washington: Third Century, 1975), pp. 215, 37–38, 43, 40–41, 225, 255–65, and chap. 8.
32. Ibid., p. 44.
33. Ibid., pp. 46–47, 26, 61–62, 50, and 55.
34. Ibid., pp. 57 and 60.
35. Ibid., p. 201.
36. Ibid., pp. xii, 51, 53, and 49; Gary K. Clabaugh, *Thunder on the Right: The Protestant Fundamentalists* (Chicago: Nelson-Hall, 1974), p. 143.
37. "Editorial," *CT*, Nov. 19, 1971, p. 27; Tunis Romein, "Freedom: Possession or Obsession?" *CT*, Jan. 17, 1969, pp. 10–11; Leon Morris, "To Be Free Men," *CT*, Oct. 12, 1973, pp. 22–24; Paul Henry, "Evangelical Christianity," in *The Cross and the Flag*, ed. Robert G. Clouse et al. (Carol Stream, Ill.: Creation House, 1972), p. 87; Ira Gal-

laway, "Liberation and Revolution," *CT*, August 25, 1972, p. 20; "Editorial: Liberation," *CT*, Jan. 19, 1973, pp. 26–27.

38. L. Nelson Bell, "Refugees!" *CT*, Oct. 23, 1970, pp. 24–25.

39. "Editorial," *CT*, Apr. 28, 1972, p. 25; "Editorial," *CT*, June 9, 1972, p. 28; "Editorial," *CT*, June 8, 1973, p. 27.

40. "Editorial: America on Its Knees?" *CT*, June 19, 1970, pp. 20–21; "Editorial: Is America Over the Hill?" *CT*, July 7, 1972, pp. 22–23.

41. "Editorial: Is Patriotism Dead?" *CT*, July 4, 1969, pp. 20–21; "Editorial: What's in a Flag?" *CT*, June 4, 1971.

42. "Editorial: The Christian as Patriot," *CT*, June 22, 1973, p. 22; "Editorial: The Place to Start," *CT*, Sept. 27, 1974.

43. Clabaugh, *Thunder*, p. 130; Richard V. Pierard, *The Unequal Yoke: Evangelical Christianity and Political Conservatism* (Philadelphia: J. B. Lippincott, 1970), pp. 117 and 121–23; John H. Redekop, *The American Far Right: A Case Study of Billy James Hargis and Christian Crusade* (Grand Rapids, Mich.: Eerdmans, 1968), pp. 17 and 169–70.

44. Billy James Hargis, *Billy James Hargis Speaks Out on the Issues* (Tulsa: Christian Crusade, 1971), p. 7.

45. Billy James Hargis, *Why I Fight for a Christian America* (Nashville: Thomas Nelson, 1974), p. 120; Redekop, *Crusade*, pp. 37–38 and chap. 2.

46. George W. Dollar, *A History of Fundamentalism in America* (Greenville, S.C.: Bob Jones University, 1973), p. 193.

47. Ibid., p. 278; Hargis, *America*, pp. 31 and 157–60.

48. Redekop, *Crusade*, p. 189.

49. Some relevant comments in *CT* in 1968: "Editor's Note," *CT*, Nov. 22, 1968, p. 2; "News: The Clergy on George Wallace," *CT*, Oct. 25, 1968, pp. 36–37.

50. "Editor's Note," *CT*, Oct. 27, 1972, p. 7; "News," *CT*, Oct. 27, 1972, pp. 38–39; "News: The Election's Religious Issues," *CT*, Dec. 8, 1972, pp. 38–39; "Let Your Yes Be Yes," *CT*, Aug. 25, 1972, p. 29; "Editorial: Objective: 1600 Pennsylvania Avenue," *CT*, July 28, 1972, p. 24.

51. "News: The Election: Who Was For Whom?" *CT*, Nov. 22, 1968, pp. 43–44; Harold Lindsell, "Editor's Notes," *CT*, Nov. 22, 1968, p. 2.

52. "Editorial: The Pardon of Richard Nixon," *CT*, Sept. 27, 1974, p. 37.

53. Harold Lindsell, "Editor's Notes," *CT*, Dec. 17, 1971, p. 11; "Editorial," *CT*, Dec. 17, 1971, pp. 22–23; e.g., J. Edgar Hoover, "An Analysis of the New Left: A Gospel of Nihilism," *CT*, Aug. 18, 1967, pp. 3–6; "Yoking Politics and Proclamation—Can It Be Done: An Interview with Bill Bright," *CT*, Oct. 24, 1976, pp. 20–22; Edward Plowman, "News: Exit John Conlon," *CT*, Oct. 24, 1976, p. 56; David Poling, *Why Billy Graham?* (Grand Rapids, Mich.: Zondervan, 1977), p. 71.

54. Russell Kirk, "Review," *CT*, Sept. 13, 1968, pp. 39–40; Thomas Howard, "Review: True Radicalism," *CT*, July 16, 1976, pp. 42–44; Erling Jorstad, "Conservative Resurgence," *CT*, July 2, 1976, p. 33; Addison H. Leitch, "Ten Years in the Wrong Direction," *CT*, Oct. 10, 1971, pp. 55–56.

55. E.g., "Editorial: The Warren Court Era," *CT*, July 19, 1968, pp. 33–34; "Review," *CT*, Dec. 22, 1972, p. 26.

56. Hargis, *Issues*, p. 14; Dollar, *America*, pp. 13 and 24.

57. Dollar, *America*, p. 191.

58. L. Nelson Bell, "Very Personal," *CT*, June 9, 1967, p. 22; L. Nelson Bell, "Beware!" *CT*, Oct. 24, 1969, pp. 24–25.

59. L. Nelson Bell, "The Church and Poverty," *CT*, Mar. 27, 1970, p. 27.

60. An example of others making the same point: Duane H. Thebeau, "On Separating Sheep from Goats," *CT*, Aug. 11, 1972, pp. 4–5; "Editorial," *CT*, Apr. 26, 1968, p. 25; and "Editorial: The Mini-City that Failed," *CT*, Mar. 27, 1970.

61. "Southern Baptists and Society," *CT*, Apr. 14, 1967, pp. 46– 47; Adon Taft, "The Gospel in a Social Context," *CT*, June 23, 1967, pp. 33– 34; "Editorial: Will American Baptists De-escalate or Advance Evangelism?" *CT*, Apr. 14, 1967, pp. 30– 31; "Editorial: Christian Social Action," *CT*, Mar. 14, 1969, pp. 24– 25; "Editorial," *CT*, Jan. 5, 1968, pp. 26– 27.

62. "Editorial," *CT*, Mar. 26, 1976, p. 25.

63. "The Lausanne Covenant," *CT*, Aug. 16, 1974, p. 23.

64. "Editorial: Statement of Purpose," *CT*, Oct. 9, 1970, pp. 30– 31; for the book review, cf. *CT*, Dec. 22, 1972, p. 28, and *CT*, Apr. 27, 1973, pp. 21– 24; see also Edwin M. Yamanchi, "How the Early Church Responded to Social Problems," *CT*, Nov. 24, 1972, pp. 6– 8.

65. Martin LaBar, "A Message to Polluters from the Bible," *CT*, July 26, 1974, pp. 8– 12; James Houston, "The Environmental Movement," *CT*, Sept. 15, 1972, pp. 8– 10.

66. "Editorial: Ecology—Dying to Live Again," *CT*, Mar. 31, 1972, pp. 22– 23; "Editorial: Waste as a Wrong," *CT*, Apr. 11, 1975, pp. 26– 27; David Gill, *CT*, July 26, 1974, pp. 29– 32; "Editorial: Living Better With Less," *CT*, Apr. 26, 1974, pp. 28– 29.

67. A point made to me by David Cook.

68. Richard M. DeVos, *Believe* (Old Tappan, N.J.: Revell, 1975), pp. 45, 99, 109, 87– 88, and chap. 1.

69. Ibid., pp. 57, 69, 39, 73– 76, 37.

70. Harold O. J. Brown, *The Protest of a Troubled Protestant* (New Rochelle, N.Y.: Arlington, 1969), p. 209.

71. Ibid.

72. Harold O. J. Brown, *Christianity and the Class Struggle* (New Rochelle, N.Y.: Arlington, 1970), pp. 199 and 171– 74.

73. Brown, *Protestant*, pp. 196, 198, and 50.

74. Ibid., pp. 196 and 48– 49.

75. Ibid., pp. 279 and 75; Harold O. J. Brown, "The Passivity of American Christians," *CT*, Jan. 16, 1976.

76. Robert Culver, *Toward a Biblical View of Civil Government* (Chicago: Moody Press, 1974), pp. 184– 85; interview.

77. Ibid., pp. 238– 39 and 233; interview.

78. Brown, *Protestant*, pp. 83 and 86; Culver, *Government*, p. 104; interview.

79. Culver, *Government*, p. 180; Brown, *Struggle*, p. 100.

80. Brown, *Struggle*, pp. 215, 30– 31, 178– 83.

81. Ibid., pp. 45 and 47.

82. Culver, *Government*, p. 99; interview.

83. Ibid., p. 186; interview.

CHAPTER THREE

1. John Pollock, *Billy Graham: The Authorized Biography* (New York: McGraw-Hill, 1966), pp. 2 and 50; David Poling, *Why Billy Graham?* (Grand Rapids, Mich.: Zondervan, 1977), p. 15; Joe E. Barnhart, *The Billy Graham Religion* (Philadelphia: United Church, 1972), pp. 62 and 219– 20.

2. Pollock, *Biography*, pp. 171– 72; Barnhart, *Religion*, p. 115.

3. E.g., William G. McLoughlin, *Modern Revivalism* (New York: Ronald Press, 1959), p. 507.

4. Ibid., pp. 503– 14.

5. E.g., Lowell D. Streiker and Gerald S. Strober, *Religion and the New Majority: Billy*

Graham, Middle America, and the Politics of the 1970's (New York: Association, 1972), p. 79.

6. Some examples: Edward Plowman, "Billy Graham Faces Berkeley Rebels," *CT*, Feb. 17, 1967, pp. 46– 47; J. D. Douglas, "He Put It Over With Love," *CT*, July 7, 1972, pp. 4– 6; James Huffman, "Graham in the Garden: New Challenges in New York," *CT*, June 20, 1969, p. 35; "Epochal Event: What God Did in Korea," *CT*, June 22, 1973, pp. 33– 34; David Kucharsky, "Graham in Raleigh: A Vote of Confidence," *CT*, Oct. 26, 1973, pp. 63– 65; Edward Plowman, *CT*, June 4, 1976, p. 156.

7. Interviews. Also Billy Graham, *Angels: God's Secret Agents* (New York: Doubleday, 1975), p. xi.

8. "Editorial: On Admiration," *CT*, Jan. 30, 1970, pp. 23– 24; John Pollock, "One Man's Furrow," *CT*, Sept. 13, 1974, pp. 14– 21; "Editorial: Twenty-five Years Later," *CT*, Sept. 13, 1974, pp. 50– 51.

9. Reported in *S*, Sept. 1977, p. 8.

10. David Frost, *Billy Graham Talks with David Frost* (Philadelphia: A. J. Holman, 1971), p. 49 and passim; Bob Arnold, "Billy Graham, Superstar," *Southern Exposure*, 4, No. 3., 1977, pp. 76– 82.

11. Graham's official biography paints Graham as an evangelist—largely nonpolitical. See Pollock, *Biography*; for a recent statement of his biblical conviction see Graham, *Angels*, p. 71.

12. T. S. Settel, *The Faith of Billy Graham* (Anderson, S.C.: Drake House, 1968), p. 88.

13. Ibid., pp. 64– 71; Billy Graham, *The Challenge* (Garden City, N.Y.: Doubleday, 1969), pp. 57, 145– 46.

14. Richard Quebedeaux, *The Young Evangelicals: Revolution in Orthodoxy* (New York: Harper & Row, 1974), p. 34; Lee Nash, "Evangelism and Social Concern," in *The Cross and the Flag*, ed. Robert G. Clouse et al. (Carol Stream, Ill.: Creation House, 1972), p. 145; Streiker and Strober, *Majority*, pp. 51– 52 and 58; David Lockhard, *The Unheard Billy Graham* (Waco, Tex.: Word, 1971), pp. 116– 26; "News: Graham in Cleveland," *CT*, Aug. 11, 1972, p. 33; Billy Graham, *World Aflame* (Garden City, N.Y.: Doubleday, 1965), p. 181; *CT*, Oct. 9, 1970, p. 52; Pollock, *Biography*, p. 98.

15. Frost, *Graham*, p. 22; "Editorial," *CT*, Apr. 13, 1973, p. 33.

16. Streiker and Strober, *Majority*, pp. 50 and 56.

17. Graham, *Challenge*, p. 10; Streiker and Strober, *Majority*, p. 57.

18. Graham, *Aflame*, pp. 175– 76.

19. "Billy Graham: Spanning the Decades," *CT*, Nov. 7, 1969, p. 34; Graham, *Aflame*, chap. 17, pp. 175– 76, and 187; Graham, *Challenge*, p. 125.

20. Graham, *Challenge*, pp. 71 and 126– 27; Lockhard, *Graham*, pp. 28 and 50.

21. James T. Baker, *A Southern Baptist in the White House* (Philadelphia: Westminster, 1977), p. 107; Settel, *Graham*, p. 34; Frost, *Graham*, p. 35; Streiker and Strober, *Majority*, pp. 46– 47.

22. Settel, *Graham*, p. 50; Lockhard, *Graham*, pp. 83– 84.

23. Billy Graham, "Why Lausanne?" *CT*, Sept. 13, 1974, p. 12; Lockhard, *Graham*, pp. 56 and 96; Billy Graham, "A Clarification," *CT*, January 19, 1973, p. 36.

24. Billy Graham, *Angels*; letter to author by David O. Moberg, Sept. 26, 1978.

25. Graham, *Challenge*, p. 97; Lockhard, *Graham*, pp. 7– 8.

26. Billy Graham, "God's Revolutionary Demand," *CT*, July 21, 1967, pp. 3– 5; Settel, *Graham*, p. 30; Billy Graham, "Three American Illusions," *CT*, Dec. 19, 1969, pp. 12– 14.

27. Graham, *Challenge*, p. 70; Graham, *Aflame*, pp. 181 and 15.

28. Graham, *Aflame*, p. 181; Billy Graham quoted in Streiker and Strober, *Majority*, p. 45.

29. Graham, *Aflame*, pp. 185– 86.

30. A bold and certainly interesting interpretation of Graham and the American order is

Marshall Frady's *Billy Graham: A Parable of American Righteousness* (Boston: Little, Brown, 1979); see also George H. Williams and Rodney L. Petersen, "Evangelicals: Society, the State, the Nation," in *The Evangelicals*, rev. ed., ed. David Wells and John D. Woodbridge (Grand Rapids, Mich.: Baker, 1975), pp. 253–54.

31. Billy Graham, "The Unfinished Dream," *CT*, July 31, 1970, p. 20.

32. Ibid., p. 21; Graham, *Aflame*, p. 26.

33. Graham, *Aflame*, pp. 15 and 2.

34. Graham, *Challenge*, p. 39; Graham, *Aflame*, pp. 20–21, 24–25, 83–84, 37–39, chaps. 4 and 7.

35. "Anaheim Crusade," *CT*, Oct. 24, 1969, pp. 40–45; Graham, *Aflame*, pp. 53–54; Lockhard, *Graham*, pp. 141–44; Arnold, "Superstar," *Southern Exposure*, p. 82; "News: Graham Preaches Peace in Viet Nam," *CT*, Jan. 20, 1967.

36. Graham, "Clarification," *CT*, p. 36; Graham, "Viet Nam," *CT*.

37. Frost, *Graham*, pp. 29-30 and 38; Billy Graham, "Watergate," *CT*, Jan. 4, 1974, pp. 18–19.

38. Poling, *Why?*, p. 78; and Pollock, *Biography*, pp. 218–19.

39. "Religion and the 1968 Candidates," *CT*, July 19, 1968, pp. 47–48; Streiker and Strober, *Majority*, pp. 65–66 and 61; "News: The Election: Who Was For Whom?" *CT*, Nov. 22, 1968, pp. 43–44; Graham, "Watergate," *CT*, p. 12; Frost, *Graham*, p. 72.

40. Billy Graham, "Inaugural Prayers," *CT*, Feb. 14, 1969, p. 27.

41. *CT*, Aug. 11, 1972, p. 27.

42. "An Act of God," *CT*, Jan. 4, 1974, pp. 48–49; *CT*, May 25, 1973, p. 46.

43. Graham, "Watergate," *CT*, p. 9.

44. Ibid., pp. 13 and 9.

45. Ibid., pp. 9 and 16.

46. Ibid., pp. 9, 19, and 12–13.

47. Ibid., p. 10; Frost, *Graham*, p. 66.

48. Streiker and Strober, *Majority*, p. 63; Poling, *Why?*, pp. 76–80.

49. Interviews; Graham, *Angels*, p. 76.

50. Pollock, *Biography*, p. 26; Barnhart, *Religion*, pp. 77–80.

51. Frost, *Graham*, p. 40; Graham, *Aflame*, pp. 177–78; Settel, *Graham*, p. 122; Lockhard, *Graham*, chap. 7.

52. Settel, *Graham*, p. 104.

53. Billy Graham, "Jesus of the Liberated Women," *Ladies' Home Journal*, December 1970.

54. Quebedeaux, *Young Evangelicals*, pp. 86–90.

55. Roger Palms, "Lonely But Loved in Lansing," *CT*, Nov. 24, 1972, p. 46; Mary Anne Pikrone, "Evangelism Plus," *CT*, June 9, 1972, p. 43; "Social Action Through Evangelism," *CT*, June 23, 1967, p. 34.

56. Leighton Ford, "Evangelism in a Day of Revolution," *CT*, Oct. 24, 1969, p. 7.

57. Leighton Ford, *One Way to Change the World* (New York: Harper & Row, 1970), p. 12.

58. Ibid., p. 42; Ford "Revolution," *CT*, p. 6.

59. Leighton Ford, *New Man, New World* (Waco, Tex.: Word, 1972), p. 102.

60. Ford, *Change*, p. 1.

61. Ibid., pp. 30 and vii.

62. Ford, "Revolution," *CT*, pp. 7–8; Ford, *Change*, p. 14; Ford, *Man*, chap. 6.

63. Ford, *Man*, p. 14.

64. Ibid., p. 28.

65. Ibid., p. 70.

66. Ford, *Change*, pp. 16, 17, and 19.

67. Ford, *Man*, pp. 28– 29, 43, and 31.
68. Ford, *Change*, p. 119.
69. Ibid., p. 78.
70. Ibid., p. 179.
71. Ford, "Revolution," *CT*, p. 9.
72. Ibid.
73. Ibid., pp. 7 and 12.
74. Ford, *Change*, p. 110; Ford, "Revolution," *CT*, p. 8.
75. Ford, *Change*, pp. 58 and 66.
76. Ibid., pp. 47– 48, 44, and 41– 42.

CHAPTER FOUR

1. Philip Yancey, "Francis Schaeffer: A Prophet For Our Time?" *CT*, Mar. 23, 1979, p. 16.
2. Francis A. Schaeffer, *Death in the City* (Downers Grove, Ill.: Inter-Varsity Press, 1969), p. 84.
3. Interview.
4. *CT*, Dec. 17, 1971, p. 60; Leighton Ford, *One Way to Change the World* (New York: Harper & Row, 1970), p. 73; Yancey, "Francis Schaeffer," *CT*.
5. "News, Evangelicals in Washington," *CT*, Mar. 26, 1976, p. 37.
6. Francis A. Schaeffer, *No Final Conflict: The Bible Without Error in All That It Affirms* (Downers Grove, Ill.: Inter-Varsity Press, 1975), p. 11; Francis A. Schaeffer, *Two Contests, Two Realities* (Downers Grove, Ill.: Inter-Varsity Press, 1975), p. 7.
7. Francis A. Schaeffer, *True Spirituality* (Wheaton, Ill.: Tyndale, 1971), p. 121; Schaeffer, *Conflict*, p. 8.
8. Francis A. Schaeffer, *The Church Before a Watching World* (Downers Grove, Ill.: Inter-Varsity Press, 1971), chap. 1; Schaeffer, *Realities*, p. 14.
9. Francis A. Schaeffer, *Genesis in Space and Time* (Downers Grove, Ill.: Inter-Varsity Press, 1972), p. 160; Francis A. Schaeffer, *No Little People* (Downers Grove, Ill.: Inter-Varsity Press, 1974), pp. 202 and 217.
10. Francis A. Schaeffer, *Back to Freedom and Dignity* (Downers Grove, Ill.: Inter-Varsity Press, 1972); Schaeffer, *City*, p. 103.
11. Francis A. Schaeffer, *The New Super Spirituality* (Downers Grove, Ill.: Inter-Varsity Press, 1972), pp. 16, 19– 20, and 12– 14; Schaeffer, *Conflict*, p. 44.
12. Francis A. Schaeffer, *The Church at the End of the 20th Century* (London: Norfolk, 1970), p. 124.
13. Francis A. Schaeffer, *How Should We Then Live?* (Old Tappan, N.J.: Revell, 1976), pp. 246, 68, 82, chap. 9 passim; Schaeffer, *Century*, pp. 37– 38.
14. Schaeffer, *City*, the later chaps.
15. Francis A. Schaeffer, *The Mark of the Christian* (Downers Grove, Ill.: Inter-Varsity Press, 1970), p. 26; Schaeffer, *World*, p. 71.
16. Schaeffer, *Christian*, p. 26.
17. Schaeffer, *World*, p. 79; Schaeffer, *People*, p. 229.
18. Schaeffer, *City*, p. 121.
19. Ibid.
20. Schaeffer, *City*, pp. 99 and 70– 71; Schaeffer, *Realities*, pp. 11, 5, and 8.
21. Schaeffer, *People*, p. 89.
22. Francis A. Schaeffer, "Race and Economics," *CT*, Jan. 4, 1974, pp. 18– 19; Schaeffer, *Realities*, p. 30.

23. Francis A. Schaeffer, "Race and Racism," *OS*, May-June 1974, p. 15; Francis A. Schaeffer, "Dragons," *OS*, Mar.-Apr. 1972, p. 44; Schaeffer, *Live*, p. 113.

24. Schaeffer, "Racism," *OS*, pp. 61, 57, and 60.

25. Schaeffer, *People*, pp. 258, 268, 184ff.; Francis A. Schaeffer, "The Universe and Two Chains," *CT*, Mar. 25, 1969, pp. 8– 11.

26. Schaeffer, *People*, p. 264; Schaeffer, *True Spirituality*, pp. 143– 44; Schaeffer, *Realities*, pp. 31– 32.

27. Francis A. Schaeffer, "How Should We Then Live?" *CT*, Oct. 8, 1976, p. 20; Schaeffer, *Century*, pp. 126– 27, 130– 31, and 135; Schaeffer, *Live*, pp. 114– 16.

28. Schaeffer, "Live," *CT*, p. 20.

29. Schaeffer, *Live*, p. 215; Schaeffer, *Realities*, pp. 31– 32; Schaeffer, "Race and Economics," *CT*.

30. Schaeffer, *Super Spirituality*, p. 15; Schaeffer, *True Spirituality*, p. 118; Schaeffer, *Realities*, p. 11.

31. Schaeffer, *People*, p. 140.

32. Schaeffer, *Christian*, pp. 35 and 10.

33. Schaeffer, *World*, p. 63; Schaeffer, *True Spirituality*, pp. 157 and 153; Schaeffer, *People*, p. 187.

34. Schaeffer, *People*; Schaeffer, *True Spirituality*, p. 94.

35. Schaeffer, *Century*, pp. 45 and 35.

36. Schaeffer, *City*, p. 12.

37. Ibid.

38. Ibid.

39. Schaeffer, "Dragons," *OS*, p. 44; Schaeffer, *Century*, pp. 67– 68 and 50.

40. Schaeffer, "Live," *CT*.

41. Schaeffer, *Live*, p. 210.

42. Ibid., pp. 254 and 124.

43. Francis A. Schaeffer, *Pollution and the Death of Man: The Christian View of Ecology* (Wheaton, Ill.: Tyndale, 1970), p. 24.

44. Ibid., p. 27. Schaeffer obviously agrees quite closely with Ellul here.

45. Ibid., pp. 54, 28, 30– 31, 47, and 40.

46. Ibid., pp. 70 and 74.

47. Ibid., pp. 82, 87, and 67– 68.

48. Ibid., p. 52.

49. Schaeffer, *Century*, pp. 97– 98 and 39; Schaeffer, *People*, pp. 43 and 45.

50. Schaeffer, *True Spirituality*, pp. 104– 5; Schaeffer, *People*, pp. 67-68 and chap. 1.

51. Schaeffer, *People*, p. 48; Schaeffer, *True Spirituality*, pp. 135– 37; Schaeffer, *Century*, chap. 7.

52. Schaeffer, *City*, pp. 11 and 21.

53. Ibid., p. 21.

54. Ibid., p. 36.

55. Ibid., pp. 50 passim.

56. Clark Pinnock, "Schaefferism as a World View," *S*, July 1977, pp. 32– 35; Jack Rogers, "Francis Schaeffer," *RJ*, June 1977, pp. 15– 19; interviews.

57. Interviews. A point made to me repeatedly.

58. Interviews.

59. Yancey, "Francis Schaeffer," *CT*, p. 18.

60. "Schaeffer on Schaeffer," *CT*, Mar. 23, 1979.

61. Edith Schaeffer, "Poured-in Protection," *CT*, Aug. 8, 1975, pp. 24–25; Edith Schaeffer, "What Harvest?" *CT*, Dec. 19, 1975, pp. 26–27; Edith Schaeffer, "Barren Reform," *CT*, July 4, 1975, pp. 23–24; Edith Schaeffer, "Flavored Sawdust," *CT*, Aug. 29, 1975, pp. 30–31; Edith Schaeffer, "Careful Conversation," *CT*, Feb. 14, 1975, pp. 29–30; Edith Schaeffer, "Who is the Snob?" *CT*, Nov. 22, 1974, pp. 34–36.

62. Edith Schaeffer, *What is a Family?* (Old Tappan, N.J.: Revell, 1975), p. 22; see also Edith Schaeffer, *L'Abri* (Wheaton, Ill.: Tyndale, 1969), chap. 19.

63. E. Schaeffer, *Family?*, pp. 151–52, 159, 44, 38, 107, 74–75, 37, 236, 64, 222, and chap. 5.

64. E. Schaeffer, "Reform," *CT*, pp. 23–24; E. Schaeffer, "Sawdust," *CT*, pp. 30–31; E. Schaeffer, "Careful," *CT*, pp. 29–30; E. Schaeffer, "Snob?" *CT*, pp. 34–36.

65. E. Schaeffer, *Family?* p. 48.

66. Ibid., pp. 50–51 and 41–42.

67. Ibid., pp. 162 and 149.

68. Ibid., pp. 238–39, 45, and 127–28.

69. Yancey, "Francis Schaeffer," *CT*, p. 17.

CHAPTER FIVE

1. Carl F. H. Henry, "The Purpose of God," in *The New Face of Evangelicalism: An International Symposium on the Lausanne Covenant*, ed. C. René Padilla (Downers Grove, Ill.: Inter-Varsity Press, 1976), p. 23.

2. Carl F. H. Henry, *Aspects of Christian Social Ethics* (Grand Rapids, Mich.: Eerdmans, 1964), pp. 16 and 127.

3. Carl F. H. Henry, "The West at Midnight," *CT*, Oct. 10, 1975, p. 33; Carl F. H. Henry, *Evangelicals in Search of Identity* (Waco, Tex.: Word Books, 1976), p. 69.

4. Carl F. H. Henry, *New Strides of Faith* (Chicago: Moody Press, 1972), pp. 123–24.

5. Carl F. H. Henry, "Evangelical Social Concern," *CT*, Mar. 1, 1974, p. 99; Carl F. H. Henry, "What Is Evangelical Liberation?" *CT*, Feb. 14, 1975, p. 34.

6. Henry, *Ethics*, pp. 120–21.

7. Ibid., pp. 118 and 9.

8. Ibid., p. 81.

9. Ibid., pp. 166, 160–61, 154–55, 158, 185, 117, 101–4, 72, and 92.

10. Ibid., p. 16.

11. Ibid., p. 122.

12. Ibid., p. 186.

13. Ibid., p. 81.

14. Ibid., pp. 82, 221, and 123.

15. Ibid., p. 186.

16. Ibid., pp. 105–6; Carl F. H. Henry, "A Challenge to Ecumenical Politicians," *CT*, Sept, 15, 1967.

17. Henry, *Ethics*, p. 20.

18. Ibid., pp. 112–13.

19. Henry, "Politicians," *CT*.

20. Carl F. H. Henry, ed., *Prophecy in the Making* (Carol Stream, Ill.: Creation House, 1971), p. 171.

21. Henry, *Faith*, pp. 24 and 130.

22. Ibid., p. 129.

23. Henry, "Concern," *CT*, pp. 99–100; Henry, *Identity*; Carl F. H. Henry, "The Gospel and Society," *CT*, Sept. 13, 1974, pp. 66–67.

24. John Howard Yoder, *The Politics of Jesus* (Grand Rapids, Mich.: Eerdmans, 1972), p. 131, n. 32; Carl F. H. Henry, "Plight of the Evangelicals," *CT*, July 5, 1968, pp. 25–27.

25. Carl F. H. Henry, "Moving on Public Frontiers," *CT*, Dec. 9, 1975, pp. 40–41; Carl F. H. Henry, "Of Bicentennial Concerns and Patriotic Symbols," *CT*, July 2, 1976; Carl F. H. Henry, "Has Democracy a Future?" *CT*, July 5, 1974, pp. 26–27.

26. Henry, "Symbols," *CT*.

27. Carl F. H. Henry, "Reflections on Women's Liberation," *CT*, January 3, 1975, pp. 25–26.

28. Carl F. H. Henry, "Further Thoughts About Women," *CT*, June 6, 1975, pp. 36–37; Carl F. H. Henry, *CT*, July 4, 1975, pp. 45–46.

29. Henry, *Ethics*, pp. 118 and 9.

30. Henry, "Frontiers," *CT*, pp. 6 and 8; Carl F. H. Henry, "What Is Man On Earth For?" in Carl F. H. Henry et al., *Quest for Reality: Christianity and the Counter-Culture* (Downers Grove, Ill.: Inter-Varsity Press, 1973), pp. 156–76.

31. Henry, *Ethics*, p. 28; Carl F. H. Henry, "Jesus and Political Justice," *CT*, Dec. 6, 1974, p. 34.

32. Carl F. H. Henry, "Revolt on Evangelical Frontiers," *CT*, Apr. 26, 1974, p. 6; Henry, *Ethics*, pp. 96 and 93.

33. Henry, "Evangelical Frontiers," *CT*, p. 6.

34. Henry, "Man on Earth," *Counter-Culture*, p. 161.

35. Carl F. H. Henry, "The Judgment of America," *CT*, Nov. 8, 1974, pp. 22–24; Henry, "Society," *CT*, p. 67.

36. Henry, *Identity*, pp. 23 and 69; Carl F. H. Henry, "Reaction and Realignment," *CT*, July 2, 1976.

37. Henry, *Identity*, p. 40; and, for example, Carl F. H. Henry, "Conflict over Biblical Inerrancy," *CT*, May 7, 1976, pp. 23–25.

38. Interview.

39. Henry, "Realignment," *CT*; Henry, *Identity*, chap. 5 and pp. 47 and 40.

40. Carl F. H. Henry, "Towards a Brighter Day," *CT*, Aug. 6, 1976, p. 28; Henry, *Faith*, p. 17; Henry, "Realignment," *CT*; Henry, *Identity*, p. 91.

41. Henry, *Identity*, pp. 74 and 93.

42. John R. W. Stott, *Christ the Controversialist* (Wheaton, Ill.: Creation, 1970), p. 145.

43. Sherwood Eliot Wirt, *The Social Conscience of the Evangelical* (New York: Harper & Row, 1968), pp. 47–48 and 135; John Warwick Montgomery, "Target: Social Neglect," *CT*, September 26, 1969, p. 44; Paul S. Rees, *Don't Sleep through the Revolution* (Waco, Tex.: Word Books, 1969), p. 108.

44. John B. Anderson, *Vision and Betrayal in America* (Waco, Tex.: Word Books, 1975), pp. 149, 145, and 148; Norman L. Geisler, *Ethics: Alternatives and Issues* (Grand Rapids, Mich.: Zondervan, 1971), p. 190.

45. Wirt, *Evangelical*, pp. 52 and 11; Montgomery, "Neglect," *CT*, p. 44.

46. Wirt, *Evangelical*, p. 41.

47. John Warwick Montgomery, *The Shaping of America* (Minneapolis: Bethany, 1976), pp. 172–73; Stott, *Controversialist*, p. 190; Vernard Eller, *The Simple Life: The Christian Stance Toward Possessions* (Grand Rapids, Mich.: Eerdmans, 1973), p. 43.

48. Stott, *Controversialist*, pp. 182–85; Rees, *Revolution*, p. 32; Montgomery, *America*, p. 175; John Warwick Montgomery, " 'If You Can't Beat 'Em Separate From 'Em'," *CT*, July 2, 1976.

49. For example, Wirt, *Evangelical*, chap. 9, pp. 80, 89, and 86.

50. Ibid., chap. 13 and p. 54; John B. Anderson, *Between Two Worlds* (Grand Rapids, Mich.:

Zondervan, 1970), chap. 1; Wesley Pippert, *Faith at the Top* (Elgin, Ill.: Cook, 1973), pp. 11– 13.

51. Wirt, *Evangelical*, pp. 84– 85.
52. John Warwick Montgomery, "Shaky Moral Foundations," *CT*, Oct. 9, 1970, pp. 25– 28; Wirt, *Evangelical*, pp. 140– 46.
53. Anderson, *America*, p. 14.
54. Montgomery, *America*, p. 184.
55. John Warwick Montgomery, "From Enlightenment to Extermination," *CT*, Oct. 11, 1974, pp. 57– 58; Montgomery, *America*, pp. 195– 96 and chap. 3.
56. Perry C. Cotham, *Politics, Americanism, and Christianity* (Grand Rapids, Mich.: Baker, 1976), pp. 192– 93, 8, passim; Wirt, *Evangelical*, chap. 12 and p. 70.
57. John Warwick Montgomery, "Marcuse," *CT*, July 3, 1970, p. 47; Anderson, *America*, p. 51.
58. Stephen V. Monsma, *The Unraveling of America* (Downers Grove, Ill.: Inter-Varsity Press, 1974), pp. 30– 31; Elton Trueblood, "The Life of Service," *CT*, Jan. 30, 1970, p. 4. Monsma is more a change-oriented evangelical than Trueblood, and Monsma, a Humphrey-style Democrat, was not fully comfortable with Trueblood's view.
59. Monsma, *America*, pp. 26ff. and 37; Trueblood, "Service," *CT*, p. 5; John B. Anderson, "Get Active Politically?" *CT*, March 26, 1978, pp. 10 and 12.
60. Cotham, *Christianity*, pp. 203, 206, and 211– 13.
61. Montgomery, *America*, p. 14; Nicholas Wolterstorff, "Reflections on Patriotism," *RJ*, July-Aug. 1976, pp. 10– 13. On most questions, Wolterstorff was unquestionably a change-oriented evangelical.
62. John W. Montgomery, "God's Country," *CT*, Jan. 30, 1970, p. 40; Montgomery, *America*, pp. 50– 51 and 57– 59; John Warwick Montgomery, "Should We Export the American Way?" *CT*, Apr. 23, 1976, pp. 57– 58.
63. Anderson, *America*, p. 12.
64. Cotham, *Christianity*, pp. 251– 52, 290– 92, and 306; Montgomery, *America*, pp. 102– 4 and 135; Anderson, *America*, p. 12.
65. Cotham, *Christianity*, p. 234; John Warwick Montgomery, "Neither Marx nor Jesus," *CT*, Oct. 8, 1971, p. 61.
66. Montgomery, *America*, pp. 109– 33 and 188– 89; Robert Benne and Philip Hefner, *Defining America: A Christian Critique of the American Dream* (Philadelphia: Fortress, 1974), p. 142.
67. Wirt, *Evangelical*, p. 124; Montgomery, *America*, pp. 65, 136, 140, and 138.
68. Anderson, *America*, pp. 23, 122– 23, and 17.
69. Ibid., p. 50.
70. Anderson, *Worlds*, p. 38; Anderson, *America*, p. 118; John W. Montgomery, "Washington Christianity," *CT*, Aug. 8, 1975, pp. 37– 38.
71. D. Elton Trueblood, "The Self and Community," in Henry et al., *Counter-Culture*, pp. 31– 40; Cotham, *Christianity*, p. 238; Rees, *Revolution*, p. 21; Monsma, *America*, pp. 39, 51, and 49; Wirt, *Evangelical*, pp. 99 and 75.
72. A complaint a number of conservative interviewees made to me.

CHAPTER SIX

1. Fred Pearson, *They Dared to Hope: Student Protest and Christian Response* (Grand Rapids, Mich.: Eerdmans, 1969), p. 85.
2. William Pannell, "Evangelicals and Social Concern: The Present and the Future," in *The Chicago Declaration*, ed. Ronald J. Sider (Carol Stream, Ill.: Creation House, 1974), p. 56.

3. Robert E. Webber, "History, Conflict, and Love," *OS*, May-June 1975, p. 56; David O. Moberg, *The Great Reversal* (Philadelphia: Lippincott, 1972), pp. 160–61, 170, and 167–68.

4. Wallace E. Fisher, *Politics, Poker and Piety* (Nashville: Abingdon, 1972), chap. 3; Paul B. Henry, "Reflections," in Sider, ed., *Declaration*.

5. George DeVries, Jr., "A Faith in Power?" *RJ*, July-Aug. 1975, pp. 7–8.

6. Melvin Gingerich, *The Christian and Revolution* (Scottdale, Pa.: Herald Press, 1968), chap. 1.

7. Timothy L. Smith, "A 'Fortress Mentality': Shackling the Spirit's Power," *CT*, Nov. 19, 1976, pp. 22–26.

8. Moberg, *Reversal*, pp. 88–94 and chap. 7.

9. Ronald J. Sider, "An Historic Moment for Biblical Social Concern," in Sider, ed., *Declaration*, pp. 11–42.

10. Foy Valentine, "Engagement—the Christian's Agenda," in Sider, ed., *Declaration*, pp. 57–77.

11. Paul B. Henry, *Politics for Evangelicals* (Valley Forge, Pa.: Judson, 1974), p. 104.

12. Sider, ed., *Declaration*, p. 1.

13. Henry, *Evangelicals*, p. 104.

14. Vernard Eller, *The Simple Life: The Christian Stance Toward Possessions* (Grand Rapids, Mich.: Eerdmans, 1973), p. 38.

15. Sider, ed., *Declaration*, p. 1.

16. Ibid., p. 2; Eller, *Life*; Sider, ed., *Declaration*; Henry, *Evangelicals*.

17. David O. Moberg, *Inasmuch* (Grand Rapids, Mich.: Eerdmans, 1965), p. 66.

18. E.g., Henry B. Clark, *Escape from the Money Trap* (Valley Forge, Pa.: Judson, 1973), pp. 62–65.

19. Moberg, *Reversal*, chap. 3; Jack Rogers, *Confessions of a Conservative Evangelical* (Philadelphia: Westminster, 1974), pp. 107–8; Henry, *Evangelicals*, pp. 54–55.

20. Robert G. Clouse et al., eds., *The Cross and the Flag* (Carol Stream, Ill.: Creation House, 1972), p. 15.

21. Vernon Grounds, *Revolution and the Christian Faith* (Philadelphia: Lippincott, 1971), pp. 208–9.

22. Richard Quebedeaux, *The Young Evangelicals: Revolution in Orthodoxy* (New York: Harper & Row, 1974), p. 53.

23. Ibid., pp. 37–38, 74–75, and 101–2.

24. Moberg, *Reversal*, pp. 25, 162, and 147.

25. Henry, *Evangelicals*; interview.

26. "Second Annual Thanksgiving Workshop of Evangelicals for Social Action," *OS*, Jan.-Feb. 1975, pp. 34–35.

27. Donald W. Dayton, *Discovering an Evangelical Heritage* (New York: Harper, 1976), pp. 4, 2, and chap. 10.

28. Linda K. Pritchard, "Religious Change in Nineteenth-Century America," in Sider, ed., *Declaration*, chap. 14.

29. Sydney Ahlstrom, *A Religious History of the American People* (New Haven: Yale University Press, 1972), chap. 39.

30. Timothy Smith, *Revivalism and Social Reform in Nineteenth-Century America* (New York: Abingdon, 1957); Dayton, *Heritage*, pp. 125–26; Martin E. Marty, *Righteous Empire* (New York: Dial, 1970), p. 93.

31. Smith, *America*, chap. 11; Dayton, *Heritage*, chap. 8; Donald W. and Lucille Sider Dayton, "Women as Preachers: Evangelical Precedents," *CT*, May 23, 1975, pp. 4–7.

32. Donald W. and Lucille Sider Dayton, "Recovering a Heritage: Evangelical Feminism," *PA*, 3, No. 6 (1974).

33. E.g., John A. DeJong, "Social Concerns," in *Piety and Patriotism: Bicentennial Studies of the Reformed Church in America, 1776–1976*, ed. James W. Van Hoeven (Grand Rapids, Mich.: Eerdmans, 1976), pp. 114–15 and passim.

34. Smith, *America*, chap. 7; Dayton, *Heritage*, chaps. 4, 5, and 7; Donald W. Dayton, "Recovering a Heritage: The Tappan Brothers: Businessmen and Reformers," *PA*, 4, No. 4 (1975); "Recovering a Heritage: Orange Scott and the Wesleyan Methodists," *PA*, 4, No. 1 (1975); "Recovering a Heritage: Theodore Weld: Evangelical Reformer," *PA*, 4, No. 3 (1975).

35. Marty, *Empire*, p. 98; DeJong, "Concerns," p. 116; Smith, *America*, chap. 12.

36. Sidney E. Mead, *The Lively Experiment: The Shaping of Christianity in America* (New York: Harper & Row, 1963); Marty, *Empire*, chap. 11 and p. 95; Paul Carter, *The Decline and Revival of the Social Gospel: Social and Political Liberalism in American Protestant Churches, 1920–1940* (Ithaca, N.Y.: Cornell University Press, 1954), pp. 8–9.

37. Perry C. Cotham, *Politics, Americanism, and Christianity* (Grand Rapids, Mich.: Baker, 1976), p. 93; George Marsden, "Evangelical Social Concern—Dusting Off the Heritage," *CT*, May 12, 1972, p. 5.

38. F. Dean Lueking, *A Century of Caring: The Welfare Ministry Among Missouri Synod Lutherans, 1868–1968* (St. Louis: Lutheran Church-Missouri Synod, 1968); Ahlstrom, *People*, pp. 694–95 and 858-72.

39. Marty, *Empire*, chap. 14, pp. 150 and 180; Mead, *America*, pp. 137–38 and 158–59; Dayton, *Heritage*, pp. 128 and 131–32; Philip S. Benjamin, *The Philadelphia Quakers in the Industrial Age 1865–1920* (Philadelphia: Temple University Press, 1976).

40. Marty, *Empire*, chap. 19; Mead, *America*, pp. 177–83.

41. Mead, *America*, p. 142.

42. Dayton, *Heritage*, pp. 113–14 and 109; Norris Magnuson, *Salvation in the Slums: Evangelical Social Work 1865–1920* (Metuchen, N.J.: Scarecrow, 1977), pp. 38, 101, chaps. 12, 15, and passim.

43. Dayton, *Heritage*, p. 101.

44. James W. Van Hoeven, "The American Frontier," in Van Hoeven, ed., *Patriotism*, pp. 49–50.

45. William G. McLoughlin, *Modern Revivalism* (New York: Ronald Press, 1959), pp. 444 and 438.

46. Robert D. Linder, "Fifty Years After Scopes: Lesson to Learn, A Heritage to Reclaim," *CT*, July 18, 1975, pp. 7–10.

47. Carter, *Gospel*, pp. 94–95 and chaps. 4 and 10; Robert D. Linder, "The Resurgence of Evangelical Social Concern," in *The Evangelicals*, ed. David Wells and John D. Woodbridge (Grand Rapids, Mich.: Baker, 1975), p. 218.

48. Moberg, *Reversal*, pp. 30–31 and 34–39; Carter, *Gospel*, p. 178 and chap. 11.

49. Wesley Pippert, *Memo for 1976: Some Political Options* (Downers Grove, Ill.: InterVarsity Press, 1974), pp. 87 and 89; Henry, *Evangelicals*, p. 74.

50. Quebedeaux, *Evangelicals*, p. 81.

51. Moberg, *Inasmuch*, pp. 148, 43, and 39–40; Calvin Redekop, *The Free Church and Seductive Culture* (Scottdale, Pa.: Herald Press, 1970), p. 142; John Howard Yoder, *The Politics of Jesus* (Grand Rapids, Mich.: Eerdmans, 1972), pp. 189–90; Rogers, *Evangelical*, pp. 47, 26–27, and 100.

52. Wesley Pippert, *Faith at the Top* (Elgin, Ill.: Cook, 1973), p. 67.

53. Mark Hatfield, *Conflict and Conscience* (Waco, Tex.: Word, 1971), p. 36; Robert Eells and Bartell Nyberg, *Lonely Walk: The Life of Senator Mark Hatfield* (Chappaqua, N.Y.: Christian Herald Books, 1979), pp. 30, 36, 40–41.

54. Hatfield, *Conscience,* p. 20; Mark Hatfield, *Between a Rock and a Hard Place* (Waco, Tex.: Word, 1976), pp. 22–25 and 110–11.
55. Mark Hatfield, *Not Quite So Simple* (New York: Harper, 1968), pp. 286, 278–79, 281–82, 244, 183, 250, 206–9, 131, 138–43, 121, and chap. 6; Eells and Nyberg, *Life,* chap. 8 and p. 154.
56. Hatfield, *Conscience,* pp. 67–68, 161, and 65.
57. Hatfield, *Place,* p. 91.
58. Ibid., chap. 7 and p. 103.
59. Hatfield, *Conscience,* p. 50.
60. Ibid., p. 58.
61. Ibid., p. 42; Mark O. Hatfield, "The Greed of Men and the Will of God," *OS,* Nov.-Dec. 1974, pp. 8–13 and 62–64.
62. Hatfield, *Place,* p. 191.
63. Ibid., p. 37.
64. Ibid., p. 208.
65. Mark O. Hatfield, "Celebrating the Year of Liberation," *CT,* Mar. 26, 1976, p. 37; see also *CT,* Nov. 21, 1975, p. 47; Eells and Nyberg, *Life,* chap. 13.
66. Hatfield, *Place,* pp. 211–12; Hatfield, "Liberation," *CT,* p. 47; Mark O. Hatfield, "An Economics to Sustain Humanity," *PA,* 4, No. 3 (1975).
67. Pippert, *Options,* p. 587; Hatfield, *Place,* pp. 29 and 23.
68. Hatfield, *Conscience,* p. 57.
69. Ibid., p. 73.
70. Ibid., pp. 54 and 28–29; Clouse et al., eds., *Flag.,* p. 16.
71. Hatfield, *Place,* p. 16; Henry, *Evangelicals,* pp. 7–9.
72. Mark Hatfield, "The CIA: Keeping Close," *CT,* Jan. 2, 1976, p. 37.
73. Hatfield, *Place,* pp. 42–43 and 69.
74. Hatfield, *Conscience,* pp. 120, 110, and 112.
75. Ibid., p. 26; "News on Watergate," *CT,* May 25, 1973, p. 46.
76. Mark Hatfield, "The Vulnerability of Leadership," *CT,* June 22, 1973, pp. 4–5.
77. Mark O. Hatfield, "Repentance, Politics and Power," *PA,* 3, No. 1 (1974), p. 14; Eells and Nyberg, *Life,* pp. 82–83.
78. Ibid.
79. Pippert, *Top,* p. 72.
80. Hatfield, *Place,* p. 28.
81. Hatfield, *Conscience,* pp. 157 and 159.
82. Hatfield, *Place,* pp. 183–84 and 172–74.
83. Ibid., p. 177; Hatfield, *Conscience,* pp. 110–12.
84. Hatfield, *Place,* p. 190; Hatfield, "Liberation," *CT,* p. 13.
85. Hatfield, *Place,* pp. 37 and 61–68; Hatfield, *Conscience,* pp. 166–68.
86. Hatfield, *Place,* pp. 64 and 66; Hatfield, *Conscience,* p. 162.
87. Clouse et al., eds., *Flag,* p. 9; Hatfield, *Conscience,* p. 167; Hatfield, *Place,* pp. 72–73.
88. Hatfield, *Not Quite,* chap. 7.
89. Hatfield, *Place,* pp. 153–57, 118, and 120.
90. Elisabeth O'Connor, *Call to Commitment* (New York: Harper & Row, 1963).
91. Ibid., pp. 158, 126–29, 35–37, and passim.
92. Elisabeth O'Connor, *Journey Inward, Journey Outward* (New York: Harper & Row, 1968), p. ix; O'Connor, *Commitment,* pp. 160–64 and chap. 5.

93. O'Connor, *Outward*, p. 33; O'Connor, *Commitment*, chap. 3 and p. 100.

94. O'Connor, *Commitment*, p. 185 and chaps. 9 and 11; O'Connor, *Outward*, chaps. 9, 4, 10, 6, and 7.

95. James and Marti Hefley, *The Church That Takes on Trouble* (Elgin, Ill.: Cook, 1976), p. 223.

96. Ibid., p. 207, chap. 12, and passim; Richard Quebedeaux, *The Worldly Evangelicals* (New York: Harper & Row, 1978), p. 109.

CHAPTER SEVEN

1. Jim Wallis, "Reflections," in *The Chicago Declaration*, ed. Ronald J. Sider (Carol Stream, Ill.: Creation House, 1974), pp. 140–42.

2. Jim Wallis, *S*, Jan. 1977, p. 16.

3. Dennis Lane, "The Place to Start (Reconsidered)," *CT*, Mar.-Apr. 1975, pp. 11–16; Jim Wallis, "Revolt on Evangelical Frontiers: A Response," *CT*, June 21, 1974, pp. 20–21.

4. John F. Alexander, "Some Inerrant Thoughts on Scripture," *OS*, May-June 1976, p. 9; John F. Alexander, "Editorial: The Authority of Scripture," *OS*, Jan.-Feb. 1973, pp. 2–3, 45–48.

5. Wallis, "Revolt," *CT*, p. 20.

6. Donald Dayton, *OS*, May-June 1976, pp. 36–39.

7. Alexander, "Inerrant Thoughts," *OS*, p. 10.

8. Virginia R. Mollenkott, *Adamant and Stone Chips* (Waco, Tex.: Word, 1967), pp. 13, 96, 72, and 70.

9. A point suggested to me by David Cook.

10. Richard Quebedeaux, *The Worldly Evangelicals* (New York: Harper & Row, 1978), pp. 151–52.

11. Ibid., p. 151; John F. Alexander, "Editorial," *OS*, July-Aug. 1975, p. 63.

12. Jim Wallis, "Post-American Christianity," *PA*, 1, No. 1 (1971).

13. "What is the People's Christian Coalition?" *PA*, 1, No. 1 (1971), 5.

14. Jim Wallis, "The Future of the *Post-American*," *PA*, 3, No. 8 (1974), 3.

15. Ibid.

16. Jim Wallis, "The Move to Washington, D.C.," *PA*, 4, No. 7 (1975), 4.

17. Jim Wallis, "Sojourners," *PA*, 4, No. 8 (1975), 3–4.

18. John Howard Yoder, *Nevertheless: A Meditation on the Varieties and Shortcomings of Religious Pacifism* (Scottdale, Pa.: Herald, 1971), p. 123.

19. Jim Wallis, "The Vehicle for the Vision," *S*, Jan. 1977, p. 3.

20. Mollenkott, *Chips*, p. 23.

21. James W. Jones, "The Practice of Peoplehood," *S*, May 1977, p. 9.

22. Yoder, *Nevertheless*, p. 124; Wallis, "Vehicle," *S*, p. 3.

23. Yoder, *Nevertheless*, p. 125; Diane MacDonald, "They Hold All Things in Common," *PA*, 4, No. 6 (1975).

24. Juan Mateus, "The Message of Jesus," *S*, June 1977, pp. 8–16.

25. Virgil Vogt, "Economic Koinonia," *S*, Jan. 1977, pp. 96–97; Virgil Vogt, "Economic Koinonia," *PA*, 4, No. 6 (1975).

26. Wallis, "Vehicle," *S*, p. 3.

27. Clark H. Pinnock, "An Evangelical Theology of Human Liberation," *S*, Jan. 1977, p. 54.

28. Jones, "Peoplehood," *S*; Art Gish, "Community: First Fruits of the New Order," *S*, Jan. 1977, pp. 94–95.

29. Yoder, *Nevertheless*, p. 78.

30. Jim Wallis, "Movemental Church," *PA*, 1, No. 2 (1972), 3.

31. Jim Wallis, "The Issue of 1972," *PA*, 1, No. 5 (1972).

32. Dave and Neta Jackson, "Living in Community, Being the Church," *OS*, May-June 1973, pp. 8–13; Arthur Gish, *The New Left and Christian Radicalism* (Grand Rapids, Mich.: Eerdmans, 1970), p. 132.

33. Jim Wallis, "A Community of Communities," *S*, 5, No. 2 (1976).

34. Wallis, "Vehicle," *S*, p. 4.

35. Gordon Cosby, "The Power of Undeflected Obedience," *S*, Apr. 1977, p. 27.

36. Wallis, "Vehicle," *S*, p. 3; Wes Michaelson, "Alternative Reality," *S*, Jan. 1977, pp. 4–5; dialogue with Conrad Hoover, Karin Michaelson, Wes Michaelson, Betty O'Connor, and Beth Burbank, *PA*, 4, No. 7 (1975); "A Portrait of Sojourners Fellowship," *S*, Jan. 1977.

37. Jones, "Peoplehood," *S*, p. 8.

38. Graham Pulkingham, "The Shape of the Church to Come," in *S*, Nov. 1976, p. 13; and *S*, Dec. 1976, p. 11; Graham Pulkingham, "Interview," Jan. 1977, pp. 21–23.

39. Adam Finnerty, "The Christian Model," *PA*, 2, No. 4 (1974); Clark Pinnock, "The Christian as a Revolutionary Man," *PA*, 1, No. 4 (1972); Carlton B. Turner, "A New Man," *PA*, 1, No. 1 (1971).

40. Alan Walker, *God, the Disturber* (Waco, Tex.: Word, 1973), pp. 15 and 63.

41. Gish, *Christian Radicalism*, p. 94.

42. William Stringfellow, *An Ethic for Christians and Other Aliens in a Strange Land* (Waco, Tex.: Word, 1976), p. 31.

43. Gish, *Christian Radicalism*, pp. 123, and 88–89; Bill Lane, "Lessons from Vietnam," *PA*, 2, No. 2 (1973); Stringfellow, *Aliens*, p. 18; Pinnock, "Christian Revolution," *PA*.

44. Gish, *Christian Radicalism*, p. 106; Jim Wallis, "Election Reflections," *PA*, 2, No. 1 (1973); Arthur G. Gish, "Love as Church Discipline," *OS*, Mar.-Apr. 1973, pp. 12–15 and 40; Wallis, "Post-American Christianity," *PA*; Robert Sabath, "Politics of Worship," *PA*, 2, No. 5 (1972).

45. Ed Guinan, "In Communion with Trampled Bodies," *PA*, 4, No. 4 (1975).

46. Jim Wallis, "The Call to Discipleship," *PA*, 3, No. 4 (1974); Jim Wallis and Robert Sabath, "In Quest of Discipleship," *PA*, 2, No. 3 (1973).

47. Cosby, "Obedience," *S*, p. 26.

48. *PA*, 1, No. 4 (1972), cover.

49. Art Gish, "Simplicity," *PA*, 1, No. 2 (1972); see also Art Gish, "Simplicity," *OS*, May-June 1973, pp. 14–16; Richard K. Taylor, *Economics and the Gospel* (Philadelphia: United Church Press, 1973), p. 21.

50. Clark H. Pinnock, "The Secular Prophets and the Christian Faith," in *Quest for Reality: Christianity and the Counter-Culture*, ed. Carl F. H. Henry et al. (Downers Grove, Ill.: Inter-Varsity Press, 1973), pp. 133–35; Etta L. Worthington, "Simplicity," *PA*, 4, No. 2 (1975); Etta L. Worthington, "Eat That Garbage," *PA*, 3, No. 4 (1974); Wes Michaelson, "Carter's Energy Plan: Conserving the American Way," *S*, July 1977, pp. 4–7; Adam Finnerty, "The Shakertown Pledge," *PA*, 3, No. 5 (1974); "Man and Technology," *PA*, 1, No. 2 (1972).

51. John F. Alexander, "What Matters?" *OS*, July-Aug. 1974, p. 4; Mark Olson, "For the Birds," *OS*, May-June 1973, pp. 42–43.

52. Clark Pinnock, "Second Mile Lifestyle," *S*, June 1977, pp. 31–32.

53. Peggy Herbert, "Cost of Silence," *PA*, 1, No. 4 (1972), p. 9; Gish, *Christian Radicalism*, p. 110.

54. John F. Alexander, "On Being Tenderhearted," *OS*, Nov.-Dec. 1974, pp. 2–4 and 60–62; Jim Wallis, "Editorial," *S*, Dec. 1976, p. 4; Dale Brown, "Revolutionary Implications of the Atonement," *PA*, 2, No. 3 (1973).

55. Taylor, *Economics*, pp. 22–23.

56. Gordon Cosby, "A Sermon on Power and Servanthood," *PA*, 4, No. 6 (1975).

57. John F. Alexander, "The Bible and *The Other Side*," *OS*, Sept.-Oct. 1975, pp. 56–65.

58. Ibid., pp. 59–60.

59. Robert Sabath, "The Bible and the Poor," *PA*, 3, No. 2 (1974); Alexander, "Bible," *OS*, pp. 62–63 and 56-59; John F. Alexander, "Jesus Said, Follow Me," *OS*, May-June 1975, p. 62; Peter Davids, "The People of God and the Wealth of the People," *PA*, 4, No. 6 (1975).

60. John F. Alexander, "Hard Heads and Soft Hearts," *OS*, Jan.-Feb. 1975, pp. 2–3 and 54–58; John F. Alexander, "A Politics of Love," *OS*, July-Aug. 1972, pp. 2–3 and 42–44.

61. Herbert, "Silence," *PA*; Sabath, "Politics of Worship," *PA*; Stringfellow, *Aliens*, pp. 14–15, 27, and 54; William Stringfellow, "The Bible and Ideology," *S*, Jan. 1977, pp. 92–93.

62. Taylor, *Economics*, pp. 78–82; Jim Wallis, "Of Rich and Poor," *PA*, 3, No. 2 (1974); Wes Michaelson, "Politics and Spirituality," *PA*, 3, No. 3 (1974); John F. Alexander, "Politics, Repentance, and Vision," *OS*, Mar.-Apr. 1974, pp. 2–3.

63. Alexander, "Vision," *OS*, pp. 2–4 and 52–54.

64. Wallis, "1972," *PA*; Jim Wallis, "The New Regime," *PA*, 3, No. 7 (1974), 30.

65. Jim Wallis, "The Election and Cheap Grace," *S*, 5, No. 8 (1976); Wes Michaelson, "Demythologizing the Presidency," *S*, 5, No. 2 (1976).

66. Wallis, "1972," *PA*; Gish, *Christian Radicalism*, p. 79.

67. Gish, *Christian Radicalism*, p. 79; John Alexander, "Editorial," *OS*, July-Aug. 1975, p. 63.

68. Alexander, "Editorial," *OS*, 1975, p. 64.

69. Stringfellow, *Aliens*, p. 151; Robert A. Sabath, "Paul's View of the State," *PA*, 3, No. 3 (1974).

70. John Howard Yoder, "The National Ritual: Realism and the Election," *S*, 5, No. 8 (1976).

71. Gish, *Christian Radicalism*, p. 136; Charles Fager, "Ethics, Principalities and Nonviolence," *PA*, 3, No. 8 (1974); Richard K. Taylor, "A Manual for Nonviolent Direct Action," *PA*, 3, No. 8 (1974); Taylor, *Economics*, p. 113.

72. Gish, *Christian Radicalism*, p. 74; Clark Pinnock, "The Radical Reformation," *PA*, 1, No. 5 (1972); Alexander, "Editorial," *OS*, 1975, p. 59.

73. Wallis, "1972," *PA*, p. 3.

74. John Howard Yoder, "The Biblical Mandate," *PA*, 3, No. 3 (1974).

75. Jim Wallis, "What Does Washington Have to Say to Grand Rapids," *S*, July 1977, pp. 3–4; Clark Pinnock, "The Christian Revolution," *PA*, 1 (1971); Pinnock, "Human Liberation," *S*, p. 51; Clark H. Pinnock, "An Evangelical Theology of Human Liberation," Part I, *S*, 5, No. 2 (1976); Clark H. Pinnock, "An Evangelical Theology of Human Liberation," Part II, *S*, 5, No. 3 (1976).

76. Jim Wallis, *S*, Jan. 1977, pp. 18–19; Wallis, "Washington . . . Grand Rapids," *S*.

77. Lucille Sider Dayton, "The Feminist Movement," *PA*, 3, No. 6 (1974); e.g., Sharon Gallagher, "The Second-Rate Rib," *PA*, 3, No. 6 (1974); Donald Dayton, "A Dialogue on Women, Hierarchy, and Equality," *PA*, 4, No. 5 (1975); Jim Wallis, "Our Common Struggle," *PA*, 3, No. 6 (1974).

78. Lee Griffith, "Confession and Captivity," *S*, Feb. 1977, pp. 27–29.

79. Jim Wallis, "Many to Belief, but Few to Obedience," *S*, Jan. 1977, pp. 6–9.

80. Walker, *God*, p. 66.

81. Jim Wallis, "An Agenda For Tomorrow," *OS*, July-Aug. 1975, pp. 47–52.

82. John F. Alexander, "The Making of a Young Evangelical," *OS*, Mar.-Apr. 1975, pp. 2–4, 62, and 60.

83. Ibid., p. 62.

84. Jim Wallis, "Evangelism in Babylon," *PA*, 1, No. 4 (1972), p. 6.

85. Dennis MacDonald, "Christian Transcendence: Dope or Hope?" *PA*, 1, No. 2 (1972); Dennis MacDonald, "Prophetic Resistance," *PA*, 1, No. 3 (1972).

86. Pinnock, "Christian Revolution," *PA*; Dennis MacDonald, "A Call to Costly Grace," *PA*, 2, No. 1 (1973); Wallis, "Evangelism in Babylon," *PA* (1972), p. 6; Wallis, "Movemental Church," *PA*.

87. Deane A. Kemper, "Growing Up Christian," *OS*, Mar.-Apr. 1975, pp. 22–29.

88. John Oliver, "A Failure of Evangelical Conscience," *PA*, 4, No. 5 (1975).

89. Interviews.

90. William Pannell, "Evangelicals and Social Crisis," *S*, Jan. 1977, pp. 39–42.

91. E.g., see M. J. Van Elderen, "Won't You Please Come to Chicago?" *RJ*, Apr. 1976, pp. 20–23; Richard V. Pierard, "Floundering in the Rain," *RJ*, Oct. 1975, pp. 6–8.

92. Jim Stenzel, "The Anti-Communist Captivity of the Church," *S*, Apr. 1977, pp. 15–19; Jim Wallis and Wes Michaelson, "The Plan to Save America," *S*, Jan. 1977, pp. 43–47.

93. Donald Dayton, "Recovering a Heritage: The 'Christian Radicalism' of Oberlin College," *PA*, 3, No. 8 (1974); Donald W. Dayton, "Recovering a Heritage, The Oberlin-Wellington Rescue Case," *PA*, 3, No. 9 (1974); Donald W. Dayton, "Recovering a Heritage: The Lane Rebellion and the Founding of Oberlin College," *PA*, 3, No. 7 (1974).

94. Clark Pinnock, "Election Reflections," *PA*, 2, No. 1 (1973); Art Gish, "Election Reflections," *PA*, 2, No. 1 (1973).

95. Stringfellow, *Aliens*, pp. 154–55. True, Stringfellow, an Episcopalian, was not an evangelical by, say, the standards of Harold Lindsell. But he was very much so in the world of *Sojourners*.

96. Ibid., p. 32.

97. Ibid., pp. 32–33.

98. Bill Pannell, "Lawlessness American Style," *PA*, 1, No. 5 (1972); Jim Wallis, "Election Reflections," *PA*, 2, No. 1 (1973).

99. Stringfellow, *Aliens*, pp. 31 and 28; William Stringfellow, "The Relevance of Babylon," *S*, Jan. 1977, pp. 27–29; Richard J. Mouw, *Politics and the Biblical Drama* (Grand Rapids, Mich.: Eerdmans, 1976), pp. 124–29.

100. Stringfellow, *Aliens*, p. 13; Sabath, "Politics of Worship," *PA*.

101. *PA*, 1, No. 5 (1972), cover.

102. Wallis, "1972," *PA*, p. 2.

103. Jim Roose, "American Civil Religion," *PA*, 1, No. 3 (1972).

104. Glen Melnik, "Awake Thou That Sleepest Or Who Are YOU Sleeping With?" *PA*, 1, No. 1 (1971), 7.

105. Wallis, "1972," *PA*, p. 2; and Jim Wallis, "Air War!" *PA*, 1, No. 3 (1972).

106. Jim Wallis, "Nuclear War by 1999?" *S*, Feb. 1977, p. 4; Dick McSorley, "It's a Sin to Build a Nuclear Weapon," *S*, Feb. 1977, p. 16.

107. Jim Wallis, "The Invisible Empire," *PA*, 2, No. 5 (1973); John Perkins, "The Reconciled Community in a World at War," *S*, July 1977, pp. 21–24 and 39.

108. John F. Alexander, "Editorial," *OS*, Nov.-Dec. 1974.

109. Van Elderen, "Come to Chicago?" *RJ*, p. 21.

110. Jim Wallis, *Agenda for a Biblical People* (New York: Harper & Row, 1976), p. xi.

111. Ibid., pp. 12, 10, and 6.

112. Ibid., p. 1.

113. Ibid., p. x.

114. Ibid., p. 11.

115. Ibid., p. x.

116. Ibid., pp. 133 and 53.

117. Ibid., pp. 96, 23, and 19.
118. Ibid., p. 3.
119. Ibid., p. 133.
120. Ibid., p. 2.
121. Ibid., p. 1.
122. Ibid., p. 24.
123. Ibid., p. 100.
124. Ibid., p. 9.
125. Ibid., p. 2.
126. Ibid., p. 5.
127. Ibid., pp. 30–31.
128. Ibid., pp. 50–51.
129. Ibid., p. 8.
130. Ibid., pp. 59 and 12.
131. Ibid., p. 137.
132. Ibid., p. 126.
133. Ibid., pp. 35 and passim.
134. Ibid., p. 4.
135. Ibid., chap. 5, pp. 5, 117, and 114.
136. Ibid., p. 108.
137. Ibid., p. 139.

CHAPTER EIGHT

1. Robert Culver, *Toward a Biblical View of Civil Government* (Chicago: Moody Press, 1974), p. 184.
2. Perry C. Cotham, *Politics, Americanism, and Christianity* (Grand Rapids, Mich.: Baker, 1976), pp. 36–37.
3. Leighton Ford, *One Way to Change the World* (New York: Harper & Row, 1970), p. vii; "Editorial: 'The Liberator Has Come,' " *CT*, Jan. 29, 1971, pp. 20–21; Bill Bright, *Come Help Change the World* (Old Tappan, N.J.: Revell, 1970), p. 184.
4. Vernon C. Grounds, "Bomb or Bibles?" *CT*, July 19, 1968, p. 6.
5. Carl F. H. Henry, *Evangelicals in Search of Identity* (Waco, Tex.: Word, 1976), pp. 17–18; Frank Bellinger, "Moral Absolutes and Political Ambiguities," *OS*, July-Aug. 1972, pp. 14–17.
6. Culver, *Government*, p. 18.
7. Harold Lindsell, "Uppsala 1968," *CT*, Aug. 16, 1968, pp. 3–7.
8. Wallace E. Fisher, *Politics, Poker, and Piety* (Nashville: Abingdon, 1972), p. 113.
9. Ronald H. Nash, "Marcuse, Reich, and the Rational," in *Quest for Reality: Christianity and the Counter Culture*, ed. Carl F. H. Henry et al. (Downers Grove, Ill.: Inter-Varsity Press, 1973), pp. 52–68.
10. "Editorial: The Student Revolution," *CT*, Feb. 14, 1969, pp. 24–25; "Editorial," *CT*, Nov. 8, 1968, pp. 31–32.
11. "Editorial: Fair Harvard," *CT*, May 9, 1969; L. Nelson Bell, "It Can Happen Here," *CT*, Jan. 2, 1970, pp. 20–21.
12. Joel H. Nederhood, "Christians and Revolution," *CT*, Jan. 1, 1971, p. 9.
13. James Daane, "Selfhood and the Protests of Youth," in Henry et al., eds., *Counter Culture*, pp. 15–28.

14. Arthur G. Gish, *The New Left and Christian Radicalism* (Grand Rapids, Mich.: Eerdmans, 1970), p. 46; Stephen V. Monsma, *The Unraveling of America* (Downers Grove, Ill.: Inter-Varsity, 1974), p. 110; George Mavrodes, "The Counter-Culture: A Flight Toward Reality?," in Henry et al., eds., *Counter Culture*, pp. 77– 86; Paul Henry, "Evangelical Christianity and the Radical Left," in *The Cross and the Flag*, ed. Robert G. Clouse et al. (Carol Stream, Ill.: Creation House, 1972), pp. 94– 96; Fisher, *Piety*, chap. 4; Fred Pearson, *They Dared to Hope: Student Protest and Christian Response* (Grand Rapids, Mich.: Eerdmans, 1969), p. 65.

15. Calvin D. Linton, "The Search for Reality," in Henry et al., eds., *Counter Culture*, p. 147.

16. Clark Pinnock, "Christian Revolution," *PA*, 1, No. 1 (1971); Gish, *Radicalism*, pp. 47 and 46; Monsma, *America*, pp. 111– 13.

17. John Perkins, "A Strategy for Change," *S*, supplement to Jan. 1977, pp. 10– 41.

18. L. Nelson Bell, "Very Personal," *CT*, June 9, 1967, p. 22.

19. Tom Skinner, *Words of Revolution* (Grand Rapids, Mich.: Zondervan, 1970), pp. 171 and 153 and introduction.

20. Often the most thoroughgoing exponents of this view were better seen as fundamentalists, as was true of Hal Lindsey, *The Liberation of Planet Earth* (Grand Rapids, Mich.: Zondervan, 1974), pp. 187– 88 and chap. 5.

21. Ibid., p. 47.

22. Ibid., pp. 27– 28.

23. Carl F. H. Henry, *Aspects of Christian Social Ethics* (Grand Rapids, Mich.: Eerdmans, 1964), p. 16.

24. Paul S. Rees, "Prayer and Social Concern," in *The Chicago Declaration*, ed. Ronald J. Sider (Carol Stream, Ill.: Creation House, 1974), pp. 78– 87.

25. L. Nelson Bell, "Prayer is Practical," *CT*, Dec. 4, 1970, pp. 22– 23; Rees, "Concern," p. 78; Harold O. J. Brown, *Christianity and the Class Struggle* (New Rochelle, N.Y.: Arlington House, 1970), pp. 30– 31.

26. L. Nelson Bell, "Beware," *CT*, Oct. 24, 1969, pp. 24– 25; "Old Serpent, New Strategy," *CT*, May 23, 1975, pp. 17– 20.

27. Clay Ford, *Berkeley Journal: Jesus and the Street People* (New York: Harper & Row, 1972), p. 14; George Edwards, *Jesus and the Politics of Violence* (New York: Harper & Row, 1972), p. 104; Paul B. Henry, *Politics for Evangelicals* (Valley Forge, Pa.: Judson Press, 1974), pp. 50– 51; Fisher, *Piety*, pp. 155– 56; Peggy Herbert, "Cost of Silence," *PA*, 1, No. 4 (1972).

28. "Editorial: Christian Social Action," *CT*, Mar. 14, 1969, pp. 24– 25; David O. Moberg, *Inasmuch*, (Grand Rapids, Mich.: Eerdmans, 1965), pp. 166– 67; Culver, *Government*, p. 100; "Editorial: If My People . . . Pray," *CT*, July 2, 1976, p. 25.

29. David R. Wilkerson, *The Cross and the Switchblade* (New York: Bernard Geis, 1963), p. 49.

30. Al Palmquist, *Miracle at City Hall* (Minneapolis: Bethany, 1974).

31. Nicky Cruz, *The Corruptors* (Old Tappan, N.J.: Revell, 1974), chaps. 2, 4, 10, and 5, and pp. 61 and 129.

32. Wilkerson, *Switchblade*, p. 187; also see Gordon R. McLean, *Man, I Need Help!* (Minneapolis: Bethany, 1975).

33. John Gimenez, *Up Tight!* (Waco, Tex.: Word, 1972); George Edwards, *Crawling Out* (Grand Rapids, Mich.: Zondervan, 1973); Johnny Cash, *Man in Black* (Grand Rapids, Mich.: Zondervan, 1975).

34. For example, James M. Hutchens, *Beyond Combat* (Chicago: Moody Press, 1968); Howard and Phyllis Rutledge, *In the Presence of Mine Enemies 1965– 1973* (Old Tappan, N.J.: Revell, 1973).

35. Rutledge, *Enemies*.

36. For example, Corrie ten Boom, *The Hiding Place* (Washington Depot, Conn.: Chosen

Books, 1971); David R. Wilkerson with Claire Cox, *Parents on Trial: Why Kids Go Wrong—Or Right* (New York: Hawthorne, 1967); Wilkerson, *Switchblade.*

37. Cash, *Black*; Gimenez, *Tight*, p. 23; Wilkerson and Cox, *Trial*, pp. 179, 119, 137, and chap. 8.

38. Wilkerson, *Switchblade*, p. 95.

39. For example, Don Wilkerson and Herm Weiskopf, *The Gutter and the Ghetto* (Waco, Tex.: Word, 1969), chap. 7; Cruz, *Corruptors*, pp. 63 and 110; Rutledge, *Enemies*, pp. 74–75 and 86; Boom, *Place*, p. 156 and passim; Gimenez, *Tight*, pp. 152–53; Wilkerson, *Switchblade*, pp. 134 and 63–64.

40. Wilkerson and Cox, *Trial*, pp. 184–88 and 107; Boom, *Place*, p. 169; McLean, *Help!*, p. 138.

41. Wilkerson and Weiskopf, *Ghetto*, pp. 57–58; Wilkerson and Cox, *Trial*, p. 107.

42. Edward Plowman, *The Jesus Movement* (Elgin, Ill.: Cook, 1971), pp. 10 and passim.

43. Donald M. Williams, "Close-Up of the Jesus People," *CT*, Aug. 27, 1971, pp. 5–7.

44. Marlin Van Elderen, *RJ*, May-June 1971.

45. "Editorial: The New Christians," *CT*, July 16, 1971, pp. 20–21; Ronald M. Enroth, Edward E. Ericson, Jr., and C. Breckenridge Peters, *The Jesus People* (Grand Rapids, Mich.: Eerdmans, 1972), pp. 17 and 10.

46. Enroth et al., *People*, p. 240.

47. Jerry Halliday, *Spaced Out and Gathered In* (Old Tappan, N.J.: Revell, 1972), pp. 35, 101, 61, and 119.

48. Ibid., pp. 15 and 35.

49. Ibid., pp. 123, 109, 117–18, and 108.

50. Interview.

51. Culver, *Government*, pp. 77 and 87.

52. John Howard Yoder, *The Politics of Jesus* (Grand Rapids, Mich.: Eerdmans, 1972), p. 204; James Montgomery Boice, *The Sermon on the Mount* (Grand Rapids, Mich.: Zondervan, 1972), pp. 206–7.

53. Fisher, *Piety*, p. 131; Robert D. Linder, "Christian Faith and Loyalty to the State: Meaning for Today?" in *God and Caesar*, ed. Robert D. Linder (Longview, Tex.: Conference on Faith and History, 1971), pp. 79–80.

54. Culver, *Government*, pp. 88 and 47.

55. Rene de V. Williamson, "The Theology of Liberation," *CT*, Aug. 8, 1975, p. 13; Culver, *Government*, pp. 244–56, 264, 260–61, and 266; Richard W. De Haan, *The World on Trial* (Grand Rapids, Mich.: Zondervan, 1970).

56. William R. Newell, *Romans Verse by Verse* (Chicago: Moody Press, 1976 [1938]), p. 484.

57. William S. Plumer, *Commentary on Romans* (Grand Rapids, Mich.: Kregel, 1971 [1870]), pp. 587–88.

58. Ibid., p. 590.

59. Culver, *Government*, pp. 183 and 239.

60. Bob Sabath, "The State: An Apostolic View," *S*, supplement to Jan. 1977, p. 32.

61. Ibid., p. 34; Bob Sabath, "Emily Post and Richard Nixon Revisited," *PA*, 1, No. 3 (1972).

62. Jim Wallis, "What Does Washington Have to Say to Grand Rapids?" *S*, July 1977; Yoder, *Jesus*, p. 150.

63. Archie Penner, "Get Active Politically? No Not Necessarily," *CT*, Mar. 26, 1976, pp. 11–12; John Howard Yoder, "The Biblical Mandate," *S*, supplement to Jan. 1977, pp. 15–18.

64. "Editorial," *CT*, June 9, 1972, p. 28; Brown, *Struggle*, p. 45; "Editorial: We Are Sick," *CT*, Apr. 14, 1972, p. 34; C. Henry, *Ethics*, pp. 160–61, 154–55, and 158.

65. Carl McIntire, *Outside the Gate* (Collingswood, N.J.: Christian Beacon Press, 1967). pp. 260 and 215; Erling Jorstad, *The Politics of Doomsday: Fundamentalists of the Far Right* (Nashville: Abingdon, 1970), pp. 140–41.
66. C. Henry, *Ethics*, pp. 120-21.
67. Monsma, *America*, p. 65; Hutchens, *Combat*, p. 51.
68. "Editorial," *CT*, June 8, 1973, p. 26.
69. John Warwick Montgomery, *The Shaping of America* (Minneapolis: Bethany, 1976), pp. 154–55.
70. See Chapter Ten for discussion on abortion.
71. P. Henry, *Evangelicals*, p. 38; Paul B. Henry, "A Christian Trial of the Campaign Trail," *OS*, Sept.-Oct. 1972, pp. 6–11.
72. Robert D. Linder, "The Christian and Political Involvement in Today's World," in Clouse et al., eds., *Flag*, p. 39.
73. Wesley Pippert, *Memo for 1976: Some Political Options* (Downers Grove, Ill.: Inter-Varsity Press, 1974), chap. 2.
74. Monsma, *America*, pp. 122 and 125–33; Moberg, *Inasmuch*, pp. 128–33 and 113; James Johnson, "Evangelical Christianity and Poverty," in Clouse et al., eds., *Flag*, pp. 172–73.
75. Linder, "Today's World," pp. 36–37; Monsma, *America*, pp. 85–91.
76. Robert D. Linder and Richard V. Pierard, "Politics: The Case for Christian Action," *OS*, Mar.-Apr. 1974, pp. 8, 10, 12, and 46–51.
77. P. Henry, *Evangelicals*, pp. 68–70 and 78.
78. Ibid., p. 101.
79. Herbert, "Silence," *PA*; see also Pearson, *Christian Response*, p. 90.
80. Moberg, *Inasmuch*, pp. 49–50.
81. Fisher, *Piety*, p. 170.
82. P. Henry, *Evangelicals*, p. 107.
83. Fisher, *Piety*, pp. 170 and 146; Cotham, *Christianity*, pp. 80–81.
84. Moberg, *Inasmuch*, pp. 91–97.
85. C. Walton Gaddy, *Profile of a Christian Citizen* (Nashville: Broadman, 1974), pp. 22–23, 88, and chap. 5.
86. George W. Dollar, *A History of Fundamentalism in America* (Greenville, S.C.: Bob Jones University, 1973), p. 191.
87. McIntire, *Gate*, pp. 287 and 269.
88. C. Henry, *Ethics*, pp. 186, 82, and 121–23.
89. Ibid., pp. 112–13.
90. Ibid., pp. 105–8.
91. Billy Graham, *World Aflame* (Garden City, N.Y.: Doubleday, 1965), pp. 181 and 230–35; Sherwood Eliot Wirt, *The Social Conscience of the Evangelical* (New York: Harper & Row, 1968), p. 134; Malcolm Nygren, "The Church and Political Action," *CT*, Mar. 14, 1969, pp. 9–12; Richard J. Mouw, *Political Evangelism* (Grand Rapids, Mich.: Eerdmans, 1973), p. 82.
92. "Editorial: The Off-Year Ballot," *CT*, Oct. 24, 1969, p. 30; Reo Christenson, "The Church and Public Policy," *CT*, Jan. 5, 1973, pp. 12–15.
93. Jeffrey K. Hadden, *The Gathering Storm in the Churches* (Garden City, N.Y.: Doubleday, 1969), pp. 136–37.
94. Lowell D. Streiker and Gerald S. Strober, *Religion and the New Majority: Billy Graham, Middle America, and the Politics of the 1970s* (New York: Association, 1972), p. 45.
95. L. Nelson Bell, "Hearts That Burn," *CT*, July 16, 1971, pp. 27–28; "Those Church Pronouncements," *CT*, Feb. 12, 1971, pp. 38–39; Ilion T. Jones, "The Church's Defec-

tion From a Divine Mission," *CT*, May 24, 1968, pp. 3–5; "Editorial: Putting First Things Second," *CT*, Mar. 1, 1968, p. 27; L. Nelson Bell, "Lay Concern," *CT*, Mar. 1, 1968, pp. 19–20.

96. "Editorial: Who Speaks For the Church?" *CT*, June 9, 1967, pp. 26–27.

97. Edmund P. Clowney, "A Critique of the 'Political Gospel'," *CT*, Apr. 28, 1967, pp. 7–11.

98. Ibid.

99. Wallace Henley, *Enter At Your Own Risk* (Old Tappan, N.J.: Revell, 1974), chaps. 6 and 2, pp. 133–34 and 43.

100. Brendan F. J. Furnish, "The Cultural Seduction of the Church," *CT*, June 18, 1976, pp. 4–6; George Marsden, "Did Success Spoil American Protestantism?" *CT*, Sept. 29, 1967, pp. 4–7.

101. Calvin Redekop, *The Free Church and Seductive Culture* (Scottdale, Pa.: Herald Press, 1970), pp. 47–48, 59, and 72-80; Elisabeth O'Connor, *Journey Inward, Journey Outward* (New York: Harper & Row, 1968), chap. 9; Elisabeth O'Connor, *Call to Commitment* (New York: Harper & Row, 1963), p. 185; Bill Lane, "Lessons from Vietnam," *PA*, 2, No. 2 (1973); Clark Pinnock, "The Radical Reformation," *PA*, 1, No. 5 (1972).

102. Jim Wallis, "The Issue of 1972," *PA*, 1, No. 4 (1972); Jim Wallis, "Of Rich and Poor," *PA*, 3, No. 2 (1974); Wes Michaelson, "Politics and Spirituality," *PA*, 3, No. 3 (1974); Charles Fager, "Ethics, Principalities and Nonviolence," *PA*, 3, No. 8 (1974).

103. Donald Durnbaugh, "Is 'Withdrawal' Involvement?," *OS*, Mar.-Apr. 1974, pp. 21–23; Dale W. Brown, "Faithfulness in Witness: Liberal or Radical," *OS*, Mar.-Apr. 1974, pp. 9, 11, 13, and 51.

104. John F. Alexander, "Editorial," *OS*, July-Aug. 1975, p. 63; John F. Alexander, "Editorial: Politics, Repentance and Vision," *OS*, Mar.-Apr. 1974, pp. 2–3.

105. Alexander, "Editorial: Politics," *OS*.

106. Yoder, *Jesus*, p. 158; also see John H. Yoder, "The Biblical Mandate," in Sider, ed., *Declaration*, pp. 88–116.

107. Dale W. Brown, *The Christian Revolutionary* (Grand Rapids, Mich.: Eerdmans, 1971), pp. 61, 107–8, and 41–42.

108. Ibid., pp. 110 and 77.

109. Richard J. Mouw, *Politics and the Biblical Drama* (Grand Rapids, Mich.: Eerdmans, 1976), pp. 112–13, 98ff, and 137–38.

110. Stephen Charles Mott, "The Politics of Jesus and Our Response," *RJ*, Feb., 1976, pp. 7–10.

111. Edwards, *Violence*, pp. 22–37 and 64ff.; Yoder, *Jesus*, pp. 50–51; Vernon Grounds, *Revolution and the Christian Faith* (Philadelphia: Lippincott, 1971), chap. 6.

112. E.g., "Editorial," *CT*, Apr. 13, 1973, p. 33.

113. Mark Hatfield, *Between a Rock and a Hard Place* (Waco, Tex.: Word, 1976), p. 114; Yoder, *Jesus*, pp. 242–43.

114. Grounds, *Faith*, chap. 8; Harold B. Kuhn, "A Theology of Violence," *CT*, Nov. 22, 1968, p. 43; Cotham, *Christianity*, p. 102.

115. Grounds, *Faith*, pp. 162, 164–65, 176, 175, and 181.

116. Norman L. Geisler, *Ethics: Alternatives and Issues* (Grand Rapids, Mich.: Zondervan, 1971), p. 89; Bloom, *Place*, p. 123.

117. Grounds, *Faith*, pp. 104, 140, and chap. 7.

118. Ralph B. Potter, *War and Moral Discourse* (Richmond, Va.: John Knox, 1969), p. 280; George W. Knight, III, "Can a Christian Go To War?" *CT*, Nov. 21, 1975, pp. 4–7; Geisler, *Issues*, chap. 9; Hutchens, *Combat*, pp. 49–50.

119. Vernard Eller, *King Jesus' Manual of Arms for the Armless* (Nashville: Abingdon, 1973), pp. 80, 35–37, 153, and 73.

120. William Nix in *Our Society in Turmoil*, ed. Gary R. Collins (Carol Stream, Ill.: Creation House, 1970), chap. 15.

121. Alan Walker, *God, the Disturber* (Waco, Tex.: Word, 1973), p. 25.

122. Gish, *Radicalism*, pp. 138–39; Walker, *Disturber*, chap. 10; Lane, "Vietnam," *PA*; Myron S. Augsburger, "Beating Swords into Plowshares," *CT*, Nov. 21, 1975, pp. 7–9.

123. John Howard Yoder, *Nevertheless: A Meditation on the Varieties and Shortcomings of Religious Pacifism* (Scottdale, Pa.: Herald Press, 1971).

124. Delton Franz, "Channeling War Taxes to Peace," *S*, Mar. 1977, pp. 21–23; Donald Kaufman, "Paying for War," *S*, Mar. 1977, pp. 16–19.

125. Yoder, *Jesus*, p. 250.

126. Cotham, *Christianity*, chap. 6; Richard K. Taylor, "A Manual for Nonviolent Direct Action," *PA*, 3, No. 8 (1974).

127. MacDonald, "Prophetic Resistance," *PA*, 1, No. 3 (1972), 1–3.

128. John Howard Yoder, "Why I Didn't Pay All My Income Tax," *S*, Mar. 1977, pp. 11–12.

129. Brown, *Revolutionary*, pp. 139, 130–34, 100, and 130.

130. "Editorial: Civil Disobedience," *CT*, June 5, 1970, p. 26.

CHAPTER NINE

1. L. Nelson Bell, "The Church and Poverty," *CT*, Mar. 27, 1970, p. 27.

2. W. A. Criswell, *What to Do Until Jesus Comes Back?* (Nashville: Broadman, 1975), pp. 49, 52–54, 135–36, and 130.

3. Harold Lindsell, *The World, the Flesh, and the Devil* (Washington: Canon Press, 1973), pp. 197–98.

4. Charles Y. Furness, *The Christian and Social Action* (Old Tappan, N.J.: Revell, 1972), pp. 101 and 109; Martin H. Scharlemann, *The Church's Social Responsibilities* (St. Louis: Concordia, 1971), chap. 3 and p. 71.

5. Scharlemann, *Responsibilities*, p. 29.

6. Ibid., p. 37.

7. Ibid., pp. 64, 68–69, and 71; Furness, *Action*, chap. 7 and pp. 98 and 93.

8. Scharlemann, *Responsibilities*, pp. 13 and 76; Furness, *Action*, p. 241.

9. Paul B. Henry, "Social Ethics," *CT*, Jan. 2, 1970, pp. 28–29.

10. John W. Montgomery, *CT*, Sept. 26, 1969, p. 44.

11. David O. Moberg, *Inasmuch* (Grand Rapids, Mich.: Eerdmans, 1965), p. 22.

12. Richard Mouw, "Saving Our Ship," *S*, May 1977, p. 34.

13. John R. W. Stott, *Christ the Controversialist* (Wheaton, Ill.: Tyndale Press, 1970), p. 145; Ronald J. Sider, "Evangelism or Social Justice: Eliminating the Options," *CT*, Oct. 8, 1976, pp. 26–29; Moberg, *Inasmuch*, p. 33.

14. Lee Nash, "Evangelism and Social Concern" in *The Cross and the Flag*, ed. Robert Clouse et al. (Carol Stream, Ill.: Creation House, 1972), p. 154; cf. Richard J. Mouw, *Political Evangelism* (Grand Rapids, Mich.: Eerdmans, 1973), pp. 93–94.

15. John W. Montgomery, "Evangelical Social Responsibility," in *Our Society in Turmoil*, ed. Gary R. Collins (Carol Stream, Ill.: Creation House, 1970), p. 15.

16. Melvin Gingerich, *The Christian and Revolution* (Scottdale, Pa.: Herald Press, 1968), p. 115; Ronald J. Sider, ed., *The Chicago Declaration* (Carol Stream, Ill.: Creation House, 1974).

17. Calvin Redekop, *The Free Church and Seductive Culture* (Scottdale, Pa.: Herald Press, 1970), p. 32.

18. Boyd Reese, "Justice 1972," *PA*, 2, No. 1 (1973).

19. Gary K. Clabaugh, *Thunder on the Right: The Protestant Fundamentalists* (Chicago:

Nelson-Hall, 1974), p. 196; William E. Pannell, *My Friend, The Enemy* (Waco, Tex.: Word, 1968), p. 53.

20. Carl McIntire, *Outside the Gate* (Christian Beacon Press, 1967), pp. 79–80; Virginia Mollenkott, "Up from Ignorance: Awareness-Training and Racism," *CT*, Mar. 26, 1971, p. 7; Bob Harrison and Jim Montgomery, *When God Was Black* (Grand Rapids, Mich.: Zondervan, 1971), p. 18 and chap. 5.

21. McIntire, *Gate*, pp. 62 and 59–60.

22. Billy James Hargis, *Why I Fight for a Christian America* (Nashville: Thomas Nelson, 1974), pp. 163 and 121; Billy James Hargis, *Billy James Hargis Speaks Out on the Issues* (Tulsa: Christian Crusade, 1971), pp. 16 and 18.

23. Harrison and Montgomery, *Black*, chap. 11; Pannell, *Enemy*, p. 33.

24. Harrison and Montgomery, *Black*, chap. 3; Mollenkott, "Racism," *CT*, p. 7.

25. Ada Lum, *Jesus the Radical* (Downers Grove, Ill.: Inter-Varsity Press, 1970), p. 19; Gingerich, *Revolution*, p. 118; Paul S. Rees, *Don't Sleep Through the Revolution* (Waco, Tex.: Word, 1969), p. 41; Pannell, *Enemy*, pp. 122–23; Francis A. Schaeffer, *Two Contests, Two Realities* (Downers Grove, Ill.: Inter-Varsity Press, 1974), p. 30.

26. Thomas O. Figart, *A Biblical Perspective on the Race Problem* (Grand Rapids, Mich.: Baker, 1973), chaps. 1–4, and pp. 120, 146, and 132; also see Columbus Salley and Ronald Behm, *Your God is Too White* (Downers Grove, Ill.: Inter-Varsity Press, 1970), chap. 6.

27. Mollenkott, "Racism," *CT*, pp. 6–7.

28. Francis A. Schaeffer, *How Should We Then Live?* (Old Tappan, N.J.: Revell, 1976), p. 13; "An Interview with Francis A. Schaeffer," *OS*, Mar.-Apr. 1972, p. 44; Francis A. Schaeffer, "Race and Reason," *OS*, May-June 1974, p. 61.

29. John F. Alexander, "Plastic Domes," *OS*, Jan.-Feb. 1972, pp. 3 and 50–51; John F. Alexander, "A Manifesto for White Christians," *OS*, Jan.-Feb. 1974, pp. 4–6 and 48–53.

30. E.g., "Editorial," *CT*, Nov. 10, 1972, p. 37; *CT*, Jan. 30, 1970, p. 3; Robert Brown, "The Curse of Ham," *CT*, Oct. 26, 1973, p. 30; "Editorial: Subject: Racism," *CT*, July 4, 1969, pp. 21–22; "Editorial: A Cordial Welcome—If You're White," *CT*, Jan. 16, 1970.

31. Joseph Daniels, "The Psychopathology of Racism," *CT*, July 19, 1968, pp. 7–8; James M. Boice, "A Stirring of Conscience," *CT*, May 24, 1968, pp. 45–46; "Editorial," *CT*, Nov. 22, 1968, p. 26; Calvin Linton, "And Pilate Said, 'Make It As Sure As Ye Can', " *CT*, Apr. 13, 1973, pp. 4–10; "Black Baptists," *CT*, Oct. 12, 1973, p. 568; Edward R. Plowman, "News," *CT*, Apr. 25, 1975, pp. 34–42; "News," *CT*, June 9, 1972, p. 45; Edward Plowman, "Baptists Face Issues," *CT*, June 6, 1969, p. 41.

32. "News: Urban Mutiny," *CT*, Aug. 18, 1967, pp. 43–44; "Editorial: Confronting the Racial Crisis," *CT*, Feb. 16, 1968, pp. 26–28; William Willoughby, "Memphis a Year Later," *CT*, Apr. 11, 1975, pp. 42–43; "Editorial: The Making of a Revolution?" *CT*, Jan. 5, 1973, p. 30.

33. "Editorial: Bob Jones University and the I.R.S.," *CT*, July 19, 1968, p. 22.

34. "Editorial," *CT*, Apr. 26, 1968, p. 25.

35. "Editorial: The Churches and James Farmer," *CT*, June 6, 1969, pp. 27–28; "Editorial: Union Seminary," *CT*, June 6, 1969, p. 27; "Editorial: Reparations in Black and White," *CT*, Sept. 26, 1969, p. 37; "News," *CT*, June 6, 1969, pp. 42–43.

36. C. Ralston Smith book review of *Where Do We Go From Here? CT*, Sept. 29, 1967, p. 39; "Abernathy Woos Communists as U.S. Backing Drops," *CT*, Oct. 22, 1971, pp. 43–44.

37. "Editorial: Johnson, King, and Ho Chi Minh," *CT*, Apr. 26, 1968, pp. 24–25.

38. Morris A. Inch, "Anatomy of a Symbol," *CT*, Apr. 11, 1969, pp. 5–7; "Editorial: Panthers and 'Pigs', " *CT*, Jan. 16, 1970, p. 25; Harold B. Kuhn, "Does Theology Come in Colors?" *CT*, Apr. 23, 1971, pp. 43–44.

39. Tom Skinner, *Black and Free* (Grand Rapids, Mich.: Zondervan, 1970), passim; Tom Skinner, *Words of Revolution* (Grand Rapids, Mich.: Zondervan, 1970), pp. i– iii.
40. Skinner, *Free*, pp. 54– 55, 105, and 92– 95.
41. Ibid., p. 93.
42. Richard Quebedeaux, *The Young Evangelicals: Revolution in Orthodoxy* (New York: Harper & Row, 1974), p. 116; "News," *CT*, June 4, 1971, p. 27.
43. Skinner, *Free*, pp. 147– 48; Skinner, *Revolution*, pp. 103– 5 and 36– 37; Tom Skinner, *How Black is the Gospel?* (Philadelphia: Lippincott, 1970), p. 76; Tom Skinner, "Black Power," *OS*, Jan.-Feb. 1972, pp. 7– 11 and 46– 47.
44. Tom Skinner, "Modern Youth in Biblical Perspective," in *Prophecy in the Making*, ed. Carl F. H. Henry et al. (Carol Stream, Ill.: Creation House, 1971), p. 291.
45. Skinner, *Revolution*, pp. 85– 86, 71, 61, and 135; Skinner, "Perspective."
46. Skinner, "Perspective," p. 264.
47. Skinner, *Free*, p. 152; Tom Skinner, *OS*, July-Aug. 1975, p. 29.
48. Skinner, "Perspective," p. 273; Skinner, *Gospel?*, p. 121.
49. Skinner, *OS*, July-Aug. 1975, p. 28.
50. Skinner, *Gospel?*, p. 77; Skinner, "Perspective," pp. 282– 83.
51. Skinner, *Revolution*, pp. 167, 62– 63, and 117; Skinner, *Gospel?*, pp. 16, 50– 51, 45– 46, 70, and 39; Skinner, *Free*, pp. 140– 42.
52. John Perkins, *Let Justice Roll Down* (Glendale, Calif.: Regal, 1976), chap. 18, pp. 111, 107, 103– 4, chap. 17, p. 195, and chap. 15.
53. Pannell, *Enemy*, pp. 31 and 16.
54. Ibid., pp. 92, 96, 63– 64, and 30.
55. John Perkins, "Black Religion," *OS*, Jan.-Feb. 1972, pp. 24– 29; William Pannell, "The Religious Heritage of Blacks," in *The Evangelicals*, rev. ed., ed. David Wells and John D. Woodbridge (Grand Rapids, Mich.: Baker, 1975), chap. 5; William H. Bentley, "Bible Believers in the Black Community," in Wells and Woodbridge, eds., *Evangelicals*, chap. 6; William H. Bentley, "Reflections," in Sider, ed., *Declaration*, pp. 135– 36.
56. Salley and Behm, *White*, chaps. 5 and 7, pp. 83 and 72.
57. John Perkins, "Integration or Development," *OS*, Jan.-Feb. 1974, pp. 10– 13 and 46– 48; "An Interview with John Perkins," *PA*.
58. Cf. Rufus Jones, "Christ and Culture," *OS*, Jan.-Feb. 1974, p. 23.
59. E.g., B. Sam Hart, "Questions and Answers," *OS*, Jan.-Feb. 1972, pp. 44– 45.
60. E.g., Barrie Doyle, "News: Famine in Africa: It's Worse," *CT*, pp. 48– 50; "Editorial: Lord, When Did We See the Hungry?" *CT*, Sept. 14, 1973, pp. 31– 32; "News: Africa's Creeping Calamity," *CT*, Sept. 14, 1973, pp. 42– 44.
61. See entire issue of *Christianity Today*, July 16, 1976; "Editorial," *CT*, July 20, 1973, pp. 29– 30; "Editorial: The Specter of World Hunger," *CT*, Nov. 10, 1967, pp. 34– 36.
62. L. Nelson Bell, "Not Bread Alone," *CT*, pp. 22– 23; "The Spectre of Famine," *CT*, Aug. 8, 1975, pp. 26– 27.
63. "Editorial: Full Hearts and Empty Stomach," *CT*, Nov. 21, 1975, pp. 47– 48.
64. Henry B. Clark, *Escape From the Money Trap* (Valley Forge, Pa.: Judson Press, 1973), pp. 83– 89.
65. Wells and Woodbridge, eds., *Evangelicals*; W. Stanley Mooneyham, "Ministering to the Hunger Belt," *CT*, Jan. 3, 1975, p. 10; W. Stanley Mooneyham, *What Do You Say to a Hungry World?* (Waco, Tex.: Word, 1975), pp. 19, 12– 13, and 144– 46.
66. Mooneyham, *World?*, pp. 173 and 16; W. Stanley Mooneyham, "Ministering to the Hunger Belt," *CT*, Jan. 3, 1975, p. 6.
67. Mooneyham, *World?*, pp. 131 and 123– 25.

68. John Perkins, "Rich Man, Poor Man," *S*, Feb. 1977, p. 32; Mark Hatfield, *Between a Rock and a Hard Place* (Waco, Tex.: Word, 1976), p. 208.

69. E.g., Mooneyham, *World?*, chap. 12; Karin Harnden, "Kicking the Meat and Potatoes Habit," *OS*, Sept.-Oct. 1975, pp. 40–43; Stanley C. Baldwin, "A Case Against Waste and Other Excesses," *CT*, July 16, 1976, pp. 10 and 4; "Editorial: Sacrificial Living, Sacrificial Giving," *CT*, July 16, 1976, pp. 32–33; James Montgomery Boice, *The Sermon on the Mount* (Grand Rapids, Mich.: Zondervan, 1972), chap. 33.

70. Arthur Simon, "Hunger: Twenty Easy Questions, No Easy Answers," *CT*, July 16, 1976, pp. 19–22; Mooneyham, *World?*, pp. 210–11.

71. George DeVries, Jr., "System and Hunger," *RJ*, Apr. 1975, pp. 4–5.

72. Francis A. Schaeffer, *The Church at the End of the Twentieth Century* (London: Norfolk Press, 1970), p. 126; Schaeffer, *Realities*, pp. 31–32; Elton Trueblood, "The Life of Service," *CT*, Jan. 30, 1970, pp. 3–5; William Stringfellow, *An Ethic for Christians and Other Aliens in a Strange Land* (Waco, Tex.: Word, 1973), p. 125; Jim Wallis, *S*, Dec. 1976, p. 4.

73. Alan R. Gruber, "Poverty," in Collins, ed., *Turmoil*, pp. 113–21.

74. Hans-Lutz Poetsch, *Marxism and Christianity* (St. Louis: Concordia, 1973), p. 37.

75. Robert Culver, *Toward a Biblical View of Civil Government* (Chicago: Moody Press, 1974), pp. 156–57.

76. Vernard Eller, *The Simple Life: The Christian Stance Toward Possessions* (Grand Rapids, Mich.: Eerdmans, 1973), p. 38.

77. Paul B. Henry, *Politics for Evangelicals* (Valley Forge, Pa.: Judson Press, 1974), p. 105.

78. Karen DeVos, "Do We Really Want Justice?" *RJ*, Jan. 1976, p. 2.

79. John R. Alexander, "The Bible and the Other Side," *OS*, Sept.-Oct. 1975, p. 62; cover, *OS*, Nov.-Dec. 1974; Robert Sabath, "The Bible and the Poor," *PA*, 3, No. 2 (1974); Peter Davids, "The People of God and the Wealth of the People," *PA*, 4, No. 6 (1975); Richard K. Taylor, *Economics and the Gospel* (Philadelphia: United Church Press, 1973), pp. 22–23; Alexander, "Other Side," *OS*.

80. Leighton Ford, *One Way to Change the World* (New York: Harper & Row, 1970), p. 44; Jim Wallis, *S*, Jan. 1977, p. 28; Moberg, *Inasmuch*, p. 47.

81. Richard V. Pierard, "Evangelical Christianity and the Radical Right," in Clouse et al., eds., *Flag*, p. 116.

82. Hatfield, *Place*, p. 42; Richard Batey, *Jesus and the Poor* (New York: Harper & Row, 1972), chap. 3; Clarence Hilliard, "Down With the Honky Christ—Up With the Funky Jesus," *CT*, Jan. 30, 1978, pp. 6–8.

83. Batey, *Poor*, p. 81; Poetsch, *Christianity*, p. 34; Boice, *Mount*, p. 247; Robert and Homer McLaren, *All To the Good: A Guide to Christian Ethics* (New York: World, 1969), p. 63; Frank Breish, "Paul's Answer to Social Evil," *OS*, Jan.-Feb. 1973, pp. 12–15.

84. Clark, *Trap*, pp. 37–42 and 20–27; McLaren, *Ethics*, p. 63.

85. Lum, *Radical*, p. 11.

86. John F. Alexander, "Editorial: What Matters?" *OS*, July-Aug. 1974, pp. 2–4 and 52–53.

87. E.g., "Editorial: Ministering to the Jobless," *CT*, July 19, 1968, pp. 24–25; L. Nelson Bell, "A Guaranteed Income?" *CT*, July 5, 1968, p. 29; "Editorial: Capitalism: 'Basically Unjust'?" *CT*, Oct. 24, 1975, pp. 31–32; Bell, "Income," *CT*, pp. 29–30; Harold O. J. Brown, *Christianity and the Class Struggle* (New Rochelle, N.Y.: Arlington House, 1970), p. 26.

88. See *CT*, Feb. 12, 1971, p. 35.

89. "Editorial: Jobless," *CT*, pp. 24–25; H. Edward Rowe, "Poverty," *OS*, July-Aug. 1972, pp. 23–29.

90. "Editorial: Capitalism vs. Communism," *CT*, Feb. 12, 1971, pp. 34–35; Brown, *Struggle*, p. 59.

91. Culver, *Government*, p. 99.

92. Ibid., p. 186.

93. Rowe, "Poverty," *OS*, p. 27.

94. Criticisms suggested to me particularly by Mark Kann.

CHAPTER TEN

1. Richard Quebedeaux, *The Worldly Evangelicals* (New York: Harper & Row, 1978), pp. 16– 17.

2. Harold B. Kuhn, "The Nuclear Family," *CT*, May 23, 1975, pp. 62– 64; Donald N. Bastian, "Sex in a Theological Perspective," *CT*, July 19, 1968, p. 8; James M. Boice, *The Sermon on the Mount* (Grand Rapids, Mich.: Zondervan, 1972), chap. 16; Russ Walton, *One Nation Under God* (Washington: Third Century, 1975), chap. 5 and p. 79.

3. Harold Lindsell, *The World, the Flesh, and the Devil* (Washington: Canon Press, 1973), p. 138; Boice, *Mount*, pp. 136– 37; Andre Bustanoby, "When Wedlock Becomes Deadlock I," *CT*, June 20, 1975, pp. 4– 6; Andre Bustanoby, "When Wedlock Becomes Deadlock II," *CT*, July 18, 1975, pp. 11– 14.

4. Lindsell, *Devil*, pp. 123, 97– 101, and 122.

5. L. Nelson Bell, "Poison in the Cup," *CT*, Sept. 11, 1970, pp. 38– 39; "Editorial: The Debilitating Revolt," *CT*, July 21, 1967, pp. 24– 25; "Editorial: Sophist's Guide to Sex," *CT*, Apr. 12, 1974, p. 31; Robert B. and Homer D. McLaren, *All To the Good: A Guide To Christian Ethics* (New York: World, 1969), p. 83; Bastian, "Perspective," *CT*, p. 8; "Editorial," *CT*, Dec. 8, 1972, pp. 29– 30; Orville S. Walters, "Contraceptives and the Single Person," *CT*, Nov. 8, 1968, pp. 16– 17; "Sex in the College Dorm," *CT*, May 21, 1971, pp. 33– 34; Tim LaHaye, *The Beginning of the End* (Wheaton, Ill.: Tyndale, 1976), p. 102.

6. Carl Henry, James Doane, John W. Montgomery, and Leon Morris, "The Bible and the New Morality," *CT*, July 21, 1967, pp. 5– 9.

7. Dwight Henry Small, *Christian: Celebrate Your Sexuality* (Old Tappan, N.J.: Revell, 1974), pp. 186, 203, 154, 190, chap. 8, and p. 151.

8. Quebedeaux, *Worldly*, p. 78.

9. Anita Bryant, *Amazing Grace* (Old Tappan, N.J.: Revell, 1971); the sad irony of subsequent events in the Bryant family merits no repetition here.

10. Perry C. Cotham, *Obscenity, Pornography, and Censorship* (Grand Rapids, Mich.: Baker, 1973), pp. 52, 68, 59– 60, and 43; Milton D. Hunnex, "Sex and the Evangelical," *CT*, June 6, 1975, p. 20.

11. Cotham, *Censorship*, pp. 169, 73, 139– 47, 131– 36, and chap. 2; Hunnex, "Evangelical," p. 20; "Editorial: Platform for Permissiveness," *CT*, Oct. 23, 1970, pp. 27– 28; John W. Drakeford and Jack Hamm, *Pornography: The Sexual Mirage* (Nashville: Thomas Nelson, 1973), chap. 11.

12. James. L. Adams, "N.A.E. Hits Hard at Pornography," *CT*, May 9, 1969, pp. 46– 47; Hunnex, "Evangelical," p. 18; "Editorial: Pornography in a Free Society," *CT*, May 22, 1970, pp. 20– 21; Drakeford and Hamm, *Mirage*, chap. 12; Addison H. Leitch, "Hole in Your Head," *CT*, Apr. 25, 1969, pp. 38– 39.

13. Cotham, *Censorship*, chap. 6 and p. 100; Hunnex, "Evangelical," *CT*, pp. 18– 20.

14. Cotham, *Censorship*, pp. 88 and 183– 87; "Editorial: How Much Censorship Is Too Much?" *CT*, Aug. 8, 1975, pp. 21– 22.

15. Richard J. Mouw, "On Being Permissive about Filth," *RJ*, Feb. 1976.

16. John F. Alexander, "Editorial: Spirituality and Decency," *OS*, Sept.-Oct. 1973, pp. 2– 3 and 49– 50.

17. "Editorial: Is Abortion a Catholic Issue?," *CT*, Jan. 16, 1976; Francis A. Schaeffer, *How Should We Then Live?* (Old Tappan, N.J.: Revell, 1976), pp. 219 and 223.

18. Clifford E. Bajema, *Abortion and the Meaning of Personhood* (Grand Rapids, Mich.:

Baker, 1974), chaps. 1 and 5; Bruce K. Waltke, "The Old Testament and Birth Control," *CT*, Nov. 8, 1968; Paul K. Jewett, "The Relation of the Soul to the Fetus," *CT*, Nov. 8, 1968.

19. Robert Meye, "New Testament Texts Bearing on the Issues," in Walter O. Spitzer and Carlyle L. Saylor, *Birth Control and the Christian* (Wheaton, Ill.: Tyndale, 1969), pp. 40–41; Bruce K. Waltke, "Old Testament Texts Bearing on the Issues," in Spitzer and Saylor, *Birth Control*, pp. 12–13; John Warwick Montgomery, "The Christian View of the Fetus," in Spitzer and Saylor, *Birth Control*; Waltke, "Birth Control," *CT*, pp. 3–4; Norman L. Geisler, *Ethics: Alternatives and Issues* (Grand Rapids, Mich.: Zondervan, 1971), pp. 218–19; Jack W. Coltrell, "Abortion and the Mosaic Law," *CT*, Mar. 16, 1973, pp. 66–69.

20. See all of Bajema, *Personhood*.

21. E.g., Robert Culver, *Toward a Biblical View of Civil Government* (Chicago: Moody Press, 1974), p. 150; Walton, *God*, pp. 87–94.

22. Lindsell, *Devil*, p. 104; also see, "Editorial: Abortions and the Courts," *CT*, Feb. 16, 1973, pp. 32–33; "Editorial: A License to Live," *CT*, July 26, 1974, pp. 32–33.

23. Montgomery, "Fetus," p. 83.

24. Richard Selzer, "What I Saw at the Abortion," *CT*, Jan. 16, 1976, pp. 11–12; "Editorial: What Price Abortion?" *CT*, Mar. 2, 1973, p. 39.

25. Philip E. Hughes, "Theological Principles in the Control of Human Life," in Spitzer and Saylor, *Birth Control*, p. 93; Lindsell, *Devil*, pp. 102–5.

26. "Editorial: Where Silence is Guilt," *CT*, Jan. 18, 1974, pp. 32–33; Harold O. J. Brown, "The Passivity of American Christians," *CT*, Jan. 16, 1976; Bajema, *Personhood*, chap. 6.

27. Nancy B. Barcus, "Thinking Straight About Abortion," *CT*, Jan. 17, 1975, pp. 8–11.

28. Wesley Pippert, *Faith at the Top* (Elgin, Ill.: Cook, 1973), p. 75; Henry Stob, "The Right-to-Life Amendment," *RJ*, Feb. 1976, pp. 2–3; David Busby, "Rape, Incest and Multiple Illegitimacy as Indications for Therapeutic Abortion," in Spitzer and Saylor, *Birth Control*; Geisler, *Issues*, p. 220; Bajema, *Personhood*, chap. 8; Hughes, "Life"; John Scanzoni, "A Sociological Perspective on Abortion and Sterilization," in Spitzer and Saylor, *Birth Control*, chap. 16.

29. David R. Wilkerson, with Claire Cox, *Parents on Trial: Why Kids Go Wrong—Or Right* (New York: Hawthorne, 1967), pp. 118–19; "Editorial: Gay Demands," *CT*, Dec. 4, 1970; Harold Lindsell, "Homosexuals and the Church," *CT*, Sept. 28, 1973, pp. 8–12; "Editorial: Assignment For Christian Citizens," *CT*, Sept. 15, 1972, pp. 34–35; "Editorial: A Setback for 'Gay Liberation'," *CT*, Apr. 23, 1976; Klaus Bockmühl, "Homosexuality in Biblical Perspective," *CT*, Feb. 16, 1973, pp. 12–18.

30. "Editorial," *CT*, June 23, 1972, p. 28; B. L. Smith, "Homosexuality in the Bible and the Law," *CT*, June 6, 1969, pp. 7–10.

31. "Editorial," *CT*, May 12, 1972, pp. 20–21; "Editorial: A Case for Sexual Restraint," *CT*, Feb. 27, 1970, pp. 31–32; Guy Charles, "Gay Liberation Confronts the Church," *CT*, Sept. 12, 1975, pp. 14ff.; Letha Scanzoni, "On Friendship and Homosexuality," *CT*, Sept. 27, 1974, pp. 11–16.

32. Letha Scanzoni and Nancy Hardesty, *All We're Meant to Be—A Biblical Approach to Women's Liberation* (Waco, Tex.: Word, 1976), chap. 15; Wallace E. Fisher, *Politics, Poker and Piety* (Nashville: Abingdon, 1972), p. 125.

33. Nancy Hardesty, "Reflections," in *The Chicago Declaration*, ed. Ronald J. Sider (Carol Stream, Ill.: Creation House, 1974), pp. 123-26.

34. Sharon Gallagher, "The Soul of the Total Woman," *S*, May 1977, p. 31; Letha Scanzoni, "The Great Chain of Being and the Chain of Command," *RJ*, Oct. 1976, pp. 14–18.

35. Letha Scanzoni, "Mystique and Machismo," *OS*, July-Aug. 1973, pp. 12–15 and 37–38.

36. Letha Scanzoni, "How to Live With a Liberated Wife," *CT*, June 4, 1976; Scanzoni and Hardesty, *Liberation*, chap. 14 and p. 12.

37. Scanzoni and Hardesty, *Liberation*, p. 15; Virginia Mollenkott, "Feminism and the Kingdom," *S*, June 1977.
38. Scanzoni and Hardesty, *Liberation*, pp. 98–100 and 106; Scanzoni, "Wife," *CT*, pp. 8–9.
39. Paul K. Jewett, "Why I Favor Ordination of Women," *CT*, June 6, 1975, pp. 7–12; Scanzoni and Hardesty, *Liberation*, chap. 13; Letha Scanzoni, "Women's Ordination," *CT*, June 6, 1975; Virginia Mollenkott, "Church Women, Theologians, and the Burden of Proof (II)," *RJ*, Sept. 1975, p. 20.
40. Virginia Mollenkott's *Women, Men and the Bible* (Nashville: Abingdon, 1977) was written after our period, but is the best work by a biblical feminist. Scanzoni and Hardesty, *Liberation*, chaps. 4 and 5; Mollenkott, "Kingdom," *S*; Judith Sanderson, "Jesus Women," *OS*, July-Aug. 1973, pp. 16–21 and 35–36; "Jesus Was No Chauvinist!" *PA*, 4, No. 1 (1972).
41. Scanzoni and Hardesty, *Liberation*, p. 37.
42. Virginia R. Mollenkott, "Evangelicalism: A Feminist Perspective," *Union Seminary Quarterly Review*, Winter 1977, p. 101.
43. Nancy Hardesty, "Toward a Total Woman Theology," *S*, supplement to Jan. 1977, pp. 58–59.
44. "A Conversation With Virginia Mollenkott," *OS*, May-June 1976, p. 26.
45. Ibid., p. 30; Kathryn Lindskoog, "Paul's Bad News for Women," *OS*, July-Aug. 1973, p. 8.
46. Mollenkott, "Perspective," *Union Review*, p. 99.
47. Ibid.; Lucille Sider Dayton, "The Feminist Movement in Scripture," *S*, supplement to Jan. 1977, p. 64; Ruth A. Schmidt, "Second-Class Citizenship in the Kingdom of God," *CT*, Jan. 1, 1971, p. 13.
48. Scanzoni and Hardesty, *Liberation*, p. 20.
49. Dick and Joyce Boldrey, "Technology and Women's Liberation," *PA*, 1, No. 4 (1972), p. 8; Dayton, "Scripture," *S*, p. 64; Sharon Gallagher, "The Second-Rate," *S*, supplement to Jan. 1977, p. 60.
50. Scanzoni and Hardesty, *Liberation*, chap. 6 and pp. 67–69 and 71.
51. Mollenkott, "Proof," (II), *RJ*, p. 17.
52. Judy Alexander, "Editorial: Servanthood and Submission," *OS*, July-Aug. 1973, pp. 2–4 and 43.
53. Scanzoni and Hardesty, *Liberation*, p. 139; Dayton, "Scripture," *S*, p. 63; Virginia Mollenkott, "Church Women, Theologians, and the Burden of Proof (I)," *RJ*, Aug. 1975, p. 20.
54. Mollenkott, "Perspective," *Union Review*, p. 99; Nancy Hardesty, "Women and Evangelical Christianity," in *The Cross and the Flag*, ed. Robert G. Clouse et al. (Carol Stream, Ill.: Creation House, 1972), p. 71.
55. Paul K. Jewett, *Man as Male and Female* (Grand Rapids, Mich.: Eerdmans, 1975), pp. 19 and 33.
56. Ibid., pp. 142, 160–70, 188, 85, chap. 3, and p. 124.
57. Ibid., p. 86.
58. "Mrs. Billy Graham," *CT*, Oct. 24, 1969, p. 45; Joe E. Barnhart, *The Billy Graham Religion* (Philadelphia: United Church, 1972), pp. 77–80.
59. John W. Montgomery, "Acknowledgements," *The Shaping of America* (Minneapolis: Bethany, 1976).
60. Bert Block, "The Liberated Wife," *RJ*, Oct. 1975, pp. 17–19.
61. Lindsell, *Devil*, pp. 149–51.
62. Ibid., pp. 151–52.
63. "Editorial," *CT*, Apr. 13, 1973, pp. 31–32; "Editorial: Hearkening to Harkness," *CT*, Sept. 13, 1974, p. 51.

64. Lindsell, *Devil*, p. 153.

65. "Editorial: That Women's Rights Amendment," *CT*, Nov. 6, 1970, p. 34; "Editorial," *CT*, Apr. 13, 1973, pp. 31–32.

66. Culver, *Government*, p. 22; Boice, *Mount*, pp. 126–27; Harold Lindsell, "Egalitarianism and Scriptural Infallibility," *CT*, Mar. 26, 1976; Maxine Hancock, *Love, Honor — and Be Free* (Chicago: Moody, 1975).

67. Hancock, *Free*, pp. 32–35 and chap. 19; pp. 179 and 28.

68. Ibid., pp. 28 and 41–42.

69. Andre S. Bustanoby, "Love, Honor, and Obey," *CT*, June 6, 1969, pp. 3–4; George W. Knight III, "Male and Female Related He Them," *CT*, Apr. 9, 1976, pp. 13–17.

70. Gladys Hunt, *Ms. Means Myself* (Grand Rapids, Mich.: Zondervan, 1972), pp. 40–41.

71. Ibid., pp. 47, 115–16, 97, 120, 54, and 91.

72. Hancock, *Free*, pp. 66, 71, and 85; Mary Bouma, "Liberated Mothers," *CT*, May 7, 1971, pp. 4–6.

73. Elizabeth Elliot, *Let Me Be a Woman* (Wheaton, Ill.: Tyndale, 1976), pp. 22 and 145.

74. Ibid., p. 148.

75. Ibid., pp. 62 and 53–54.

76. Ibid., pp. 125 and 64.

77. Ibid., p. 75.

78. Ruth Graham, "Women's Ordination," *CT*, June 6, 1975, p. 32; Elizabeth Elliot, "Why I Oppose the Ordination of Women," *CT*, June 6, 1975, pp. 12–16; Hancock, *Free*, pp. 183–84.

79. E.g., Walton, *God*, pp. 94–99; Hancock, *Free*, p. 57.

80. Edith Schaeffer, *What Is a Family?* (Old Tappan, N.J.: Revell, 1975), pp. 48 and 50–51.

81. Ibid., pp. 162 and 149.

82. Larry Christenson, *The Christian Family* (Minneapolis: Bethany, 1970), pp. 54, 17, 47, chap. 2, and pp. 24–27.

83. Ibid., chap. 5.

84. Quebedeaux, *Worldly*, p. 71.

85. Marabel Morgan, *The Total Woman* (Old Tappan, N.J.: Revell, 1973), chap. 13 and p. 13; "Interview: Marabel Morgan Preferring One Another," *CT*, Oct. 10, 1976, pp. 13–14.

86. Morgan, *Woman*, p. 58.

87. Ibid., p. 86.

88. Ibid., pp. 57 and 59 and chap. 5.

89. Ibid., pp. 52, 49, 84, and chap. 6.

90. "Marabel Morgan," *CT*, p. 13; Morgan, *Woman*, p. 69.

91. Morgan, *Woman*, pp. 95 and 92.

92. Ibid., chaps. 9 and 10.

93. Ibid., p. 80.

94. Quebedeaux, *Worldly*, p. 122.

CHAPTER ELEVEN

1. Billy James Hargis, *Why I Fight For a Christian America* (Nashville: Thomas Nelson, 1974), p. 42; Gary K. Clabaugh, *Thunder on the Right: The Protestant Fundamentalist* (Chicago: Nelson-Hall, 1974), p. 96; also see *CT*, Mar. 17, 1972, p. 39; and Erling Jorstad, *The Politics of Doomsday: Fundamentalists of the Far Right* (Nashville: Abingdon, 1970).

2. John Harold Redekop, *The American Far Right: A Case Study of Billy James Hargis and Christian Crusade* (Grand Rapids, Mich.: Eerdmans, 1968), pp. 61, 17–18, 53, and chap. 4.

3. Billy James Hargis, *Billy James Hargis Speaks Out on the Issues* (Tulsa: Christian Crusade, 1971), p. 5.

4. Ibid., p. 10; Redekop, *Crusade*, pp. 44–45; Jorstad, *Right*, pp. 82–83; Carl McIntire, *Outside the Gate* (Christian Beacon Press, 1967), pp. 77–78, 226–27, and chap. 12.

5. Hargis, *America*, pp. 79, 38, 53, 77, and 139.

6. William Cantelon, *The Day the Dollar Dies* (Plainfield, N.J.: Logos, 1973), chaps. 11 and 12; Hargis, *America*, p. 76.

7. Hargis, *Issues*, p. 3.

8. Hargis, *America*, pp. 174 and 155.

9. Jim Stenzel, "The Anti-Communist Captivity of the Church," *S*, Apr. 1977, pp. 15–19; Jim Wallis and Wes Michaelson, "The Plan to Save America," *S*, Jan. 1977, pp. 43–47.

10. E.g., Ralph B. Potter, *War and Moral Discourse* (Richmond, Va.: John Knox, 1969), pp. 107–11; Hans-Lutz Poetsch, *Marxism and Christianity* (St. Louis: Concordia, 1973).

11. "Editorial: The Marxist Never-Never Land," *CT*, Dec. 20, 1974, pp. 19–20; Poetsch, *Christianity*, p. 44; James M. Hutchens, *Beyond Combat* (Chicago: Moody Press, 1968), p. 25; "Editorial: The Danger of Christian-Marxist Dialogue," *CT*, Oct. 27, 1967, pp. 26–27.

12. Melvin Gingerich, *The Christian and Revolution* (Scottdale, Pa.: Herald Press, 1968), p. 63; "Editorial: Is Christian-Marxist Dialogue Possible?," *CT*, Jan. 6, 1967, pp. 26–27; Francis D. Breisch and Karl E. Keefer, *Isms on the Prowl* (Wheaton, Ill.: Victor Books, 1974), p. 4; Harold Lindsell, *The World, the Flesh, and the Devil* (Washington: Canon Press, 1973), p. 47.

13. Gingerich, *Revolution*, p. 61; Sherwood Eliot Wirt, *The Social Conscience of the Evangelical* (New York: Harper & Row, 1968), p. 123; Klaus Buckmühl, "The Marxist New Man," *CT*, Dec. 9, 1975, pp. 53–54; Thomas Finger, "Christians and Marxists . . . The Debate Goes On," *S*, Apr. 1977, p. 35.

14. "Editorial: Marxism: A Missing Person Report," *CT*, May 23, 1975, pp. 43–44.

15. Breisch and Keefer, *Isms*, p. 24.

16. Finger, "Marxists," *S*, p. 36.

17. "Interview with Samuel Escobar," *S*, Jan. 1977, pp. 76–80.

18. Harold O. J. Brown, *Christianity and the Class Struggle* (New Rochelle, N.Y.: Arlington, 1970), p. 28.

19. Robert B. McLaren and Homer D. McLaren, *All to the Good: A Guide to Christian Ethics* (New York: World, 1969), p. 125; Clark Pinnock, "An Evangelical Theology of Human Liberation," *S*, Jan. 1977, p. 41.

20. Buckmühl, "Man," *CT*; Finger, "Marxists," *S*, p. 35.

21. Elton Trueblood, "The Life of Service," *CT*, Jan. 30, 1970, p. 4; Rene de Visme Williamson, "The Theology of Liberation," *CT*, Aug. 8, 1975, p. 12; "Interview With Samuel Escobar," *S*, p. 79.

22. Dale W. Brown, *The Christian Revolutionary* (Grand Rapids, Mich.: Eerdmans, 1971), pp. 122–23.

23. E.g., Poetsch, *Christianity*, p. 46.

24. Gingerich, *Revolution*, pp. 63–64.

25. Daniel Poling et al., "Churchmen Look at Communism," *CT*, June 23, 1967, p. 12; Francis Schaeffer, "How Should We Then Live?" *CT*, Oct. 8, 1976, p. 23; Cantelon, *Dollar Dies*, chap. 13.

26. Poling et al., "Communism," *CT*, pp. 13–14.

27. Williamson, "Liberation," *CT*, pp. 7–8; Poetsch, *Christianity*, pp. 58–59.

28. C. Rene Padilla, "The Theology of Liberation," *CT*, Nov. 9, 1973, pp. 69–70.

29. Richard V. Pierard, *The Unequal Yoke: Evangelical Christianity and Political Conservativism* (Philadelphia: J. B. Lippincott, 1970), p. 90.

30. Hutchens, *Combat*, p. 26; Schaeffer, "Live?" *CT*, p. 27; H. Brown, *Struggle*, pp. 135 and 13–15; Rus Walton, *One Nation Under God* (Washington: Third Century, 1975), pp. 283ff.; Francis A. Schaeffer, *How Should We Then Live?* (Old Tappan, N.J.: Revell, 1976), p. 215; Samuel Hugh Moffett, "A Lesson in World-Winning," *CT*, Oct. 10, 1971, pp. 4–6.

31. Winrich Scheffbuch, *Christians Under the Hammer and Sickle* (Grand Rapids, Mich.: Zondervan, 1972); Edward E. Plowman, "News: Carrying the Cross in the U.S.S.R.," *CT*, Dec. 20, 1974, pp. 26–27; "Repression in the U.S.S.R.," *CT*, May 10, 1974, pp. 54–55.

32. David Benson, *Miracle in Moscow* (Glendale, Calif.: Regal Books, 1975), pp. 208 and 167.

33. Ibid., p. 262.

34. Janice A. Brown, "Evangelism in the U.S.S.R.," *CT*, June 21, 1974, pp. 11–16; "Confronting the Kremlin," *CT*, Feb. 28, 1975, pp. 41–42; David E. Kucharsky, "Against Such, No Law," *CT*, June 23, 1972, pp. 45–50; Paul D. Steeves, "Baptists as Subversives in the Contemporary Soviet Union," in *God and Caesar*, ed. Robert D. Linder (Longview, Tex.: Conference on Faith and History, 1971), pp. 59–73; J. D. Douglas, "The Limits of Valor," *CT*, Apr. 25, 1975, pp. 49–50; Richard Wurmbrank, *If That Were Christ, Would You Give Him Your Blanket?* (Waco, Tex.: Word, 1971); Benson, *Miracle*, p. 176 and passim.

35. Richard V. Pierard and Robert D. Linder, "Christianity in East Europe," *CT*, Jan. 21, 1972, pp. 12–13; Edward Plowman, "Revival and Repression in Romania," *CT*, Nov. 22, 1974, pp. 52–55; Wurmbrank, *Blanket?*, chap. 9.

36. Michael Browne, "Red Guards: China's Mini-Mao Revivalists," *CT*, Feb. 3, 1967, pp. 48–49; Forrest J. Boyd, "News: The Church in China," *CT*, Mar. 17, 1972, pp. 37–38; "Editorial," *CT*, Feb. 4, 1972, pp. 20–21; George N. Patterson, "To China by Bridge," *CT*, June 9, 1972, pp. 12–14; Dick Hillis, "Who Will Mourn Chairman Mao?" *CT*, Nov. 24, 1972, pp. 4–5.

37. J. D. Douglas, "Cuba Revisited," *CT*, Feb. 17, 1967, pp. 54–55; Lawrence A. Rankin, "The Cuban Revolution: Letter From a Sympathetic Dissenter," *PA*, 2, No. 5 (1972), 29–30; "Chile: Church and Caesar," *CT*, Jan. 17, 1975, pp. 34–36; "Editorial: The Options of Modern Man," *CT*, Nov. 7, 1969, pp. 30–31.

38. E.g., "Revival in Indochina," *CT*, May 26, 1972, pp. 32–34; Edward Plowman, "News: The Peace of God in South Viet Nam," *CT*, Dec. 22, 1972, pp. 32–33; Orvel N. Steinkamp, *The Holy Spirit in Vietnam* (Carol Stream, Ill.: Creation House, 1974); James C. Hefley, *By Life or by Death* (Grand Rapids, Mich.: Zondervan, 1969); Wesley G. Pippert, "Review of *By Life or by Death*," *CT*, July 18, 1969.

39. George H. Williams and Rodney L. Petersen, "Evangelicals: Society, the State, the Nation," in *The Evangelicals*, ed. David Wells and John D. Woodbridge (Grand Rapids, Mich.: Baker, 1975), p. 251.

40. Wirt, *Evangelical*, pp. 122 and 125.

41. Harold O. J. Brown, *The Protest of a Troubled Protestant* (New Rochelle, N.Y.: Arlington House, 1969), p. 209.

42. Harold John Ockenga, "Report From Viet Nam," *CT*, Mar. 15, 1968, p. 35.

43. Carl F. H. Henry, "A Nation in Trouble," *CT*, Sept. 12, 1969, pp. 37–38.

44. E.g., Mark Hatfield, *Conflict and Conscience* (Waco, Tex.: Word, 1971), p. 55; see Chapter Six for a full discussion of Hatfield and Vietnam.

45. "Editorial: Vietnam a Moral Dilemma," *CT*, Jan. 20, 1967, pp. 27–28; "Editorial: Spock, Coffin, and Viet Nam," *CT*, July 5, 1968, p. 28.

46. "Moratorium Day in Retrospect," *CT*, Nov. 7, 1969, p. 133; "Editorial: Open Letter to Mr. Nixon," *CT*, October 10, 1969, p. 34.

47. "Editorial: The President's Viet Nam Policy," *CT*, Nov. 21, 1969, p. 25; "Editorial: Nixon and the Logjam," *CT*, Oct. 23, 1970, p. 27; "Editorial," *CT*, Oct. 13, 1972, p. 36; "Editorial," *CT*, May 26, 1972, p. 27.

48. "Editorial: The Violent New Breed," *CT*, Nov. 24, 1967, pp. 25–26; "Editorial: War and Peace in Viet Nam," *CT*, Feb. 17, 1967, p. 29; "Editorial: America Faces Critical Decisions," *CT*, Jan. 20, 1967, pp. 24–25; "Editorial: Vandalism in the Name of Peace," *CT*, Apr. 11, 1969, p. 29; "Editorial: Hooray For Ho?," *CT*, Oct. 10, 1969, p. 33; "Editorial: The Peace March: A Post-Mortem," *CT*, Dec. 5, 1969, pp. 25–26; "Editorial," *CT*, Feb. 16, 1968, p. 28; "Editorial: Lawbreaking Lawmakers," *CT*, July 4, 1969, p. 22.

49. Glen Melnik, "Awake Thou That Sleepest or Who Are YOU Sleeping With?," *PA*, 1, No. 1 (1971), 7.

50. Jim Wallis, "Air War!," *PA*, 1, No. 3 (1972), p. 5.

51. Jim Wallis, "The Issues of 1972," *PA*, 2, No. 5 (1972), 2; *PA*, 1, No. 2 (1972), cover.

52. "A Joint Treaty . . . ," *PA*, 1, No. 1 (1971), 15.

53. "Editorial: The Vietnam Pact," *CT*, Feb. 16, 1973, p. 34; "Editorial: What to Remember About Vietnam," *CT*, May 23, 1975, pp. 45–46; "Editorial: The Indochina Fiasco," *CT*, Apr. 25, 1975, p. 27; "Others Say," *CT*, May 9, 1975, p. 28; "Editorial," *CT*, July 4, 1975, pp. 47–48; "Left Behind in South Viet Nam," *CT*, May 9, 1975, pp. 42–43.

54. John B. Anderson, *Vision and Betrayal in America* (Waco, Tex.: Word, 1975), p. 90.

55. Jim Wallis, "Vietnam and Repentance," *PA*, 4, No. 5 (May 1975), p. 17; Jim Wallis, "The Desire to Forget," *PA*, 2, No. 2 (1973).

56. Bill Lane, "Lessons from Vietnam," *PA*, 2, No. 2 (1973); Dale Suderman, "A Failure of Liberalism," *PA*, 4, No. 8 (1975).

57. Wes Michaelson, "The Postwar Plight of a People," *S*, Nov. 1976, p. 23; Jim Wallis, "Back to Normal, Arrogantly," *S*, Nov. 1976, pp. 3–5.

CHAPTER TWELVE

1. "Editorial," *CT*, June 8, 1973.

2. "Editorial," *CT*, Nov. 24, 1972, p. 29; "Editorial," *CT*, June 22, 1973, p. 22.

3. David Kucharsky, *The Mind and Spirit of Jimmy Carter* (New York: Harper & Row, 1976), p. 69.

4. "Message to the President," *CT*, Nov. 9, 1973, pp. 40–41; "The Appeal to Resign," *CT*, Nov. 23, 1973, p. 41; "Should Nixon Resign?" *CT*, June 7, 1974, pp. 28–29; John B. Anderson, *Vision and Betrayal in America* (Waco, Tex.: Word, 1975), p. 91.

5. "Editorial: Fifteen Turbulent Years," *CT*, Aug. 30, 1974, p. 24.

6. "Editorial: The Pardon of Richard Nixon," *CT*, Sept. 27, 1974, p. 37; Harold B. Kuhn, "A Boon from the Secular," *CT*, Dec. 6, 1974, pp. 49–50.

7. James Hefley and Edward Plowman, *Washington: Christians in the Corridors of Power* (Wheaton, Ill.: Tyndale, 1975), p. 31.

8. Anderson, *America*, pp. 106–18.

9. Billy Graham, "Watergate," *CT*, January 4, 1974, p. 9.

10. John A. Huffman, Jr., "Biblical Lessons from Watergate," *CT*, Mar. 15, 1974, p. 12; Perry C. Cotham, *Politics, Americanism, and Christianity* (Grand Rapids, Mich.: Baker, 1976), p. 292; "Editorial: What Good from Watergate?" *CT*, Aug. 10, 1973; Jack N. Spark, "Will You Rob God?" in *A Nation Under God?*, ed. C. E. Gallivan (Waco, Tex.: Word, 1976), chap. 6.

11. Huffman, "Watergate," *CT*, p. 9; Paul B. Henry, *Politics for Evangelicals* (Valley Forge, Pa.: Judson Press, 1974), pp. 85–86; Cotham, *Christianity*, pp. 283–85 and 295–98.

12. Huffman, "Watergate," *CT*, p. 8; also see report on Huffman in *CT*, Aug. 30, 1974.

13. Cotham, *Christianity*, pp. 276–77, 172–73, and 271–72; Huffman, "Watergate," *CT*, p. 10.

14. *OS*, Mar.-Apr. 1975, p. 27.

15. "Watergate and Religion," *CT*, Aug. 31, 1973, pp. 27–28; Harold B. Kuhn, "Personal Pietism and Watergate," *CT*, Sept. 28, 1973, pp. 61–62.

16. Delton Franz, "Reflections on the Watergate," *OS*, May-June 1973.

17. Dale Brown, "We Have Seen the Enemy," *PA*, 4, No. 4 (1975).

18. Jim Wallis, "The Lesson of Watergate," *PA*, 3, No. 1 (1974).

19. Kucharsky, *Carter*, pp. 76–77.

20. L. Nelson Bell, "Changing the Rules," *CT*, Aug. 18, 1967, pp. 26–27.

21. Joseph Fletcher and John Warwick Montgomery, *Situation Ethics* (Minneapolis: Bethany, 1972), pp. 35ff.; Norman L. Geisler, *Ethics: Alternatives and Issues* (Grand Rapids, Mich.: Zondervan, 1971), chap. 4.

22. Erwin W. Lutzer, *The Morality Gap: An Evangelical Response to Situation Ethics* (Chicago: Moody Press, 1972), pp. 41 and 86.

23. Fletcher and Montgomery, *Ethics*, pp. 34–35, 47, and 43–44.

24. Ibid., pp. 69–70 and 51; Lutzer, *Ethics*, p. 89.

25. Lutzer, *Ethics*, pp. 65 and 36; Fletcher and Montgomery, *Ethics*, p. 79.

26. Harold B. Kuhn, "Pietism and Watergate," *CT*, pp. 61–62; "Editorial," *CT*, July 6, 1973, p. 31; Francis W. Lutzer, "Watergate Ethics," *CT*, Sept. 13, 1974, pp. 26–27; Huffman, "Watergate," *CT*, p. 9; Lutzer, *Ethics*, pp. 75ff.

27. "Editorial," *CT*, June 22, 1973, p. 22; "Editorial: Fifteen Turbulent Years," *CT*, Aug. 30, 1974, p. 24; Kucharsky, *Carter*, p. 86.

28. Wesley Pippert, "Rebirth," *RJ*, July-Aug. 1976, pp. 29–30.

29. Charles Colson, *Born Again* (Old Tappan, N.J.: Revell, 1977), p. 11; Hefley and Plowman, *Washington*, pp. 38–55; Wallace Henley, *The White House Mystique* (Old Tappan, N.J.: Revell, 1976), p. 109; "Watergate or Something Like It Was Inevitable — Interview with Charles Colson," *CT*, Mar. 12, 1976, p. 4.

30. Colson, *Again*, pp. 72 and 11.

31. Henley, *Mystique*, p. 12.

32. Ibid., p. 55.

33. Colson, *Again*, p. 61.

34. Henley, *Mystique*, pp. 56 and 58.

35. Ibid., pp. 74, 77–78, and 96–98.

36. Colson, *Again*, pp. 181 and 198.

37. Ibid., pp. 85–86; "It Was Inevitable," *CT*, p. 4.

38. "It Was Inevitable," *CT*, pp. 5–7.

39. Henley, *Mystique*, p. 31.

40. See Albert J. Menendez, *Religion at the Polls* (Philadelphia: Westminster, 1977).

41. Barrie Doyle and James C. Hefley, "The New President," *CT*, Aug. 30, 1974, pp. 33–34; "Editorial: Time for Something Different," *CT*, Nov. 8, 1974, p. 30; Edward Plowman, "The Democrats: God in the Garden?" *CT*, Aug. 6, 1976, pp. 34–36; Arthur H. Matthews, "Crusade for the White House: Skirmishes in a 'Holy War'," *CT*, Nov. 19, 1976, pp. 48–51; Edward Plowman, "An Election Year to Remember," *CT*, May 7, 1976.

42. "Sunday Brunch at Jerry's Place," *CT*, Mar. 12, 1976, pp. 48–49; "Evangelicals in Washington," *CT*, Mar. 26, 1976, pp. 36–37; Edward Plowman, "Southern Baptists: Platform for President," *CT*, July 16, 1976, pp. 48–51; see, for example, *CT*, Oct. 8, 1976, pp. 66–68.

43. "Graham Undecided," *CT*, Oct. 8, 1976, p. 65; "Editorial: Election 1976—The Push Potential," *CT*, Oct. 8, 1976, pp. 38–40.
44. Harold Lindsell, *CT*, Oct. 22, 1976, p. 5.
45. Harold Lindsell, *CT*, Nov. 19, 1976, p. 5; "Editorial: The Political Peak Is Also the Brink," *CT*, Nov. 19, 1976, pp. 33–34.
46. See *RJ*, December 1975, pp. 8–9.
47. Nicholas Wolterstorff, "Carter's Religion," *RJ*, Sept. 1976, pp. 4–5.
48. Jim Wallis, "The Election and Cheap Grace," *S*, 5, No. 8 (1976).
49. Wes Michaelson, "The Piety and Ambition of Jimmy Carter," *S*, 5, No. 8 (1976); earlier, Wes Michaelson, "Demythologizing the Presidency," *S*, 5, No. 2 (1976).
50. Wes Michaelson, "The Fall, the Elect, and the Elections," *S*, 5, No. 8 (1976).
51. William Stringfellow, "An Open Letter to Jimmy Carter," *S*, 5, No. 8 (1976).
52. Howard Norton and Bob Slosser, *The Miracle of Jimmy Carter* (Plainfield, N.J.: Logos, 1976), chap. 8 and pp. 133 and passim.
53. Kucharsky, *Carter*, p. 9.
54. Ibid., p. 117.
55. Ibid., p. 37.
56. Ibid., pp. 7–8.
57. Ibid., pp. 18–19.
58. Ibid., p. 138.
59. Jimmy Carter, *Why Not the Best?* (New York: Bantam, 1976), pp. 151–57.
60. See Richard Quebedeaux, *The Worldly Evangelicals* (New York: Harper & Row, 1978).

BIBLIOGRAPHY

PERIODICALS SYSTEMATICALLY CONSULTED

Christianty Today
Daughters of Sarah
The Other Side
The Post-American (Sojourners)
The Reformed Journal
Union Seminary Quarterly Review

BOOKS

Ahlstrom, Sydney. *A Religious History of the American People.* New Haven: Yale University Press, 1972.

Anderson, John B. *Between Two Worlds.* Grand Rapids, Mich.: Zondervan, 1970.

————. *Vision and Betrayal in America.* Waco, Tex.: Word, 1975.

Armstrong, O.K., and Armstrong, Marjorie M. *The Indomitable Baptists.* Garden City, N.Y.: Doubleday, 1967.

Bajema, Clifford E. *Abortion and the Meaning of Personhood.* Grand Rapids: Michigan: Baker, 1974.

Baker, James T. *A Southern Baptist in the White House.* Philadelphia: Westminster, 1979.

Baker, Robert A. *The Southern Baptist Convention and Its People, 1607–1972.* Nashville: Broadman, 1974.

Barnhart, Joe. E. *The Billy Graham Religion.* Philadelphia: United Church, 1972.

Batey, Richard. *Jesus and the Poor.* New York: Harper & Row, 1972.

Bellah, Robert N. *Beyond Belief.* New York: Harper & Row, 1970.

————. *The Broken Covenant: American Civil Religion in Time of Trial.* New York: Seabury, 1975.

Benjamin, Philip S. *The Philadelphia Quakers in the Industrial Age, 1965–1920.* Philadelphia: Temple University Press, 1976.

Benne, Robert, and Hefner, Philip. *Defining America: A Christian Critique of the American Dream.* Philadelphia: Fortress, 1974.

Benson, David. *Miracle in Moscow.* Glendale, Calif.: Regal Books, 1975.

Bloesch, Donald G. *The Evangelical Renaissance.* Grand Rapids, Mich.: Eerdmans, 1973.

Boice, James Montgomery. *The Sermon on the Mount.* Grand Rapids, Mich.: Zondervan, 1972.

Boom, Corrie ten. *The Hiding Place.* Washington Depot, Conn.: Chosen, 1971.

Breisch, Francis D. and Karl E. Keefer. *Isms on the Prowl.* Wheaton, Ill.: Victor Books, 1974.

Bright, Bill. *Come Help Change the World.* Old Tappan, N.J.: Revell, 1970.

Brown, Dale W. *The Christian Revolutionary.* Grand Rapids, Mich.: Eerdmans, 1971.

Brown, Harold O. J. *Christianity and the Class Struggle.* New Rochelle, N.Y.: Arlington House, 1970.

_____. *The Protest of a Troubled Protestant.* New Rochelle, N.Y.: Arlington House, 1969.

Bryant, Anita. *Amazing Grace.* Old Tappan, N.J.: Revell, 1971.

Cantelon, William. *The Day the Dollar Dies.* Plainfield, N.J.: Logos, 1973.

Carter, Jimmy. *Why Not the Best?* New York: Bantam, 1976.

Carter, Paul. *The Decline and Revival of the Social Gospel: Social and Political Liberalism in American Protestant Churches, 1920–1940.* Ithaca, N.Y.: Cornell University Press, 1954.

_____. "The Fundamentalist Defense of the Faith." In *Change and Continuity in Twentieth-Century America: The 1920's.* Edited by John Braeman et al. Columbus: Ohio State University Press, 1968.

Cash, Johnny. *Man in Black.* Grand Rapids, Mich.: Zondervan, 1975.

Christenson, Larry. *The Christian Family.* Minneapolis: Bethany, 1970.

_____. *Social Action: Jesus Style.* Minneapolis: Dimension, 1976.

Clabaugh, Gary K. *Thunder on the Right: The Protestant Fundamentalists.* Chicago: Nelson-Hall, 1974.

Clark, Elmer T. *The Small Sects in America.* Nashville: Cokesbury, 1937.

Clark, Henry B. *Escape from the Money Trap.* Valley Forge, Pa.: Judson, 1973.

Clouse, Robert G., Robert D. Linder, and Richard V. Pierard, eds. *The Cross and the Flag.* Carol Stream, Ill.: Creation House, 1972.

Collins, Gary R., ed. *Our Society in Turmoil.* Carol Stream, Ill.: Creation House, 1970.

Colson, Charles. *Born Again.* Old Tappan, N.J.: Revell, 1977.

Cotham, Perry C. *Obscenity, Pornography, and Censorship.* Grand Rapids, Mich.: Baker, 1973.

_____. *Politics, Americanism, and Christianity.* Grand Rapids, Mich.: Baker, 1976.

Criswell, W. A. *What to Do Until Jesus Comes Back?* Nashville: Broadman, 1975.

Cruz, Nicky. *The Corruptors.* Old Tappan, N.J.: Revell, 1974.

Culver, Robert. *Toward a Biblical View of Civil Government.* Chicago: Moody Press, 1974.

Dayton, Donald W. *Discovering an Evangelical Heritage.* New York: Harper, 1976.

De Haan, Richard W. *The World on Trial.* Grand Rapids, Mich.: Zondervan, 1970.

De Vos, Richard M. *Believe.* Old Tappan, N.J.: Revell, 1975.

Dollar, George W. *A History of Fundamentalism in America.* Greenville, S.C.: Bob Jones University, 1973.

Drakeford, John W., and Hamm, Jack. *Pornography: The Sexual Mirage.* Nashville: Thomas Nelson, 1973.

Edwards, George. *Crawling Out.* Grand Rapids, Mich.: Zondervan, 1973.

_____. *Jesus and the Politics of Violence.* New York: Harper & Row, 1972.

Eighmy, John Lee. *Churches in Cultural Captivity.* Knoxville: University of Tennessee, 1972.

Eells, Robert and Bartell Nyberg. *Lonely Walk: The Life of Senator Mark Hatfield.* Chappaqua, N.Y.: Christian Herald Books, 1979.

Eller, Vernard. *King Jesus' Manual of Arms for the Armless.* Nashville: Abingdon, 1973.

_____. *The Simple Life: The Christian Stance Toward Possessions.* Grand Rapids, Mich.: Eerdmans, 1973.

Elliot, Elizabeth. *Let Me Be A Woman.* Wheaton, Ill.: Tyndale, 1976.

Enroth, Ronald M.; Edward E. Ericson, Jr.; and Peter C. Breckenridge. *The Jesus People.* Grand Rapids, Mich.: Eerdmans, 1972.

Figart, Thomas O. *A Biblical Perspective on the Race Problem.* Grand Rapids, Mich.: Baker, 1973.

Fisher, Wallace E. *Politics, Poker and Piety.* Nashville: Abingdon, 1972.

Fletcher, Joseph, and John Warwick Montgomery. *Situation Ethics.* Minneapolis: Bethany, 1972.

Ford, Clay. *Berkeley Journal: Jesus and the Street People.* New York: Harper and Row, 1972.

Ford, Leighton. *New Man, New World.* Waco, Tex.: Word, 1972.

_____. *One Way to Change the World.* New York: Harper & Row, 1970.

Frady, Marshall. *Billy Graham: A Parable of American Righteousness.* Boston: Little, Brown, 1979.
Frost, David. *Billy Graham Talks with David Frost.* Philadelphia: A. J. Holman, 1971.
Furness, Charles Y. *The Christian and Social Action.* Old Tappan, N.J.: Revell, 1972.
Gaddy, C. Welton. *Profile of a Christian Citizen.* Nashville: Broadman, 1974.
Gallivan, C. E., ed. *A Nation Under God?* Waco, Tex.: Word, 1976.
Geisler, Norman L. *Ethics: Alternatives and Issues.* Grand Rapids, Mich.: Zondervan, 1971.
Gimenez, John. *Up Tight.* Waco, Tex.: Word, 1972.
Gingerich, Melvin. *The Christian and Revolution.* Scottdale, Pa.: Herald Press, 1968.
Gish, Arthur G. *The New Left and Christian Radicalism.* Grand Rapids, Mich.: Eerdmans, 1970.
Graham, Billy. *Angels: God's Secret Agents.* New York: Doubleday, 1975.
――――. *The Challenge.* Garden City, N.Y.: Doubleday, 1969.
――――. *World Aflame.* Garden City, N.Y.: Doubleday, 1965.
Greenfield, Robert. *The Spiritual Supermarket.* New York: Saturday Review Press, 1975.
Grounds, Vernon. *Revolution and the Christian Faith.* Philadelphia: Lippincott, 1971.
Gustafson, James M. *Christ and the Moral Life.* New York: Harper & Row, 1968.
Hadden, Jeffrey K. *The Gathering Storm in the Churches.* Garden City, N.Y.: Doubleday, 1969.
Halliday, Jerry. *Spaced Out and Gathered In.* Old Tappan, N.J.: Revell, 1972.
Hancock, Maxine. *Love, Honor—and Be Free.* Chicago: Moody Press, 1975.
Hargis, Billy James. *Billy James Hargis Speaks Out on the Issues.* Tulsa, Okla.: Christian Crusade, 1971.
――――. *Why I Fight for a Christian America.* Nashville: Thomas Nelson, 1974.
Harrison, Bob, and Jim Montgomery. *When God Was Black.* Grand Rapids, Mich.: Zondervan, 1971.
Hatfield, Mark. *Between a Rock and a Hard Place.* Waco, Tex.: Word, 1976.
――――. *Conflict and Conscience.* Waco, Tex.: Word, 1971.
――――. *Not Quite So Simple.* New York: Harper and Row, 1968.
Hatfield, Mark, et al. *Amnesty? The Unsettled Question of Vietnam.* Croton-on-Hudson, N.Y.: Sun River Press, 1973.
Hefley, James C. *By Life or by Death.* Grand Rapids, Mich.: Zondervan, 1969.
Hefley, James and Marti Hefley. *The Church That Takes on Trouble.* Elgin, Ill.: Cook, 1976.
Hefley, James and Edward Plowman. *Washington: Christians in the Corridors of Power.* Wheaton, Ill.: Tyndale, 1975.
Henley, Wallace. *Enter At Your Own Risk.* Old Tappan, N.J.: Revell, 1974.
――――. *The White House Mystique.* Old Tappan, N.J.: Revell, 1976.
Henry, Carl F. H. *Aspects of Christian Social Ethics.* Grand Rapids, Mich.: Eerdmans, 1964.
――――. *Evangelicals in Search of Identity.* Waco, Tex.: Word, 1976.
――――. *New Strides of Faith.* Chicago: Moody Press, 1972.
Henry, Carl F. H., et al., eds. *Prophecy in the Making.* Carol Stream, Ill.: Creation House, 1971.
――――. *Quest For Reality: Christianity and the Counter Culture.* Downers Grove, Ill.: Inter-Varsity, 1973.
Henry, Paul B. *Politics for Evangelicals.* Valley Forge, Pa: Judson Press, 1974.
Herberg, Will. *Protestant Catholic Jew.* Rev. ed. Garden City, N.Y.: Anchor, 1960.
Hopkins, Charles H. *The Rise of the Social Gospel.* New Haven: Yale, 1940.
Hudson, Winthrop S. *Religion in America.* New York: Scribner's, 1965.
Hunt, George, ed. *Calvinism and the Political Order.* Philadelphia: Westminster Press, 1965.
Hunt, Gladys. *Ms. Means Myself.* Grand Rapids, Mich.: Zondervan, 1972.
Hutchens, James M. *Beyond Combat.* Chicago: Moody Press, 1968.
Jewett, Paul K. *Man as Male and Female.* Grand Rapids, Mich.: Eerdmans, 1975.
Jorstad, Erling. *The Politics of Doomsday: Fundamentalists of the Far Right.* Nashville: Abingdon, 1970.
Judah, J. Stillson. *The History and Philosophy of the Metaphysical Movements in America.* Philadelphia, Pa: Westminster, 1967.
Kelley, Dean. *Why Conservative Churches are Growing.* New York: Harper & Row, 1972.

Kelsey, George. *Social Ethics Among Southern Baptists, 1917–1969.* Metuchen, N.J.: Scarecrow, 1972.

Kersten, Lawrence. *The Lutheran Ethic.* Detroit: Wayne State, 1970.

Kucharsky, David. *The Mind and Spirit of Jimmy Carter.* New York: Harper & Row, 1976.

LaHaye, Tim. *The Beginning of the End.* Wheaton, Ill.: Tyndale, 1976.

Linder, Robert D., ed. *God and Caesar.* Longview, Tex.: Conference on Faith and History, 1971.

Lindsell, Harold. *The Battle for the Bible.* Grand Rapids, Mich.: Zondervan, 1976.

———. *The World, the Flesh, and the Devil.* Washington: Canon Press, 1973.

Lindsey, Hal. *The Liberation of Planet Earth.* Grand Rapids, Mich.: Zondervan, 1974.

Littell, F. H. *From Church to Pluralism.* Garden City, N.Y.: Doubleday, 1962.

Lockhard, David. *The Unheard Billy Graham.* Waco, Tex.: Word, 1971.

Lueking, F. Dean. *A Century of Caring: The Welfare Ministry Among Missouri Synod Lutherans, 1868–1968.* St. Louis: Lutheran Church-Missouri Synod, 1968.

Lum, Ada. *Jesus the Radical.* Downers Grove, Ill.: Inter-Varsity, 1970.

Lutzer, Erwin W. *The Morality Gap: An Evangelical Response to Situation Ethics.* Chicago: Moody Press, 1972.

Magnuson, Norris. *Salvation in the Slums: Evangelical Social Work, 1865–1920.* Metuchen, N.J.: Scarecrow, 1977.

Marsden, George. *Fundamentalism and American Culture: The Shaping of Twentieth Century Evangelicalism: 1870–1925.* New York: Oxford, 1980.

Martin, Walter R. *The Kingdom of the Cults.* Minneapolis: Bethany, 1965.

Marty, Martin E. *A Nation of Behavers.* Chicago: University of Chicago Press, 1976.

———. *The Pro and Con Book of Religious America: A Bicentennial Argument.* Waco, Tex.: Word, 1975.

———. *Righteous Empire.* New York: Dial, 1970.

McIntire, Carl. *Outside the Gate.* Collingswood, N.J.: Christian Beacon Press, 1967.

McLaren, Robert B., and Homer D. McLaren. *All to the Good: A Guide to Christian Ethics.* New York: World, 1969.

McLean, Gordon R. *Man, I Need Help!* Minneapolis: Bethany, 1975.

McLoughlin, William G. *Modern Revivalism.* New York: Ronald Press, 1959.

———. *Revivals, Awakenings and Reform: An Essay on Religion and Social Change in America, 1607–1977.* Chicago: University of Chicago, 1978.

———., and Robert N. Bellah. *Religion in America.* Boston: Houghton-Mifflin, 1968.

Mead, Frank S. *Handbook of Denominations in the United States.* Nashville: Abingdon, 1975.

Mead, Sidney E. *The Lively Experiment: The Shaping of Christianity in America.* New York: Harper & Row, 1963.

Menendez, Albert J. *Religion at the Polls.* Philadelphia: Westminster Press, 1977.

Minear, Paul S. *Commands of Christ.* Nashville: Abingdon, 1972.

Moberg, David O. *The Great Reversal.* Philadelphia: J. B. Lippincott, 1972.

———. *Inasmuch.* Grand Rapids, Mich.: Eerdmans, 1965.

Mollenkott, Virginia R. *Adamant and Stone Chips.* Waco, Tex.: Word, 1967.

———. *Women, Men and the Bible.* Nashville: Abingdon, 1977.

Monsma, Stephen V. *The Unraveling of America.* Downers Grove, Ill.: Inter-Varsity, 1974.

Montgomery, John Warwick. *The Shaping of America.* Minneapolis: Bethany, 1976.

Mooneyham, W. Stanley. *What Do You Say to a Hungry World?* Waco, Tex.: Word, 1975.

Morgan, Marabel. *The Total Woman.* Old Tappan, N.J.: Revell, 1973.

Mouw, Richard J. *Political Evangelism.* Grand Rapids, Mich.: Eerdmans, 1973.

———. *Politics and the Biblical Drama.* Grand Rapids, Mich.: Eerdmans, 1976.

Needleman, Jacob. *The New Religions.* Garden City, N.Y.: Doubleday, 1970.

Newell, William R. *Romans Verse by Verse.* Chicago: Moody Press, 1976 [1938].

Niebuhr, H. Richard. *The Kingdom of God in America.* Hamden, Conn.: Shoe String Press, 1956.

Norton, Howard, and Bob Slossen. *The Miracle of Jimmy Carter.* Plainfield, N.J.: Logos, 1976.

O'Connor, Elisabeth. *Call to Commitment.* New York: Harper & Row, 1963.

———. *Journey Inward, Journey Outward.* New York: Harper & Row, 1963.

Padilla, C. René, ed. *The New Face of Evangelicalism: An International Symposium on the Lausanne Covenant.* Downers Grove, Ill.: Inter-Varsity, 1976.
Palmer, Earl F. *Salvation by Surprise.* Waco, Tex.: Word, 1975.
Palmquist, Al. *Miracle at City Hall.* Minneapolis: Bethany, 1974.
Pannell, William E. *My Friend, the Enemy.* Waco, Tex.: Word, 1968.
Pearson, Fred. *They Dared to Hope: Student Protest and Christian Response.* Grand Rapids, Mich.: Eerdmans, 1969.
Perkins, John. *Let Justice Roll Down.* Glendale Calif.: Regal, 1976.
Pierard, Richard V. *The Unequal Yoke: Evangelical Christianity and Political Conservatism.* Philadelphia: J. B. Lippincott, 1970.
Pippert, Wesley. *Faith at the Top.* Elgin, Ill.: Cook, 1973.
_____. *Memo for 1976: Some Political Options.* Downers Grove, Ill.: Inter-Varsity, 1974.
Plowman, Edward. *The Jesus Movement.* Elgin, Ill.: Cook, 1971.
Plumer, William S. *Commentary on Romans.* Grand Rapids, Mich.: Kregel, 1971 [1870].
Poetsch, Hans-Lutz. *Marxism and Christianity.* St. Louis: Concordia, 1973.
Poling, David. *Why Billy Graham?* Grand Rapids, Mich.: Zondervan, 1977.
Pollock, John. *Billy Graham: The Authorized Biography.* New York: McGraw-Hill, 1966.
Potter, Ralph B. *War and Moral Discourse.* Richmond, Va.: John Knox, 1969.
Price, Eugenia. *The Unique World of Women.* Grand Rapids, Mich.: Zondervan, 1969.
Quebedeaux, Richard. *The New Charismatics.* Garden City, N.Y.: Doubleday, 1976.
_____. *The Worldly Evangelicals.* New York: Harper & Row, 1978.
_____. *The Young Evangelicals: Revolution in Orthodoxy.* New York: Harper & Row, 1974.
Ramm, Bernard L. *The Evangelical Heritage.* Waco, Tex.: Word, 1973.
Redekop, Calvin. *The Free Church and Seductive Culture.* Scottdale, Pa.: Herald Press, 1970.
Redekop, John Harold. *The American Far Right: A Case Study of Billy James Hargis and Christian Crusade.* Grand Rapids, Mich.: Eerdmans, 1968.
Rees, Paul S. *Don't Sleep Through the Revolution.* Waco, Tex.: Word, 1969.
Richey, Russell E., and Donald G. Jones. *American Civil Religion.* New York: Harper & Row, 1974.
Rogers, Dale Evans. *Let Freedom Ring.* Old Tappan, N.J.: Revell, 1975.
Rogers, Jack. *Confessions of a Conservative Evangelical.* Philadelphia: Westminster, 1974.
Rust, Eric. *Nature—Garden or Desert?* Waco, Tex.: Word, 1971.
Rutledge, Howard and Phyllis Rutledge. *In the Presence of Mine Enemies, 1965–1973.* Old Tappan, N.J.: Revell, 1973.
Salley, Columbus and Ronald Behm. *Your God is Too White.* Downers Grove, Ill.: Inter-Varsity, 1970.
Sanders, Thomas G. *Protestant Concepts of Church and State.* New York: Holt, Rinehart & Winston, 1964.
Sandeen, Ernest R. *The Roots of Fundamentalism.* Chicago: University of Chicago Press, 1970.
Scanzoni, Letha and Nancy Hardesty. *All We're Meant To Be—A Biblical Approach to Women's Liberation.* Waco, Tex.: Word, 1974.
Schaeffer, Edith. *L'Abri.* Wheaton, Ill.: Tyndale, 1969.
_____. *Back to Freedom and Dignity.* Downers Grove, Ill.: Inter-Varsity, 1972.
_____. *The Church at the End of the Twentieth Century.* London: Norfolk Press, 1970.
_____. *The Church Before a Watching World.* Downers Grove, Ill.: Inter-Varsity, 1971.
_____. *Death in the City.* Downers Grove, Ill.: Inter-Varsity, 1969.
Schaeffer, Francis A. *Genesis in Space and Time.* Downers Grove, Ill.: Inter-Varsity, 1972.
_____. *How Should We Then Live?* Old Tappan, N.J.: Revell, 1976.
_____. *The Mark of the Christian.* Downers Grove, Ill.: Inter-Varsity, 1970.
_____. *The New Super Spirituality.* Downers Grove, Ill.: Inter-Varsity, 1972.
_____. *No Final Conflict: The Bible Without Error in All That It Affirms.* Downers Grove, Ill.: Inter-Varsity, 1975.
_____. *No Little People.* Downers Grove, Ill.: Inter-Varsity, 1974.
_____. *Pollution and the Death of Man: The Christian View of Ecology.* Wheaton, Ill.: Tyndale, 1970.
_____. *True Spirituality.* Wheaton, Ill.: Tyndale, 1971.

_____. *Two Contests, Two Realities.* Downers Grove. Ill.: Inter-Varsity, 1974.

Scharlemann, Martin H. *The Church's Social Responsibilities.* St. Louis: Concordia, 1971.

Scheffbuch, Winrich. *Christians Under the Hammer and Sickle.* Grand Rapids, Mich.: Zondervan, 1972.

Settel, T. S. *The Faith of Billy Graham.* Anderson, S.C.: Drake House, 1968.

Sider, Ronald J., ed. *The Chicago Declaration.* Carol Stream, Ill.: Creation, 1974.

_____. *Rich Christians in an Age of Hunger.* Downers Grove, Ill.: Inter-Varsity, 1977.

Simon, Arthur. *Bread For the World.* Grand Rapids, Mich.: Eerdmans, 1975.

Skinner, Tom. *Black and Free.* Grand Rapids, Mich.: Zondervan, 1970.

_____. *How Black is the Gospel?* Philadelphia: J. B. Lippincott, 1970.

_____. *Words of Revolution.* Grand Rapids, Mich.: Zondervan, 1970.

Small, Dwight H. *Christian: Celebrate Your Sexuality.* Old Tappan, N.J.: Revell, 1974.

Smith, Timothy. *Revivalism and Social Reform in Nineteenth Century America.* New York: Abingdon, 1957.

Smith, James Ward and A. Leland Jamison, eds., *Religion in American Life.* Princeton: Princeton University Press, 1961.

Sontag, Rufus B. *At Ease in Zion: Social History of Southern Baptists, 1865–1900.* Nashville: Vanderbilt, 1967 [1961].

Spike, Robert W. *The Freedom Revolution and the Churches.* New York: Association, 1965.

Spitzer, Walter O., and Carlyle L. Saylor. *Birth Control and the Christian.* Wheaton, Ill.: Tyndale, 1969.

Steinkamp, Orvel N. *The Holy Spirit in Viet Nam.* Carol Stream, Ill.: Creation House, 1974.

Stott, John R. W. *Christ the Controversialist.* Wheaton, Ill.: Tyndale Press, 1970.

Streiker, Lowell D., and Gerald S. Strober. *Religion and the New Majority: Billy Graham, Middle America, and the Politics of the 1970's.* New York: Association, 1972.

Stringfellow, William. *An Ethic for Christians and Other Aliens in a Strange Land.* Waco, Tex.: Word, 1973.

Strout, Cushing. *The New Heavens and New Earth: Political Religion in America.* New York: Harper & Row, 1974.

Taylor, Richard K. *Economics and the Gospel.* Philadelphia: United Church Press, 1973.

Van Hoeven, James W., ed. *Piety and Patriotism: Bicentennial Studies of the Reformed Church in America, 1776–1976.* Grand Rapids, Mich.: Eerdmans, 1976.

Van Til, Henry R. *The Calvinistic Concept of Culture.* Grand Rapids, Mich.: Baker, 1959.

Walker, Alan. *God, The Disturber.* Waco, Tex.: Word, 1973.

Wallis, Jim. *Agenda for a Biblical People.* New York: Harper & Row, 1976.

Walton, Rus. *One Nation Under God.* Washington: Third Century, 1975.

Webber, Robert. *Common Roots.* Grand Rapids, Mich.: Zondervan, 1978.

Webber, Robert, and Donald Bloesch. *The Other Orthodox Evangelicals.* Nashville: Thomas Nelson, 1978.

Wells, David, and John D. Woodbridge, eds. *The Evangelicals.* Rev. ed. Grand Rapids, Mich.: Baker, 1975.

Werning, Waldo J. *The Stewardship Call.* St. Louis: Concordia, 1970.

Wilkerson, David R. *The Cross and the Switchblade.* New York: Bernard Geis, 1963.

Wilkerson, David, with Claire Cox. *Parents on Trial: Why Kids Go Wrong—Or Right.* New York: Hawthorne, 1967.

Wilkerson, Don, and Herm Weiskopf. *The Gutter and the Ghetto.* Waco, Tex.: Word, 1969.

Wirt, Sherwood Eliot. *The Social Conscience of the Evangelical.* New York: Harper & Row, 1968.

Wurmbrank, Richard. *If that were Christ, Would You Give Him Your Blanket?* Waco, Tex.: Word, 1971.

Yinger, J. Milton. *The Scientific Study of Religion.* New York: Macmillan, 1970.

_____. *Sociology Looks at Religion.* New York: Macmillan, 1961.

Yoder, John Howard. *Nevertheless: A Meditation on the Varieties and Shortcomings of Religious Pacifism.* Scottdale, Pa.: Herald Press, 1971.

_____. *The Politics of Jesus.* Grand Rapids, Mich.: Eerdmans, 1972.

Zaretsky, Irving, and Mark Leone, eds. *Religious Movements in Contemporary America.* Princeton: Princeton University Press, 1974.

INDEX